TWENTY
CONTEMPORARY ONE-ACT PLAYS
(AMERICAN)

Fifty Contemporary One-Act Plays

Edited by
FRANK SHAY and PIERRE LOVING

THIS volume contains FIFTY REPRESENTATIVE ONE-ACT PLAYS of the MODERN THEATER, chosen from the dramatic works of contemporary writers all over the world and is the second volume in *The Appleton Dramatic Anthologies*, the first being European Theories of the Drama, by Barrett H. Clark, which has been so enthusiastically received.

The editors have scrupulously sifted countless plays and have selected the best available in English. One-half the plays have never before been published in book form; thirty-one are no longer available in any other edition.

The work satisfies a long-felt want for a handy collection of the choicest plays produced by the art theaters all over the world. It is a complete repertory for a little theater, a volume for the study of the modern drama, a representative collection of the world's best short plays.

CONTENTS

Large 8vo, 585 pages. Net, $5.00
Special India Paper Edition, less than one-half inch thick.
Limp Cloth, net, $6.00; Limp Leather, net, $7.50.

Twenty Contemporary One-Act Plays

(AMERICAN)

Selected and Edited by

FRANK SHAY

D. APPLETON AND COMPANY

NEW YORK: LONDON: MCMXXV

WARNING

The plays in this volume are for reading purposes only. The fact that you have purchased this volume does not give you permission to produce any play in it unless you have received permission to do so from the owner of copyright in the play, or from his agent. Directions are given before each play in the volume concerning the name and address of the owner of copyright, or his agent.

The plays in this volume are fully protected in all countries. No performance, professional or amateur, no public reading, no radio broadcast may be given without permission of the owner of copyright, or his agent.

Performances of each play in this volume are subject to royalty. Anyone presenting any of these plays without the consent of the owner of the play, or his authorized agent, will be liable to the penalties provided by law:

"Section 4966:—Any person publicly performing or representing any dramatic or musical composition for which copyright has been obtained, without the consent of the proprietor of said dramatic or musical composition, or his heirs and assigns, shall be liable for damages, thereof, such damages, in all cases to be assessed at such sum, not less than one hundred dollars for the first and fifty dollars for every subsequent performance, as to the court shall appear to be just. If the unlawful performance and presentation be wilful and for profit, such person or persons shall be guilty of a misdemeanor, and upon conviction shall be imprisoned for a period not exceeding one year."—U. S. Revised Statutes: Title 60, Chap. 3.

TO
EUGENE O'NEILL

FOREWORD

The present collection of short plays must be considered as a supplementary volume to *Fifty Contemporary One-Act Plays* issued early in 1921. The same conditions surrounded its development and completion.

The lot of the anthologist is not a happy one. He must either select his plays because of the fame of the authors, or, he must use a trace of critical judgment and include only those plays, regardless of the literary standing of their authors, which he feels are the best that have come to his attention. Whatever his course may be, it is always open to criticism.

The editor has read several hundred one-act plays since the previous volume was completed. Indeed he has become so inured to meeting persons who have plays they want published that he is inclined to fly every time a person appears with a manuscript under his arm. So many merely good one-act plays are being written and acted these days the editor early concluded that selecting the best was not so much of a task as eliminating the almost good. In this collection I have ignored individual fame and have selected the best plays I could find.

I would have liked to include Eugene G. O'Neill's

The Emperor Jones, and Edna St. Vincent Millay's *Aria da Capo.* The former is so tied up in copyrights that it could not be used. In the bibliography, which is appended, the reader will find the play easily accessible to all interested. Miss Millay's play, fortunately or unfortunately, was included in the Fifty Contemporary One-Act Plays. These two are unquestionably the outstanding plays of the last year. They mark, in no small way, the high accomplishments of the art theatre in America.

F. S.

New York.

CONTENTS

MIRAGE

A PLAY IN ONE ACT

by GEORGE M. P. BAIRD

The first performance of MIRAGE was given at the University of Pittsburgh by the Pitt Players on the evening of April 11, 1916, with the following cast:

POLAINA, *a Hopi Girl*, - - - HARRIET SMITH

GRAYSON STONE, *an Ethnologist*, - RIDDEL CRAMBLET

CHRISTINE, *his Wife*, - - - - IRENE GARRISON

HORMEK, *a Psychiatrist*, - - DANIEL T. R. DICKSON

FIRST HOPI WOMAN, - - - AUGUSTA SCHMELTZ

SECOND HOPI WOMAN, - - - CLAUDIA CHAMBERS

Scenery, costumes, and properties designed by the author and executed by the Pitt Players.

MIRAGE

CONCERNING THE PEOPLE OF THE PLAY

Polaina,[1] the niece of Chief Loloamai, is a nine-teen-year-old daughter of an ancient Amarind tribe, and heir to a civilization different from, but in no essential sense inferior to, that of the paler peoples who have invaded its demesne. She is a "child of nature" perhaps, but by no means a simple one. Passion and stoicism, intellectual curiosity and superstition, frankness and guile, craving and custom, struggle within her. She is neither a pathetic fool nor a sentimental wanton, but a strong woman with an intense desire for hap-piness, an ardent love of life, and the courage to attempt their satisfaction whatever the cost. Po-laina is dressed in a wrapper-like, blue, cotton gown which reaches slightly below the knees. Her right shoulder and arm are bare, and a scarlet blanket is flung over the left shoulder and fastened beneath the right armpit. There are brightly beaded moccasins upon her feet, and her legs are wound about with strips of white cotton cloth. Her blue-black hair is parted in the center and rolled in elaborate "butterfly" coils above her ears. These coils, together with the yellow squash blos-

---

[1] Polaina = Butterfly.

*soms which ornament them, are a badge of virgin-
ity among the Hopi Indians. Her necklace,
bracelets, and large, square ear-pendants are of
hammered silver set with raw turquoise.*

*The First Hopi Woman is a middle-aged squaw,
while the Second Hopi Woman is probably about
ten years her senior. The faces of both are wrinkled
with a thousand little lines. Their hair is stiffly
braided, and their garments are similar to those of
Polaina, though much more subdued in color.
These women are the sibyls of the play, their function being not unlike that of a Greek chorus.*

*Grayson Stone is a tall, somewhat emaciated man,
about thirty-five years of age. He is suffering from
amnesia, superinduced by sunstroke and exposure,
and has reverted to type. His hair and beard are
brown in color and quite unkempt, while his face,
arms, and bare feet are deeply tanned. He is
dressed, Hopi fashion, in a faded blue shirt and
nondescript tan cotton trousers. He wears a band
of red cloth about his head.*

*Christine is a well-poised, good-looking young
woman, blonde as to complexion, and obviously
Back Bay as to social status. She wears an écru
pongee motor coat over a blue summer frock, sun-
hat, tourist veil, and stout walking boots.*

*Dr. James Hormek is a short, somewhat stout per-
son, who would be singled out anywhere as a successful physician. He has a generous, sentimental nature which he tries to disguise by a
brusque manner and clipped, incisive mode of*

speech. He is dressed in tweeds, golf cap, and tortoise-shell glasses, and carries motor gauntlets.

The action takes place upon the roof of an adobe house, which forms one of the higher terraces in a Hopi pueblo. To the right and left the walls of another course of dwellings rise and are lost to sight in the flies. At the rear is a low battlement of sun-baked bricks, beyond which the silent desert and the purple waste of space stretch illimitably. A rude ladder leans against the wall, right, and the top of another can be seen projecting above the battlement. It is the hour before dawn on an August morning. Polaina is discovered at a stone corn-trough, down-stage, left.

POLAINA (*grinding corn and singing*)
  I-o-ho wonder-water,
  I-o-ho wonder-water,
  Life anew to him who drinks!
  Look where southwest clouds are bringing rain;
  Look where southeast clouds are bringing rain;
  Life anew to him who drinks!
  I-o-ho wonder-water,
  I-o-ho wonder water,
  Life anew to him who drinks!*

(*Two Hopi women bearing water-jars upon their heads enter from the left, rear. They put down the jars and squat beside them.*)

FIRST WOMAN (*wearily*)
  Dry!

---

* See note on page 40.

SECOND WOMAN

The rock pools are empty.

FIRST WOMAN

The Well of the Eagles has failed.

POLAINA

But the spring beneath the yuccas, at the foot of the mesa? Even in the moon of thirst it has always given sweet water.

FIRST WOMAN

Dry, too. The clay bottom is a crust of mud burned like adobe.

SECOND WOMAN

Only the poisoned pool yields its palmful of bad medicine.

POLAINA

The old men say that there has never been so parched a summer; never so great a drouth in all the years since the gods, our fathers, fled to this mesa from the falling mountains.

FIRST WOMAN (*taking a gourd bottle from the folds of her blanket*)

I have brought the witch-water from the poisoned pool.

POLAINA (*surprised*)

What will you do with that?

SECOND WOMAN (*significantly*)

The thirst will soon be upon us. This is the milk of forgetfulness from the breasts of Death.

FIRST WOMAN (*nodding assent*)

When the throat is afire and the tongue hangs

like a blackened bean-pod between cracked, swollen lips, swift death will be good medicine.

POLAINA (*cheerfully*)
Do not speak of death; the rains must come soon. Uncle Loloamai and the priests have been three days in the Kivas below the earth, weaving the ceremonial cords of many colors and binding feathers upon the sacred bahos.[1] When the yellow line brightens in the east we shall plant them upon the edge of the mesa toward the dawn, and the climbing sun will bear our prayers for rain aloft.

SECOND WOMAN (*skeptically*)
Bahos! What virtue is there in prayers breathed to the turkey feathers and eagle feathers upon a painted stick?

POLAINA
Last year the Blue Flutes danced, the women planted bahos in the white dawn, and at sunset the rain clouds kissed the painted desert with a crystal kiss.

SECOND WOMAN (*looking sharply at Polaina*)
Some say it was not Hevebe, the Rain Lord, but the White Bahana[2], who brought luck, for it was on that day that our herdsmen found him nearly dead with thirst in the desert, and brought him to the pueblo.

FIRST WOMAN
The Great Spirit behind the sun had touched him, and the Drouth Demons feared him. The Heyapo, the rushing clouds, followed the trail

---

[1] Bahos = votive prayer-sticks.
[2] Bahana = white man.

of the mad white stranger. (*Touching her head.*)
The queer are good medicine.

SECOND WOMAN

Polaina, this Bahana is your lover. Can you
not make him work his strong rain-charm again?

POLAINA

He says that he makes no medicine, that he has
no power. He does not even know whence he
came, or his name, or the home of his people.

FIRST WOMAN

The sun brings forgetfulness.

SECOND WOMAN

He is not a man, but a child of the sun.

POLAINA

He is a man! (*Enigmatically.*) It is not well
that a woman should be spouse to the child of a
god.

FIRST WOMAN

Then you are to be his woman?

POLAINA (*touching the great wing whorls of hair
on the sides of her head*)

I would cast aside the blossom of the squash for
no other. For him alone would I let down these
coils of maidenhood and plait them in wifely
fashion.

SECOND WOMAN

The white corn and the red corn do not grow on
one stock.

POLAINA

No, but they are ground in the same trough,
and when the pika[1] is baked it is as sweet as
bread from unmingled meal.

---

[1] Pika = cakes—"paper bread."

FIRST WOMAN

You know nothing of the Bahana's tribe. What if the gods should give back his memory and he should carry you far from your people to the Eastland, where the sun grows cold with cloud?

POLAINA

I should be happy anywhere with him.

FIRST WOMAN

Perhaps he already has a white woman for wife. Some day he may remember. The eagle flies far; but when the blood of dying day is red upon the canyon crest, he returns to his nest among the rocks.

POLAINA

For my Bahana there are no yesterdays. He was born again of the desert and the sun. The past is a mirage. Nothing is real but our love, and in it are all the to-morrows.

SECOND WOMAN (*dully*)

Unless the rains come there will be no to-morrow for the children of Muyinguava.[1]

(*A pause. Polaina continues at her work. The First Woman points toward the east, where the first light of dawn is brightening.*)

FIRST WOMAN

The spirits of the dawn are bending a yellow line in the east like a string to the great bow of the sky, and soon the blazing arrow of the sun will shoot upward to the cloudless heavens.

(*From below and at some distance comes the*

---

[1] Muyinguava = life-giving god — spirit of growth and fertility.

17

rhythmic chant of the men as they file up from the Kivas or council chambers to make invocation to the Great-Spirit-Behind-the-Sun for the life-giving rains. They approach slowly. Their song increasing in volume for a time dies gradually as they move eastward toward the edge of the mesa.[1])

(Grayson Stone climbs halfway down the ladder, right, and stands silent for a moment, a dark silhouette against the growing light. He speaks slowly, almost colorlessly.)

STONE

May you have good in your hearts, O women!

POLAINA AND WOMEN

May you have good in your heart, O Bahana!

(He descends.)

STONE

Will there be rain to-day?

POLAINA *(approaching him)*

Listen! The men are marching to the eastern cliff to pray for it. If the Demons keep the breath of the prayer-sticks from the Great-Spirit-Behind-the-Sun, the young men and the Antelope Priests must dance the dance of the rattlesnake to-morrow. Then surely there will be rain.

SECOND WOMAN

There will be no rain.

STONE

The sun is still beneath the rim of the desert, but it is already fever-hot. Give me to drink.

---

[1] Chant should be accompanied by drum (tom-tom) and Indian flute.

FIRST WOMAN
The springs are dried up. We have no water.

POLAINA
Is it true, my Bahana, as these women say, that in your country it rains many times and the sun is as pale as the moon?

STONE
My country! I have no country but this. I remember nothing earlier than my first sight of you as you bent above me and poured the living water, drop by drop, upon my tortured tongue. I have tried to recall the past, for I know that I have not lived here always. I must be of another —another tribe. But it's no use. When I strive to remember, I am like one in the darkness of a strange house where still things and living things are vaguely sensed, but are not seen or known.

POLAINA
Some day you will remember; and in that day I shall be forgotten.

STONE (*takes her hand*)
I must go on trying, but I shall never pierce the darkness. Yet, even if the lost should come back to me, if I should learn to remember, it would make no difference in our love, Polaina.

POLAINA
Are you sure, Bahana? That is a fear that is with me always. The call of the tribe is strong and blood will answer blood.

STONE
No, my Butterfly, love is a mightier magic, greater than all the powers, stronger than death

itself. You are my tribe, and when my arms are about you I embrace my only people. Love sits with us in the Council Kiva of Life, and who shall dare to make evil medicine where he abides? O little Butterfly, have you begun to doubt me? Have you ceased to trust my love?

POLAINA

No, no, I trust you! . . . And yet I am afraid. Though the coyote-cub be suckled by a dog on the roof of a chief's house, time comes when the ancient longing for the wide waste of moonwhite desert leaps in his heart and he answers the summons of the far-off pack.

STONE

I am not a wolf, but a man. I shall remain upon the roof of the chief's house.

POLAINA

You say that because you have not come to remember. Perhaps you once loved another woman, and when the thought of her returns I shall be left alone.

STONE

There can be no other woman, Butterfly.

POLAINA

The wells fail, the Demons are angry, and we must die of thirst unless the rains come swiftly. If you heard the call to return to the land of cloud and rivers, the call of life and love and your own people, you would go.

STONE

In life or death you are mine; I would not go. (*Pause.*) Come, you shall plant a baho for me on the edge of the mesa.

20

POLAINA

You are a white man, a Bahana! Can you believe in Hopi magic?

STONE

Our souls are of one tribe, and I believe in you. Come!

(*They go off stage, right, hand in hand.*)

FIRST WOMAN (*grinding corn*)

I grind the red corn and the white corn in one trough.

SECOND WOMAN

Meal is not bread until it has felt the fire.

FIRST WOMAN

How lies the corn in the Kivas on the Altar of the Six Directions?

SECOND WOMAN (*sorting corn*)

A yellow ear to the north, and a blue ear to the west, a sugar ear for the zenith of the sun, and a black ear for its nadir, a red ear to the south, and a white ear to the east. It is a powerful charm to lay them so, but to mingle them is bad medicine.

(*The southern dawn has come swiftly, and the desert begins to glow with the growing warmth of the summer sun. The light and heat increase in intensity throughout the rest of the action.*)

(*Christine and Dr. Hormek enter, left.*)

FIRST WOMAN

A red ear to the south and a white ear to the east; an evil charm and a bad medicine if they be mingled.

21

CHRISTINE (*advancing*)
Good-morning.

WOMEN
May good be in your hearts!

CHRISTINE (*illustrating her words with gesture and raising her voice as one does when one thinks the hearer unfamiliar with one's language*)
We wish to buy pottery—jars, you know.

(*The women indicate that they understand.*)

SECOND WOMAN
We have many beautiful pots. We will show.

(*The First Woman goes off stage, right.*)

DR. HORMEK
Now, don't be long, Christine. It's hot on this roof already, and in an hour it'll be unbearable.

CHRISTINE
Five minutes will be long enough, Dr. Hormek.

DR. HORMEK (*humorously petulant*)
That's what you said at Acoma, and it took two hours. O, you women! When the bargaining instinct gets you, the devil himself couldn't drag you away.

CHRISTINE (*bantering him*)
You'll remember, doctor, that I didn't ask you to come with me.

HORMEK
O, you didn't, eh? I suppose I'm to let you go wandering all over this godforsaken desert alone! I never should have permitted you to leave Havordton.

CHRISTINE (*tossing her head*)

Do you think that you could have prevented my coming?

HORMEK

No, I suppose not. But you'll have to admit that the whole thing has been a wild-goose chase. Now, hasn't it?

CHRISTINE (*seriously*)

I have not given up hope.

HORMEK

Ah, but you have! I can see it in your eyes. Your voice cries out, "No hope," even when you are protesting the opposite. Come, Christine, give up this silly business. It can mean but unhappiness for both of us.

CHRISTINE

I shall not give up until I have found Grayson, or have conclusive proof that he is dead.

HORMEK

Proof! Great Scott! Haven't you the word of the guides and the government agent for it? Your brother, who spent months searching the desert for him, believes he is dead. No man could live without food or water through an August week in these wastes.

CHRISTINE

The very fact that they found no trace of him convinces me that he is still alive.

HORMEK

For quixotic obstinacy, go to a woman, especially a married one! Here am I, trailing you all over this damned—I beg your pardon—this infernal country like a love-sick crusader when I ought to be back home with my patients. Many of them are not half so crazy as I am.

CHRISTINE (*coolly*)

Well, why not take a train to-morrow? By starting now you will have plenty of time to reach the railroad.

HORMEK

I shan't leave without you; you know that.

CHRISTINE (*banteringly*)

For quixotic obstinacy, go to a man, especially an unmarried one.

HORMEK

I'm not good at repartee. Hang it all, Christine, I want to marry you, can't you understand that? (*She smiles.*) Oh, it's damned humorous, no doubt, and I'm making seven kinds of an ass of myself, but I can't help it. It's enough to make any red-blooded man fighting mad, to have a woman like you within his reach and be denied her by this gho—(*He is about to say "ghost," but changes it to*)—this romantic fancy of yours.

CHRISTINE (*serious again*)

Please don't say any more.

HORMEK

I shan't, if it pains you, dear, but honestly now—

CHRISTINE

There, you're beginning all over again!

HORMEK

Well, let me have my word out now, and I swear I won't trouble you again. We've been at every pueblo and white settlement in this benighted

region; you're ruining your health, and still no
word of Grayson. I want you to promise that
you'll go back home with me at the end of this
week. (*He seizes her hand.*) Will you, Christine?

(*The First Woman returns with a back-load of
pottery.*)

CHRISTINE (*hesitant*)
I—I don't know.

SECOND WOMAN
Pots of the butterfly and pots of the eagle,
bowls of the rain-beast, and jars with the sign
of Hevebe.

FIRST WOMAN (*displaying her wares*)
Paint cups, corn bowls, and water-jars.

CHRISTINE (*examining the collection with the eye of a
connoisseur*)
The burning is not so good as that of Acoma.
(*Holding up a small bowl.*) How much?

FIRST WOMAN
Three dollar?

CHRISTINE
One.

SECOND WOMAN (*protesting*)
The lady knows the best. Three dollar it is
little.

CHRISTINE (*firmly*)
One.

FIRST WOMAN
Two dollar?

HORMEK
Give it to her and let's get out of here. (*Takes
two silver dollars from purse.*)

CHRISTINE

It's not worth that much. (*Hormek is about to give the coins to the woman.*) She means two dollars Mexican; one of those is sufficient.

(*Hormek pays; Christine turns to go.*)

FIRST WOMAN (*taking a small jar out of a larger one and holding it up*)
Good medicine!

HORMEK (*taking the jar*)
I say, Christine, look at this one! Red and white, Greek fret, and (*Examining it closely*), by George, Greek letters—Alpha, Pi, Sigma!

CHRISTINE (*as if stricken by a blow*)
Why, so it is! (*To woman*) Where did you get this? It's not Hopi.

SECOND WOMAN
We make; Bahana paint.

HORMEK
Who?

FIRST WOMAN
Bahana, white man.

HORMEK
How'd he come to paint it? Who is he?

FIRST WOMAN (*touching her forehead significantly*)
A child of the mirage touched by the Great-Spirit-Behind-the-Sun.

SECOND WOMAN
The forgetful one who gives us luck.

CHRISTINE
Oh, if it is he!

HORMEK
> Bring him here.

(Second Woman nods and goes out, right.)

CHRISTINE
> How long has the white man been with you?

FIRST WOMAN
> Since this time last year. We found him dying in the desert just before the rains came.

HORMEK
> And he remembers nothing?

FIRST WOMAN
> His mind is like a bowl before it is painted.

CHRISTINE (*moving impulsively toward the right*)
> I must go to him!

HORMEK (*detaining her*)
> No, stay here. Try to calm yourself. It may be a mistake. It may be someone else.

CHRISTINE (*hysterically*)
> Let me go! You don't want me to find him, you, you—

HORMEK
> Good God, Christine! Do you think I'm such a cad? You're getting hysterical. Brace up, girl, I don't fancy having a collapse patient on my hands in the middle of this blasted desert.

(Stone and Polaina enter slowly, right. His arm is about her waist.)

CHRISTINE (*rushing to Stone and embracing him*)
> Grayson!

HORMEK (*the sentimentalist*)
> O faith of woman!

27

POLAINA (*interposing and pushing Christine away*)
Go 'way, white woman!

CHRISTINE
He is my husband. (*She attempts to seize Stone's hands.*) Speak to me, Gray!

(*Grayson stands dazed and embarrassed and gives no sign of recognition. Polaina looks at him questioningly, and then turns scornfully to Christine.*)

POLAINA
Let him choose!

STONE (*oblivious of the newcomers*)
Come along, Butterfly.

(*Polaina smiles in triumph and puts her arm about him. Christine sinks to a seat on the ground and sobs hysterically.*)

HORMEK (*professionally*)
Brace up, I need your help. It's a case of fugue, I think. Pull yourself together and we'll save him yet.

(*Stone and Polaina move off. Christine stiffens and sits with tensely clasped hands. Hormek seizes Stone's arm and forces him to look at the "Greek" jar.*)

HORMEK
Did you paint this?

STONE (*slowly*)
Yes. . . . Yes, I painted it.

HORMEK (*pointing to the design and speaking in the even, deliberate tone which one uses with a hypnotic subject*)

Greek! Does that suggest anything? Alpha, Pi, Sigma! Greek!

(*Stone traces the letters with a labored finger and speaks dreamily*)

STONE
Alpha . . . Pi . . . Sigma . . . Greek . . . Greek letter.

HORMEK
Fraternity.

STONE
My fraternity . . . We . . . there was a girl . . . We danced there.

HORMEK
Our last college dance. Do you recall the girl's name? Christine?

STONE (*groping*)
I think, I think it was Christine. . . . Yes, that was it, Christine.

HORMEK
It was in May, our commencement night.

STONE (*piecing the ideas together laboriously*)
Christine, . . . moonlight, . . . Campus trees, . . . elm trees . . . Commencement . . . Christine . . . I asked her and she . . . she promised to marry me.

(*Christine is about to cry out, but is stopped by a warning gesture of Hormek*)

HORMEK
You married her. You married Christine.

STONE (*very slowly, as one emerging from sleep*)
Yes, I married her. (*Showing interest for first time.*) Where is she? Where am I?

CHRISTINE (*throwing her arms about him*)
Here I am. Don't you know me, Gray?

STONE (*his voice and manner changing to that of an alert, cultured man*)
Of course I know you. Why shouldn't I? How did you get here? (*Looking about.*) I don't remember coming to this pueblo. Where's the rest of the expedition?

HORMEK (*soothingly*)
In good time, in good time, old man. You've been very sick, y' know. Sunstroke.

STONE
Nonsense! Never felt better. What's the joke? How did *you* get here, Chrisie?

CHRISTINE
I came to find you.

HORMEK
And the devil's own time she's had of it.

STONE (*impulsively seizing Hormek's hand*)
Why, Jim Hormek, you old villain! You here, too? So I've been sick. How long have I been here?

CHRISTINE (*caressing him*)
A year, dearest.

STONE (*incredulously*)
A year? Surely not! Why, it was only this morning I left camp to look for a poison pool the natives told me of.

HORMEK
A year ago these Indians found you dying of thirst out yonder in the desert.

CHRISTINE
We have been searching for you ever since

Brother Jack reported your disappearance, and
at last . . . Thank God! (*She clings to him.*)
(*Pause.*)

HORMEK

I had given you up for dead.

STONE

And yet you kept up the search, like the faithful
old friend you are.

HORMEK (*looking at Christine*)

Selfishness often travels the same road with
love. You have only Christine to thank.

CHRISTINE

I could not have restored his memory; that part
was yours.

HORMEK

Let it be for my atonement.

STONE

What have I been doing here? I remember
nothing.

HORMEK

Living the life of a native, I should think;
eating, sleeping . . . (*He stops abruptly and
looks at Polaina. Christine does the same.
Hormek and Christine exchange glances.*)

STONE (*apparently seeing Polaina for the first time*)

Why do you look at that girl so strangely?

(*There is an embarrassing silence. Hormek and
Christine are evidently trying to think of the dip-
lomatic thing to say. Christine succeeds first and
says gently—*)

CHRISTINE

I—I think she has been very good to you, Gray.

STONE
Has she? Strange that I can't remember her.

(*Polaina clutches at her heart*).

SECOND WOMAN (*grinding corn*)
The eagle returns to his nest.

FIRST WOMAN (*sorting corn*)
A white ear to the east, a red ear to the south, and an evil medicine if they be mingled.

CHRISTINE (*weakly*)
I feel faint. (*She sways; Stone supports her.*)

HORMEK
The heat is becoming unbearable. (*To the women*) Any water there? (*They nod denial.*) You've both been under a big strain. Let's get out of here.

STONE
Yes, but first I must thank these Indians. (*Feels for money, but discovers that he is wearing the pocketless clothes of the Hopi.*) Have you any money with you, Jim?

HORMEK (*handing Stone a purse*)
I'll take Christine down into the shade. We'll start for civilization as soon as you can make your adieux. Don't linger, now.

STONE
Trust me, I shan't be long. (*He kisses Christine.*) Wait for me, dearest.

CHRISTINE
I shall wait for you. (*Christine, supported by Hormek, goes out.*)

(*Stone goes over to Polaina.*)

STONE (*formally*)

I have you and your people to thank for my life, and I am truly grateful. Take this, not in payment, but as a poor token of my gratitude. (*He closes her hand about the purse. She puts her hands behind her back, the purse drops unnoticed.*) What is your name?

POLAINA

You called me Butterfly.

STONE (*indulgently, as to a child*)

Did I? What a pretty name!

POLAINA

You are going away?

STONE (*in a matter-of-fact voice*)

Yes, I must go back to my people.

POLAINA

The coyote answers the summons of the pack. The eagle circles low at the she-eagle's call.

STONE (*somewhat puzzled*)

You mean that the white lady is my wife, and that I am going back with her?

POLAINA

Yes. What of me?

STONE (*mystified*)

You? I'm afraid I don't understand.

POLAINA (*passionately*)

Am I not your people, am I not your woman? Have you forgotten your oath, have you forgotten the kisses of Polaina? You loved me, and I gave you all my love—all! all!

STONE (*starting back*)

I kissed you? I said I loved you? I can't remember. No, no, I never did that!

POLAINA (*unwinding her maiden coils of black hair*)
Look! it was for you that I came out from among the maidens.

FIRST WOMAN
She spoke truly.

SECOND WOMAN
She was his woman.

STONE (*suddenly realizing her meaning*)
Not that! O, my God! What have I done?

POLAINA
In the sight of your gods and of my gods, I am your woman.

STONE
How shall a man atone for a sin he never willed to do? (*An agonized pause.*) What do you wish?

POLAINA
You, your love.

STONE
Whatever may have been, that is impossible now. I am already married.

POLAINA
She has no children?

STONE
No, but—

POLAINA
Judge then, which of us is more truly your wife.

STONE
I must go to her. I must go to her.

POLAINA (*strangely stoical*)
Yes, you must go. It is useless to fight against

34

the spell of blood, but in the eyes of the gods you will always be mine.

STONE (*torn with remorse*)
Is there nothing I can do, nothing that will give you back your life, your happiness?

POLAINA
The wells have failed, and the rains are not yet. A little while and I, with all my people, must journey to the country of the dead. My suffering is less than yours, for you must live with your thoughts.

(*A new light comes into her eyes, her body stiffens with purpose. Stone is too busy with his trouble to discern the change in her. She smiles.*)

STONE
Yes, life is often more cruel than death.

POLAINA (*lifting the gourd bottle*)
This is the last water I shall ever taste. Will you drink it with me for good-bye?

STONE
I cannot take it, when you need it so much. It may keep you alive until the rain.

POLAINA (*coaxingly*)
Will you deny me this last little joy? Drink, drink!

(*Stone drinks, hands the gourd to Polaina and she, too, drinks.*)

FIRST WOMAN (*springing up*)
They have drunk the—

SECOND WOMAN (*drawing her down*)
Peace! The milk of forgetfulness. It is better so.

(Polaina raises and lowers her arms rhythmically toward the heavens. Her lips move rapidly as in prayer.)

FIRST WOMAN

She is praying to the Master of the Rods of Life, she is praying for the rains.

SECOND WOMAN

No, she does not face the East. She is praying to the Demons against the rains. She wishes to die.

(Polaina regains her composure. She seats herself and motions for Stone to sit beside her. He obeys.)

POLAINA *(calmly)*

Forgive me. The sun has made me mad. *(She touches Stone's forehead.)* You, too, are fevered.

STONE

Yes, I feel as if I were in a burning forest.

POLAINA *(slowly, in a soothing voice, almost like an incantation)*

Your head throbs, your lips are like charred embers.

STONE

My throat is parching.

POLAINA

The morning wind is dead.

STONE

My eyes burn.

POLAINA

The desert is burning. It is wrapped in the flame of the sun.

STONE

The heat curves and wavers. The air stifles me.

POLAINA

You are very thirsty, very thirsty.

STONE

Yes, yes!

POLAINA

Your tongue thickens, your throat is a tortured coal. Thirsty, thirsty.

STONE

The sun beats like—like a thousand hammers on my head. I think I am dying.

POLAINA

Come, I will shade you with my blanket. (*She draws him to her and puts her blanket about him.*) You are very thirsty.

STONE (*weakly*)

I must go; they are waiting.

POLAINA

You wish to drink, to drink, to drink. You are thirsty, very thirsty.

STONE

Water! Water!

POLAINA (*her arms about him, holds the gourd to his lips*)

Drink! (*He drinks.*)

STONE

My brain reels. (*He struggles to rise, but is restrained by Polaina.*)

I—must—go to—to—to drink! to drink! to DRINK!

POLAINA

No, not yet, my Bahana. You thirst. But you will not go.

STONE (*dreamily and in his first manner*)
Come, we will find cold water, and you shall plant a baho for me on the edge of the desert.

POLAINA
You have no wife. You have no wife, and you are thirsty. No wife, only Polaina.

STONE (*wandering*)
A wife? Don't tease me! You are my wife, Polaina.

POLAINA
The white woman is waiting, but you will not go. You will stay with Polaina, for you are very thirsty.

STONE
I know no woman but you. Water! Water!

POLAINA (*passionately*)
Kiss me. (*He kisses her.*) Have you forgotten your people?

STONE
I have no people. (*He claws at his throat.*) I'm dying with thirst. Water!

POLAINA (*holding the gourd upside down*)
There is no more water.

STONE (*frenzied*)
No water? You lie! (*Getting to his feet unsteadily and pointing into the desert.*) Look! The lake! Water! The lake, the lake!

POLAINA (*laughing, but without mirth*)
Mirage, like our lives.

STONE
No! No! It's real, I tell you. Water! Water! Come. (*He moves to the left.*)

POLAINA (*triumphantly*)
The desert gave you to me; the desert is my mother. I will go. We shall die in the beautiful desert!

STONE
We shall not die. We shall live our love beside the sweet waters.

POLAINA (*ecstatically*)
Our love shall not die. It shall laugh on the wind of the desert, when the morrow's sands drift over us. Come, my Bahana.

STONE (*embracing her*)
Butterfly!

(*They go out, left, in each other's arms. The voice of Hormek is heard below, offstage, right.*)

HORMEK
Ready to leave, Grayson?

FIRST WOMAN
The desert has conquered. They follow the mirage.

SECOND WOMAN (*grinding corn*)
White corn and red corn are ground and mingled. The pika smokes on the oven stones.

FIRST WOMAN (*in benediction*)
May good be in their hearts!

SECOND WOMAN
May good be in their hearts!

VOICE OF CHRISTINE (*calling*)
Gray, ho Gray!

FIRST WOMAN (*rising and turning her water-jar upside down*)
Tenkia! It is all finished.

SECOND WOMAN (*following her example*)
Aye, Tenkia!

(*They pass out slowly toward the left as the curtain falls.*)

MUSIC

Polaina's song is the "Laguna Corn-grinding Song," while the Men's Chant is the "Lene Tawi" (Hopi Flute Song.) The words and music are to be found only in "The Indians' Book," by Natalie Curtis [Natalie Curtis Burlin].

NAPOLEON'S BARBER

A PLAY

by ARTHUR CAESAR

CHARACTERS

NAPOLEON JOSEPHINE

BARBER PIERRE

NAPOLEON'S BARBER

PLACE.—*The village of Plombiers, about two kilometres outside the city of Dijon.*

TIME.—*Late one evening in the latter part of the eighteenth century, just before Napoleon's Spanish campaign.*

SCENE.—*An eighteenth-century barber shop in a small French village. Leading from the shop, up-stage, are three short steps which one mounts to enter the living quarters of the Barber. The shop is divided from the dwelling quarters by portières, which are almost always left undrawn so that the Barber's wife may know all that goes on in the shop. With rise of curtain the Barber is observed pacing to and fro in his shop, gesticulating wildly and reading from a manuscript a poem of his own composition.*

BARBER (*reciting his poem in a loud voice and with wild gesticulation*)

To arms! To arms! my braves!

Are ye but slaves?

The tools of knaves?

Such you are. Napoleon lives.

(*With the commencement of the reading, the Barber's wife stands in the doorway of the living chambers, listening to the Barber. The Barber, knowing she is there, pretends not to notice her, and goes on louder than ever with his poetry, expecting the approval of his wife.*)

Napoleon, beware!
Tyrant, have a care!
Had I you in my power,
I'd cut you ear to ear!

WIFE (*smiling, descends into the shop*)

That I believe. Some poor innocent client will be found here some day by the police, headless or earless or both, if you don't stop being a poet and reformer of France.

BARBER

There you go, defending Napoleon.

WIFE

Bah! Defending Napoleon! I never said anything about Napoleon. What have I to do with the business of kings and emperors? I leave them to the perfumed ladies of Paris. They can take care of them very well. I married a barber, who told my parents he was the best in Dijon, and could earn a real respectable livelihood, and now woe is me. I find I have been tricked. He has become the worst poet in France, and has made a business of being Napoleon's best enemy.

BARBER

Madame, you do not understand. A woman never understands. La Belle France is in danger. A tyrant is sapping its life's blood— (*Grows very emotional and stutters*) We must arouse the people of France to—to—t—to—

WIFE

To look after clients and save France by ceasing to chase away your patrons with long speeches and bad haircuts. (*Goes to him and puts her hand on his shoulder.*) Forget the stories of your ne'er-do-well brother in Paris. If he had something profitable to do, he wouldn't know nor care how many times a day a man beats his wife, even if that fellow were Napoleon. You were the best barber in France, and now you are merely the worst rhymester in the world. Give it up, I beg you.

BARBER

I can't— (*Very emotional*) I can't. Do you remember General Du Bois?

WIFE

Yes, the kind old man in charge of the Dijon section.

BARBER

Exactly. He is dead. A suicide.

WIFE

Dead! A suicide? Why?

BARBER

Napoleon insulted him.

WIFE

Poor man.

BARBER

Yes, he found him off duty. Is that such a crime, I ask you? And told him in front of several people, after recalling that he had decorated him with the Legion of Honor, he would shoot him in the very field where the old general had received the decoration, and with as much ceremony, if he found him away again without permission. Is that the way to talk to an old soldier?

WIFE

Well, I don't know, dear, but it seems to me that the General ought to have been soldier

enough to stick at his work, even as you ought
to be barber enough to shave, shave, shave.

BARBER

My God, woman, are you in love with that
devil? Oh, if I could have him here now, I
would cut his neck from ear to ear! I would,
may God help me!

(*During this speech the door leading from the
street into the shop has been quietly opened, and
in the doorway, listening, stands a private soldier. He is unshaven, his shoulders are stooped,
and his hair in the back is noticeably long.*)

NAPOLEON (*bows*)

Pardon. May a tired soldier of France be
shaved here?

(*Madame makes a hasty exit up the steps which
lead to the living quarters, enters the dwelling
chambers, and draws the curtain. The Barber
fumbles nervously with the manuscript and then
thrusts it into his blouse.*)

BARBER (*nervously*)

Eh, good day, my friend. Certainly, gladly.
Seat yourself. You must be tired.

NAPOLEON (*goes to chair and sits in it with a great
sigh of relief*)

I am tired. War is very hard work. It is
very hard for me, because I don't like seeing
blood. I hate red. If I could but stop for a
moment marking time for Fate. Destiny is a
hard master. He punishes and rewards you
within the minute; he ruins you while you
sleep. To him, a lost minute is eternity.

(*Stretches and sighs.*) Ah, but for a rest, without anxiety and fear.

BARBER (*with cup in hand, and not quite understanding*)

Without fear? Poor fellow! Do the officers beat you?

NAPOLEON

Yes, sometimes, when I'm not paying attention. When I'm off guard.

BARBER (*putting down the cup*)

Ah, it must be a hard life for you. Nothing to do but kill and avoid being killed.

NAPOLEON

You talk as if death were the thing to be feared. Ah, no; ah, no. It is life which holds out the promise of tomorrow. Death is the messenger of yesterday. I know of Cæsar and Rome, but what do I know of tomorrow?

BARBER

Oh, yes; quite right. Tomorrow you may be dead, poor fellow—

NAPOLEON

Do you read the stars? Is this prediction—

BARBER

I hear of men dying in the thousands. I hear strange stories of their blessing him who sends them to their death. (*Gets excited.*) Why? Sir—for whom do they die?

NAPOLEON

It is true, they bless him as they die—but why they should bless him as they die, I cannot say. (*Napoleon noticeably affected.*) I will never forget the lad who stood beside him, a messenger, in one of the battles of our last campaign. He was hardly fifteen, a child from the province of Dordogne, a dispatch carrier. I saw him shot through the heart, but still grasping the message, he saluted the Emperor: "God bless you, sire, your generals are victorious." (*Shakes his head.*) Poor lad, why should he have died blessing him, I wonder?

BARBER

Why, indeed, poor son of his miserable parents— Why, indeed, for a ridiculous little man they call Napoleon a tyrant, sucking the life's blood of France?

NAPOLEON

Quite right. A noʋoʋy, a ridiculous little man, the son of a bandit, bred in a bandit cave, who walked hungry through the streets of Paris, making promises to his stomach that it would sometime be fed power. The tears which flowed down his cheeks from his sleepless eyes watered this will to power.

BARBER (*very much encouraged. At last he has found a client who agrees with him, he thinks*) Ah, how well you put it! Such elegant language! You should be a journalist. He is a traitor, too; we mustn't forget that. He betrayed the Revolution.

NAPOLEON

Traitor, traitor; that's it. He cut off the hot heads and heated the cold ones. He turned the tide of blood-stained reason from suicide to system and order. And for such a reward; for a ridiculous eagle no handsomer than Hannibal's, but weighing a good deal heavier.

Traitor, indeed! He should be murdered in a bathtub by some kind mistress.

BARBER

Or a barber shop. Would it were mine.

NAPOLEON

You really hate him? You must know him well.

BARBER

Know him? Know him? I certainly do. He beats his wife, hates children, insults his generals, kills innocent soldiers for sport.

NAPOLEON

What does this monster look like who feeds on the blood of men?

BARBER

Just like the devil. Short, with popping eyes which burn into you like hot coals; a big head like a cabbage. Sometimes he looks like an imbecile and sometimes like a bloodthirsty monster whose compressed lips hide carnivorous teeth.

NAPOLEON (*sighs*)

You know him well, very well. A few mistakes in observation here and there, but for the rest you know him like a poor relation.

BARBER

Ah, then you know him, too.

NAPOLEON

Not too well.

BARBER

You served under him?

NAPOLEON

I served for him. I was his bodyguard; aye, his soul guard, too, if you please, for I saw to it that naught got to him which would interfere with his course for a moment. I knew that there was ever present the germ of his own destruction in himself. He is sentimental and sensitive.

BARBER (*with much awe*)
Then you were close to him?

NAPOLEON
So near to him I could hurt him with a word, a look. I could have permitted jealousy to smuggle its vicious sting into his consciousness, or dangerous doubting, or perhaps, the most destructive of all, indigestion. But I chal lenged them all.

BARBER
Yet you are still a private. What was your reward from the ungrateful one?

NAPOLEON
Reward was ever present in the game. The harder I watched, the greater his warning to watch harder, more carefully. The smaller the danger the greater was my carefulness. "For Fate," he would say, "lurks in strange places, and Destiny chooses strange moments for his practical jokes."

BARBER
Did he never say a kind word to you, the tyrant?

NAPOLEON
Yes, I remember one night when he was very kind to me. He reviewed his entire life for me. We had been in retreat for several days. During this time we had not tasted meat. The first day we had settled ourselves more or less

permanently, he ordered a full-course supper.
When the cook served it to him he ate it
ravishedly. That night he was sick. He sighed
and groaned and tossed about.

BARBER

Oh, had he died, what a blessing that would
have been.

NAPOLEON

Early that morning I heard him call my name.
"What is it, sire?" I asked. "Indigestion," he
replied, "my worst enemy. Listen, soldier.
Some day I shall lose all I have worked for because of my stomach. I have mastered all
elemental passions and emotions, but my desire
to eat, my ravishing desire to eat." Then,
pointing to his stomach, he said: "There lies
the source of victory and defeat; there lies the
fate of England and the world and Napoleon.
Achilles has bequeathed me his vulnerable heel
and I have swallowed it."

BARBER

I would have relieved him of his misery quickly,
the vicious dragon.

NAPOLEON

I think his ravishing appetite is responsible
for his speaking nights.

BARBER

His conscience, my friend. How can one rest
when he is responsible for the bloody deaths of
thousands? His heart must be as heavy as
lead—

NAPOLEON (*sighs*)

Nearly crushed, I should think.

BARBER

What does he say in his sleep? (*Anxiously*)
What does he do?

NAPOLEON

He is usually weeping. "Ah, woe is me!" he
cries, "woe is me. My generals lie to me; they
betray me. They promise to bring me the
hearts of ten thousand enemies, and I only get
one thousand."

BARBER (*disgusted*)

Hearts of men, the snake!

NAPOLEON (*continues*)

Then he calls the names of his marshals.
"Ney," he cries, "bring me the Colosseum. This
day, Blücher, spare no children! General,
bring me the Pope's ring this noon!"

BARBER (*very much excited*)

Heathen! Devil! No respect for God or
man! Oh, I could make short of him! May
God appoint me his executioner!

NAPOLEON (*reaches his climax in these gross exag-
gerations now. He draws the barber nearer by
speaking very quietly and dramatically*)

That is not the worst, for it is in the early
morning that he sends a chill running up and
down my spine. He repeats this tale every
night. I think it is a fixed thought with him.

BARBER (*anxiously*)

What is it?

NAPOLEON

You know how fond he is of the Orient. It
appeals to his dramatic sense—the pomp and
ceremony. Well, he has planned for himself a
gorgeous Oriental funeral. He directs that his

successor gather together five thousand Frenchmen. They must represent every trade and
profession—mechanics, tradesmen, lawyers, doc-
tors, and barbers. Every small village is to
give up its quota in barbers, et cetera. These
are to be buried with him in Oriental fashion to
keep him company. "I love France and
Frenchmen!" he cries. "I must have them in
death even as in life."

BARBER

Horrible ghoul! What an idea! Phew! (*Gets
very excited.*) Oh, if I only had him here—

NAPOLEON

Seeing you so excited, my dear friend, about the
trials of La Belle France, makes me a little bit
afraid that you might cut me.

BARBER (*very proudly*)

Not at all; not at all. I am the best barber in
Dijon. (*Now very profoundly*) And, besides,
shaving has nothing to do with revolution. I
keep them separate. One is an ideal and the
other a job. You understand.

NAPOLEON

Except when you have Napoleon for a customer. I suppose then the ideal and the job
meet.

(*Napoleon and the Barber laugh. The Barber
proceeds to lather Napoleon's face. He has one
side completely lathered when he suddenly stops
and searches through his blouse for the poem.*)

BARBER

I am going to read you my revolutionary
masterpiece.

NAPOLEON

Do you mind completing the art you have already commenced? The soap is drying on my face.

BARBER (*pays no attention to him, but wildly gesticulating, recites the poem, while Napoleon smiles and squirms uncomfortably in his chair. Starts to lather Napoleon's face again, and this time begins the shaving of him*)

In those funeral arrangements did he include barbers? Are you sure he expects to get one at least from every village?

NAPOLEON

Quite sure. I remember his distinctly saying barbers. Sometimes he would miss a doctor or a lawyer, but a barber never.

BARBER

Oh, if the man who shaves him only knew! If I were his barber—oh, if he were my customer, I would give him his funeral.

NAPOLEON

What can a barber do to Napoleon?

BARBER (*very much surprised. He gives his razor an energetic honing, lifts the head of Napoleon by the chin a little higher so that the head is thrown back, exposing the neck advantageously, then he turns his razor so that the blunt edge meets the neck of Napoleon*)

Look. Just this—(*runs the blunt edge across Napoleon's neck from ear to ear*) and no more Napoleon, no more tyranny, and a barber is the saviour of France.

NAPOLEON

True. A freak stroke of fate, and a barber succeeds where kings and emperors fail.

(*Napoleon throws his head back and shuts his
eyes and the Barber completes the shaving of
Napoleon, whistling Revolutionary tunes as he
proceeds.*)

BARBER (*pats Napoleon on the face*)

Ah! Now you look like a young bridegroom
all ready for— (*Whispers in Napoleon's ear and
laughs. Napoleon has an accommodating smile.*)
My Josephine likes me smooth-shaven. She
says she does not like me unshaven; it scratches
her skin. Vain women. They are strange,
aren't they?

NAPOLEON (*startled, repeats*)

Josephine—Josephine.

BARBER

Yes, that's the name of my wife, the woman
you saw here when you entered.

NAPOLEON

Josephine—your wife?

BARBER

Certainly, my good friend. Are you dreaming?
Certainly my wife.

NAPOLEON (*more to himself, with his back to the
Barber. He has turned about in the chair and
looks out into the dirt path which leads to the
barber shop. The sun is setting and it is growing
darker*)

Strange what images the sound of a name can
conjure up. The mention of that name has
driven from my mind the plans of empire,

wiped from my will the ambitions of a lifetime.
I am one with him, just male, just male, crowded
with sentimental yearnings of love and father-
hood and—

BARBER

Speaking to yourself?

NAPOLEON (*pays no heed. Still to himself, while
the Barber hones a razor*)

Strange how the years are destroyed by that
name. There she stands, in that drawing-
room, surrounded by the pampered pale aris-
tocracy of Paris. She, an Amazon in their
midst. The heat of the southern sun which
colored her ancestors gave her the passion of
its soul. Oh, Josephine, (*quietly*) Josephine,
you are mine in Egypt, on the battlefield, in
my tent in Italy, in victory and defeat, Josephine.

BARBER

Pardon. Have you ever heard Napoleon speak
of his Josephine? The poor woman does not
miss him and his beatings, I suppose. Do you
think he ever gives a thought to her—the
devil? I hear because of him she is not invited
to the salons of Paris. She is left lonely, poor
woman.

NAPOLEON (*with much disgust*)

Insects creep without much sense of honor or
loyalty. Today they ignore her, but tomorrow they will fawn at her feet and, like
lice, feed on the bounty and glory which she
may be able to bestow upon them. Phew!
Weep if you will about the destruction of
thousands on the battlefields. To one strong

oak there are thousands of fungi which must be destroyed before the strong can serve.

BARBER (*slowing growing conscious of a great personality. He takes sidelong looks at his patron as he hones his razors. He speaks little now, but keeps constantly honing a razor, listening and testing its sharpness*)
Don't lose your kindness, sir. Perhaps it's because of her recent caprices with a young army lieutenant.

NAPOLEON (*has heard this rumor before. He rises in the chair in a rage. The Barber hones*)
Lying lepers, slimy things which lie awake in the still night, planning the destruction of the fittest. Vultures, whose claws dig deepest when one is most helpless. Dark scientists of tears and laughter who study the human emotions, will, and intellect for their cowardly profit. They know to the gram the kind of stuff to feed the emotions until such time when it will in its desperation ride wildly over the will and intellect, destroying the victim of their unscrupulousness. But they shall eat the entrails of the weaker great, not the really great, for such caliber of food is too rich for their fluttering hearts.

(*The Barber listens to this speech not really meant for his ears, honing his razors and testing them. A look of suspicion has come into the face of the Barber. Napoleon knows he has betrayed himself. There enters from the street Pierre, the Barber's son. He is about ten years old, and is singing a French song. He spies the soldier and runs to him. Napoleon takes him up in his lap and kisses him.*)

PIERRE
Hello! Are you a soldier with Napoleon?

NAPOLEON
Yes, my little friend.

PIERRE
I want to be a soldier with Napoleon.

NAPOLEON
Do you? And why?

PIERRE
I like to fight, to sleep in tents, to march to the drum.

(*The Barber looks disapprovingly at his son, but continues to hone razors.*)

NAPOLEON
You may be a general some day.

PIERRE
My father doesn't like generals.

NAPOLEON
Why?

PIERRE
I don't know. He says they murder people. But mother says they sometimes make real men out of what look like people.

NAPOLEON (*laughs*)
That's true.

PIERRE
I can recite.

NAPOLEON (*pressing the boy closer to his breast*)
What?

PIERRE
Egalité, fraternité—liberté.

NAPOLEON

That's fine—a soldier in their name. A good sentiment.

(*From behind the portières is heard the calling of the name "Pierre."*)

PIERRE

I must go now. Mother will want an explanation for my staying so long after school was out. But I played war and won the battle.

(*Pierre by this time has gotten off Napoleon's lap and is walking toward the steps which lead up to the living quarters.*)

NAPOLEON

Fine boy.

PIERRE

Goodbye, father.

(*Barber, continuing to hone, says goodbye to the boy rather absent-mindedly.*)

NAPOLEON

Wait a moment, Pierre. Did you say that you won that battle?

PIERRE

Yes—the battle of Dijon.

NAPOLEON

Come here, my general!

(*Pierre approaches Napoleon. Napoleon fumbles in his coat for a medal of the Legion of Honor, pins it on him, kisses him, and salutes him. Pierre runs up the steps shouting.*)

PIERRE

Mother! Mother! See what I have!

(The Barber has watched this proceeding with great awe. By this time he has laid out all his razors with their blades extended.)

BARBER
But, sir, only he can do this—give the medal of the Legion. Are you—

NAPOLEON
Whom?

(Both men look at each other intensely. There is in the face of the Barber a knowledge of the certain identity of Napoleon. Napoleon seems to read the thoughts of the Barber as he gazes at the newly sharpened razors.)

NAPOLEON *(runs his hands over his neck)*
You have not quite finished. My neck here—it is a little rough in spots. It will take but a moment.

BARBER *(anxious and nervous)*
Only a minute, sir.

(Chooses one of the newly sharpened razors, hones it again, pulls from his head a hair, and tests it. A smile of satisfaction lights up his face. Napoleon watches him intensely. He lays his head back, staring firmly up into the face of the barber. The Barber grows more and more nervous as he commences to shave Napoleon's neck. Napoleon watches him intensely. His eyes hold those of the barber firmly fixed upon him. The hand of the Barber shakes noticeably.)

NAPOLEON *(just audibly)*
No accidents, my friend. This requires will-power. I cannot be the victim of accident.

BARBER (*throws his razor to the ground, falls to his knees before him, and shrieks in a high pitch nervously*)

My God! I can't! You are too human! I can't! You are too strong! You are the Emperor! Forgive me.

(*Enter from the living quarters the Barber's wife and her son. They hear the last words—"You are the Emperor." The Barber's wife falls to her knees; Pierre runs to Napoleon's side.*)

WIFE

Forgive him. He is a good barber and a good husband, but a fool.

NAPOLEON (*holding Pierre's hand*)

Rise, madame. You are forgiven for marrying a fool. You are punished beyond measure.

BARBER

Forgive me. I did not mean to preach revolution. I did not know you were a man. I thought you were a devil. I did not mean to preach revolt. Forgive me.

NAPOLEON (*acting up to the situation, feigning anger*)

Forgive you? Listen, Barber. You held the fate of France in your hand; aye, perhaps the entire world, and you had not the courage to go on. That, Mr. Barber, is the real difference between us—personality, the will to power. I can forgive you your revolutionary rantings. I love those who hate me; they prove my invincibility. I am too vain to hang those that oppose me. The spirits of Hannibal and Constantine, Alexander and Cæsar live within me.

I cannot hang barbers for opposing me, but listen: The next time you take the imperial name in vain to rhyme with an impossible word, you have my word that you will hang for it. I can forgive bad shaving, but bad poetry never.

(*He turns swiftly on his heels in military fashion. It has grown quite dark now, and there is just barely seen the figure of Napoleon disappearing through the street door.*)

BARBER (*as he rises to his feet exclaims to his wife*) Think of it, Josephine! Think of it! I have been honored by the Emperor!

CURTAIN

GOAT ALLEY

A PLAY IN ONE ACT

by ERNEST HOWARD CULBERTSON

CHARACTERS

LUCY BELLE DORSEY
"SLIM" DORSEY, *her Brother*
AUNT REBECCA, *an Old Negress*
LIZZIE GIBBS, *a Mulatto Woman*
SAM REED, *alias "Mule" Reed*
FANNY DORSEY, ⎫
ISRAEL DORSEY, ⎬ *Children*
POLICEMAN
A YOUNG BABY

GOAT ALLEY is here published as a One-Act Play. It was later re-written and made into a long play. The extended version may be had from the publishers, D. Appleton and Company, 35 West 32d Street, New York City, N. Y.

GOAT ALLEY

The curtain rises on the sitting-room of a negro's squalid dwelling in Goat Alley, Washington, D. C. At the Right Back there is a door giving directly on the street, and when it is open one gets a glimpse of the miserable, tumble-down houses on the opposite side. At Left Back is a window, one pane of which is broken out and an old shirt stuck in the hole. The one or two filthy rag-carpet rugs which lie on the floor serve only in a small measure to cover its bareness. Several old, broken, and battered chairs stand here and there about the room. At Left Center is a door leading into the other room of the house. Between it and the wall at Back is a door opening into a closet. Near the door, Left Center, and toward the front stands a battered table on which lie, in disordered array, papers and one or two dog-eared books with their backs off. It is night and a lighted oil lamp, with the chimney badly smoked, rests in the center. The wick is turned low, and the guttering flame causes countless shadows to disport themselves eerily about the room. Flamboyant lithographs, a gilt-framed picture of Jack Johnson, wearing his golden smile, an engraved portrait of Abraham Lincoln, and several grotesque crayon portraits, presumably of members of the family (crassly inexpressive), adorn the dirty and discolored walls. An old corset, a half-eaten roll, and a doll, with the head off,

*lie about on the floor. A horseshoe is nailed over
the center of the door, Back.*

*Aunt Rebecca, an old, coal-black negress, enters,
Back, with a shawl thrown over her shoulders. She
has the appearance of an animated mummy. Her
eyes are small and bead-like, and shine with an
uncanny lustre; her hands, long and bony, re-
sembling the talons of a hawk. She glances about
inquiringly, gives an impatient grunt, then turns
and slowly closes the door.*

AUNT REBECCA (*in high-pitched, raspy tones, as she
moves to the Center*)
Lucy Belle! Oh, Lucy Belle!

LUCY BELLE (*from the next room*)
Yassum! Jes' a minute.

(*Aunt Rebecca moves slowly about the room,
mumbling to herself. Presently Lucy Belle enters,
Left, wearing a black straw sailor hat, badly
misshapen, and carrying a basket of washing.
She is a frail, light-brown, young negress of about
twenty-eight. She has a nervous, hesitating manner.*)

LUCY BELLE
Oh! I'se so glad yo's yere. Yo' kin stay a
while, kain't yo'? (*Aunt Rebecca grunts and
nods.*) I wants yo' ter stay wid de chillen while
I runs out wid dis yere washin'. Only take a
minute—'roun ter Miss Erminie's. (*Lucy Belle
deposits the washing on a chair.*) Seem mighty
good ter have yo' so handy onct more. Jes' like
ole times. Les' see—how long yo' all been
'way?

66

AUNT REBECCA (*reflectively, as she sits.*)

Um! Um! (*Puts a hand to her head.*) Dat gin got mah haid all tangle up. Um! I keep tellin' G'orge whiskey suit me bettah—but he like gin. How long? Um! Um! Gawd-a-massy! Be two yeahs in Feb-wary! (*Lucy Belle exclaims incredulously.*) Sho' has! I was a yeah in Cumberlan' wid Sadie—she's de slim yallar one, yo' know—got a mole on her right cheek. Some say dat reason she so lucky—an' den mos' six mon's wid Em'ly—she dat lil' fat, brown gal. (*Lucy Belle nods.*) An' den fo' mon's in Frederick wid Henry. (*Shaking her head proudly.*) Henry a great big fine lookin' niggah. Ain' so lucky dough. Bawn in de da'k ob de moon.

LUCY BELLE

I 'member him. I 'member seein' him w'en his fawther died—ole Uncle Henry.

AUNT REBECCA (*scornfully*)

Dat niggah wasn't his fawther. No indeedy! Dat lil' scrootchin' monkey wasn't calc'lated ter be de fawther ob no boy like Henry. (*Lucy Belle gives an exclamation of surprise. Aunt Rebecca sits in perplexed preoccupation for several moments. At length she speaks slowly.*) 'Deed, chile, I kain't seem ter 'member who Henry's fawther was. Dat gin got mah haid all tangle up.

LUCY BELLE (*turning and moving toward Left*)

I reckon I bettah bring dat baby out yere. No tellin' what dem chillen liable ter do to it.

(*She hurries out, Left. In a moment or two she returns, carrying a very young negro baby.*)

AUNT 'REBECCA
Yo' want me ter hol' him?

LUCY BELLE
I reckon yo' might as well. (*She places the baby in Aunt Rebecca's arms.*)

(*Fanny Dorsey, a little negro girl of eight, and Israel Dorsey, a little negro boy of six, run in, Left. Both wear nightgowns.*)

FANNY
Mamma! Where yo' all gwine?

ISRAEL
Mamma! Git me some candy!

LUCY BELLE (*harshly*)
Yo' all hush! Git right back ter bed! Go 'long!

FANNY (*whimpering*)
I'se scar't ob de night doctahs.

LUCY BELLE
Hush, chile! Night doctahs ain' gwine ter git yo' in yere. Go 'long! (*Threateningly.*) Do yo' wan' me ter beat yo'?

ISRAEL
Mamma! Git me—

(*Lucy Belle grabs them roughly and pushes them through door, Left, closing it after them. Their cries are heard for several moments and then gradually cease.*)

LUCY BELLE
Some day I'se gwine ter git good an' mad an' knock dere haids off! (*Dropping into a chair and drawing a hand across her forhead.*) I ain' nevah had no luck. Some gals gits by widout no trouble at all. I ain' one-a dem kin'. Nuffin'

68

I evah done come out right—nuffin at all! Ef
I starts ana'thing its boun' ter go wrong. I—
I'se cunjuhed fer life!

AUNT REBECCA

Hush, chile! Don' git down in de mouf like dat!
Yo' luck liable change any minute. Min' did
aftah I gits rid-a dem warts.

LUCY BELLE

I ain' got no business wid all dese chillen. I'se
a fool—Gawd knows I is! Ain' only one niggah
evah treated me decent.

AUNT REBECCA

Who dat?

LUCY BELLE

Sam Reed. Gawd knows he treated me right!
An' now he's in jail!

AUNT REBECCA

Honey!

LUCY BELLE

I loves him. He's de onliest niggah I evah did
love! I thinks 'bout him all de time! (*A moment's pause. She stares into space.*)

AUNT REBECCA

How long he been in jail?

LUCY BELLE

I reckon it's been pretty near two yeahs.
Weren't long aftah yo' lef' I knows.

AUNT REBECCA

Is he yere?

LUCY BELLE (*shaking her head*)

Down at Moun'sville. He kain't write, an' so
I don' nevah yere from him. (*A moment's
pause.*)

AUNT REBECCA (*cautiously*)
What did he do?

LUCY BELLE (*disconsolately, as she stares into space*)
Cut a man. (*With feeling.*) He done it fer me!
Jim Bisbee come foolin' roun' aftah me—mos'
allas drunk—an' one day Sam seen him—aw,
dere wasn't nuffin' to it. Jim, he blubbered like
a baby. He was so scar't he didn't know what
ter do. Deed he was a sight!

AUNT REBECCA
An' de *po*-lice git him?

LUCY BELLE (*sadly*)
Yas, indeed. (*Rises slowly and takes up the
basket.*) I ain' nevah gwine ter meet up wid
anoder niggah like Sam. He's de bes' ole buddy
in de worl'!

AUNT REBECCA
How long did dey send him up fo'?

LUCY BELLE
Fo' yeahs. (*A silence. She moves toward door,
Back.*)

LUCY BELLE (*at door*)
I ain' gwine ter be gone but a minute.

(*Aunt Rebecca nods. Lucy Belle passes out, Back.
Aunt Rebecca chants in a low monotone to herself.*)

AUNT REBECCA
Um—aum—a—um—a—um—a—um — a —
um! Trouble in mah soul! Um—a—um—a—
um—a—um—a—um—a! Trouble in mah soul!
(*High treble*) Um—a—um—a—um—a—um—a!

(*Footsteps and someone whistling are heard offstage, Back. Aunt Rebecca stops and listens. The
door opens and "Slim" Dorsey enters, Back. He*

70

is a tall, slender, light-colored, young negro of about twenty-four. He wears a cap and old ragged suit of clothes.)

SLIM

Hello, Aun' Becky. What yo' all doin' yere?

AUNT REBECCA

Mindin' de chillen fo' Lucy Belle.

SLIM

Whar she?

AUNT REBECCA

Takin' washin' 'roun' ter Miss Erminie.

(*Slim proceeds to roll a cigarette.*)

SLIM

Dat gal ain' no good. She'd make twict as much ef she was ter wuk out.

AUNT REBECCA

What kin' a brudder is yo'? Dat ain' no way ter talk. What would she do wid de chillen?

SLIM (*licking the cigarette*)

Ter hell wid dem.

AUNT REBECCA

Shame on yo'—shame on yo'—talkin' like dat! She doin' de bes' she kin! An' yo' all ies' lay 'roun' an' let her keep yo'.

SLIM

Dat's a lie! I wuks a damn sight harder den she do.

AUNT REBBECA

Where yo' wuk?

SLIM

On de wharf—shuckin' oysters.

AUNT REBECCA

Dat steady?

SLIM

Steady in season. I fishes w'en I ain' wukkin dere. Dat's why we move ovah yere—ter be handy ter de rivah. Don' yo' all go lyin' 'bout me livin' off Lucy Belle.

(*Aunt Rebecca glowers at him and remains silent for several moments.*)

AUNT REBECCA (*suddenly to Slim and nodding toward Left*)

What niggah de fader dese chillen ob Lucy Belle's?

SLIM

Dat gal Fanny is Ed Cales'. (*Shaking his head.*) Gawd knows who's de fader ob de oder two. (*A moment's silence. Slim lights the cigarette.*)

AUNT REBECCA

She got too many children.

SLIM

Ain' nobody knows dat bettah den I do. No niggah ain' gwine ter take up wid her now. Ed Cales was crazy fo' ter marry her one time. Huh—he wouldn't look sideways at her ef he was ter see her in de street.

(*The wind blows and whistles through the cracks. Aunt Rebecca sits erect and the whites of her eyes show.*)

AUNT REBECCA (*in low, frightened tones*)

Gawd—a—massy! Yo' ain' gwine ter git me— yo' ole hussy!

SLIM

What's matter?

AUNT REBECCA
  Dat's Lil Mundy tryin' ter git back at me.
SLIM (*with a laugh*)
  What fer?
AUNT REBECCA
  Fer kickin' dat ole dog ob hern off my do' step.

  (*Lucy Belle enters, Back, at this point, carrying the empty basket.*)

AUNT REBECCA (*exclaiming*)
  Lan' sake, chile! It ain' takin' yo' long.
LUCY BELLE
  Yo' don' see me wastin' no time on a night like dis. Hello, Slim.
SLIM (*jumping up*)
  "Luce," Sam's yere!
LUCY BELLE (*dropping the basket with a cry*)
  What d' yo' mean?
SLIM
  He's back yere in Wash'nin.
LUCY BELLE (*with a gasp*)
  Oh, Gawd!
SLIM
  "Mink" Hall jes' tol' me. He's lookin' fo' yo'.
LUCY BELLE
  Sam!
SLIM
  Yas. Yo' see he done los' track of us since we move.
LUCY BELLE (*huskily*)
  How—how did he git out so soon?
SLIM
  Got his sentence cut short fo' bein' good.

73

LUCY BELLE (*agitatedly*)
Does Mink Hall know whar we live?

SLIM
He didn'. I jes' tol' him.

LUCY BELLE (*with a cry of anger*)
Yo' was a damn fool ter do dat—widout comin'
an' tellin' me! Oh! (*Moves agitatedly about.*)

SLIM
No use ter keep my mouf shet. Sam gwine ter
find out somehow or 'nother.

LUCY BELLE
Yo' ain' got no sense! Nevah did have no
sense! Damn yo'!

SLIM (*moving toward door, Back*)
Keep on talkin' ef yo' wan' ter lan' in de hospital.

LUCY BELLE (*imploringly*)
Slim—Slim—ef—ef yo' see him duck—duck.
I'se gwine over to Mag's fo' a few days—in de
mawnin'. I—I don' want ter see him fo' a day
or two.

SLIM
I ain' botherin' 'bout him.

LUCY BELLE
Slim—yo'll duck, won't yo? Won't yo', honey?

(*Slim slowly nods, then turns and passes out,
Back.*)

LUCY BELLE (*slowly removing her hat and coat*)
Oh, Gawd! I didn't have no kind-a idea Sam
'ud git out so soon. (*Rapturously.*) Sam! Mah,
Sam! (*Then fearfully.*) But I kain't see him
yet awhile.

74

AUNT REBECCA

What's de mattah, honey?

LUCY BELLE (*wringing her hands*)

I tol' yo' I nevah had no luck! What kin a po' gal like me do? Yo'—yo' see I got dat baby. It—it's free months ole now. Ef he sees dat— Oh, Gawd!

AUNT REBECCA

Yo' reckon—

LUCY BELLE

He'd kill me! Sho' as yo' bawn! Yo' see—Oh, Gawd! Ef he could only know what I been up against! I—I promised him I wouldn't look at a niggah while he was gone. Ef I'd a had any kind-a luck, nuffin' in de worl' would a made me break it! I loves Sam—I loves him bettah den anybody. He knows I does. (*A moment's pause. Her eyes rove space.*) Las' wintah I couldn't git nuffin' much ter do—an' Slim he didn't have no job—an' Chick Avery, he come 'roun'. Chick is a barber an' makes good money. Him an' me went ter school togeder. (*Slowly.*) I let's him stay yere fo' a while. (*A moment's pause, then she points at the baby.*) Dat's his chile.

AUNT REBECCA (*shaking her head*)

Yo' po', po' chile!

LUCY BELLE

When Sam an' me fust met he says: "Lucy Belle, I don't care nuffin' at all 'bout what yo' done fo' I knowed yo'. Dat's all pas' an' some'fin' yo' an' me ain' gwine ter boder our haids 'bout." (*She stares into space.*) But den

he said he'd kill me ef I evah had anything ter
do wid anoder niggah.

AUNT REBECCA

Nevah min'! He ain' gwine ter do nuffin' like
dat! Don' yo' worry!

LUCY BELLE (*smiling faintly*)

He's de onliest niggah dat evah done an'thing
much fo' me. He done mos' eva'thing I ask
him. Take me downtown on pay day an' buy
me clothes. Onct him an' me was 'rested fo'
gittin' drunk—an' he lies off an' takes all de
blame hisself. (*A moment's pause.*) An'—an'
yo' see he's comin' right back ter me now he's
out.

AUNT REBECCA

Yas, indeed!

LUCY BELLE (*clenching her hands*)

Oh, Gawd!

AUNT REBECCA

Don' yo' worry, honey!

LUCY BELLE

Sam nevah boder his haid 'bout oder gals—not
since he know me. Long, long time ago he wen'
wid ole Lizzie Gibbs. Yo' know dat hard, ole
yallaw gal? (*Aunt Rebecca nods.*) De whole
yeah fo' he wen' ter jail she keep aftah him all
de time! Nevah did see nuffin' like it. He don'
care no mo' fo' her den he do a rat! But I'se
scar't a her. She'd blackguard me in a minute
ef she thought she had some'fin on me. (*Fearfully.*) Dat's de onliest thing I'm scar't of—is
dat niggahs will lie an' blackguard on me!

AUNT REBECCA (*indicating the baby*)

Who all know yo' got dis yere chile?

76

LUCY BELLE

Only Slim an' Mag an' yo'. Mag's mah sister dat lives ovah in Anacostia. Yo' see we move from Carter St. ovah yere ter Goat Alley—an' we didn't tell nobody where we was gwine. Dat's why Sam cain't fin' me.

AUNT REBECCA

Ef I didn't have dem gran'chillen I'd keep de baby fo' yo'.

LUCY BELLE

No, no! Wouldn't wan' yo' ter do nuffin' like dat.

AUNT REBECCA

What do yo' calc'late yo' do?

LUCY BELLE (*pacing about agitatedly*)

I don' know, I don' know! I ain' done no mo' den oder gals—an'—an' Sam gotta fo'give me!

(*A knock sounds on the door, Back. Lucy Belle starts.*)

LUCY BELLE (*in a low voice to Aunt Rebecca*)

Take him in dere. (*Points off, Left.*)

(*Aunt Rebecca rises, carrying baby, and hurries out, Left.*)

LUCY BELLE (*as she disappears*)

Come in!

(*The door, Back, opens and Lizzie Gibbs enters. She is a large, voluptuous, loud-mouthed mulatto. She has straight hair and a sinister countenance. She wears no hat, but has a light shawl thrown over her shoulders.*)

LIZZIE (*slouching in*)

Hello!

LUCY BELLE (*starting back*)
Hel—hello, Lizzie.

LIZZIE
How is yo'?

LUCY BELLE
I'se all right.

LIZZIE
Thought I'd fin' yo' flyin' 'roun' wid yo' eyes popin' out-a yo' haid.

LUCY BELLE (*with studied complacency*)
No, indeed! I don' know what yo' all talkin' 'bout.

LIZZIE (*with a sarcastic laugh*)
Ha! Ha! Ain' got nuffin' on yo' min', eh?

LUCY BELLE
Not a thing!

LIZZIE
A good frien' of yo's is back in town.

LUCY BELLE
Now yo' said some'fin'. Who?

LIZZIE (*darkly*)
Dat's right—preten' yo' don' know nuffin' 'bout it—yo' damn little hussy!

LUCY BELLE (*hotly*)
Don' yo' call me no hussy!

LIZZIE
Don' yo' stan' up dere an' tell me yo' don' know Sam Reed ain' home.

LUCY BELLE (*simulating surprise*)
Sam! No! Is yo' seen him?

LIZZIE (*mysteriously*)
Ha! Ha! I guess he don' fergit ole friends.

LUCY BELLE (*sharply*)
Huh! I bet he ain'! I bet yo' all I got he ain'!

78

LIZZIE

Yo' all got de idee yo' got some kin' of a strangle hol' on Sam, ain' yo'?

LUCY BELLE

I knows damn well he ain' gwine ter fool 'roun' an' ole wench like yo'!

LIZZIE (*menacingly*)

Ef yo' say anything like dat agin I'll bus' yo' in yo' mouf. (*Lucy Belle laughs.*) Lemme tell yo', gal, I knows a thing or two 'bout yo'.

LUCY BELLE

Nuffin' but what yo' make up out-a yo' own haid.

LIZZIE

Gawd knows how many times I seen yo' on de street las' wintah wid Chick Avery.

LUCY BELLE (*quickly*)

Yo' nevah! Yo' lie!

LIZZIE (*with a laugh*)

Oh, yas, yo' little angel-face! Yo' nevah done nuffin' wrong in yo' life! (*Darkly.*) Lemme tell yo' one thing—keep yo' han's off dat niggah. If I yere he's been foolin' 'roun' yo' all, I'se gwine ter raise some hell. (*She turns toward the door.*)

LUCY BELLE

Yo' won't do nuffin'!

LIZZIE (*turning for a moment*)

Ask anybody dat knows me ef I don' allas make good. I'll clean up fo' yo' all! I'll fix dat face ob yo's so it won' nevah look de same!

LUCY BELLE

Yo' ain' gwine ter do nuffin'!

6   79

LIZZIE (*at the door*)

Ain' I? Yo' wait an' see? I'se gwine ter make dat face-a yo's look like a piece-a sausage. Don' yo' come tryin' ter play any ob dat doll-baby business wid me! Ha! Ha! Yo' damn lil' hussy, yo'! (*She passes out, Back.*)

(*Lucy Belle stands gazing angrily after her. Presently, Aunt Rebecca enters, Left.*)

AUNT REBECCA

Whew-me! Gawd-a-massy! Sweah out a warrant fo' her! Go 'long! Don' yo' let no niggah blackguard yo' like dat!

LUCY BELLE

I'll git her mahse'f! Ef I don', Slim will. (*Fiercely.*) Some night I'll ketch her alone an' I'll knock her haid off!

AUNT REBECCA

Low down yallaw wench!

LUCY BELLE

I ain' gwine ter stan' fo' no niggah talkin' ter me like dat! (*Moving agitatedly about.*) 'Deed I ain'! What she anyway? Stuck up kase she got straight hair. Nevah done a lick-a wuk in her life.

AUNT REBECCA

Hush, honey! Ain' no use ter git all wukked up!

LUCY BELLE (*with an hysterical laugh*)

Ha! Ha! She think she kin keep Sam away from me! I like ter see her! I like ter see her!

AUNT REBECCA

Nevah min'! Nevah min'!

(*A knock on the back door. Lucy Belle and Aunt Rebecca start.*)

LUCY BELLE (*calling in tremulous tones*)
Who dat?

SAM (*off, Back*)
Me!

LUCY BELLE (*with a gasp*)
It Sam! (*She motions to Aunt Rebecca to leave the room. The latter hurries out, Left.*)

(*Lucy Belle hesitates a moment, then goes to door, Back, and opens it. Sam Reed enters. He is a big, powerful negro—brown in color—of about thirty-five. He wears an old ragged suit of clothes, an old felt hat, and no collar.*)

SAM (*with a cry of joy*)
Gal!

LUCY BELLE (*rushing to him*)
Sam!

SAM (*taking her in his arms and smothering her with kisses*)
Honey baby! Honey baby!

LUCY BELLE (*murmuring softly*)
Baby! Baby!

SAM
Yo' ain' forgot yo' ole Sam, is yo'?

LUCY BELLE
No, no! Oh, Sam, Sam! Mah ole Sam-boy! (*Clutching him tight.*) Oh, I'se so glad ter see yo'! Gawd bless yo'!

SAM
Honey baby! Honey baby!

LUCY BELLE
Ole Sam-boy! I'se *so* glad ter see yo'!

SAM
Yo' all didn't 'spec' me, did yo'?

LUCY BELLE

No, no! Didn't have no idea in de worl' I'd see yo' so soon! Not until jes' a minute ago! Slim come an' tol' me! Mink Hall tol' him. Ah, Sam-boy! Yo' ain' nevah gwine ter leave me agin, is yo'?

SAM

No, indeedy! Not unless dey takes me away in a box!

LUCY BELLE

Yo's de bes' ole baby in de worl'!

SAM

Seem ter me I only had ter shet mah eyes— night or day—an' see yo' face. Only thinkin' 'bout yo' kept me from killin' everybody in sight when I'se breakin' mah back on dem rock piles. Yo' don' know what kin'-a hell I been through, gal. Kin'-a hell dat sets a man crazy —'less he's careful.

LUCY BELLE

I know, I know. Mus'—a been turrible—turrible. Oh, Gawd!

SAM

What made yo' all move?

LUCY BELLE (*quickly*)

It's nearer fo' Slim—nearer to de rivah.

SAM

Nobody knowed whar yo' was.

LUCY BELLE

No, no! We sort-a los' track of all dem ole niggahs ovah dere.

SAM

Yo' lookin' mighty thin.

LUCY BELLE

I'se been wukkin' hard, Sam. 'Tain't easy fo'
a gal alone an'—an' wid two chillen.

SAM

I reckon not. Yo' po' kid!

LUCY BELLE

Sam—Sam-boy, le's yo' an' me go to Baltimo'.

SAM

Baltimo'!

LUCY BELLE

Yas. Dey's mo' wuk ovah dere. Everybody
say so. An'—an' dey pay bettah wages.

SAM

I don' know, honey.

LUCY BELLE

De *po*-lice be aftah yo' all de time.

SAM

No, dey won't.

LUCY BELLE

Dey will—yo' know dey will. Eva' time dey's a
little trouble dey'll pick yo' up. An'—an' I ain'
nevah had no luck in dis town.

SAM

I'll study 'bout if fo' awhile.

LUCY BELLE

Ain' near de chances ter git wuk dat dere is dere.

SAM

What put it in yo' haid ter go dere?

LUCY BELLE

I wants ter git away. I gotta feelin' dat things
ain' nevah gwine right long as we stay yere.

SAM

Wait until de fust of de week—an' den maybe
I'll go.

LUCY BELLE

Baby, it's bes'—I knows it is. Yo' an' me nevah had no luck in dis town.

SAM

All right, honey baby. Ef dat's what yo' wants to do we'll go.

LUCY BELLE (*throwing her arms about him*)

Baby, baby! Gawd bless yo'! Mah Sam-boy! Mah Sam-boy!

(*Aunt Rebecca enters, Left.*)

LUCY BELLE (*breaking away from Sam*)

Oh, Aun' Becky!

SAM (*rushing forward and shaking her hand*)

Aun' Becky! Glad ter see yo'!

AUNT REBECCA

Sam! Gawd bless yo'!

SAM

How yo' all been?

AUNT REBECCA

. 'Tolable! 'Tolable! I kain't complain. I'se mighty glad yo's out.

SAM

I'se mighty glad ter be out.

AUNT REBECCA

Mus' 'scuse me. I got ter git home an' cook some supper fo' mah ole man.

LUCY BELLE

Don' run away, Aun' Becky.

AUNT REBECCA

Mus', mah chile! See yo' some mo'.

SAM

Good-bye.

(*Aunt Rebecca passes out, Back.*)

LUCY BELLE (*moving toward Left*)
Honey baby, 'scuse me a minute.

SAM
Whar yo' gwine?

LUCY BELLE (*nodding toward Left*)
In yere. I'll be right back.

(*Sam nods. She passes out, Back. Sam moves
slowly about the room. Presently, there is a loud
knock on the door, Back. Sam starts toward the
door. As he nears it, it opens and Lizzie rushes
in.*)

LIZZIE (*halting abruptly*)
Sam!

SAM
What in hell are yo' doin' yere?

LIZZIE (*ingratiatingly*)
Sam, kid—come on wid me!

SAM
Go 'long! Ef yo' keep foolin' 'roun' me yo's
gwine ter git hurt.

LIZZIE
Sam—Sam, ole baby—what did I evah do ter
make yo' treat me like yo' have?

SAM
Go 'long! D' yo' yere me?

LIZZIE (*her manner gradually changing*)
Yo's a damn fool fo' stickin' ter dis gal.

SAM (*menacingly*)
Yo' shet up!

LIZZIE
She don' care nuffin' 'bout yo'!

SAM (*stepping toward her*)
I bet I'll bus' yo' in de mouf.

LIZZIE

Sam—I'se gwine ter git a good job uptown—
Monday. I'll keep yo' dis wintah, Sam. Yo'
won' haf ter do no wuk. I don' want ter see no
fellah like yo' git tied up wid a wench like her.

SAM

Git out-a yere—d' yo' yere me? 'Go long!

LIZZIE (*nastily*)

Yo's a great big stiff ter let a gal like her take
yo' in!

(*The door, Left, opens slightly and Lucy Belle can
be seen listening.*)

SAM (*hotly*)

Shet up!

LIZZIE

She been runnin' 'roun' wid Chick Avery—
evah since yo' lef'. Ha! Ha!

SAM

Dat's a lie!

LIZZIE

So help me **Gawd,** dat's de tru'f—an' I kin
prove it!

SAM (*menacingly*)

It's a lie!

LIZZIE

She'll bleed yo' ter deaf an' den tu'n yo' loose.
Dat's what I'm telling yo'!

SAM (*hitting her on the jaw*)

Shet up!

LIZZIE (*shrieking*)

Murder! Murder! Po-lice! Po-lice! Murder!

(*Sam darts out the door, Back. Lucy Belle closes
the door, Left. Hurried footsteps are heard at*

Back. Lizzie glances out of window, Back, gives a little gasp, hesitates a moment, then darts into the closet, Left Back, closing the door after her. A policeman enters, Back.)

POLICEMAN (*calling out*)
What's the trouble here? (*He stands surveying the room for a moment or two, then advances toward door, Left. The door suddenly opens and Lucy Belle enters.*)

POLICEMAN (*gruffly*)
What's the matter?

LUCY BELLE
Nuffin'—nuffin' at all, sir.

POLICEMAN
There was so! (*Marching over to her.*) Who was that yellin'?

LUCY BELLE
I—I don' know, sir. It wasn't yere.

POLICEMAN
I know better!

LUCY BELLE
No, no! Hones' to Gawd!

POLICEMAN
Don't try to give me any gaff like that! (*Striding over to the door, Left.*) Who's in here?

LUCY BELLE
Jas' mah chillen.

(*He passes in. She stands watching him. He re-enters in a moment.*)

POLICEMAN (*moving toward Back*)
I've a good mind to lock you up anyway.

LUCY BELLE (*With a wail*)
Oh—Oh, please, sir—I nevah done nuffin'!

POLICEMAN (*hesitating at the door*)

You'd better look out. I ain't goin' to stand for any monkey business around this neighborhood. (*He passes out, Back, closing the door after him.*)

(*Lucy Belle stands gazing after him for a moment or two. Eventually she turns and passes hurriedly out, Left. She re-enters immediately, carrying the baby. Fanny—in her nightgown—runs in, Left.*)

FANNY

Mamma!

LUCY BELLE

Hush, chile!

FANNY

Whar yo' gwine?

LUCY BELLE

I'se gwine ter take de baby ovah to yo' Aun' Rebecca's. Yo' go right back ter bed. Go 'long!

(*Fanny turns and runs out, Left, closing the door after her. Lucy Belle starts toward Back. Lizzie steps out from the closet.*)

LIZZIE

So dat's yo' baby, is it?

LUCY BELLE (*with a cry*)

Oh! Oh, mah Gawd!

LIZZIE

I knowed I'd git yo'! Pretendin' ter be such a little angel! Ha! Ha! Been up ter all kin'-a tricks, ain' yo'?

LUCY BELLE (*commanding herself*)
Git out-a yere!

LIZZIE (*slouching slowly toward Back*)
I got yo' numbah, now! Ha! Ha!

LUCY BELLE
What in hell d' yo' mean? It ain' mah chile!

LIZZIE
Ha! Ha! Ha! Ain' yo' chile! Ain' yo' chile!
Yo's a good little liah, ain' yo?

LUCY BELLE (*defiantly*)
No, it ain'—yo' blackguardin' hussy!

LIZZIE
Ha! Ha! It certainly do look like Chick—jes'
'zactly. Wait until I tells Sạm. He's one-a
dem kin' dat ain' so particular. He don' min'
accidents now an' den! Ha! Ha! (*She
slouches out, Back, laughing fiendishly.*)

(*Lucy Belle stands staring to the front. Suddenly
a look of desperation comes over her face and she
dashes out, Back. In the course of a moment or
two Aunt Rebecca enters, Back, and moves about
the room.*)

AUNT REBECCA (*calling*)
Lucy Belle! Oh, Lucy Belle!

(*Fanny runs in, Left.*)

FANNY
Mamma's gone ovah to yo' house wid de baby.

AUNT REBECCA
Mah house!

FANNY
Dat what she say.

AUNT REBECCA

'Deed, chile, yo' all mus' been dreamin'.

FANNY (*with a whimper*)

Den—den I don' know whar she is.

AUNT REBECCA

Yo' been dreamin'. Go 'long back ter bed.

(*Fanny reluctantly passes out, Left. Aunt Rebecca sits down in a chair and chants to herself.*)

AUNT REBECCA

Devil gwine ter git yo'! Um—a—um—a—um—a—um—a—um—a! Devil gwine ter git yo'! Um — a — um — a — um — a — um—a—um—a! Devil gwine ter git yo'!

(*Suddenly Slim rushes in, Back, wild-eyed.*)

SLIM (*breathlessly*)

Aun' Becky!

AUNT REBECCA

Yas! Yas!

SLIM

Lucy Belle drown de baby!

AUNT REBECCA (*jumping up with a shriek*)

Oh! Oh, mah Gawd! Oh, oh!

SLIM (*rapidly*)

I seen her runnin' ter de rivah an' I follows her. She th'u' it in an' den run in behin' dem coal chutes. I stop an' see ef I could save it. Wasn' no use 'dough—it was too dark. I believe she gone plum crazy.

AUNT REBECCA

Oh, mah Gawd! Dat po' chile! I knowed somefin turrible gwine ter happen!

SLIM

Come on! Le's see ef we kin fin' her.

(Aunt Rebecca and Slim rush out, Back. In the course of several moments Lucy Belle steals in, Back. She wears a terrified expression and moves agitatedly about the room, twining and intertwining her fingers. Presently Sam enters, Back.)

SAM

Lucy Belle!

LUCY BELLE *(in tremulous tones)*

Sam-boy!

SAM

I wasn't gwine ter take no chances.

LUCY BELLE *(avoiding his gaze)*

No, no! Honey baby! Mah ole honey baby! I'se so scar't I didn't know what ter do.

SAM *(darkly)*

Did yo' yere what she was tellin' me?

LUCY BELLE *(lying)*

I yere jes' a little—

SAM *(fiercely)*

She say yo' all been gwine 'roun' wid Chick Avery.

LUCY BELLE

Dat's a lie! Ain' a wud of truf' in dat!

SAM *(grabbing her)*

Have yo'?

LUCY BELLE

No, no! Sam! Fo' Gawd's sake! Yo' don' believe a devil like her, do yo'?

SAM

Ef I ketch yo' runnin' wid anybody else I'se gwine ter kill yo'

LUCY BELLE

Sam-boy! Hones' to Gawd—I ain' had nuffin' ter do wid nobody since yo' been gone! Nuffin' at all!

(*Lizzie enters, Back.*)

LIZZIE (*with a cry of triumph*)

I knowed I'd git yo' numbah!

SAM

Git out-a yere! D' yo' want me ter kill yo'?

LIZZIE

Sam—Sam—she got-a baby! It Chick Avery's. It's yere! Dat's de way she treat yo' all! Ha! Ha! Makin' a damn fool of yo'! I allas knowed yo's an easy mark!

LUCY BELLE (*screaming*)

It's a lie! It's a lie! No, no!

(*Sam starts for Lizzie. She backs out of the door.*)

LIZZIE (*outside*)

I tol' yo' I'd git yo'! I tol' yo' I'd git yo'! Ha! Ha!

(*Sam starts to rush out after her. He hesitates, however, and finally bangs the door shut and turns to Lucy Belle.*)

SAM (*between his teeth*)

Yo' yere what she say?

LUCY BELLE (*palsied with fear*)

It ain' so! It's a lie! Yo' know she couldn't tell de truf! Yo' don' believe her, do yo'?

SAM (*gruffly*)

Lemme look 'roun' yere!

92

LUCY BELLE

Yo' won' see nuffin'! Yo' won' see nuffin', Sam!

SAM (*shoving her aside roughly*)

Lemme look! (*Starts toward Left.*)

FANNY

Ain' nobody but Fanny an' Israel in dere!

SAM (*shouting*)

Ef yo' try any funny business wid me I'll kill yo'! Damn yo' heart to hell!

(*He passes out, Left, followed by Lucy Belle. The door stands open and their voices can be heard.*)

LUCY BELLE (*off, Left*)

See, Sam—ain' nobody but Fanny an' Israel. Don' wake 'em up! Jes' mah clothes, Sam-boy! Aw, yo' believe me—don' yo'? Yo' don' believe an ole hussy like her!

SAM (*savagely*)

Chick Avery been comin' yere?

LUCY BELLE

No, no! I swear ter Gawd he ain' nevah been in dis house! No, no! It's all a dirty lie! See, Sam—see—ain' no baby 'roun' yere! Lizzie allas has blackguarded me—don' yo' know she has—evah since yo' an' me met up! She jealous of me! She say anything—anything at all ter git back at me!

(*They re-enter, Left.*)

SAM (*grabbing her by the shoulder*)

Yo' has seen Chick Avery!

93

LUCY BELLE

No—no—I ain'—I swear ter Gawd I ain'! Aw, Sam, yo' believe yo' honey baby, don' yo'?

(*A tense pause. He stares into her face.*)

SAM (*at length*)

Ef she keep on blackguardin' yo' I'se gwine ter kill her!

LUCY BELLE

No, no, Sam-boy! Yo' an' me wants ter git away from dis town. It'll be bettah fo' us bo'f. We ain' nevah had no luck yere! (*Caressingly.*) Bes' ole buddy in de worl'! I wants yo' Sam,— jes' yo'—nuffin' else.

SAM (*muttering*)

I'll clean up fo' dat gal!

LUCY BELLE

Yo' loves me, don' yo'—don' yo'?

SAM (*impulsively takes her in his arms and holds her tightly*)

Kid, yo's all I got in de worl'! Ef yo' fools me I'll tu'n bad fo' life.

LUCY BELLE

Sam, baby, mah ole Sam-boy baby! Ain' nuffin' on Gawd's ear'f I wouldn' do fo' yo'! (*Looking up into his face.*) Yo' an' me's gwine ter Baltimo', ain' we? (*Sam nods.*)

SAM

Honey baby! Honey baby! Jes' mah lil' gal! Yo's mine—mine fo' life!

(*Aunt Rebecca rushes in excitedly, Back.*)

AUNT REBECCA
> Lucy Belle! Mah Gawd! Lucy Belle! Is yo'
> crazy? Dey fish him out—de baby! Oh, mah
> Gawd!

> (*Lucy Belle gives a stifled cry and breaks away
> from Sam.*)

SAM (*exclaiming savagely*)
> Baby! What d' yo' mean?

> (*A tense silence of a moment or two. At length
> Sam divines her meaning. Aunt Rebecca staggers
> back, realizing what the consequences of her reve-
> lation are likely to be. Lucy Belle stands at one
> side, moaning softly. Sam rushes at Aunt Rebecca,
> hits her and knocks her out through door, Back.
> She screams. He rushes over, closes the door, and
> locks it.*)

SAM (*rushing at Lucy Belle*)
> Damn yo' black heart to hell! (*She gives an
> unearthly scream.*) Yo' will double-cross me!
> Dis is de way yo' pays me up fo' all I done
> fo' yo'!

LUCY BELLE (*dropping to her knees*)
> Sam—Sam-boy—listen! Lemme tell yo'! Oh,
> Gawd! It ain'—

SAM (*grabbing her*)
> I'll show yo' how ter play dat kin' of a game!

LUCH BELLE (*screaming*)
> Sam! Sam!

SAM
   I'll fix yo'!

(*He takes her by the throat and slowly chokes her to death. She struggles frantically to release herself. At length she grows quiet and her body limp. He throws her on the floor, stands gazing at her for a moment or two, grabs up his hat, slinks to the door, Back, opens it cautiously and passes out, closing it after him.*)

CURTAIN

SWEET AND TWENTY

A COMEDY IN ONE ACT

by FLOYD DELL

First produced by the Provincetown Players, New York City, January 25, 1918, with the following cast:

THE YOUNG WOMAN,   -   EDNA ST. VINCENT MILLAY

THE YOUNG MAN,   -   -   -   -   ORDWAY TEAD

THE AGENT,   -   -   -   -   -   OTTO LIVERIGHT

THE GUARD,   -   -   -   -   -   -   LOUIS ELL

SWEET AND TWENTY

SCENE—*A corner of the cherry orchard on the country place of the late Mr. Boggley, now on sale and open for inspection to prospective buyers. The cherry orchard, now in full bloom, is a very pleasant place. There is a green-painted rustic bench beside the path. . . .*
(*This scene can be effectively produced on a small stage by a back-drop painted a blue-green color, with a single conventionalized cherry branch painted across it, and two three-leaved screens masking the wings, painted in blue-green with a spray of cherry blossoms*).

A young woman, dressed in a light summer frock and carrying a parasol, drifts in from the back. She sees the bench, comes over to it and sits down with an air of petulant weariness.

A handsome young man enters from the right. He stops short in surprise on seeing the charming stranger who lolls upon the bench. He takes off his hat.

HE

Oh, I beg your pardon!

SHE

Oh, you needn't! I've no right to be here, either.

HE

(*Coming down to her*) Now what do you mean by that?

SHE

I thought perhaps you were playing truant, as I am.

99

HE

Playing truant?

SHE

I was looking at the house, you know. And I got tired and ran away.

HE

Well, to tell the truth, so did I. It's dull work, isn't it?

SHE

I've been upstairs and down for two hours. That family portrait gallery finished me. It was so old and gloomy and dead that I felt as if I were dead myself. I just had to do something. I wanted to jab my parasol through the window-pane. I understood just how the suffragettes felt. But I was afraid of shocking the agent. He is such a meek little man, and he seemed to think so well of me. If I had broken the window I would have shattered his ideals of womanhood, too, I'm afraid. So I just slipped away quietly and came here.

HE

I've only been there half an hour and we— I've only been in the basement. That's why our tours of inspection didn't bring us together sooner. I've been cross-examining the furnace. Do you understand furnaces? (*He sits down beside her*) I don't.

SHE

Do you like family portraits? I hate 'em!

HE

What! Do the family portraits go with the house?

SHE

No, thank heaven. They've been bequeathed to the Metropolitan Museum of Horrors, I understand. They're valuable historically—early colonial governors and all that sort of stuff. But there is someone with me who—who takes a deep interest in such things.

HE

(*frowning at a sudden memory*) Hm. Didn't I see you at that real estate office in New York yesterday?

SHE

Yes. *He* was with me then.

HE (*compassionately*)

I—I thought I remembered seeing you with—with him

SHE (*cheerfully*)

Isn't he *just* the sort of man who would be interested in family portraits?

HE (*confused*)

Well—since you ask me—I—!

SHE

Oh, that's all right. Tubby's a dear, in spite of his funny old ideas. I like him very much.

HE

(*gulping the pill*) Yes. . . .

SHE

He's so anxious to please me in buying this house. I suppose it's all right to have a house, but I'd like to become acquainted with it gradually. I'd like to feel that there was always some corner left to explore—some mystery saved up for a rainy day. Tubby can't understand that. He drags me everywhere, explaining how we'll keep this and change that—dormer windows here and perhaps a new wing there. . . . I suppose you've been rebuilding the house, too?

HE

No. Merely decided to turn that sunny south room into a study. It would make a very pleasant place to work. But if you really want the place, I'd hate to take it away from you.

SHE

I was just going to say that if *you* really wanted it, *I'd* withdraw. It was Tubby's idea to buy it, you know—not mine. You *do* want it, don't you?

HE

I can't say that I do. It's so infernally big. But Maria thinks I ought to have it. (*Explanatorily*) Maria is—

SHE (*gently*)

She's—the one who *is* interested in furnaces, I understand. I saw her with you at the real-estate office yesterday. Well—furnaces are necessary, I suppose. (*There is a pause, which she breaks suddenly*) Do you see that bee?

HE

A bee? (*He follows her gaze up to a cluster of blossoms.*)

SHE

Yes—there! (*Affectionately*) The rascal! There he goes. (*Their eyes follow the flight of the bee across the orchard. There is a silence, in which*

Maria and Tubby drift into the limbo of forgotten things. Alone together beneath the blossoms, a spell seems to have fallen upon them. She tries to think of something to say—and at last succeeds.)

SHE

Have you heard the story of the people who used to live here?

HE

No; why?

SHE

An agent was telling us. It's quite romantic— and rather sad. You see, the man that built this house was in love with a girl. He was building it for her—as a surprise. But he had neglected to mention to her that he was in love with her. And so, in pique, she married another man, though she was really in love with him. The news came just when he had finished the house. He shut it up for a year or two, but eventually married someone else, and they lived here for ten years—most unhappily. Then they went abroad, and the house was sold. It was bought, curiously enough, by the husband of the girl he had been in love with. They lived here till they died—hating each other to the end, the agent says.

HE

It gives me the shivers. To think of that house, haunted by the memories of wasted love! Which of us, I wonder, will have to live in it? I don't want to.

SHE (*prosaically*)

Oh, don't take it so seriously as all that. If

one can't live in a house where there's been an unhappy marriage, why, good heavens, where *is* one going to live? Most marriages, I fancy, are unhappy.

HE

A bitter philosophy for one so—

SHE

Nonsense! But listen to the rest of the story. The most interesting part is about this very orchard.

HE

Really!

SHE

Yes. This orchard, it seems, was here before the house was. It was part of an old farm where he and she—the unhappy lovers, you know—stopped one day, while they were out driving, and asked for something to eat. The farmer's wife was busy, but she gave them each a glass of milk, and told them they could eat all the cherries they wanted. So they picked a hatful of cherries, and ate them, sitting on a bench like this one. And then he fell in love with her. . . .

HE

And . . . didn't tell her so. . . . (*She glances at him in alarm. His self-possession has vanished. He is pale and frightened, but there is a desperate look in his eyes, as if some unknown power were forcing him to do something very rash. In short, he seems like a young man who has just fallen in love.*)

SHE (*hastily*)
So you see this orchard is haunted, too!

HE
I feel it. I seem to hear the ghost of that old-time lover whispering to me. . . .

SHE (*provocatively*)
Indeed! What does he say?

HE
He says: "I was a coward; you must be bold. I was silent; you must speak out."

SHE (*mischievously*)
That's very curious—because that old lover isn't dead at all. He's a baronet or something in England.

HE (*earnestly*)
His youth is dead; and it is his youth that speaks to me.

SHE (*quickly*)
You mustn't believe all that ghosts tell you.

HE
Oh, but I must. For they know the folly of silence—the bitterness of cowardice.

SHE
The circumstances were—slightly—different, weren't they?

HE (*stubbornly*)
I don't care!

SHE (*soberly*)
You know perfectly well it's no use.

HE
I can't help that!

SHE

Please! You simply mustn't! It's disgraceful!

HE

What's disgraceful?

SHE (*confused*)

What you are going to say.

HE (*simply*)

Only that I love you. What is there disgraceful about that? It's beautiful!

SHE

It's wrong.

HE

It's inevitable.

SHE

Why inevitable? Can't you talk with a girl in a cherry orchard for half an hour without falling in love with her?

HE

Not if the girl is you.

SHE

But why especially *me?*

HE

I don't know. Love—is a mystery. I only know that I was destined to love you.

SHE

How can you be so sure?

HE

Because you have changed the world for me. It's as though I had been groping about in the dark, and then—sunrise! And there's a queer feeling here. (*He puts his hand on his heart*) To tell the honest truth, there's a still queerer feeling in the pit of my stomach. It's a gone feeling, if you must know. And my knees are weak. I know now why men used to fall on their knees when they told a girl they loved her; it was because they couldn't stand up. And there's a feeling in my feet as though I were walking on air. And—

SHE (*faintly*)

That's enough!

HE

And I could die for you and be glad of the chance. It's perfectly absurd, but it's absolutely true. I've never spoken to you before, and heaven knows I may never get a chance to speak to you again, but I'd never forgive myself if I didn't say this to you now. I love you! love you! love you! Now tell me I'm a fool. Tell me to go. Anything—I've said my say. . . . Why don't you speak?

SHE

I—I've nothing to say—except—except that I —well— (*almost inaudibly*) I feel some of those symptoms myself.

HE (*triumphantly*)

You love me!

SHE

I—don't know. Yes. Perhaps.

HE

Then kiss me!

SHE (*doubtfully*)

No. . . .

HE

Kiss me!

SHE (*tormentedly*)
  Oh, what's the use?

HE
  I don't know. I don't care. I only know that
  we love each other.

SHE
  (*after a moment's hesitation, desperately*) I don't
  care, either! I *do* want to kiss you. (*She does.
  . . . He is the first to awake from the ecstasy.*)

HE
  It is wicked—
SHE (*absently*)
  Is it?

HE
  But, oh heaven! kiss me again! (*She does.*)

SHE
  Darling!

HE
  Do you suppose anyone is likely to come this
  way?

SHE
  No.

HE (*speculatively*) Your husband is probably still
  in the portrait gallery. . . .

SHE
  My husband! (*Drawing away*) What do you
  mean? (*Thoroughly awake now*) You didn't
  think—? (*She jumps up and laughs convulsively*) He thought poor old Tubby was my
  husband!!

HE
  (*staring up at her bewildered*) Why, isn't he
  your husband?

SHE (*scornfully*)

    No!! He's my uncle!

HE

    Your unc—

SHE

    Yes, of course! (*Indignantly*) Do you suppose I would be married to a man that's fat and bald and forty years old?

HE (*distressed*)

    I—I beg your pardon. I did think so.

SHE

    Just because you saw me with him? How ridiculous!

HE

    It was a silly mistake. But—the things you said! You spoke so—realistically—about marriage.

SHE

    It was *your* marriage I was speaking about. (*With hasty compunction*) Oh, I beg your—

HE

    My marriage! (*He rises*) Good heavens! And to whom, pray, did you think I was married? (*A light dawning*) To Maria? Why, Maria is my aunt!

SHE

    Yes—of course. How stupid of me.

HE

    Let's get this straight. Are you married to *anybody?*

SHE

    Certainly not. As if I would let anybody make love to me if I were!

HE

Now don't put on airs. You did something quite as improper. You kissed a married man.

SHE

I didn't.

HE

It's the same thing. You *thought* I was married.

SHE

But you *aren't*.

HE

No. I'm *not* married. And—and—*you're* not married. (*The logic of the situation striking him all of a sudden*) In fact—! (*He pauses, rather alarmed.*)

SHE

Yes?

HE

In fact—well—there's no reason in the world why we *shouldn't* make love to each other!

SHE

(*equally startled*) Why—that's so!

HE

Then—then—shall we?

SHE

(*sitting down and looking demurely at her toes*) Oh, not if you don't want to!

HE

(*adjusting himself to the situation*) Well—under the circumstances—I suppose I ought to begin by asking you to marry me. . . .

SHE

(*languidly, with a provoking glance*) You don't seem very anxious to.

HE

> (*feeling at a disadvantage*) It isn't that—but—well—

SHE (*lightly*)

> Well what?

HE

> Dash it all, I don't know your name!

SHE

> (*looking at him with wild curiosity*) That didn't seem to stop you a while ago. . . .

HE (*doggedly*)

> Well, then—will you marry me?

SHE (*promptly*)

> No.

HE (*surprised*)

> No! Why do you say that?

SHE (*coolly*)

> Why should I marry you? I know nothing about you. I've known you for less than an hour.

HE (*sardonically*)

> That fact didn't seem to keep you from kissing me.

SHE

> Besides—I don't like the way you go about it. If you'd propose the same way you made love to me, maybe I'd accept you.

HE

> All right. (*Dropping on one knee before her*) Beloved! (*An awkward pause*) No, I can't do it. (*He gets up and distractedly dusts off his knees with his handkerchief*) I'm very sorry.

SHE

(*with calm inquiry*) Perhaps it's because you don't love me any more?

HE (*fretfully*)

Of course I love you!

SHE (*coldly*)

But you don't want to marry me. . . . I see.

HE

Not at all! I *do* want to marry you. But—

SHE

Well?

HE

Marriage is a serious matter. Now don't take offense! I only meant that—well— (*He starts again*) We *are* in love with each other, and that's the important thing. But, as you said, we don't know each other. I've no doubt that when we get acquainted we will like each other better still. But we've got to get acquainted first.

SHE (*rising*)

You're just like Tubby buying a house. You want to know all about it. Well! I warn you that you'll never know all about me. So you needn't try.

HE (*apologetically*)

It was *your* suggestion.

SHE (*impatiently*)

Oh, all right! Go ahead and cross-examine me if you like. I'll tell you to begin with that I'm perfectly healthy, and that there's no T. B., insanity, or Socialism in my family. What else do you want to know?

HE (*hesitantly*)

Why did you put Socialism in?

SHE

Oh, just for fun. You aren't a Socialist, are you?

HE

Yes. (*Earnestly*) Do you know what Socialism is?

SHE (*innocently*)

It's the same thing as Anarchy, isn't it?

HE (*gently*)

No. At least not my kind. I believe in municipal ownership of street cars, and all that sort of thing. I'll give you some books to read

SHE

Well, I never ride in street cars, so I don't care whether they're municipally owned or not. By the way, do you dance?

HE

No.

SHE

You must learn right away. I can't bother to teach you myself, but I know where you can get private lessons and become really good in a month. It is stupid not to be able to dance.

HE

(*as if he had tasted quinine*) I can see myself doing the tango! Grr!

SHE

The tango went out long ago, my dear.

HE

(*with great decision*) Well—I *won't* learn to dance. You might as well know that to begin with.

SHE

And I won't read your old books on Socialism. You might as well know *that to begin with!*

HE

Come, come! This will never do. You see, my dear, it's simply that I *can't* dance, and there's no use for me to try to learn.

SHE

Anybody can learn. I've made expert dancers out of the awkwardest men!

HE

But, you see, I've no inclination toward dancing. It's out of my world.

SHE

And I've no inclination toward municipal ownership. *It's* out of *my* world!

HE

It ought not to be out of the world of any intelligent person.

SHE

(*turning her back on him*) All right—if you want to call me stupid!

HE

(*turning and looking away meditatively*) It appears that we have very few tastes in common.

SHE

(*tapping her foot*) So it seems.

HE

If we married we might be happy for a month—

SHE

Perhaps. (*They remain standing with their backs to each other.*)

HE

And then—the old story. Quarrels. . . .

SHE

I never could bear quarrels. . . .

HE

An unhappy marriage. . . .

SHE

(*realizing it*) Oh!

HE

(*hopelessly turning toward her*) I can't marry you.

SHE

(*recovering quickly and facing him with a smile*) Nobody asked you, sir, she said!

HE

(*with a gesture of finality*) Well—there seems to be no more to say.

SHE (*sweetly*)

Except good-bye.

HE (*firmly*)

Good-bye, then. (*He holds out his hand.*)

SHE

(*taking it*) Good-bye!

HE

(*taking her other hand—after a pause, helplessly*) Good-bye!

SHE

(*drawing in his eyes*) Good-bye! (*They cling to each other, and are presently lost in a passionate embrace. He breaks loose and stamps away, then turns to her.*)

HE
  Damn it all, we *do* love each other!

SHE
  (*wiping her eyes*) What a pity that is the only
  taste we have in common!

HE
  Do you suppose that is enough?

SHE
  I wish it were!

HE
  A month of happiness—

SHE
  Yes!

HE
  And then—wretchedness.

SHE
  No—never!

HE
  We mustn't do it.

SHE
  I suppose not.

HE
  Come, let us control ourselves.

SHE
  Yes, let's. (*They take hands again.*)

HE
  (*with an effort*) I wish you happiness. I—I'll
  go to Europe for a year. Try to forget me.

SHE
  I shall be married when you get back—perhaps.

HE
  I hope it's somebody that's not bald and fat
  and forty. Otherwise—!

SHE

And you—for goodness sake! marry a girl that's very young and very, very pretty. That will help.

HE

We mustn't prolong this. If we stay together another minute—

SHE

Then go!

HE

I can't go!

SHE

You must, darling! You must!

HE

Oh, if somebody would only come along! (*They are leaning toward each other, dizzy upon the brink of another kiss, when somebody does come— a short, mild-looking man in a Derby hat. There is an odd gleam in his eyes*).

THE INTRUDER (*startled*)

Excuse me! (*They turn and stare at him, but their hands cling fast to each other.*)

SHE (*faintly*)

The Agent!

THE AGENT

(*in despairing accents*) Too late! Too late!

THE YOUNG MAN

No! Just in time!

THE AGENT

Too late, I say! I will go. (*He turns.*)

THE YOUNG MAN

No! Stay!

THE AGENT
> What's the use? It has already begun. What good can I do now?

THE YOUNG MAN
> I'll show you what good you can do now. Come here! (*The Agent approaches*) Can you unloose my hands from those of this young woman?

THE YOUNG WOMAN
> (*haughtily releasing herself and walking away*) You needn't trouble! I can do it myself.

THE YOUNG MAN
> Thank you. It was utterly beyond my power. (*To the Agent*) Will you kindly take hold of me and move me over *there?* (*The Agent propels him away from the girl*) Thank you. At this distance I can perhaps make my farewell in a seemly and innocuous manner.

THE AGENT
> Young man, you will not say farewell to that young lady for ten days—and perhaps never!

THE YOUNG WOMAN
> What!

THE AGENT
> They have arranged it all.

THE YOUNG MAN
> *Who* has arranged *what?*

THE AGENT
> Your aunt, Miss Brooke—and (*to the young woman*) your uncle, Mr. Egerton— (*The young people turn and stare at each other in amazement.*)

THE YOUNG MAN
> Egerton! Are you Helen Egerton?

HELEN

And are you George Brooke?

THE AGENT

Your aunt and uncle have just discovered each other up at the house, and they have arranged for you all to take dinner together to-night, and then go to a ten-day house-party at Mr. Egerton's place on Long Island. (*Grimly*) The reason of all this will be plain to you. They want you two to get married.

GEORGE

Then we're done for! We'll have to get married now whether we want to or not!

HELEN

What! Just to please *them?* I shan't do it!

GEORGE (*gloomily*)

You don't know my Aunt Maria.

HELEN

And Tubby will try to bully me, I suppose. But I won't do it—no matter what he says!

THE AGENT

Pardon what may seem an impertinence, Miss; but is it really true that you don't want to marry this young man?

HELEN (*flaming*)

I suppose because you saw me in his arms—! Oh, I want to, all right, but—

THE AGENT (*mildly*)

Then what seems to be the trouble?

HELEN

I—oh, you explain to him, George. (*She goes to the bench and sits down.*)

GEORGE

Well, it's this way. As you may have deduced from what you saw, we are madly in love with each other—

HELEN

(*from the bench*) But I'm not madly in love with municipal ownership. That's the chief difficulty.

GEORGE

No, the chief difficulty is that I refuse to entertain even a platonic affection for the tango.

HELEN (*irritably*)

I told you the tango had gone out long ago!

GEORGE

Well, then, the maxixe.

HELEN

Stupid!

GEORGE

And there you have it! No doubt it seems ridiculous to you.

THE AGENT (*gravely*)

Not at all, my boy. I've known marriage to go to smash on far less than that. When you come to think of it, a taste for dancing and a taste for municipal ownership stand at the two ends of the earth away from each other. They represent two different ways of taking life. And if two people who live in the same house can't agree on those two things, they'd disagree on ten thousand things that came up every day. And what's the use for two different kinds of beings to try to live together? It doesn't work, no matter how much love there is between them.

GEORGE

(*rushing up to him in surprise and gratification, and shaking his hand warmly*) Then you're our friend. You will help us not to get married!

THE AGENT

Your aunt is very set on it—and your uncle, too, Miss!

HELEN

We must find some way to get out of it, or they'll have us cooped up together in that house before we know it. (*Rising and coming over to the Agent*) Can't you think up some scheme?

THE AGENT

Perhaps I can, and perhaps I can't. I'm a bachelor myself, Miss, and that means that I've thought up many a scheme to get out of marriage myself.

HELEN (*outraged*)

You old scoundrel!

THE AGENT

Oh, it's not so bad as you may think, Miss. I've always gone through the marriage cere-mony to please them. But that's not what I call marriage.

GEORGE

Then what do you call marriage?

HELEN

Yes, I'd like to know!

THE AGENT

Marriage, my young friends, is an iniquitous arrangement devised by the Devil himself for driving all the love out of the hearts of lovers. They start out as much in love with each other as you two are to-day, and they end by being as sick of the sight of each other as you two will be twenty years hence if I don't find a way of saving you alive out of the Devil's own trap. It's not lack of love that's the trouble with marriage—it's marriage itself. And when I say marriage, I don't mean promising to love, honor, and obey, for richer, for poorer, in sickness and in health till death do you part— that's only human nature to wish and to attempt. And it might be done if it weren't for the iniquitous arrangement of marriage.

GEORGE (*puzzled*)

But what *is* the iniquitous arrangement?

THE AGENT

Ah, that's the trouble! If I tell you, you won't believe me. You'll go ahead and try it out, and find out what all the unhappy ones have found out before you. Listen to me, my children. Did you ever go on a picnic? (*He looks from one to the other—they stand astonished and silent*) Of course you have. Everyone has. There is an instinct in us which makes us go back to the ways of our savage ancestors—to gather about a fire in the forest, to cook meat on a pointed stick, and eat it with our fingers. But how many books would you write, young man, if you had to go back to the camp-fire every day for your lunch? And how many new dances would *you* invent if you lived eternally in the picnic stage of civilization? No! the picnic is incompatible with everyday living. As incompatible as marriage.

GEORGE

But—

HELEN

But—

THE AGENT

Marriage is the nest-building instinct, turned by the Devil himself into an institution to hold the human soul in chains. The whole story of marriage is told in the old riddle: "Why do birds in their nests agree? Because if they don't, they'll fall out." That's it. Marriage is a nest so small that there is no room in it for disagreement. Now it may be all right for birds to agree, but human beings are not built that way. They disagree, and home becomes a little hell. Or else they do agree, at the expense of the soul's freedom stifled in one or both.

HELEN

Yes, but tell me—

GEORGE

Ssh!

THE AGENT

Yet there *is* the nest-building instinct. You feel it, both of you. If you don't now, you will as soon as you are married. If you are fools, you will try to live all your lives in a love-nest; and you will imprison your souls within it, and the Devil will laugh.

HELEN

(*to George*) I am beginning to be afraid of him.

GEORGE

So am I.

THE AGENT

If you are wise, you will build yourselves a little nest secretly in the woods, away from civilization, and you will run away together to that nest whenever you are in the mood. A nest so small that it will hold only two beings and one thought—the thought of love. And then you will come back refreshed to civilization, where every soul is different from every other soul—you will let each other alone, forget each other, and do your own work in peace. Do you understand?

HELEN

He means we should occupy separate sides of the house, I think. Or else that we should live apart and only see each other on week-ends. I'm not sure which.

THE AGENT (*passionately*)

I mean that you should not stifle love with civilization, nor encumber civilization with love. What have they to do with each other? You think you want a fellow student of economics. You are wrong. *You* think you want a dancing partner. You are mistaken. You want a revelation of the glory of the universe.

HELEN

(*to George, confidentially*) It's blithering nonsense, of course. But it *was* something like that—a while ago.

GEORGE (*bewilderedly*)

Yes; when we knew it was our first kiss and thought it was to be our last.

THE AGENT (*fiercely*)

A kiss is always the first kiss and the last—or it is nothing.

HELEN (*conclusively*)

He's quite mad.

GEORGE

Absolutely.

THE AGENT

Mad? Of course I am mad. But— (*He turns suddenly, and subsides as a man in a guard's uniform enters.*)

THE GUARD

Ah, here you are! Thought you'd given us the slip, did you? (*To the others*) Escaped from the Asylum, he did, a week ago, and got a job here. We've been huntin' him high and low. Come along now!

GEORGE

(*recovering with difficulty the power of speech*) What—what's the matter with him?

GUARD

Matter with him? He went crazy, he did, readin' the works of Bernard Shaw. And if he wasn't in the insane asylum he'd be in jail. He's a bigamist, he is. He married fourteen women. But none of 'em would go on the witness stand against him. Said he was an ideal husband, they did. Fourteen of 'em! But otherwise he's perfectly harmless. Come now!

THE AGENT (*pleasantly*)

Perfectly harmless! Yes, perfectly harmless! (*He is led out.*)

HELEN

That explains it all!

GEORGE

Yes—and yet I feel there was something in what he was saying.

HELEN

Well—are we going to get married or not? We've got to decide that before we face my uncle and your aunt.

GEORGE

Of course we'll get married. You have your work and I mine, and—

HELEN

Well, if we do, then you can't have that sunny south room for a study. I want it for the nursery.

GEORGE

The nursery!

HELEN

Yes; babies, you know!

GEORGE

Good heavens!

[CURTAIN]

TICKLESS TIME

A COMEDY IN ONE ACT

by SUSAN GLASPELL AND GEORGE CRAM COOK

First performed by the Provincetown Players, New York, December 20, 1918, with the following cast:

IAN JOYCE, *Who Has Made a Sun-dial*,	JAMES LIGHT
ELOISE JOYCE, *Wedded to the Sun-dial*,	NORMA MILLAY
MRS. STUBBS, *a Native*,	JEAN ROBB
EDDY KNIGHT, *a Standardized Mind*,	HUTCHINSON COLLINS
ALICE KNIGHT, *a Standardized Wife*,	ALICE MACDOUGAL
ANNIE, *Who Cooks by the Joyces' Clock*,	
	EDNA ST. VINCENT MILLAY

TICKLESS TIME

SCENE:

A garden in Provincetown. On the spectator's right a two-story house runs back from the proscenium—a door towards the front, a second-story window towards the back. Across the back runs a thick-set row of sunflowers nearly concealing a fence or wall. Back of this are trees and sky. There is a gate at the left rear corner of the garden. People entering it come straight toward the front, down the left side and, to reach the house door, pass across the front of the stage. A fence with sunflowers like that at the back closes off the left wing of the stage—a tree behind this left fence.

The sun-dial stands on a broad step or pedestal which partly masks the digging which takes place behind it. The position of the sun-dial is to the left of the center of the stage midway between front and back.

From behind the tree on the left the late afternoon sun throws a well-defined beam of light upon the horizontal plate of the sun-dial and upon the shaft which supports it. On this shaft is the accompanying diagram: two feet high and clearly visible. On the plate of the sun-dial stands the alarm clock.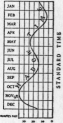

A huge shovel leans against the wall of the house-corner at the back.

Ian is at the sun-dial. He sights over the style to some distant stake left rear, marking the north. He then sights over the east and left line toward the six

129

o'clock sun. Looks at shadow. Looks at alarm clock. Is intensely pleased.

IAN (*turning toward the house and calling excitedly*)
Eloise! Oh, Eloise!

ELOISE (*inside house*)
Hello!

IAN
Come quick! You'll miss it.

ELOISE (*poking her head out of the second-story window; she cranes her neck to look straight up in the air.*)
What is it?

IAN
Come down here quick or you'll miss it.

ELOISE (*disappears from window. A moment later comes running out, one braid of hair up and one braid down. Again looks wildly up in the air.*)
Where is it?

IAN (*absorbed in the sun-dial*)
Where's what?

ELOISE
The airplane.

IAN
Airplane? It's the sun-dial. It's right. Just look at this six-o'clock shadow. (*She goes around to the other side of it.*) It's absolutely, mathematically—you're in the way of the sun, Eloise. (*She steps aside.*) Look! the style is set square on the true north—this is the fifteenth of June —the clock is checked to the second by telegraph with the observatory at Washington, and see!

the clock is exactly nineteen minutes and twenty seconds behind the shadow—the precise difference between Provincetown local time and standard Eastern time.

ELOISE

Then the sun-dial's really finished—and working right! After all these words! Oh, Ian! (*She embraces him.*)

IAN

It's good to get it right after all those mistakes. (*With vision.*) Why, Eloise, getting this right has been a symbol of man's whole search for truth—the discovery and correction of error—the mind compelled to conform step by step to astronomical fact—to truth.

ELOISE (*going to it again*)

And to think that it's the sun-dial which is true and the clock—all the clocks—are wrong! I'm glad it is true. Alice Knight has been here talking to me for an hour. I want to think that something's true.

IAN

That's just it, Eloise. The sun-dial is more than sun-dial. It's a first-hand relation with truth. A personal relation. When you take your time from a clock you are mechanically getting information from a machine. You're nothing but a clock yourself.

ELOISE

Like Alice Knight.

IAN

But the sun-dial—this shadow is an original document—a scholar's source.

ELOISE

To tell time by the shadow of the sun—so large and simple.

IAN

I wouldn't call it simple. Here on this diagram I have worked out—

ELOISE

Dearest, you know I can't understand diagrams. But I get the feeling of it, Ian—the sun, the North star. I love to think that this (*placing her hands on the style*) is set by the North star. (*Her right hand remains on the style, her left prolongs its line heavenward.*) Why, if I could go on long enough I'd get *to* the North star!

IAN (*impressively*)

The line that passes along the edge of this style joins the two poles of the heavens. (*Eloise pulls away her hand as one who fears an electric shock.*) Look at this slow shadow, and what you see is the spin of the earth on its axis. It is not so much the measure of time, as time itself made visible.

ELOISE (*knitting her brows to get this—escaping to an impetuous generality*)

Ian, which do you think is the more wonderful—space *or* time?

IAN (*again sighting over his east and west lines. Good-humoredly*)

Both are a little large for our approbation.

ELOISE (*sitting on the steps and putting up the other braid*)

Do you know, Ian, that's the one thing about them I don't quite like. You can't get very intimate with them, can you? They make you so humble. That's one nice thing about a clock. A clock is sometimes wrong.

IAN

Don't you want to live in a first-hand relation to truth?

ELOISE

Yes; yes, I do—generally.

IAN

I have a feeling as of having touched vast forces. To work directly with worlds—it lifts me out of that little routine of our lives which is itself a clock.

ELOISE (*catching his exultation*)

Let us *be* like this! Let us have done with clocks!

IAN

Eloise, how wonderful! Can the clocks and live by the sun-dial? Live by the non-automatic sun-dial— as a pledge that we ourselves refuse to be automatons!

ELOISE

Like Alice Knight. (*She takes clock from dial and puts it face downward on the ground.*) I shall never again have anything to do with a clock!

IAN

Eloise! How corking of you! I didn't think you had it in you. (*Raising his right hand.*) Do you solemnly swear to live by the truth, the whole truth, and nothing but the truth?

ELOISE (*her hand upon the sun-dial*)

I swear.

IAN

Bring them!

ELOISE

Bring—?

IAN

The clocks! Bring them! (*Seizes the spade over by the house; begins to dig a grave behind the sun-dial.*) Bring every one! We will bury the clocks before the sun-dial—an offering, a living sacrifice. I tell you this is *great*, Eloise. What is a clock? Something agreed upon and arbitrarily imposed upon us. Standard time. Not true time. Symbolizing the whole standardization of our lives. Clocks! Why, it is clockiness that makes America mechanical and mean! Clock-minded! A clock is a little machine that shuts us out from the wonder of time. (*A large gesture with the shovel.*) Who thinks of spinning worlds when looking at a clock? How *dare* clocks do this to us? But the sun-dial—because there was creation, because there are worlds outside our world, because space is rhythm and time is flow that shadow falls precisely there and not elsewhere! Bring them, Eloise! I am digging the graves of the clocks!

(*Eloise, swept up by this ecstasy, yet frightened at what it is bringing her to, hesitates, then runs to house. Ian digs with rhythmic vigor. A moment later Eloise is seen peering down at him from window, in her arms a cuckoo clock. It begins to cuckoo, startling Eloise.*)

IAN

That damned cuckoo!

(*A moment later Eloise comes out, bearing a cuckoo clock and an old-fashioned clock. Ian's back is to her; she has to pass the alarm clock, lying where she left it, prone on the ground. She hesitates, then carefully holding the other two clocks in one arm, she stealthily goes rear and puts the alarm clock behind the sunflowers. Then advances with the other two.)*

IAN (*while digging*)

Into these graves go all that is clocklike in our minds. All that a clock world has made of us lies buried here!

(Eloise stands rather appalled at the idea of so much of herself going into a grave. Puts the old-fashioned clock carefully on the ground. Gingerly fits the cuckoo clock into the completed grave. With an exclamation of horror lifts it out of the grave. Listens to its tick. Puts her ear to the sun-dial; listens vainly.)

ELOISE

The sun-dial doesn't tick, does it, Ian?

IAN

Why should it tick?

ELOISE

Do you know, Ian, I (*timidly*)—I like to hear the ticking of a clock. (*No reply. Eloise holds up the cuckoo clock.*) This was a wedding present.

IAN

No wonder marriage fails. (*He moves to take it from her.*)

ELOISE

I wonder if we hadn't better leave the cuckoo until tomorrow.

IAN

Flaming worlds! A cuckoo!

ELOISE

Eddie and Alice gave us the cuckoo. You know they're coming back. I asked them for dinner. They might not understand our burying their clock.

IAN

Their failure to understand need not limit our lives. (*Puts the cuckoo clock in its grave and begins to cover it.*)

ELOISE (*as the earth goes on*)

I liked the cuckoo! I liked to see him popping out!

IAN (*kindly*)

You will grow, Eloise. You will go out to large things now that you have done with small ones.

ELOISE

I hope so. It will be hard on me if I don't.

(*Ian reaches for the other clock.*)

ELOISE (*snatching it*)

Oh, Ian, I don't think I ought to bury this one. It's the clock my grandmother started housekeeping with!

IAN (*firmly taking clock*)

And see what it did to her. Meticulous old woman! (*Puts it in its grave.*)

ELOISE

You were glad enough to get her pies and buckwheat cakes.

IAN

She had all the small virtues. But a standardized mind. (*Trampling down the grave.*) She lacked scope. And now—a little grave for little clocks. (*Takes out his watch, puts it in its grave.*) Your watch, Eloise.

ELOISE (*holding to her wrist watch*)

I thought I'd keep my watch, Ian. (*Hastily.*) For an ornament, you know.

IAN

We are going to let truth be your ornament, Eloise.

ELOISE

Nobody sees the truth. (*With a fresh outburst.*) This watch is my graduation present!

IAN

Symbolizing all the standardized arbitrary things you were taught! Commemorating the clocklike way your mind was made to run. Free yourself of that watch, Eloise. (*Eloise reluctantly frees herself. Ian briskly covers the watches. Moves to the unfilled grave.*) Is there nothing for this grave? (*Eloise shakes her head.*) Sure—the alarm clock!

ELOISE (*running to the sunflowers and spreading out her skirts before them.*)

Oh, Ian, *not* the alarm clock! How would we ever go to Boston? The train doesn't run by the sun.

IAN

Then the train is wrong.

ELOISE

But, Ian, if the train is wrong we have to be wrong to catch the train.

IAN

That's civilization. (*Stands resolutely by the grave.*) The alarm clock, Eloise. The grave awaits it.

ELOISE (*taking it up, her arms folded around it*)
  I wanted to go to Boston and buy a hat!

IAN
  The sun will fall upon your dear head and give
  you life.

ELOISE (*about to cry*)
  But no style! It ticks so loud and sure!

IAN
  All false things are loud and sure.

ELOISE
  I need a tick! I am afraid of tickless time!
  (*Holding the clock in both hands she places it
  against her left ear.*)

IAN (*spade still in his right hand, he places his left
  arm around her reassuringly*)
  You will grow, Eloise. You are growing.
  (*He takes the clock as he is saying this. She
  turns her head backward following the departing
  clock with surprised and helpless eyes. Disconsolately watches him bury it.*)

ELOISE (*an inspiration*)
  Ian! Couldn't you fix the sun-dial to be set
  and go off?

IAN (*pained*)
  "Set and go off?" (*Pause; regards the sun.*)
  Sine sole silio.

ELOISE
  What did you say, Ian?

IAN
  I said: *Sine sole silio.*

ELOISE
  Well, I don't know what you say when you say
  that.

IAN

It's a Latin motto I've just thought of for the sun-dial. It means, "Without sun, I am silent." Silence is a great virtue. (*Having finished the grave, he looks around, making sure there are no more clocks. Joyously.*) Now we are freed! Eloise, think what life is going to be! Done with approximations. Done with machine thinking. In a world content with false time, we are true.

ELOISE (*sitting on the steps*)

Yes, it's beautiful. I want to be true. It's just that it's a little hard to be true in a false world. For instance, tomorrow I have an appointment with the dentist. If I come on sun-time, I suppose I'll be twenty minutes—

IAN (*eagerly. Going to the sun-dial and pointing*)

If you will just let me explain this table— (*Eloise shrinks back. Ian gives it up.*) Oh, well, tell him you are living by the truth.

ELOISE

I'm afraid he'll charge me for it. And when we ask people for dinner at seven, they'll get here at twenty minutes of seven. Or will it be twenty minutes *after* seven?

IAN (*smoothing down the graves*)

It will be a part of eternal time.

ELOISE

Yes—*that's* true. Only the roast isn't so eternal. Why do they have clocks wrong?

IAN

Oh, Eloise, I've explained it so many times. You —living in Provincetown, three hundred miles to the eastward, are living by the mean solar time of Philadelphia. (*Venomously.*) Do you *want* to live by the mean solar time of Philadelphia?

ELOISE

Certainly *not.* (*An idea.*) Then has Philadelphia got the right time?

IAN

It's right six miles this side of Philadelphia.

ELOISE

We might move to Philadelphia.

(*Enter, through gate, Mrs. Stubbs, a Provincetown "native."*)

MRS. STUBBS

Now, Mr. Joyce, this sun clock—is it running?

IAN

It doesn't "run," Mrs. Stubbs. It is acted upon.

MRS. STUBBS

Oh? Well, is it being acted upon?

IAN

As surely as the sun shines.

MRS. STUBBS (*looking at the sun*)

And it is shining today, isn't it? Well, will you tell me the time? My clock has stopped and I want to set it.

IAN (*happily*)

You hear, Eloise? Her clock has stopped.

MRS. STUBBS

Yes, I forgot to wind it.

ELOISE (*grieved to think of any one living in such a world*)

Wind it!

IAN

Do you not see, Mrs. Stubbs, where the shadow

falls? (*She comes up the steps.*) From its millions of spinn— You're in the way of the sun,
Mrs. Stubbs. (*She steps aside.*) Its millions of
spinning miles, the sun casts that shadow and
here we know that it is eight minutes past six.

MRS. STUBBS

Now, ain't that wonderful? Dear, dear, I
wish Mr. Stubbs could make a sun clock. But
he's not handy around the house. Past six.
Well, I must hurry back. They work tonight
at the cold storage but Mr. Stubbs gets home
for his supper at half past six. (*Starts away,
reaching the gate.*)

ELOISE (*running to her*)

Oh, Mrs. Stubbs! Don't get his supper by sun
time. It wouldn't be ready. It— (*with a
hesitant look at Ian*) might get cold. (*Mrs.
Stubbs stares.*) You see, Mr. Stubbs is coming
home by the mean solar time of Philadelphia.

MRS. STUBBS (*loyal to Mr. Stubbs*)

Who said he was?

ELOISE (*in distress*)

Oh, it's all so false! And arbitrary! (*To Ian.*)
But I think Mrs. Stubbs had better be false
and arbitrary, too. Mr. Stubbs might rather
have his supper than the truth.

MRS. STUBBS (*advancing a little*)

What is this about my being false? And—
arbitrary?

ELOISE

You see, you have to be, Mrs. Stubbs. We
don't blame you. How can you live by the truth
if Mr. Stubbs doesn't work by it?

MRS. STUBBS

This is the first word I ever heard said against Johnnie Stubbs's way of freezin' fish.

ELOISE

Oh, Mrs. Stubbs, if it were *merely* his way of freezing fish!

IAN

Since you are not trying to establish a direct relation with truth, set your clock at five minutes of six. The clocks, as would be clear to you if you would establish a first-hand relation with this diagram, Eloise, are slow.

MRS. STUBBS

You mean your sun clock's wrong.

IAN

All other clocks are wrong.

ELOISE

You live by the mean solar time of Philadelphia.

MRS. STUBBS

I do no such thing!

ELOISE

Yes, you do, Mrs. Stubbs. You see the sun can't be both here and in Philadelphia at the same time. Now, could it? So we have to pretend to be where it is in Philadelphia.

MRS. STUBBS

Who said we did?

ELOISE

Well, (*after a look at Ian*) the Government.

MRS. STUBBS

Them congressmen!

ELOISE

But Mr. Joyce and I— You're standing on a grave, Mrs. Stubbs. (*Mrs. Stubbs jumps.*) The grave of my grandmother's clock. (*In reply to Mrs. Stubbs's look of amazement.*) Oh, yes! That clock has done harm enough. Mrs. Subbs, think what time is—and then consider my grandmother's clock! Tick, tick! Tick, tick! Messing up eternity like that!

MRS. STUBBS (*after failing to think of anything adequate*) I must get Mr. Stubbs his supper! (*Frightened exit.*)

IAN (*standing near house door*)
Eloise, how I love you when feeling lifts you out of routine! Do you know, dearest, you are very sensitive in the way you feel feeling? Sometimes I think that the way to feel feeling is greater than to feel. You're like the dial. Your sensitiveness is the style—the gnomon—to cast the shadow of the feeling all around you and mark what has been felt. (*They embrace.*)

(*Eddy and Alice open the gate.*)

EDDY
Ahem! (*He comes down.*) Ahem! We seem to have come ahead of time.

ELOISE
Oh, Eddy! Alice! (*Moving toward Eddy but not passing the dial.*) We are living by sun time now. You haven't arrived for twenty minutes.

EDDY
We haven't arrived for twenty minutes? (*Feeling of himself.*) Why do I seem to be here?

ALICE (*approaching dial*)
So this is the famous sun-dial? How very interesting it is!

ELOISE
It's more than that.

ALICE
Yes, it's really beautiful, isn't it?

ELOISE
It's more than that.

EDDY
Is it?

ELOISE
It's a symbol. It means that Ian and I are done
with approximations arbitrarily and falsely imposed upon us.

EDDY
Well, I should think you would be. Who's been
doing that to you?

ELOISE
Don't step on the graves, please, Alice.

ALICE (*starting back in horror*)
Graves?

ELOISE (*pointing down*)
The lies we inherited lie buried there.

EDDY
Well, I should think that might make quite a
graveyard. So the sun-dial is built on lies.

ELOISE
Indeed it is not!

ALICE
Does it keep time?

IAN
It doesn't "keep" time. It gives it.

EDDY (*comparing with his watch*)
Well, it gives it wrong. It's twenty minutes fast.

(*Ian and Eloise smile at one another in a superior
way.*)

144

ALICE

You couldn't expect a home-made clock to be perfectly accurate. I think it's doing very well to come within twenty minutes of the true time.

IAN

It *is* true time.

ELOISE

You think it's twenty minutes fast because your puny, meticulous little watch is twenty minutes slow.

ALICE

Why, is it, Eddy? (*Comparing watches across the sun-dial.*) No, Eddy's watch is right by mine.

IAN

And neither of you is right by the truth.

ELOISE (*pityingly*)

Don't you know that you are running by the mean solar time of Philadelphia?

EDDY

Well, isn't everybody else running that way?

ELOISE

Does that make it right?

EDDY

I get you. You are going to cast off standard time and live by solar time.

ELOISE

Lies for truth.

EDDY

But how are you going to connect up with other people?

IAN

We can allow for their mistakes.

ELOISE

We will connect with other people in so far as other people are capable of connecting with the truth!

EDDY

I'm afraid you'll be awful lonesome sometimes.

ALICE

But, Eloise, do you mean to say that you are going to insist on being right when other people are wrong?

ELOISE

I insist upon it.

ALICE

What a life!

EDDY

Come, now, what difference does it make if we're wrong, if we're all wrong together?

IAN

That idea has made a clock of the human mind.

(*Enter Annie.*)

ANNIE

Mrs. Joyce, can't I have my clock back now? I don't know when to start dinner.

IAN (*consulting dial*)

By true time, Annie, it is twenty minutes past six.

ELOISE (*confidentially*)

By false time it is six.

ANNIE

I have to have my kitchen clock back. (*She looks around for it.*)

IAN

We are done with clocks, Annie.

ANNIE
You mean I'm *not* to have it back?

ELOISE
It lies buried there.

ANNIE
Buried? My clock buried? It's not *dead!*

IAN
It's dead to us, Annie.

ANNIE (*after looking at the grave*)
Do I get a new clock?

ELOISE
We are going to establish a first-hand relation with truth.

ANNIE
You can't cook without a clock.

IAN
A superstition. And, anyway—have you not the sun?

ANNIE (*after regarding the sun*)
I'd rather have a clock than the sun. (*Returns to her clockless kitcken.*)

IAN
That's what clocks have made of the human mind.

EDDY (*coming to Ian*)
Of course, this is all a joke.

IAN
The attempt to reach the truth has always been thought a joke.

EDDY
But this isn't any new truth! Why re-reach it?

IAN
I'm reaching it myself. I'm getting the impact— as of a fresh truth.

ALICE
  But hasn't it all been worked out for us?

IAN
  And we take it never knowing—never *feeling*
  —what it is we take.

ELOISE
  And that has made us the mechanical things we
  are!

ANNIE (*frantically rushes in, peeling an onion*)
  Starting the sauce for the spaghetti. Fry onions
  in butter three minutes. (*Wildly regards sun-
  dial—traces curved line of diagram with knife.
  Looks despairingly at the sun. Tears back into
  the house.*)

IAN
  You get no sense of wonder in looking at a clock.

ALICE
  Yes, do you know, I do. I've always thought
  that clocks were perfectly wonderful I never
  could understand how they could run like that.

ELOISE
  I suppose you know they run wrong?

EDDY
  What do you mean "run wrong?"

ELOISE
  Why, you are running by the mean solar time
  of Philadelphia. And yet here you are in
  Provincetown where the sun is a very different
  matter. You have no direct relation with the
  sun.

EDDY
  That doesn't seem to worry me much.

IAN

No, it wouldn't worry you, Eddy. You're too perfect a product of a standardized world.

(*Eddy bows acknowledgment.*)

ANNIE (*rushing out to look at dial.*) Add meat, brown seven minutes. (*Measures seven minutes between thumb and finger, holds up this fragment of time made visible and carries it carefully into the house.*)

EDDY

That girl'll get heart disease.

IAN

Let her establish a first-hand relation to heat. If she'd take a look at the food instead of the clock—!

EDDY

Trouble is we have to establish a first-hand relation with the spaghetti. (*Eddy now comes down and regards the sun-dial. Moralizes.*) If other people have got the wrong dope, you've got to have the wrong dope or be an off ox.

IAN

Perfect product of a standardized nation!

EDDY (*pointing with his stick*)

What's this standardized snake?

IAN

That's my diagram correcting the sun?

EDDY

Does one correct the sun?

ELOISE (*from behind the dial*)

Ian! Correcting the *sun!*

IAN

You see, there are only four days in the year

when the apparent time is the same as the average time.

ELOISE (*in growing alarm*)
Do you mean to tell me the sun is not right with *itself?*

IAN
I've tried to explain it to you, Eloise, but you said you could get the feeling of it without understanding it. This curve (*pointing*) marks the variation. Here, today, you see, the shadow is "right" as you call it—that is, average. It will be right again here in September, and again on December twenty-first.

ALICE
My birthday!

ELOISE
Ian, you mean to say the sun only tells the right *sun* time four days in the year?

IAN
It always tells the "right" sun time, but here the said right sun time is fifteen minutes behind its own average, and here it is sixteen minutes ahead. This scale here across the bottom shows you the number of minutes to add or subtract.

ELOISE (*with bitterness*)
Add! Subtract! Then you and your sun are false!

IAN
No, Eloise, not false. Merely intricate. Merely not regular. Machines are regular.

ELOISE
You got me to bury the clocks and live by the

sun and now you tell me you have to *fix up* the sun.

IAN

It was you who said bury the clocks.

ELOISE

I suppose you have to do something to the North star, too!

IAN

Yes, the North star is not true north. (*He starts to point out its error, sighting over the style of the dial.*)

ELOISE

What *is* true? What *is* true?

IAN (*with vision*)

The mind of man.

ELOISE

I think I'd better have a clock. (*A new gust.*) You told me I was to live by the sun, and now —after the clocks are in their graves—what I am to live by is *that snake*. (*She points at diagram.*)

IAN

You are a victim of misplaced confidence, Eloise. Sometimes when one feels things without understanding them, one feels the wrong thing. But there's nothing to worry about. The sun and I can take care of the sun's irregularities.

EDDY

Take heart, Eloise. It's a standardized sun.

IAN

It's not a blindly accepted sun!

ANNIE (*who comes as one not to be put aside*)

What'll I do when it rains?

IAN
> You'll use your mind.

ANNIE
> To tell time by? (*Looking to Eloise.*) I think I'd better find another place.

ALICE (*coming forward, regarding this as a really serious matter*)
> No, don't do that, Annie.

ELOISE (*tearfully*)
> You don't *know* the *wonders* of your own mind!

ANNIE
> No, ma'am. (*After a look at the sun, becomes terrified.*) It's going down!

EDDY
> Yes, it goes down.

ANNIE
> How'll we tell time when it's dark?

IAN
> *Sine sole silio.*

ANNIE
> Is that saying how we'll know when it's time to go to bed?

IAN
> The doves know when to go to bed.

ANNIE
> The doves don't go to the pictures.

ELOISE (*hysterically*)
> You'll grow, Annie!

ANNIE
> I'd rather have a clock. (*Exit.*)

IAN
> She'd rather have a clock than grow.

ALICE
> Now, why can't one do both?

IAN

One doesn't—that's the answer. One merely has the clock. I'd rather be a fool than a machine.

EDDY

I never definitely elected to be either.

IAN

One can be both without electing either.

ELOISE

I want to hear the ticking of a clock!

EDDY

It's a nice thing to hear. The ticking of a clock means the minds of many men. As long as the mind of man has to—fix up the facts of nature in order to create ideal time I feel it's a little more substantial to have the minds of many men.

ALICE

As I've told you before, Eloise, you can't do better than accept the things that have been all worked out for you.

IAN

You hear them, Eloise? You see where this defense of clocks is leading?

ELOISE

Ian, I'm terribly worried—and a little hurt—about the sun. (*As one beginning a dirge.*) The sun has failed me. The North star is false.

IAN (*going to her*)

I am here, dearest.

ELOISE

Sometimes you seem so much like space. I am running by the sun—that wobbly sun (*looking at it*) and everyone else is running by Philadelphia. I want a little clock to tick to me!

IAN

You will grow, dearest.

ELOISE

There's no use growing. The things you grow
to are wrong. (*Pressing her hands to her head.*)
I need a tick in time!

IAN (*striding savagely from her*)

Very well, then; dig up the clocks.

EDDY

Now you're talking!

(*Eloise springs up.*)

IAN

Dig up the clocks! And we spend our lives
nineteen minutes and twenty seconds apart!

(*Eloise is arrested, appalled. Dreadful pause.*)

ELOISE

You mean we'd never get together?

IAN

Time would lie between us. I refuse to be
re-caught into a clock world. It was you,
Eloise, who proposed to give up the clocks and
live in this first-hand relation to truth.

ELOISE

I didn't know I was proposing a first-hand relation with that snake!

IAN

It's not a snake! It's a little piece of the long-
winding road to truth. It's the discarding of
error, the adjustment of fact. And I did it myself. And it puts me *on* that road. Oh, I know
(*to Eddy and Alice*) how you can laugh if you

yourself feel no need to *feel* truth. And you, Eloise, if you don't want to feel time—return to your mean little clock. What is a clock? A clock is the soulless—

(*The alarm clock enters a protest. Smothered sound of the alarm clock going off underground. Eloise screams.*)

ELOISE

The alarm clock! It's going off!

ALICE

Buried alive!

ELOISE

Oh, no—oh, no! How terrible! Ian, how terrible! (*She runs to him. Alarm clock, being intermittent, goes off again.*)

IAN

Eloise, if you listen to the voice of that clock—!

EDDY

How bravely it tries to function in its grave!

ALICE

The death struggle—the last gasp!

(*With another scream Eloise snatches spade, begins to dig; alarm clock gives another little gasp; spade is too slow for her: in her desperation, goes to it with her hands. Gets it and, as she holds it aloft, the alarm clock rings its triumph.*)

ELOISE (*holding it to her ear*)

It's ticking. It ticks! It ticks! Oh, it's good to hear the ticking of a clock!

(*As he hears this, Ian, after a moment of terrible silence, goes and unscrews the plate of the sundial. All watch him, afraid to speak. He takes it off, holds it above the grave from which the alarm clock has been rescued.)*

ELOISE

Ian! What are you doing? (*He does not answer, but puts the sun-dial in the alarm clock's grave.*) Ian! No! No! Not that! Not your beautiful sun-dial! Oh, no! Not that!

(*Ian, having finished the burial of the sun-dial, sees the alarm clock, and puts it on the pedestal from which the sun-dial has been taken.*

IAN

We bow down, as of old, to the mechanical. We will have no other god but it. (*He then sits on the step, sunk in gloom.*)

(*Annie appears, in her hand a panful of water.*)

ANNIE

This liver has to soak five minutes. I'll soak it here. (*Sees the alarm clock; with a cry of joy.*) My clock! My clock! (*Overcome with emotion.*) Oh! My clock! My clock! Can I take it in the house to finish dinner?

ELOISE (*in a hopeless voice*)

Yes, take it away.

(*Beaming, Annie bears it to her kitchen. Eloise now kneels behind the grave of the sun-dial.*)

EDDY

Let us leave them alone with their dead. (*Leads Alice to the corner of the house; they look off down the road.*)

(*Eloise and Ian sit there on either side of the*

grave, swaying a little, back and forth, as those who mourn.)

ELOISE *(looking at grave)*
I had thought life was going to be so beautiful.

IAN
It might have been.

ELOISE *(looking at empty pedestal)*
I suppose it will never be beautiful again.

IAN
It cannot be beautiful again...

(Suddenly, with a cry, Eloise gets up and darts to the house: comes racing back with the alarm clock, snatches spade, desperately begins to dig a grave.)

ELOISE
Ian! Ian! Don't you see what I'm doing? I'm willing to have a first-hand relation with the sun even though it's *not* regular.

(But Ian is as one who has lost hope. Eddy and Alice turn to watch the re-burial of the alarm clock. Annie strides in.)

ANNIE *(in no mood for feeling)*
Where's my alarm clock?

ELOISE
I am burying it.

ANNIE
Again? *(Looks at sun-dial.)* And even the sun clock's gone?

EDDY
All is buried. Truth. Error. We have returned to the nothing from which we came.

ANNIE

This settles it. Now I go. I leave. (*Firm with purpose, re-enters the house.*)

ALICE (*excitedly*)

Eloise! She means it!

ELOISE (*dully*)

I suppose she does. (*Continues ner grave digging.*)

ALICE

But you can't get anybody else! You can't *get* anybody now. Oh, this is madness. What does any of the rest of it matter if you have lost your cook? (*To Ian.*) Eloise can't do the work! Peel potatoes—scrub. What's the difference what's *true* if you have to clean out your own sink? (*Despairing of him, she turns to Eloise.*) Eloise, stop fussing about the moon and stars! You're losing your *cook!*

(*Annie comes from the house with suitcase, shawl-strap, and hand-bag on long strings. Marches straight to left of stage, makes a face at the sun, marches to gate left rear and off.*)

ALICE

Eddy, go *after* her! Heavens! Has *no* one a mind? Go *after* her!

EDDY

What's the good of going after her without a clock?

ALICE

Well, get a clock! For heaven's sake, get a clock! Eloise, get off the grave of the alarm clock! (*Eloise stands like a monument. To Eddy.*) Well, there are graves all around you.

Dig something else up. No! You call her back.
I'll— (*Snatches spade, which is resting against
sun-dial pedestal, begins to dig.*)

EDDY (*stands at back, calling*)
Annie! Oh, Annie! *Wait*, Annie!

ALICE (*while frantically digging*)
Say something to *interest* her, imbecile!

EDDY (*stick in one hand, straw hat in the other,
making wild signals with both.*) Come home,
Annie! Clock! Clock! (*Giving up that job and
throwing off his coat.*) You interest her and I'll
dig.

(*They change places.*)

ALICE
She's most to the bend! Eddy, don't you know
how to *dig?*

(*Eddy, who has been digging with speed and skill,
produces the clock with which Eloise's grandmother started housekeeping. Starts to dash off
with it.*)

ELOISE (*dully*)
That clock doesn't keep time. Annie hates it.

IAN (*as if irritated by all this inefficiency*)
What she wants is the alarm clock. Get off
the grave, Eloise.

(*He disinters alarm clock and with it runs after
Annie. Alice draws a long breath and rubs her
back. Eddy brings the clock he dug up and sets
it on the pedestal. Then he looks down at the
disturbed graves.*)

EDDY
Here's a watch! (*Lifts it from the grave; holds*

11

it out to Eloise; she does not take it. He puts it on the pedestal beside the clock.) Here's another watch. (*Holds up Ian's watch.*) Quite a valuable piece of ground.

(*Now is heard the smothered voice of a cuckoo.*)

ALICE (*jumping*)
What's that?

ELOISE
The cuckoo. I suppose it's lonesome.

ALICE (*outraged*)
Cuckoo! (*Pointing.*) In that grave? The cuckoo we gave you? (*Eloise nods.*) You buried our wedding present? (*Eloise again nods. Eddy and Alice draw together in indignation.*) Well, I must say, the people who try to lead the right kind of lives *always* do the wrong thing. (*Stiffly.*) I am not accustomed to having my wedding presents put in graves. Will you please dig it up, Eddy? It will do very well on the mantel in our library. And my back nearly broken digging for your cook! (*She holds her back.*)

(*While Eddy is digging up the cuckoo, Annie and Ian appear and march across from gate to house, Annie triumphantly bearing her alarm clock, Ian—a captive at her chariot wheels—following with suitcase, shawl-strap, and long strings of bag around his wrist. A moment later Ian comes out of the house, looks at each dug-up thing, stands by the grave of the sun-dial. Enter Mrs. Stubbs.*)

MRS. STUBBS

Oh, Mr. Joyce, I've come to see your sun clock again. Mr. Stubbs says *he'll* not be run from Philadelphia. He says if you have got the time straight from the sun— (*Sees that the sun-dial is gone.*) Oh, do you take it in at night?

IAN

The sun-dial lies buried there.

MRS. STUBBS

You've *buried* the sun-clock? And dug up all the *wrong* clocks? (*With a withering glance at Eloise.*) That's how a smart man's appreciated! What did you bury it for, Mr. Joyce?

(*Eddy gives the cuckoo clock to Alice.*)

IAN

It cannot live in this world where no one wants truth or feeling about truth. This is a world for clocks.

MRS. STUBBS

Well, *I* want truth! And so does Johnnie Stubbs! If you'll excuse my saying so, Mr. Joyce, after you've made a thing that's right you oughtn't to bury it, even if there is nobody to want it. And now that *I* want it— (*Mrs. Stubbs takes the spade and begins to dig up the sun-dial. Ian cannot resist this and helps her. He lifts the sun-dial, she brushes it off, and he fits it to its place on the pedestal.*) Now, there it is, Mr. Joyce, and as good as if it had never seen the grave. (*She looks at the setting sun.*) And there's time for it to make its shadow before this sun has gone.

IAN
The simple mind has beauty.

ELOISE (*coming to him*)
I want to be simpler.

MRS. STUBBS
Now what time would you say it was, Mr. Joyce?

IAN
I would say it was twenty minutes of seven, Mrs. Stubbs.

MRS. STUBBS (*looking at Eddy and Alice and the cuckoo clock*)
And *they* would say it was twenty minutes past six! Well, *I* say: let them that want sun time have sun time, and them that want tick time have tick time.

(*Annie appears at the door.*)

ANNIE (*in a flat voice*)
It's dinner time!

CURTAIN

THE HERO OF SANTA MARIA

A RIDICULOUS TRAGEDY IN ONE ACT

by KENNETH SAWYER GOODMAN AND BEN HECHT

CHARACTERS

NATHAN FISHER, *known as "Nate"*

MARTIN FISHER, *known as "Marty"*

ELMIRA FISHER,

EDWARD MARTIN FISHER,
 known as "Toady"

JAMES MERRYWEATHER HINES,
 known as the "Squire" or "Heinie"

BERNARD P. FOSS

THEODORE Q. WILKINSON

THE HERO OF SANTA MARIA was originally presented by the Washington Square Players, at the Comedy Theatre, New York, on the night of February 12, 1917.

THE HERO
OF SANTA MARIA

*The Scene is the living-room of the Fisher home.
A scrupulously neat room of the late horsehair
and wax flower period.*

*At the back is the "front door," and near it a win-
dow looking toward the street. At the left is a
door leading into Marty's bedroom, and at the
right a door leading into a room sacred to Nate.*

*Over Marty's door is a printed sign, "Trespassers
will be prosecuted to the full extent of the law."
On the right wall is a crayon portrait of Nate in
G. A. R. uniform. The uniform is draped with
small American flags.*

*In the center of the room is a table with two stiff
chairs beside it. There are other articles of furni-
ture, including another small table with a drawer
in it. Among the knick-knacks on the center
table is a plush-covered family album.*

*The time is about ten in the morning of a pleasant
spring day.*

*When the curtain rises the stage is empty. Imme-
diately the street doors open and Marty peers
cautiously into the room. He then enters and
closes the door behind him.*

MARTY

Hey! Anybody home? (*He listens, then goes
cautiously to the door at the right, opens it, and*

listens again.) Hullo, Nate! Are y' in there? (*Evidently satisfied that the room is empty, he tiptoes across to the door at the left, stands before it, and raps softly and with precision. He then squats down and addresses the occupant of the room through the keyhole.*) P-s-s-s-t! Toady! (*Receiving no response, he looks about anxiously and again speaks into the keyhold in a slightly louder voice.*) P-s-s-s-t! Toady!

A SLEEPY VOICE (*from inside*)
What d'you want?

MARTY
Open the door. It's me, Uncle Marty.

THE VOICE
Oh!

(*A bolt is shot, and Toady Fisher stands on the threshold, rubbing his eyes. Marty produces two bottles of beer and a paper bag, which he places on the center table.*)

TOADY (*stretching his arms*)
Oh hum!

MARTY
Wake up. . . . I've brought yer breakfast.

TOADY (*glancing at the clock*)
You took yer time about it.

MARTY
If I'd snuck so much as a doughnut out of our own kitchen yer Aunt Elmira'd been wise to us in a minute. She's tighter than the skin on a prize pig, she is.

TOADY
Well, what you got?

MARTY

A couple of bottles of beer and a fried egg sandwich from Hopper's Hotel.

TOADY (*examining the supplies*)

Huh, is that all?

MARTY (*looking into his hat, which he takes off for the first time*)

I had a pair of fried fish-cakes in the top of my hat. Guess I must have lost 'em when I tipped it to Mrs. Sprudder down by the corner.

TOADY (*pulling up a chair to the table*)

Say, get me a glass and a plate, can't you?

MARTY (*seizing his arm*)

No you don't; not out here. They'll spot you sure.

TOADY

Rats! Pa wouldn't have me arrested.

MARTY

You ain't lived with him for sixty-seven years like I have.

TOADY

He can't pin it on me that I ever seen his fifty dollars.

MARTY

I reckon everybody knows it left town along about the same time you did.

TOADY (*beginning to eat the sandwich*)

Well, I ain't got it now, that's a cinch.

MARTY

Look here, who's running this family reconciliation, me or you?

TOADY (*his mouth full*)

Aw, can the prodigal son stuff, can it.

MARTY

Now, Toady, don't go and spoil it all.

TOADY

I wouldn't have stopped off in no flea-bitten burg like this, only I was sick of bumming my way on freights. All I want's enough coin to get me to Chicago like a gentleman.

MARTY

You don't know how much I've missed you. Why, I can't even take a couple of drinks no more without crying. Go on in there like a good boy, and mebbe I'll run up to the barber shop and borrow the Police Gazette for you to read.

TOADY (*getting up*)

I give you fair warning. I ain't going to sit in that hole all day.

MARTY

You'll be safe. Even Elmira daresn't put her foot in my room.

TOADY (*picking up one of the beer bottles and the sandwich and moving toward the door at the left*)

Aw, all right! All right!

MARTY

I'll steal something nice for your dinner, honest to Gawd I will. Some cold banana pudding.

TOADY (*wearily*)

All right! All right!

(*Marty pushes Toady·through the door and closes it.*)

MARTY

Now lock it on the inside. An' don't you open your head except I give you the high sign.

TOADY (*from inside*)
All right!

(*The bolt is shot. Marty listens a moment, then goes back to the center table and picks up the remaining bottle of beer just as the street door opens and Elmira Fisher enters. She has a letter in her hand.*)

ELMIRA (*in a rasping voice*)
Well, what are you doing home at this time of day?

(*Marty, startled, turns and switches the bottle of beer behind him.*)

MARTY
Eh?

ELMIRA
You heard what I said.

MARTY
So help me, I—

ELMIRA
You've been drinking. I can smell it on you from here.

MARTY
That's a nice way for a sister to talk, ain't it?

ELMIRA
I'd like to forget I was your sister.

MARTY
I ain't laying nothing in the way to hinder you trying. (*He makes a move toward the street door.*)

ELMIRA
Where you going now?

MARTY

Mebbe I'm going back to sweep the court-house, and then again, mebbe I'm going fishing.

ELMIRA

Fishing! Huh!

MARTY

Well, fishing's respectable, ain't it? It's men-tioned in the Bible, ain't it? I guess that'll hold you. The Lord said to his disciples, "Go out and dig bait," or something—

ELMIRA

Martin Henry Fisher, you're a blaspheming good-for-nothing—

MARTY

Aw, dry up!

ELMIRA

You'll lose your job, and serve you right, too.

MARTY

Needn't let that wear on your nose. I'm a political appointee, I am. I've got influence in Forkville.

ELMIRA (*turning on him*)

Influence! You've got influence, all right. Bad influence, that's what you've got. It was your influence made a thief out of your own nephew Edward and damned his immortal soul for him.

MARTY

I ain't responsible for Toady. He ain't my son.

ELMIRA

It don't matter whose son he is—

MARTY

Aw, lay off!

ELMIRA

What's that you're hiding under your coat-tails?

MARTY (*realizing that further concealment of the beer bottle is useless*)

Just a plain bottle of beer, registered under the Pure Food Act, to contain five per cent alcohol.

ELMIRA

I knew it! So that's what you keep hidden in that pig-sty of a room of yours. (*She advances toward the door at the left.*)

MARTY (*in alarm*)

Hold on there. Where you going?

ELMIRA

To bust in that door if I have to take an axe to it. I'm going to clear this house of every drop of devil's rum you've had the indecency to bring into it.

MARTY (*getting between Elmira and the door*)

No you don't! I own one-third of this house the same as you and Nate. Take a squint at that sign over my door. "Trespassers will be prosecuted to the full extent of the law." You keep out of my place and I'll keep out of yours. Don't have nothing more to do with me than you can help, and I'll return the favor, all right. But, by cricky, if you so much as set one of your flat feet acrost that sill, I'll have a warrant out for you.

(*Marty has backed up against the door, and Elmira stands glaring at him. Nathan Fisher enters from the street unnoticed in time to hear the last line.*)

ELMIRA (*to Marty*)
> You—you viper!

NATE (*gruffly*)
> Here, what's going on?

MARTY
> Howdy, Nate. I was just going out.

ELMIRA
> It would be a God's mercy if you'd go for good.

NATE (*coming toward the table*)
> It ain't likely he'll oblige us that far. What can't be helped has got to be endured.

MARTY
> Amen! That goes for both sides of the family.

NATE (*picking up the letter from the table and peering at it*)
> When did this come?

ELMIRA
> I just fetched it from the post-office.

NATE (*feeling in his pockets*)
> I must have left my specks in my other coat. Here, Marty, where's it from? (*He hands the letter to Marty and sits down.*)

MARTY (*reading from the corner of the envelope*)
> Fourteen eighteen F Street, Washington, D. C.

NATE
> Huh!

ELMIRA
> Give it here to me.

MARTY
> Don't get in a twitter. I'm doing this.

NATE
> Well, why don't you open it?

(Marty deliberately tears open the envelope and shakes out the letter.)

MARTY *(reading from the letter)*
Mr. Nathan Fisher, Forkville, Indiana.

Dear Sir: Our Mr. Gray has again looked into the evidence upon which you propose to base your fourth application for pension as a veteran of the Civil War, and we regret that, in our opinion, it is not sufficient to warrant us in going further with the case. The records clearly show that you were drafted into the army March 14, 1864, and had not left training camp at the close of hostilities.

There is, however, one possibility, to which we call your attention. We understand that the Honorable Bernard P. Foss is a fellow-citizen of yours. Mr. Foss is doubtless well known to you, and if willing to bring his personal influence to bear in your behalf could undoubtedly induce the Board of Pensions to take favorable action.

We herewith enclose bill for services to date, trusting that they have been entirely satisfactory and that our suggestion in regard to Mr. Foss will prove helpful.

Yours respectfully,
DODSON & GRIFFIN,
Attorneys-at-Law.

NATE *(with bitter resignation)*
That settles it, consarn 'em! Old Foss wouldn't lift a finger if I was drowning.

ELMIRA
How much is the bill?

MARTY
Eighty-seven dollars.

ELMIRA
The robbers!

NATE (*between his teeth*)
That's it, robbers! The hull country's in the hands of a bunch of dirty political crooks. If fellers like Squire Hines and Ted Wilkinson had an ounce of red-blooded patriotism they wouldn't stand to see a soldier of the Rebellion turned out of his nation's history.

MARTY
Haw, haw!

ELMIRA
You act like you seen something funny in paying out eighty-seven dollars for nothing.

MARTY
I reckon it takes a smarter liar than Nate to fool 'em in Washington.

NATE
Who's a liar? Ain't I marched in every Decoration Day parade for forty years? Ain't I a member of the G. A. R. Post Number Ninety-two?

ELMIRA
Not to count being a deacon and an officer of the Sunday school

MARTY
Being a Bo's'un in the Baptist Church don't entitle you to nothing this side of the Golden Gate.

ELMIRA
You're a low-down blaspheming likker snake.

MARTY

Well, as Toady used to say, mebbe it's better to be soaked in rum than vinegar.

(*Elmira begins to whimper.*)

NATE

I told you never to mention that scalawag's name in this house. Ain't it enough misfortune to be cheated out of sixteen hundred dollars back pension and a regular pension twice a month without you forever reminding me that I'm the father of a thief?

MARTY (*glancing apprehensively at the bedroom door*)

You hadn't ought to be so hard and unforgiving. Like as not Toady'll turn out a credit to the family yet.

NATE (*bitterly*)

I never had an ounce of comfort out of him all the days of his life, and I never expect to.

MARTY

Supposing he was to come home—I'm only saying—supposing?

NATE (*bringing his fist down*)

I'd have him in jail, that's where I'd have him. He's a liar and a drunkard and a thief. There ain't anything bad enough to call him, nothing!

MARTY

Hold on! You don't have to yell.

ELMIRA

There's Squire Hines now.

NATE

Eh! Who?

12

175

ELMIRA
Squire Hines. He's coming up the walk!

NATE (*confused between his anger at Toady and his anger over the pension*)
He's another one of 'em, damn 'em! They're all of a piece, conspiring to keep a man out of his rights. Darn the hull pack of 'em!

ELMIRA
Nate!

NATE
He'd better keep out of here. I got scores to settle with him.

MARTY
You ain't thinking of the editorial he wrote the time Toady was up for throwing the dead calf down Eben Fosdick's well? The one where he said the father was responsible for the sins of his son?

NATE
I ain't saying what I'm thinking—

MARTY
'Cause you'd oughtn't to blame a newspaper editor for thinking things out in an uncommon way.

(*There is a knock at the door. Elmira hesitates and looks at Nate. The knock is repeated.*)

NATE (*to Elmira*)
You heard him knock, didn't you?

(*Elmira opens the street door. Squire Hines enters pompously with his hat in his hand. The others regard him suspiciously without speaking.*)

NATE

Well?

HINES

Mr. Fisher, sir, I realize that under ordinary circumstances I would not be a welcome visitor in your home.

MARTY

I guess you're about right on that.

HINES

I feel, however, that in view of what has so recently and unexpectedly transpired, all petty rancors and animosities should be swept aside. I come, friends, as the bearer of sad, but glorious news, which to-night will thrill the national conscience and set the hearts of every man and woman in the State beating high with pride and sorrow.

ELMIRA

Well, we're listening to you.

HINES

To be as brief as possible, my paper has just received a dispatch from the Associated Press, dated this morning.

MARTY

No wonder you're excited. I bet it's about the first time the Bugle's had a piece of news less than a couple of days old.

HINES (*impressively*)

Your levity, sir, is ill-timed. The dispatch to which I refer recounts the heroic death of your brother's only son, Edward Martin Fisher.

MARTY

Eh?

NATE (*taken back*)
How's that?

ELMIRA
It's all a mistake. Toady wasn't the kind to expose himself.

HINES
So I thought myself, Miss Fisher, but I was wrong. Toady, as you so lovingly call him, showed himself, when the crisis came, to be a man of honor fit to take his place beside the heroes of the past.

MARTY (*with a glance at the bedroom*)
Say, you could knock me down with a feather!

NATE
Where did it happen?

HINES
At Santa Maria del something-or-other, on the Mexican border, the Company of United States Cavalry in which your son had enlisted—

ELMIRA
Now I know it's a mistake. Toady never rode a horse in his life.

HINES (*ignoring the interruption*)
I repeat, sir, his company crossed the river under a murderous fire to dislodge a party of snipers. At the very foot of the enemy's position Edward gloriously gave up his life for our beloved flag, the first American killed.

MARTY (*wiping his face with his handkerchief*)
Phew!

NATE
You're sure of what you're saying?

HINES
When you have been duly informed of your

bereavement by the War Department, the remains will be shipped here for interment, via El Paso, Texas.

MARTY

I never was a funeral fan like Elmira, but this here corpse is one I'll take a heap of interest looking at.

ELMIRA (*to Marty*)

You're a callous, unfeeling reptile.

HINES

I have no wish to add to your burden of affliction, but I warn you in advance that the features have been mutilated beyond recognition. He was identified only by the card sewed in his uniform.

MARTY (*slapping his knee as a light suddenly dawns on him*)

Haw, haw, haw! So that's it?

ELMIRA (*seizing Marty by the collar*)

So that's what?

MARTY

Take your hands off me. I got a right to be upset by my grief the same as the rest of you, ain't I?

HINES

If I may be allowed to say so, your grief ought to be somewhat tempered by the knowledge that your loss has given the youth of America an example of noble and self-sacrificing courage.

NATE

I knew it.

MARTY

Eh?

NATE

Any son of mine was bound to have the right stuff in him. Yes, sir, I knew it all along.

MARTY

Well, I'll be damned!

NATE

And it's about time the nation waked up to what me and mine has done for it.

HINES

That's just the point I was coming to. We have decided, with your permission, Mr. Fisher, to hold a large public demonstration of Pride and Sorrow, a military funeral, the expenses of which, I am authorized to say, will be borne jointly by the Bugle, Congressman-elect Foss, and the Honorable Theodore Q. Wilkinson, our Democratic candidate for sheriff at the coming county elections.

MARTY

Seems to me the offer ain't to be sneezed at.

HINES

To be perfectly frank, that's the way I look at it.

NATE

No!

ELMIRA

You mean you ain't going to let them?

NATE

They can't pay me off cheap and make a good thing out of it for themselves at the same time.

HINES

Am I to understand—

NATE

You're to understand you can't make nothing

off me. I've suffered enough for my country and been disowned by it. I ain't going to sit by and see my own son's funeral turned into a rally for the Democratic party that wouldn't lift a finger to get me my just rights. No, sir! He'll be buried with only family members and close personal friends attending, and if there's any credit coming, it ain't going to the bunch of political shysters that has turned me down.

HINES

I give you my word, Mr. Fisher—

MARTY

Nate's right for once. If he lets you pull votes for Ted Wilkinson and boom the circulation of the Bugle, there ought to be something in it besides brass bands and immortelles.

NATE

I've given my own flesh and blood that might have been a comfort and a support to me in my old age.

ELMIRA

It's no more'n right they should do something for him.

HINES

I'm deeply pained by your attitude, deeply disappointed.

MARTY

It don't seem exactly fair we should deprive the Squire of a chance to make a couple of speeches.

HINES

The committee are at the Bugle office now, drafting a set of resolutions which we had intended to present later in the day. I feel, however, that under the circumstances any further offer from us might be misunderstood.

MARTY

You needn't be shy about making a proposition. This ain't a sensitive family.

HINES (*to Nate*)

In that case may I venture to suggest that if Mr. Foss would undertake to push your own claim for a pension, and that if the Bugle would draft and circulate a petition endorsing it?—

ELMIRA

Do you mean that?

MARTY

There's sixteen hundred dollars of back pension due him, according to his own reckoning.

HINES

I dare say the Government will not be niggardly in its recognition of your brother's patriotic service when the facts are presented by the proper persons.

NATE

I ain't saying it's a bargain.

ELMIRA

If there was some way of fixing it so as Nate's pension was mentioned in the resolutions, and Mr. Foss couldn't crawl out of it afterwards.

MARTY

I always said that woman had ought to been a lawyer.

HINES

Well?

NATE

Mebbe, if you could fix it like Elmira says.

HINES (*glancing at his watch*)

Done! A public funeral it is, then. (*He has lost his unctuousness, and the others have apparently lost sight of the gravity of the event upon which they are basing their bargain.*) I'll be back in fifteen minutes with the committee.

NATE

I ain't promising nothing yet.

HINES (*genially*)

That, sir, to put it vulgarly, is up to us. Good morning, all.

(*He goes briskly out at the street door. Elmira goes to the window and looks after him.*)

ELMIRA (*thoughtfully*)

Eighty-seven dollars from sixteen hundred—

MARTY

I never thought twenty minutes ago I'd be the uncle of a hero and the brother of a bonyfidy pensioned veteran. (*He fills his pipe.*)

ELMIRA

Well, it won't benefit you none. You'll pay your keep out of what you can earn for yourself, same as ever.

MARTY

Mebbe so, and then again, mebbe not. (*He strikes a match.*)

ELMIRA

Don't you dast light that pipe in here!

MARTY

Aw, close your face!

NATE

It's hard enough to lose an only son, without hearing you two jawing each other.

MARTY

Yes, and mebbe it's a darn sight harder'n you think to lose a son like yours.

ELMIRA

What d'you mean by that?

MARTY

There's a little piece of business has got to be settled amongst ourselves before the Squire gets back with them resolutions.

NATE (*suspiciously*)

Eh!

MARTY (*going to the bedroom door and opening it*)

Hey! Come out of there.

(*Toady appears in the doorway. Nate and Elmira regard him in speechless consternation.*)

TOADY

Howdy, Pa.

NATE (*bitterly*)

So! You wasn't killed, after all?

MARTY

At least his face ain't any worse mutilated than usual. Come on, Toady; don't be bashful. You ain't buried yet.

ELMIRA

I might have known there was some mistake.

NATE

Mistake nothing! It's a game they put up on me, the two of 'em. Yes, and Hines was in it, and Foss, and the hull damn bunch, like as not.

TOADY

No they wasn't.

MARTY

This here is just a quiet family funeral. (*He*

184

begins turning the pages of the family album on the table.)

NATE

I'll—I'll get even with you. I'll—

TOADY

There's gratitude for you.

ELMIRA

I like your impudence.

TOADY

It ain't every son has done as much for his old man as I've done for you, pa.

NATE

I'll call the constable and have you in jail. Yes, sir, and I'll have Marty—

MARTY

You needn't pay no further attention to me.

(*He extracts a photograph from the album and goes to the small table, where he opens a drawer and takes out a hammer and some tacks.*)

NATE (*to Toady*)

You heard what I said. Now git!

TOADY

I ain't in no particular rush. You can't pin nothing on me. I'll tell 'em Aunt Elmira swiped your fifty dollars for the Baptist mission.

(*Marty draws a chair to the side of the room, climbs on it, and begins tacking up the photograph in a conspicuous place.*)

ELMIRA

You're a deserter from the United States Army. They'll get you for that, anyhow.

185

TOADY

Say, you make me laugh. When I heard old Hiny shooting off that bunk about me wading acrost the Rio Grandy with a flag in my mit, you could have butchered me with a dish rag.

MARTY (*pointing with his hammer to the flags over Nate's crayon portrait*)

Will you reach me them flags, Elmira, please?

ELMIRA (*turning*)

Eh? Land of Goshen, what are you doing on my best chair.

MARTY

Just putting up an old photo of the dear departed for his loving relatives to admire.

(*He gets down from the chair and goes for the flags himself.*)

TOADY

That's right. You'd ought to have a decorated picture of the Hero of Santa Maria. I guess you can't jump over Uncle Marty for a sob artist.

ELMIRA (*advancing on Toady*)

I'm going to get to the inside of this, if I have to shake the skin off you.

TOADY

Hold on, will you? I'm busy. (*He turns to Marty, who has returned with the flags and has begun adjusting them.*) Say, Unk, you're sticking them flags a little crooked.

NATE

If Hines and Foss ain't putting up a game on me, how'll I look when they find out?

TOADY

I guess that's something you got to figure out for yourself.

NATE

You've fixed my chances for a pension. It's a conspiracy!

ELMIRA

Yes, and Marty was in it.

MARTY

So help me, I never laid eyes on Toady till he came tapping at my window last night.

ELMIRA

You needn't tell me.

TOADY

If you all shut up, I'll give you the straight dope. On the level, I will.

MARTY

Make it short if you don't want your pa to have apoplexy.

TOADY

I met a feller in the park one night last winter.

ELMIRA

What park?

TOADY

Madison Square Park, New York City. He was a little red-headed feller with bow legs, and say, but he had a bad eye, believe me! His name was Christian Dane O'Houlihan.

ELMIRA

What's that got to do with it?

TOADY

For cat's sake, who's telling this, me or you?

NATE

Let him alone.

187

TOADY

"Gee," I sez to him, "if I had a flossy label like
yours, I bet I wouldn't have to be no free
lunch hound." "If you like it," he sez, "you're
welcome to it. You can't do no worse with it
than what I've done. If I had a nice, plain
name like Edward Martin Fisher, I'd go and
enlist in the cavalry with it." "Go ahead," I
sez, "you're on." So we swapped names, and
I got a job washing dishes in a dairy lunch.

MARTY

And the red-headed feller's getting shipped
from Santa Maria, via El Paso, Texas, to be
buried at the expense of the local option Dem-
ocrats of Forkville, Indiana.

TOADY

I guess that's about the answer. My name
was more unluckier than his'n.

ELMIRA

What did you come back for? Why couldn't
you let the only sensible thing you ever done
stay done?

TOADY

Oh, I got a heart, all right. I almost had a
mind to light out and keep my mouth shut
when I saw how puffed up Pa was over having
me killed. I'd have done it, too, only I heard
you driving that bargain with Hines about my
funeral.

ELMIRA

Well, what do you want? I know you want
something.

TOADY

I give you just one guess.

NATE

No, sir, I don't give him a cent. I'll be doing my country another service by putting a crook like him behind the bars.

TOADY (*cheerfully*)

All right. Turn me up, and blooie goes the pension.

MARTY

You sort of owe it to the family reputation, Nate, to keep him dead.

ELMIRA

If your pa gives you twenty-five dollars, will you get out and leave us be?

TOADY

Come around to the other ear. You don't talk loud enough.

NATE

I tell you I won't be a party to no fraud.

ELMIRA

That ain't the question. When he's gone, we can decide what's best according to our own conscience.

MARTY

I'd like to put some money on the way 'Miry's conscience'll jump.

ELMIRA (*to Toady, paying no attention to Marty*)

Suppose he makes it fifty dollars?

TOADY

What d'you take me for, a boob? I guess I know what me and the red-headed feller has done for Pa, all right. Twenty-five per cent cash. Them's my best terms. (*He turns and surveys the decorated portrait.*) Say, Uncle Marty, that looks swell.

189

ELMIRA

I never heard such gall in my life.

TOADY

I want four hundred dollars, or I'll walk down the street to Hopper's Hotel, and get drunk where the hull town'll see me.

NATE

That's a fine way for a son to talk to his father. Here's Hines and Foss, come around to do the right thing, after ten years' crookedness, and just when it's all fixed up for me to get my just deserts—

MARTY

Hold on!

ELMIRA

Yes, and mebbe your pa'd have got his pension long ago, except for your carryings on, putting everybody against us.

TOADY

Don't make me laugh. Everybody's heard how Pa tried to buy a substitute when he was drafted, only he couldn't raise the coin.

NATE

That's a lie, you blackmailing young skunk!

TOADY

I got my feelings the same as other people, and just for that word "skunk" it'll cost you an extra hundred before I leave this house.

MARTY

They'll be back here any minute with them resolutions.

NATE (*rising*)

I'll—I'll—

MARTY

You'll get your regular thirty a month all the same.

NATE (*to Toady*)

I'll—I'll—take a stick to you. I'll beat you till there ain't a hull bone in your carcass.

(*He seizes his stick.*)

TOADY

All right, sail in. I could lick you with one hand, but I'll let you beat me if you want to.

(*Nate makes a move toward Toady.*)

ELMIRA

For the love of heaven, Nate, be careful.

TOADY

Only for every belt you give me I'll holler like the Bull of Basham. We'll have all the neighbors in here to see you basting the Hero of Santa Maria.

(*Nate stands trembling with rage, the stick clutched in his hand.*)

MARTY

Walloping the corpse back to life'll settle things quick enough.

(*A band is heard faintly in the distance. Elmira puts her hand suddenly to her heart.*)

ELMIRA

Glory be! What's that?

(*They all listen a moment.*)

MARTY

It's Heinie coming back with his bandwagon load of Pride and Sorrow.

TOADY (*cheerfully*)
Well, Pa, what's the good word?

NATE
You—you—

TOADY
I meant to be easy on you, but when they turn the courthouse corner, I'll have to make it eight hundred for the suspense you're causing me.

NATE (*inarticulate with rage*)
You'll—you'll—

(*The music grows suddenly louder.*)

MARTY
There they go around the corner into Main Street.

ELMIRA (*wringing her hands*)
You better give in, Nate. Three-quarters is better'n nothing.

TOADY
It ain't three-quarters any longer. I've been reasonable and honest, but you've kind of pushed me too far. I've got to have eight hundred cold, iron dollars.

ELMIRA
We ain't got four hundred to our names, let alone eight hundred.

(*The band stops, and there is only the sound of the drums tapping a slow march.*)

TOADY
I'll take one hundred in cash and Pa's note for eight hundred, six months at seven per cent interest. Seven hundred to the order of Christian

Dane O'Houlihan, that's me, for services rendered, and the rest to Uncle Marty for acting as my agent. How's that, Marty?

MARTY

Sounds fair to me.

TOADY

Marty can hold the notes, and if they ain't taken up on the dot, I'll come back and we'll all get jugged together for defrauding the Government.

MARTY (*at the window*)

You better decide pretty quick, Nate. They're almost in front of the house.

NATE

No, by God! You can't rob a man that's been honest all his life. I'll—

MARTY

They're stopping in the gate. Foss has got his plug hat on.

NATE

They ain't here any too quick to suit me. I'll have the both of you up for robbery and black-mail.

ELMIRA

You'd better think what you're doing, Nate.

NATE

That's fine advice for a deaconess to give, ain't it?

ELMIRA

I'm only thinking what's best in the end.

NATE

No, sir! I'm honest. and I'll see you all damned before I'll—

TOADY (*soothingly*)

It's all right, Pa. I know you ain't yourself.
I'm going back in Uncle Marty's room, and if
you want to go through with it, the stuff's on.
I mean it. I'll skin out tonight and stay a
corpse. (*He picks up the bottle of beer from the
table.*) Of course if you want me to come and
get pinched, all you got to do is call me.

NATE (*sullenly*)

I ain't saying what I'll do.

(*There is another knock. Toady goes into the
bedroom and closes the door softly. Elmira goes
to the street door and opens it, disclosing Foss,
Hines, and Wilkinson. Foss wears a frock coat
and carries a silk hat in one hand and a roll of
papers in the other. The three dignitaries advance into the room. Behind them is a group of
neighbors framed in the doorway. Wilkinson
shakes Nate by the hand rather abruptly and
awkwardly.*)

WILKINSON (*attempting to come at once to the point*)

Howdy, Mr. Fisher. The Squire's (*he indicates
Hines with a hitch of his thumb*) already put you
wise to what we're here for.

HINES (*cutting in on Wilkinson and taking Nate's
reluctant hand*)

Quite so! (*He points to the decorated portrait.*)
See, gentlemen, what loving hands have already done. Nothing we can say or do more
sincerely voices the poignancy of this moment
than those simple flags and that simple photograph.

FOSS (*taking Nate's hand in turn*)
In this room, sir, where the hero of Santa Maria so recently lived and had his being, (*Marty glances apprehensively at the bedroom door*) our sympathy must seem a poor and inadequate thing—

NATE
I ain't said I wanted your sympathy, I—

ELMIRA (*cutting in*)
Don't mind what he says, Mr. Foss. He's been that upset—

FOSS (*still wringing Nate's hand*)
Spartan firmness, M'am. I admire him for it.

WILKINSON
I'll just leave some of my campaign cards on your table, in case the neighbors—

(*Hines shoots him an ugly look.*)

FOSS
We will not intrude on you long, Mr. Fisher. I have delegated myself—

WILKINSON
Been delegated.

FOSS
Been delegated by the citizens of Forkville to act as their spokesman on this solemn occasion and to read you these er— (*He adjusts his eyeglasses.*)

WILKINSON
You'll find them O. K., Mr. Fisher.

HINES
We have inserted a clause explicitly recognizing your own patriotic services.

MARTY
> D'you hear that, Nate?

NATE
> Yes, I hear it. But I got something to say first.

> (*Elmira plants a chair against the bedroom door and sits down in it.*)

FOSS (*unrolling his document*)
> Spare yourself, my friend. We all know the strain you've been laboring under. Perhaps, later at the public demonstration—

> (*Nate glances at him.*)

HINES
> The Governor and Senator Tinblatter have wired us—

WILKINSON
> Say, that's a fine stunt. A little talk, eh? Telling the folks how Edward was always a good Democrat.

> (*Nate glares at him.*)

HINES
> The Governor and Senator Tinblatter have wired us, promising to speak. Perhaps after that.

ELMIRA
> D'you hear, Nate? The Governor and Senator Tinblatter.

NATE
> I ain't said there'd be no demonstration.

MARTY
> You'll be getting telegrams from Washington next.

WILKINSON

You bet! Joe Finks is on the piazza now with a fist full.

(*A man steps forward from the group in the door-way and hands Nate a packet of yellow envelopes. Nate looks at them helplessly.*)

MARTY

The hull Democratic party's going to see this thing done up right.

FOSS (*clearing his throat and reading from the paper*)

We, the citizens of Forkville, Indiana, offer the following: Whereas, this day has become for us a day of er—

MARTY (*under his breath*)

Pride and sorrow.

ELMIRA (*to Marty*)

Shut up!

FOSS

Whereas, facing his country's foes on foreign soil, Edward Martin Fisher, son of our respected citizen, Nathan Fisher, himself an intrepid de-fender of our national existence in the Civil War, yesterday gave up his life;

Whereas, by his courageous death and ex-ample, the said Edward Martin Fisher has per-formed an inestimable service to each and everyone of us—

MARTY

That's right!

FOSS

Be it resolved, that we evidence our esteem and gratitude to the bereaved father by circulating an endorsement of his own claim to the proper and lawful pension heretofore unaccountably denied him by the National Government.

And be it further and finally resolved, that Edward Martin Fisher be buried with full military honors and all other tokens of love and respect of which this city and the Sovereign State of Indiana are capable.

 (Signed.) BERNARD P. FOSS,
     Member of Congress,
    JAMES MERRYWEATHER HINES,
    THEODORE Q. WILKINSON,
     Committee on Arrangements.

(*Foss rolls up the paper. Elmira, unable to stand the tension, sobs in partial hysteria. Nate's face has undergone various changes during the reading. He is rapidly losing his desire for revenge on Toady under the influence of the adulation of his neighbors. He stands undecided, crumpling the telegrams in his hand.*)

WILKINSON
 I guess that about covers it.

(*They all regard Nate as if expecting a definite answer.*)

MARTY (*seeing that Nate has practically given in*)
 You better say something, Nate.

NATE
 I—I don't know exactly how to put it, gentlemen—

MARTY
 You was mighty keen to talk a minute ago.

ELMIRA (*between her sobs, afraid that Marty may spoil everything*)
Let him alone, can't you?

NATE
It's all come on me sort of sudden-like, but I guess I know what I done for the United States —yes, and what my son Edward done for 'em, too.

THE CROWD IN THE DOORWAY
Hear! Hear!

NATE
I'd kind of set my heart on a—a—

MARTY
A quiet family funeral—

FOSS
Exactly, but under the circumstances—

NATE
It ain't for me to set myself up against what's expected of me.

WILKINSON (*extending his hand*)
Put it here, Mr. Fisher.

HINES
Then we're to understand?

NATE
I reckon I got to accept your resolutions.

FOSS (*shaking Nate by the hand*)
I can see how, sir, that your son was a chip off the old block.

MARTY
That's about the truest thing anybody's said yet.

CURTAIN

ALL GUMMED UP

A SATIRICAL COMEDY

by HARRY WAGSTAFF GRIBBLE

CHARACTERS

GEORGE BARTLETT, *a Liver Specialist*
MINTER, *his Assistant*
HENRIETTA TREMAYNE,
GEOFFREY TREMAYNE, *her Husband, a Pianist*
GLORIA BARTLETT, *George's Wife*

TIME: *The Present*
SCENE: *Bartlett's Consulting Room*

ALL GUMMED UP

SCENE:

> *There is a door leading into the ante-room up R.*
> *Another door leading to another part of the house*
> *up L, at the back. A desk over L. C., with a desk-*
> *chair behind it. Fireplace at the back, C. A*
> *settee over R. C. An armchair to L of fireplace*
> *and a small chair to R of fireplace. To the L of*
> *the settee and slightly above it is a smoker's table*
> *and set. Behind the settee is a small table with a*
> *lamp on it. The window is over L, behind the*
> *desk. On the desk are a cigar ash-tray, writing*
> *materials, a desk-lamp, and a note pad, and at the*
> *rise a small, oblong tin box.*

> *As the curtain rises, Bartlett is discovered asleep*
> *in the chair behind his desk, with his feet up on the*
> *desk.*

> *Enter Minter. Minter crosses and pulls down the*
> *window shade. He puts a tin box in a drawer of*
> *the desk.*

MINTER

Seven o'clock, Mr. Bartlett. (*Bartlett does not answer. Shaking Bartlett.*) Mr. Bartlett!

BARTLETT

Eh? What?

MINTER

Seven o'clock. (*Minter switches on desk-lamp.*)

BARTLETT

Morning or evening?

MINTER
Evening. (*Minter crosses and tidies cushions on settee, afterwards switching on lamp behind settee.*)

BARTLETT
Have I had my supper?

MINTER
Yes.

BARTLETT
Well, I'm still hungry. How do you account for that?

MINTER
It's your liver.

BARTLETT
You can't tell me anything about my liver.

MINTER (*re-crossing to desk and taking ash-tray and shaking ashes into fireplace*)
If I could, I should be a liver specialist and you my assistant—instead of vice versa.

BARTLETT
My wife's going to the theater tonight, isn't she?

MINTER
Yes. And you are going with her.

BARTLETT
Who said so?

MINTER
She did.

BARTLETT
She's usually right.

MINTER
Her choice is excellent—with a few exceptions. (*Glancing at him.*)

BARTLETT (*not noticing the "dig"*)

Theaters, for instance. She likes those noisy plays that won't allow one to sleep.

MINTER

It would take several brass bands to keep you awake.

BARTLETT

What's the use of keeping awake? Nothing ever happens nowadays.

MINTER

Doesn't it? You're too sleepy to notice anything.

BARTLETT

What do you mean?

MINTER

Did you ever realize that people suffer from love as well as from liver?

BARTLETT

Who the dickens is in love?

MINTER (*going*)

Keep awake and you'll find out.

BARTLETT

Minter, do you know why I continue to employ you?

MINTER

Because I continue to stay with you.

BARTLETT

You haven't even mentioned leaving.

MINTER

I shouldn't mention it. I should go.

BARTLETT

I think you had better go. You are getting too fresh.

MINTER
>What time for breakfast?

BARTLETT
>Breakfast won't concern you.

MINTER
>It never does. I don't take it. What time for
>yours?

BARTLETT
>Minter, you're discharged. Here's your salary.

MINTER
>Well, we'll say eight o'clock.

BARTLETT
>Do you mean that you refuse to be discharged?

MINTER
>You had better get dressed for the theater.

BARTLETT
>Minter, you are almost impertinent. Try to re-
>member the difference in our stations. (*Door-
>bell rings.*)

MINTER
>There's the door-bell. Will you answer it?

BARTLETT
>What do you mean?

MINTER
>That's the difference in our stations. (*Exit.*)

BARTLETT (*rising and walking slowly to fireplace,
>where he puts on a pair of slippers*)
>Life would be very pleasant and peaceful if it
>were not for Minter. But he's an evil—an evil
>necessity. (*Re-enter Minter.*)

MINTER
>A lady to see you, Mr. Bartlett.

BARTLETT
>I'm not consulting. It's after hours.

MINTER

Sorry. Too late. Here she is. (*Enter Henrietta Tremayne.*)

BARTLETT

How do you do?

HENRIETTA

How do you do?

BARTLETT (*bringing small chair from fireplace to R of desk*)

Won't you sit down?

MINTER

The lady is not a patient.

BARTLETT

You can go, Minter.

MINTER

Sorry I spoke. Thought I'd put you wise.

BARTLETT

I'm waiting.

MINTER

All right. But don't forget. It isn't liver—it's love. (*Exit Minter.*)

BARTLETT

Please pardon this exhibition of ignorance. I'm getting rid of him shortly.

HENRIETTA

Oh, please don't. He's such a nice fellow. So handsome, and so alert.

BARTLETT

He's very alert in answering the door-bell; but he can't even do that without boasting about it.

HENRIETTA

He understood me at once.

BARTLETT

Um!

14

HENRIETTA

I know it's a scandalous hour to call on you, but I told him that it was a very important matter and he showed me in.

BARTLETT

Um! What can I do for you?

HENRIETTA

Of course, you know my husband.

BARTLETT

I haven't even the pleasure of knowing you—as yet.

HENRIETTA

My name is Tremayne. My husband is Geoffrey Tremayne—the musician.

BARTLETT

Oh, yes. I believe my wife took me to hear him sing one day.

HENRIETTA

No, no. Play the piano. He's a very fine pianist.

BARTLETT

Oh! My impression was that he sang. Perhaps someone else did. Music always confuses me.

HENRIETTA

Well, it was about Geoffrey that I came to see you.

BARTLETT

Quite so. Pianists are frequently troubled with liver complaint. Chiefly owing to the sedentary life they lead. He should take a course in dancing, and after every sixth scale, or arpeggio, should do a buck and wing, or a little Russian ballet. If you had time you could shimmie with him—that would be better still.

HENRIETTA

Oh, no, his liver is perfectly all right.

BARTLETT

Then your husband cannot interest me, madam. I specialize in the liver solely.

HENRIETTA

He's as sound as a bell, physically. It's his mental condition I want to talk to you about. You see, he's desperately in love.

BARTLETT

Don't do anything for it. It will cure itself.

HENRIETTA

Oh, perhaps you think he's in love with me. Not at present. Just now he's in love with your wife.

BARTLETT

Well, that's a perfectly natural and healthy sentiment. My wife is a very attractive girl, and anyone who was immune to her beauty would probably be suffering from some liver complaint.

HENRIETTA

Then you have no objection to their affection for each other. I'm so glad.

BARTLETT

"Their affection"—I was not aware that my wife reciprocated the attachment.

HENRIETTA

No, I thought not. Well, she does.

BARTLETT

I think there must be some mistake. My wife

is always most confidential, and she hasn't even mentioned the matter.

HENRIETTA

Well, Geoffrey is a very straightforward boy. He never lies to me, and he wouldn't tell me it was so if he weren't sure.

BARTLETT

What is the program? Do I blacken your husband's eye, or do you tear my wife's hair?

HENRIETTA

It was to avoid those very things that I came to see you. My husband is coming to call on you, and I want you to promise not to injure him in any way. I shall behave wonderfully to your wife.

BARTLETT

But shouldn't we be committing a social error by taking it so calmly?

HENRIETTA

The only way for us to cover up their social error is by committing one ourselves. Besides, why should they corner all the publicity? We should create a sensation by remaining perfectly calm.

BARTLETT

You seem quite certain that you and I should make a good partnership in this affair. I hope your proposals are strictly businesslike.

HENRIETTA

Absolutely. Don't you see that directly we introduce emotion we lose our calm. In fact, our calm is essential to balance their emotion.

BARTLETT

You have somewhat relieved my mind.

HENRIETTA

Of course, we could have a little intrigue on the side, just to amuse ourselves, and to complicate matters for them.

BARTLETT

I begin to be frightened again.

HENRIETTA

Please retain your calm. I wouldn't have suggested an intrigue had I not thought I could trace an element of sport in you. (*Rising, and crossing to sofa, where she sits at head of it.*)

BARTLETT

Oh, my dear lady, did you ever hear of a sporty liver specialist?

HENRIETTA

No; I never expected you to be like this.

BARTLETT (*crossing C*)

Er—of course, if we enter into this agreement, we do it for the sake of our respective conjugal partners—not for each other's—nor for our own.

HENRIETTA

Absolutely, it's entirely unselfish.

BARTLETT

My wife, Gloria, is a very delightful girl, and the only reason I specialized in livers was to be able to shower her with the fees from my wealthy liverish clients.

HENRIETTA

Oh, that's nothing. I have sued every street-car company, and several of the Railroads, for self-inflicted sprained ankles, and obtained damages in each case, merely to provide Geoffrey with European musical vacations.

BARTLETT

What a noble woman! We certainly have something in common. (*Sitting by her.*)

HENRIETTA

Oh, you are quite different from what I expected.

BARTLETT

I think you are the first woman who has really interested me—except Gloria.

HENRIETTA

You are almost the only man who has ever attracted me—except Geoffrey.

BARTLETT

What was it in me which suggested to you sport or intrigue?

HENRIETTA

Oh, now you are getting inquisitive.

BARTLETT

Very inquisitive.

HENRIETTA

Well, I'll tell you. It's in your eye.

BARTLETT

Really!

HENRIETTA

Yes. It's more in the way you look at a person. You seem to search one's very liver—er, I mean soul.

BARTLETT

I'm trying to search you now for your idea of an intrigue.

HENRIETTA

You are dying to be a sport.

BARTLETT

It isn't the intrigue itself—it's your idea of one —which interests me.

HENRIETTA

Then I'll tell you. For a long time I have been looking for someone to share with me a secret passion. I believe you are the person.

BARTLETT

You amaze me.

HENRIETTA

It's no ordinary passion. The famous sirens, adventuresses, and vampires never experienced a desire such as mine. Their cravings were by comparison as mild as a child's longing for sweets.

BARTLETT

I really think that I had better back out.

HENRIETTA

Oh, please don't. The force of my craving is all in the desire—the object is very simple—merely gum.

BARTLETT

Gum?

HENRIETTA

Yes, gum—chewing gum. Plain, ordinary gum will do, but I delight in the fancy kinds—the refreshing spearmint, the sensuous clove, the juicy tutti-frutti. My husband knows of my passion, and thwarts me at every turn. He won't have a piece of gum in the house. He would rather I eloped to Honolulu with a bartender than chew one little morsel of gum. But, now that he is seeking his independence, don't you think my emancipation is justifiable?

BARTLETT

Why, yes, and the amazing coincidence is just this, that I, too, have the same craving, and am thwarted by my wife in the same manner.

HENRIETTA

Oh, I knew I had come to the right man. Directly I saw you I *knew* you were my chewing-gum mate.

BARTLETT (*going to desk and opening drawer, takes out box of gum*)

I'm almost afraid to show this to anyone. I have kept it hidden so long. (*Showing her the box.*)

HENRIETTA

Oh—oh—how marvelous! Give me some!

BARTLETT

Be careful! Gloria might come in at any moment, and then there would be a terrible scene.

HENRIETTA

Oh, what do we care for Gloria, or Geoffrey, or anyone. Let's be rash—let us abandon ourselves to our delight. (*She takes a piece and unwraps it, handing it to Bartlett. He does the same thing for her.*) Oh, what rapture!

BARTLETT

It has a wonderful thrill, hasn't it?

HENRIETTA

This publicity will never do. We must meet in some secret place. What about the subway?

BARTLETT

You are right. There is no secrecy like the secrecy of a crowd.

HENRIETTA

A long trip. Just you and I and our gum. Say to the Bronx Zoo.

BARTLETT

Oh, no. The animals stare so. They always remind me of my aunts at a prayer-meeting.

HENRIETTA

Well, then Van Cortlandt Park

BARTLETT

It shall be. (*Enter Minter.*)

MINTER

Better break away—the third party is here. (*Bartlett and the Lady rise.*)

BARTLETT

What the—How dare you interrupt without knocking?

MINTER

For the simple reason that if I had knocked he would have known that you were here. I wanted to warn you. You had better beat it. I think he has a gun.

BARTLETT

Who?

MINTER

Her lawfully wedded husband.

BARTLETT

Oh—show him in.

MINTER

What?

BARTLETT

Show him in.

MINTER

On second thoughts I'll take my salary. (*Bartlett gives him some notes.*) Here's my gun. (*Takes his gun out of his pocket.)* Good-bye. (*Exit. Bartlett puts gun in drawer.*)

BARTLETT

Are you nervous?

HENRIETTA

Of Geoffrey? Not now that you know my secret. (*Re-enter Minter with Geoffrey.*)

MINTER

Mr. Tremayne.

GEOFFREY (*to Bartlett*)

How do you do? (*Seeing Henrietta.*) Henrietta! What is the meaning of this?

HENRIETTA

Oh, Geoff, you bad boy, you've come out without your overcoat.

MINTER

It's all right. I'm keeping it for him.

HENRIETTA

Thank you so much, Mr. Minter.

MINTER

Not at all. I'm delighted to do anything for you.

BARTLETT

Minter, you can go.

MINTER

I know it. (*Exit.*)

BARTLETT

Please be seated, Mr. Tremayne.

GEOFFREY

No, thank you. Henrietta, what are you doing here?

BARTLETT

Mrs. Tremayne had the goodness to call on me with reference to her liver.

GEOFFREY

That's not true.   She has no liver.

BARTLETT

Dear, dear! That makes her still more interesting.

GEOFFREY

Henrietta, you're chewing!

HENRIETTA

Just a little, dear.

GEOFFREY

How disgusting, Mr. Bartlett; I must apologize for my wife.

BARTLETT

Not at all.   You find me in the same condition. In fact I gave it to her.

GEOFFREY (*to Henrietta*)

You had better leave me alone with Mr. Bartlett.

HENRIETTA

Certainly.   Where shall I wait?

BARTLETT

Oh, please stay.   All the other rooms are so draughty.

HENRIETTA

I don't mind draughts.   I'll go and talk to Mr. Minter.   Now, Geoff, take care of yourself, and Mr. Bartlett, don't upset him, will you? (*Exit.*)

GEOFFREY

My wife leaves me in a very awkward position.

BARTLETT

Well, sit down and make yourself comfortable.

GEOFFREY

I don't wish to be comfortable.   I have a very serious matter to discuss.

BARTLETT

Quite so. I'm always more serious myself when I'm uncomfortable.

GEOFFREY

I hope you will not make fun of me. It's a very difficult situation. What was my wife telling you?

BARTLETT

About what?

GEOFFREY

About me—and my affairs?

BARTLETT

Oh, she said you sold pianos—

GEOFFREY

No, sir. I play them.

BARTLETT

I knew you did something to them.

GEOFFREY

Was your wife's name introduced—

BARTLETT

In connection with the pianos?

GEOFFREY

No, no—in connection with me?

BARTLETT

Now, let me see—

GEOFFREY

Well, if my wife tried to influence you in any way with regard to a matter which she knows I intend to put to you, I warn you not to let it have any weight.

BARTLETT

No—of course not.

GEOFFREY

Because, sir, I am adamant.

BARTLETT
  You are.   Have a cigar?

GEOFFREY
  No, thank you.

BARTLETT
  A cigarette?

GEOFFREY
  No, thank you.

BARTLETT
  How is the piano game?

GEOFFREY
  What piano game?

BARTLETT
  The piano game in general?

GEOFFREY
  Look here, Mr. Bartlett, you are evidently in
  the dark as to my mission here.

BARTLETT
  A man of your charm needs no mission.

GEOFFREY
  I have one just the same—Er—Er—I think
  you will admit to yourself, if not to me, that
  you are by nature, profession, and tempera-
  ment entirely unsuited to your wife's society.

BARTLETT
  Absolutely unsuited.

GEOFFREY (*taken aback*)
  I'm glad to find you honest about so personal
  and yet so obvious a matter.

BARTLETT
  We married men should be very thankful to be
  unsuited to our wives. A woman sticks to a man
  she can't understand.

GEOFFREY
Are you sure?

BARTLETT
Yes—as long as no one else understands him.

GEOFFREY
I think I understand *you*.

BARTLETT
You're very clever. I don't understand myself.

GEOFFREY
Do you understand your wife?

BARTLETT
Heaven forbid. She is the greatest study of my life.

GEOFFREY
Perhaps again I am clever—I think *I* understand Gloria.

BARTLETT
Well, you are accustomed to intricate mechanism. The piano must be very complicated.

GEOFFREY
Are you comparing Gloria to a piano?

BARTLETT
A piano has its limits. Gloria has none.

GEOFFREY (*rising*)
She has reached her limit, Mr. Bartlett.

BARTLETT
For heaven's sake, has she exhausted all the plays and cabarets?

GEOFFREY
Ah! that is your idea of Gloria—You have simply a superficial knowledge of her appetites. Let me tell you, you haven't begun to study her

soul! And while you have been neglecting her,
I have studied and understood her soul.

BARTLETT

How interesting! Would you mind putting
your result on one of my diagnosis forms?

GEOFFREY

Don't joke about it, Bartlett. This is a serious
matter. Yes, to be brief, we are so suited to
each other that it would be almost criminal for
us to remain separated.

BARTLETT

Who? You and I?

GEOFFREY

No, no. Your wife and I.

BARTLETT

Oh, yes.

GEOFFREY

In fact it is essential for us to be together
to fulfill our destiny. It would be useless for
you to oppose us, for we should simply elope.

BARTLETT

Oh, yes. I remember now, your wife mentioned
something of the sort.

GEOFFREY

She did?

BARTLETT

And then we began discussing a very important
matter and it passed out of my mind.

GEOFFREY

Is your wife's future not an important matter?

BARTLETT

It is so important to have had a good past, and
so interesting having a good present, that the
future is bound to take a third place.

GEOFFREY
Do you mean to say that you're countenancing my proposal?

BARTLETT
You said it was useless for me to oppose you.

GEOFFREY
You have no objections to a man coming into your house and taking your wife from under your very nose—a perfect stranger.

BARTLETT
I know nothing against you. You seem a nice clean-cut young man. If I knew you better I might have some objections to you.

GEOFFREY
But this is preposterous—it's—it's outrageous—it's absolutely immoral. Surely you will put up some fight for your wife!

BARTLETT
Well, Minter loaned me his revolver to defend myself against you. Now, I never used one of these things. Do you know how they work?

GEOFFREY
Are you trying to make an ass of me?

BARTLETT
No, no. I assure you, if it is the proper thing to do I'll shoot you. Where would you like to be shot? You see, if I kill you, you will be of no further use to Gloria. On the other hand, if I wound you severely, you will again be out of luck, because Gloria is an atrocious nurse.

GEOFFREY
I never heard anything as abominable in my life. I shan't waste another moment here. I

shall go and fetch Gloria and take her away from you at once.

BARTLETT

Try and be back by June 20th, will you? I always take Gloria to visit my aunts at French Lick. She amuses them while I give them a liver treatment.

GEOFFREY

I've tried hard to control myself, Bartlett; but your utter contempt for the common decencies, your lack of appreciation of your wife, and your general unsoundness of mind are more than I can bear. Let me tell you that of all the inane idiots I have ever met—I have never in all my life—(*Enter Minter.*)

MINTER

Excuse me, but Mrs. Tremayne says not to strain your voice as you have to lecture tomorrow—also not to bang your fingers on the table, as that will spoil your touch.

GEOFFREY

What the devil are you doing out there with my wife?

MINTER

I was telling her of my troubles since I started taking care of other people's wives.

GEOFFREY

Oh, get out!

MINTER

Don't forget about the voice. (*Enter Gloria Bartlett.*)

GLORIA

Good evening, Minter. Georgie, it's time to start for the theatre. Why, there's Geoff. How

15

are you? (*Goes over to him and pats his face.
To Bartlett.*) Darling! You aren't ready, and
you know I like to hear the overture. He's a
terrible trial, Geoff. I'll never be able to train
him.

GEOFFREY
Gloria, come away from your husband.

GLORIA
From Georgie, why? Oh, I see. You've been
chewing again! How bad of you! Throw the
horrid stuff away!

BARTLETT
Yes, dear. (*Throws his gum in waste basket.*)

GEOFFREY
Gloria, what do you mean by this familiarity
with that man? Do you realize why I came
here tonight?

GLORIA
To meet him, I suppose. Have I interrupted a
consultation? Oh, I'm so sorry. Geoff, there's
nothing wrong with your liver, is there?

GEOFFREY
Do you suppose I should come to your husband
about my liver?

GLORIA
I can't think of anything else you would want
to see him about.

GEOFFREY
Not even about you?

GLORIA
My liver's all right, isn't it, Georgie?

GEOFFREY
Have you gone out of your senses, or are you

224

trying to fool me, because it won't work—I tell
you—it won't work!

GLORIA

Whose liver won't work? Georgie, who's ill?
What's the trouble?

BARTLETT

I think you have forgotten an appointment you
had with Mr. Tremayne.

GLORIA

Oh dear, have I?

BARTLETT

He seems to think you made an agreement to
elope with him.

GLORIA

Oh, that's perfectly true, I did. Yes, dear, we
had a long talk the other evening and we decided it would be quite the latest thing for us to
do. When shall we start, Geoff?

GEOFFREY

Heavens above—am I really the only honest
person left? Am I to stay here and listen to a
wife tell her husband that she is going to elope
with me?

GLORIA

Well, Geoff, I'd have told him before, only I
forgot.

GEOFFREY

I think you are the most impossible people I
ever met; I wouldn't elope with you if you went
on your knees and begged me to. You aren't
worthy! And as for you, Bartlett, you're a hip-
pant flypocrite. (*Enter Henrietta.*)

BARTLETT

Your liver must be in a wonderful condition.

Would you let me use you as a standard type in my new book?

HENRIETTA

No—No! I absolutely refuse! Geoffrey isn't a standard. Everything about him is original and I'm sure his liver is no exception. What have they been trying to do to you, Geoff?

GEOFFREY

Oh, leave me alone, Henrietta; are you trying to make a fool of me, too?

HENRIETTA

How could you ask such a thing? (*To the others.*) Have you made a fool of Geoffrey? That's very unkind of you.

BARTLETT

I must apologize for my wife. Through a lapse of memory she omitted to mention the fact that she was about to elope with your husband. She has upset his plans and he refuses to reconsider the matter.

HENRIETTA

And I don't blame him. He has a sensitive nature, and though big things might slip his memory, he is very particular about trifles.

GEOFFREY

Trifles!

GLORIA

I seem to have made an awful mess of things.

HENRIETTA

We know you didn't do it intentionally. Come, Geoff, dear, we had better go.

BARTLETT (*to Geoffrey*)

I hope you are not tired, and I do hope we shall

meet again. I should like to hear you play Wagner on our Church organ.

GEOFFREY

Oh, that's the last straw! Your wife trifles with my emotions. You outrage my sense of decency. Henrietta defies my independence, and now you cap it all with a request for Wagner on an organ! Do you realize that an 80-piece orchestra can only begin to interpret Wagner—and you ask for him on an organ!—Where's my coat?

HENRIETTA

Minter has it, dear.

GLORIA

Come to dinner some night and bring your wife.

GEOFFREY

If we were on a desert island, and you two had the only cocoanut, I wouldn't chew a piece of the fibre. (*Exit.*)

BARTLETT

What a splendid fellow!

HENRIETTA

Oh, he's just splendid in his own way. Some day he will compose a symphony which even the critics will understand. Good-bye, Mrs. Bartlett.

GLORIA

Good-bye.

HENRIETTA

Good-bye, Mr. Bartlett.

BARTLETT

I'll see you to the door. (*Following her.*)

HENRIETTA (*at door*)

Oh, please don't trouble. (*Bartlett makes a sign to her.*)

BARTLETT (*handing her the box of chewing gum*)

One day next week—subway—bring the gum with you. (*Sotto voce.*)

HENRIETTA (*sotto voce*)

I'll wait for a message from you.

BARTLETT

I'll send Minter. (*Exit Henrietta.*)

GLORIA (*holding up a piece of paper with Bartlett's chewed gum on it*)

George, where did you get this chewing gum?

BARTLETT (*confused*)

The woman tempted me and I did eat.

GLORIA

Did *she* give it to you?

BARTLETT

Y-u-yes, dear.

GLORIA

Och! The cat! (*Throwing it back into basket.*)

BARTLETT

Now don't get angry, darling.

GLORIA

I had far rather you had bought it yourself and been honest about it. (*Going up stage.*)

BARTLETT

Oh! (*Enter Minter, with box of gum.*)

MINTER

Did you give this to Mrs. Tremayne?

BARTLETT

Certainly not.

MINTER

I thought not. I caught her trying to get away

with it. I didn't think she was that kind of person. (*He puts box back in drawer.*)

BARTLETT

What are you putting it there for?

MINTER

It belongs there, doesn't it?

BARTLETT

What makes you think that?

MINTER

I ought to know. I've had enough of it. (*Going right.*)

BARTLETT

Minter, there's your gun, go shoot yourself.

MINTER

If I did, your business would go to the devil. I'm the only lasting impression anyone gets from a consultation with you.

GLORIA

One moment, Minter, you are a witness that my husband lied to me. George, you shall pay for this—you shan't take me to the theater.

BARTLETT

Oh, dear!

GLORIA

I shall go, and just to spite you I shall sit by myself.

BARTLETT

Oh, dear!

MINTER

Perhaps I could be of assistance to you, Mrs. Bartlett.

GLORIA

Oh, thank you, Mr. Minter, you shall take me.

BARTLETT

No—no—I object! I absolutely object to your going with Minter to the theater. You should have more regard for my feelings.

GLORIA

Had you any regard for my feelings when I found you chewing in my house with another man's wife?

BARTLETT

Just the same, I absolutely refuse to let you go with Minter.

GLORIA (*turning and going*)

Oh, we shall see—

BARTLETT

But think. dear!

GLORIA

Think what?

BARTLETT

I shall have to answer the door-bell. (*Exit Gloria, angry, with Minter. Bartlett settles himself into his chair, with his feet on the table.*) Oh, dear! What an uneventful life!

CURTAIN

THOMPSON'S LUCK

A TRAGEDY IN ONE ACT

by HARRY GREENWOOD GROVER

*The author acknowledges his indebtedness for the central
idea of this play to Ben Ames Williams, whose story,
"They Grind Exceeding Small," suggested the play.*

CHARACTERS

STEPHEN THOMPSON
JANE, *his Wife*
WATERMAN HOLMES $\Big\}$ *Neighbors*
HIRAM PRATT

THOMPSON'S LUCK

The interior of a very plain farmhouse kitchen, forenoon of a gray winter day. At the right there is a kitchen range, with tea kettle and iron pot. Right front door to pantry. Back center the sink in front of a window; a pump at right end, large water-pail at the other, with tin dipper hanging over it; at left, shelves, and along the wall at right more shelves and a corner cupboard. A plain table is in center of room, with two equally plain chairs by it. There is a door, back left, which reveals, as it opens later to admit the neighbor, that it is the only one leading outdoors, although it must be through one of those shed-like contrivances, so frequent in New England, that stretch from house to barn, for, when the door opens, only a darkening results. On the left wall there is a door which leads to the "down-stairs" bedroom; near this door is an old-fashioned wooden cradle; the hooded sort, with rockers. It is turned with head towards audience. At the rise, a thin, faded, small woman of thirty-five is washing dishes at the sink. When she walks, she is a little twisted over to one side: one limb is drawn up a little so she stands on her toes. An oldish-looking, gray-haired, stoop-shouldered, and sharp-faced man, sunken, small, gray eyes, bushy overhanging brow, is seated in the center pulling off rubber boots; and, as the conversation proceeds,

233

putting on black, shiny, greased, knee-length leather boots. The woman turns round from her work, looks at him and sighs.

THOMPSON

Want anything to the store?

MRS. THOMPSON (*sadly*)

Are you going to town to-day?

THOMPSON

Yes. (*Sharply.*) What's going to hinder?

MRS. THOMPSON (*turning and wiping dish as she talks, half apologetically: as if she did not feel it her right to question or dispute with her lord and master*)

I thought mebbe that the going and the—

THOMPSON

The going? When did going ever stop me?

MRS. THOMPSON

Yes, I know. (*Falteringly, as if she had more to say, but doesn't get any further.*)

THOMPSON (*vigorously*)

I guess so. No storm is going to stop me from getting to town; there is two men owe me interest money that will be in to-day to my office. That's how I got my money, putting it out and taking care to get it back. (*He laughs very slightly, a little cackling, thin laugh without any joy in it.*)

MRS. THOMPSON

Aren't you afraid it's going to storm?

THOMPSON

No, I'm not afraid of anything! It isn't my luck to have a storm. Don't you believe what folks around here tell you about Thompson's luck. Mebbe some of my folks was unlucky, but it don't follow me. (*He chuckles a little, holding one boot in his hand; he looks at her.*) You know yourself what folks said when I married you. (*Mrs. Thompson turns with a pained expression, as if she does not care to hear what she knows so well. Thompson continues looking away so that he doesn't see the look of pain.*) Thompson's luck again! Waited until he was an old man, then married a crooked stick. (*He chuckles again, not seeing the look of hatred on her face; pulls on his boot and looks up towards her.*) But we fooled 'em. (*He rises, goes over to the cradle, kneels before it, and looks in, pushing away a bit of the blanket that covers the child within.*) Who's got a finer boy than Steve Thompson? (*Turning to her anxiously.*) What makes him sleep so much?

MRS. THOMPSON
He's got cold.

THOMPSON
Pshaw, why should he have a cold? (*Rising.*) He'll be all right. I won't have him sick!

MRS. THOMPSON
Don't you think you better get the medicine? He seemed worse last night.

(*Thompson goes over, takes a coat from a hook by the door, and takes things from its pockets and puts them into another coat, which hangs there. While he is fumblingly doing this he goes on with his talking.*)

THOMPSON
Didn't I buy medicine last week?

MRS. THOMPSON

But that was another trouble. We can't use that for this.

THOMPSON

He won't be sick.

MRS. THOMPSON (*sighing*)

I hope not, but I am afraid.

THOMPSON

You ain't afraid to spend money, I notice.

MRS. THOMPSON

But, Steve, if he needs it, you wouldn't mind spending money?

THOMPSON

But he'll be all right, I say. Can't anything happen to my boy!

(*Knock at the door is heard.*)

THOMPSON (*without looking around*)

Come in.

(*There enters a quiet, smiling man, smooth, red face, soft voice, bundled up in a big coat, with heavy mittens, a cap pulled over his ears. He is younger looking than Thompson.*)

HOLMES (*quietly*)

So you're going, are you?

THOMPSON (*sharply*)

Didn't I just telephone you I was?

HOLMES (*smiling*)

Well—(*and seeing Mrs. Thompson over in the corner*) Good morning, Miss Thompson.

MRS. THOMPSON (*nods*)

Don't you think it's going to be a blizzard?

HOLMES (*doubtfully*)

I don't know.

THOMPSON

She's afraid of Thompson's Luck. Guess she heard of it before she ever came over here to keep house for me. Wouldn't think she'd marry me, would you? (*Bitterly, fumbling in his pocket and not looking up.*) Old man and crooked stick!

MRS. THOMPSON

Steve!

THOMPSON (*laughing, turns to Holmes*)

Have you seen my boy?

HOLMES

Not since yesterday. (*Smiling.*) Is he grown up? (*He looks at Mrs. Thompson, who smiles faintly.*)

(*Thompson going over to cradle, pulls back the quilt a little; although Holmes has followed him, he speaks to himself.*)

THOMPSON

A fine boy! A fine boy! (*He gets up.*) Thompson's luck! It never hit me!

HOLMES (*dryly*)

It never does hit more than once, does it?

THOMPSON (*angrily*)

You believe in it, too, do you?

HOLMES (*quietly*)

Oh, no, I don't believe in any luck. I think, as a man sows, he will reap.

THOMPSON

Hump! (*Contemptuously.*) You think my grandfather was struck by lightning just because, after the big tree in the yard was split to kindling, he said, "Now, try Thompson!"

HOLMES

Well, I don't know.

THOMPSON

I do! But they don't hit me, I tell ye. (*He has by now dressed, and goes into the pantry, off right, returning with a basket into which he looks, turning to his wife.*) Only two dozen eggs today? Why, I brought in seven yesterday.

MRS. THOMPSON (*meekly*)

I sold a dozen day before yesterday.

THOMPSON

You did! (*Winking at Holmes.*) Where's the money?

MRS. THOMPSON (*not seeing the joke*)

You said I might keep it.

THOMPSON

That's why I asked; to see if you keep it or spend it. (*He laughs a cynical laugh in which no one joins him. Holmes looks uneasy.*) Well! (*To Holmes*) Come on. (*He goes to the water-pail at the sink, takes down the tin dipper, drinks from it, puts back the dipper, draws from his trousers' pocket a black plug of tobacco, from which he bites, and returns it to his pocket.*)

MRS. THOMPSON (*who has been standing nervously wiping a pan over and over again, now gets up her courage to speak.*)

Don't you think you better get the medicine? If anything should happen—

THOMPSON (*interrupting*)

Nonsense! I'm going to town to get money, not

to spend it. He isn't sick. I won't have him sick! (*Turns to go, takes the latch of the door in his hand, then back over his shoulder with*) Take good care of my boy! Keep him warm! Care and warmth is what he needs. (*He goes out, followed by Holmes who simply nods as he goes through the door.*)

MRS. THOMPSON (*stands by the sink, looking out the window, until there is heard outside, Thompson's voice calling, "Whoa! hold up!" Then there is a sharp jingling of sleigh-bells succeeded by quiet, and she moves a step or two, evidently to follow better with her eyes, the retreating sleigh. She mechanically puts down the pan which she has continued to hold and wipe, and stands there with the dish-towel in her hand. She turns and looks toward the cradle, then out of the window suddenly as if he had come in sight again on some far hilltop. She raises her hand threateningly and exclaims:*)

It will be your fault! (*She limps over to the cradle, kneels by it, remains there as if listening. She gets up quickly, goes to the table with great determination; makes something in a cup, goes back to the cradle and exclaims feverishly:*) I won't let him die! His boy, and he won't spend a penny for medicine! He's my boy, too, and I won't let him die. (*She puts the cup back on the table, goes to the stove, takes a brick from the top of the stove, wraps it in a large piece of cloth, carries it to the cradle, pulls up the covering at the foot, and, while putting it in, talks frantically.*) His baby! I'll show him! He wouldn't have him die! I will not let him die! His mother will save him. He's my boy! Another crooked stick! (*She shrieks hysterically; buries her face in her hands, sobbing uncontrollably.*)

SCENE II

The curtain falls for an instant to rise on the same scene with this difference. The room is filled with queer shadows made by the light from a poor, little lamp on the table. There is a large rocking-chair near the table which has been moved to the middle of the room. The shades are drawn. The cradle is over near the stove. The oven door is open and Mrs. Thompson propped up in the chair with a red, faded shawl over her shoulders seated before it. She wakens with a start at some distant, low call heard outside.

MRS. THOMPSON

Oh! (*She steps over near the cradle and listens; looks up at the clock on the mantle over the stove.*) Half-past twelve. (*A weak knock is heard at the door. She rises quickly, limps over to the door, and, with her hand on the bar, which locks the door, she calls timorously:*) Who's there? (*A weak man's voice is heard outside.*) It's me. (*To which Mrs. Thompson adds with assurance and eagerness:*) Hiram Pratt? (*Before the "yes" comes she has taken down the bar and with it the door is opened, disclosing a thin, tall, stooped man; clad in a poor-looking, old, faded overcoat; a cap pulled down over his narrow head; a big strip of cloth wound round his thin, long neck.*)

MRS. THOMPSON

Well, I'm glad you've come.

PRATT (*staggers to the chair at the left of the table; sits down as if exhausted; in a weak voice says*) Baby worse?

MRS. THOMPSON
Yes, awful; but I'll save him with the medicine.

(*Pratt begins unbuttoning his coat; then another beneath it; and, at last, painfully draws something out of his trouser's side-pocket, which Jane reaches eagerly for.*)

PRATT
I didn't fetch it, Miss Thompson. I'm sorry! (*His speech is broken off by a spasm of coughing. Her hands have fallen limp at her side, and from now, during the recital, she stands mute and sometimes as if unconscious of his story or presence, until he comes to the part Thompson had played; at which, for a moment, she shows signs of a repressed rage, which suggests strength that lies hidden beneath her pitifully weak, habitual exterior.*) You see! (*He holds out a small, dirty, white canvas bag, such as country men use to carry loose change.*) I put that dollar bill you gave me to buy the medicine in here with my money and tied this tape around it just as I always do. (*He shows the bag folded securely, with the open end turned in and a soiled piece of white tape turned around it.*) It couldn't have got lost, could it? (*Appealing to Mrs. Thompson.*) Do you see how it could?

MRS. THOMPSON (*shakes her head*)
No!

PRATT
I thought I'd do my interest business first, be-

fore I went to the store to trade. I got my mortgage on my place from Mr. Thompson, you know.

MRS. THOMPSON

No, I didn't know.

PRATT

Yes, so I went right to the office. My! but it was warm up there; up those stairs. You know how it is.

MRS. THOMPSON

No, I've never seen it.

PRATT

Hain't seen it?

MRS. THOMPSON

No, I never go to town.

PRATT

Come to think of it, I don't know as I ever did see you there; but I supposed mebbe the old man took you sometimes.

MRS. THOMPSON

No, he never has room.

PRATT

I see he had Waterman Holmes.

MRS. THOMPSON

Yes, Waterman went. (*Weakly*.) But the baby was sick.

PRATT

Waterman was there when I went in; though I was kind of blinded when I first got in, I soon made out who it was and I knew his voice. I felt so kind of queer up there, climbing the stairs and the heat and all, and my fingers were so cold, I couldn't scarce count my money. But I finally got out the $11.40 that I had. It was not enough, but Mr. Thompson took it and let me have a little more time for the rest. (*He coughs terribly.*) This has been a tough winter, all the children sick with colds and one thing or another. (*He sighs, shakes his head.*) I don't know. (*He remains silent for what seems a long time, until brought back to his story by the cold voice of Jane.*)

MRS. THOMPSON
And then?

PRATT (*starting up*)
Oh, yes! Well, I thought it wouldn't do any harm as long as I had so much bad luck, poor crops and a calf that died, and so on, to ask Mr. Thompson if he wouldn't let me off a little. (*He sighs again*)

MRS. THOMPSON (*quickly and mechanically*)
What did he say?

PRATT
I suppose I can't complain. I told him I had a big family and had lots of sickness, and he said he had a family, too, to look out for. "I know," says I. (*He pauses, looks at the cradle and around the room.*) So I got up and come out, and when I got over to the store for the medicine the dollar bill was gone. (*He pauses and looks at Jane as if looking for some sharp scolding or word of question, perhaps of sympathy, but, seeing nothing but a stare on her face, he continues pitifully.*) I always put my money in that bag, but I thought I might have put it in some back pocket, seeing it wasn't my money.

MRS. THOMPSON
And you couldn't find it in your pocket?

PRATT

> I hunted in every pocket I've got. Zack Turner finally spoke up and asked me if I had come to town to clean out my pockets. I couldn't find that dollar, Miss Thompson. I'll pay you back soon as I can. Mebbe in a month I'll get it. Will that be all right? I'm sorry. (*He rises, begins fumblingly buttoning his coat.*)

MRS. THOMPSON (*as if awakening to reality*)

> It ain't the money; it's the medicine. (*She goes over and kneels by the cradle.*) What will become of my boy? (*She sobs.*)

PRATT (*weakly*)

> I guess he'll be a'right. Harriet could come over tomorrow and help you, mebbe.

MRS. THOMPSON

> Tomorrow?

PRATT

> Well, if it stops snowin'.

MRS. THOMPSON (*as if to herself*)

> Mebbe Steve bought it and will bring it.

PRATT

> Steve won't be out tonight.

MRS. THOMPSON

> Oh, yes, he will. He would have telephoned to find out about the boy if he didn't mean to come home.

PRATT

> Telephoned! There hain't three lengths of telephone wire between here and Batesville.

MRS. THOMPSON

> Then he'll come. (*Faintly, as if she did not believe it.*) I guess.

244

PRATT

  If there's anything I could do—I'm afraid he won't come.

MRS. THOMPSON

  You got through.

PRATT

  Yes, but I had to. There was Harriet and the children.

MRS. THOMPSON

  He's got a family, too.

PRATT

  Yes, but he can afford to stay in town. He can go to the hotel.

MRS. THOMPSON

  Not him. He sleeps in his office sometimes when he's kept in late. (*She looks at the cradle.*) But he'll come before mornin'. (*As if to herself.*) He said he wouldn't let him die.

PRATT

  Humph! He don't believe in Thompson's luck. Well, I hope not. (*Turning to go.*) I'm sorry, Miss Thompson. I must be going. (*He goes, and she mechanically bars the door after him. Now she seems awake, as if she realizes that the child has no hope but her resources. She wraps up another brick taken from the stove, takes the one from the cradle, and puts in the freshly heated one. Her every movement is feverish; at times, frantic. She stoops over very close as if to listen for the breathing of the child. She rises, limpingly fetches the lamp; kneels by the cradle, turns up the wick until it smokes and seems to peer into the face of the child within. She puts the lamp back on the table, mixes at the table something in a cup, puts it down, goes over to the telephone, takes down the receiver, and, after a pause, calls faintly:)*

MRS. THOMPSON

Hello! (*Pause.*) Hello! (*A longer pause in which she moves nervously, as if she heard strange sounds or perhaps no sound in the receiver.*) Hello! (*Then, frantically*) Hello! Hello! Hello! (*The receiver drops full length of the cord from her hand, she turns slowly round; falls into a chair and laughs hysterically.*) It's coming now. Thompson's luck!

Curtain

SCENE III

When the curtain rises after a brief interval, it is to disclose the kitchen flooded with a dazzling sunlight reflected from the snow-covered world outside. It is mid-forenoon of the day following the previous events. The table is still out in the center of the room, but the cradle is gone. The back door opens and in walks Thompson, followed by Waterman Holmes.

THOMPSON (*over his shoulder*)

You might as well come in. We'll have something hot to drink. (*Loosening their coats, they sit at the table; Thompson toward the stove and away from the bedroom door. From the bedroom door Jane comes quickly. She has a strained look, is pale, with deep circles under her eyes.*)

MRS. THOMPSON

At last!

THOMPSON (*not looking at her; speaking over his shoulder*)
This isn't late. We're early. (*Looking at his watch.*) Only ten o'clock. Give us a cup of coffee, will you?

(*Mrs. Thompson, without answering, goes over to the shelf by the window, takes a spoon, a jar of coffee, and puts water from pail into the coffee-pot.*)

THOMPSON (*continuing*)
It turned out to be a big storm. I didn't see any good spending money to telephone. I see the wires are all down anyhow. I knew you would be all right; you aren't afraid.

(*Jane pauses in her preparations, looks at him with a sudden look of hatred coming over her face, but says nothing.*)

THOMPSON (*continuing*)
Never see such drifts, did you, Waterman?

HOLMES
No!

THOMPSON
Couldn't have got through last night no more than you could fly.

MRS. THOMPSON
Some did

THOMPSON (*turning around and looking at her*)
Who?

MRS. THOMPSON
Hiram Pratt.

THOMPSON (*laughing his dry, cackling laugh*)
He couldn't do anything but go through. No

place to stay and no money to put up at the hotel. (*Turning to Waterman.*) Mebbe that dollar bill he dropped at my table was his hotel expenses. (*He slaps his knee and laughs so he doesn't hear the coffee-pot come down with a thud on the shelf at the side of the sink, when Jane's nerveless hand lets it drop as she hears "dollar bill." Waterman Holmes looks around, but, as Jane manages to pick it up and go on, he turns back. Thompson continues to Jane, who now stands with her back to him.*) He was into my office yesterday afternoon to pay up his interest and dropped a dollar bill on the table while he was counting out his chicken feed to make up his $11.40. (*Turning to Holmes.*) Guess he must have saved all the change he's seen for the last six months. He did have two silver dollars, though. (*He laughs again and then resumes to Jane.*) Well, sir, he's got so little brains that, while he was counting and recounting his small change to make sure he wasn't giving me too much, he let a dollar bill slip out on the table, and, with his eyes looking straight at that table, setting there as near as Holmes and I are to this one, he never saw me cover it up with my hand (*imitating on table*) and put it in my pocket. (*He bursts out laughing. Holmes smiles a little, but stops as he perceives Jane's queer look when she hears "dollar bill."*)

HOLMES

It was too bad, though.

THOMPSON (*snorting*)

Too bad, nothing! Dum fool! Why didn't he take care of his money? He ain't got brains

enough to carry him around the corner let alone
borrow money. (*Bitterly to Jane.*) How did
you know he got back last night?

MRS. THOMPSON
He stopped here.

THOMPSON
What time?

MRS. THOMPSON
About half-past twelve.

THOMPSON
What for?

MRS. THOMPSON
I asked him to do an errand.

THOMPSON
Can't I do your errands?

MRS. THOMPSON (*doggedly*)
You wouldn't.

THOMPSON
Shucks!

MRS. THOMPSON
I asked you to buy the medicine and you said
No!

THOMPSON
Pshaw! Did he get it?

MRS. THOMPSON
No, he couldn't.

THOMPSON
Why not?

MRS. THOMPSON (*looking defiantly at him*)
He lost the money I gave him.

THOMPSON
Lost the money? Stole it, you mean. How
much did you give him?

MRS. THOMPSON (*defiantly, looking sharply at him*)
A dollar bill! (*Holmes stands up; Thompson jumps to his feet, starts toward the bedroom door, stops, turns around and asks, with a tremor in his voice:*)

THOMPSON
How's my boy?

MRS. THOMPSON (*pointing to the door of the bedroom*)
Go and see!

THOMPSON (*goes slowly, but before he reaches the door turns again and says*)
How's my boy?

MRS. THOMPSON
Dead!

CURTAIN

FATA DEORUM

A POETIC PLAY IN TWO SCENES

by CARL W. GUSKE

CHARACTERS

Marius, *a retired General*
Decius, *a Philosopher and Slave to Marius*
A Messenger from Rome
A Suevian Prisoner
Two Roman Soldiers

FATA DEORUM

TIME: About 15 A. D.
PLACE: Near Rome.

SCENE ONE. *A room in the home of Marius.*
Discovered: Marius, sitting perfectly rigid and staring blankly into space.
Enter: Decius and Messenger.

DECIUS

Stay yet awhile, for I divine that soon
This morbid melancholia,
Corroding fast the basis of his reason,
Will abate. Then in the trenchant wrath
That will ensue, as surely as the night
Succeeds the day, it is more like we'll find
A chance to broach the subject of thy message.

MESSENGER

'Tis well; I'll stay awhile, and pray the Gods
May soon repel this death incipient!
See how he stares with fixéd gaze into
Vague miles of distance, and nor hears,
Nor sees, nor knows what 'round him stirs.
Poor soul! How long hath he thus been af-
flicted?

DECIUS

Since his retirement, and day by day
Grows worse. Of nourishment he scarce par-
takes.
Moreover, when to soothing sleep at last

253

He doth succumb, 'tis not for long, but starts
With sudden, wild, incisive shriek, and cries:
"Oh, Claudius, oh, Claudius, my son!"
And then he writhes, and moans, and weeps, as
though
His heart were being cleft. Then follows wrath,
Mad, turgid wrath, when all about him he
Would tear asunder. Yet I fear it not—
Not half so much as when he sinks into
This melancholy spell. 'Tis so like death;
I am afraid!

MESSENGER

Alas, he was
Rome's bravest general. Even to-day
The Emperor proclaimed him such when he
Dispatched me here and said: "I would that he
Were well again." Where is the scroll I brought?

DECIUS

I left it there before him. Look, he wakes.
The Gods be praised!

MESSENGER

The Gods be praised!

MARIUS

Where art thou, Decius?

DECIUS

Here, master, here.

MARIUS

Say if I slept a moment since, or woke.

DECIUS

Master, I do not know. Thou wert as rigid
As a stone, and yet thine eyes were opened wide.

MARIUS

'Tis that accurséd, hideous dream that haunts
me

Even while I wake. It hangs on me,
As if a sorrow bitterer than I've
Yet known were threatening. But no, it seems
As though it were a shadow of long past
Calamity, which I in state of blissful
Ignorance escaped. How strange it was,
And yet I saw them plainly—myriads
On myriads came staggering up a hill,
It seemed, and I was at the top.
Plodding, plodding, slowly plodding, nearer,
Nearer they approached; clad in scanty
Filthy rags, fast rotting in the dampness
Of their foul, unearthly home. Poor souls!
'Though some were blind and toothless, yet they grinned
Like fiends from hell. And one there was more gruesome
To behold than all the rest; he stretched
His arms to me in dire passion as
He passed. Gods, what a sorry sight!
And what a sound their harsh, hoarse croaking,
Moaning, wailing, laughing, crying,
All at once: "Unclean, unclean, unclean!"
Why am I tortured thus? Is 't not enough
That I must bear? Why do the Gods their fury
Wreak upon the head of one poor mortal
Here below? I had a son—where is
He now? He's gone, I know not where.
Not e'en the comfort of his death is mine.
Relent thy vengeance, mighty Gods. You've racked
Enough this wretched heart; now succor it,
Lest it should rise in mutiny, and, fraught
With curses rank, defy thy punishment!

DECIUS

 Oh, master mine, thou work'st thine own destruction.

MARIUS

 What sayest, fool? That is a lie. The Gods,
 The Gods—I am a victim of their mills;
 Oh, how they grind! "Thou work'st thine own
  destruction?"
 Lie, lie, I say it is a lie. The Gods
 Have planned it all, and I am doomed. They
  laugh
 To scorn my fervent prayers, whilst I, full help-
  less,
 Bear their cruel blows. Whence came this
  scroll?

DECIUS

 'Twas brought to thee by yonder messenger
 From Emperor Tiberius.

MARIUS

        Then read it,
 Decius. My temples rock, mine eyes
 Are almost blind! Read what Tiberius says.

DECIUS (*reading*)

 "Rome greets thee, Noble Marius:
         Now hast
 Thou rested forty days, and hope runs high
 In Rome that soon thy health will be restored.
 Thou mayest know how keen our forces
 Feel thine absence, when that we do send to
  thee,
 While still thy pulses rage, this matter for at-
  tention.
 The Gods have dealt us graciously the capture
 Of a Suevian prisoner—the charge

'Gainst whom, in full, the bearer will impart to
    thee."

MARIUS

Where is the prisoner?

MESSENGER

                              Without, my lord.

MARIUS

Go, fetch him in.   Come hither, Decius,
(*Exit Messenger*)
Come, sit thou here; I would a while consult
With thee.   For years and years I've trusted
    thee
With duties sacred in my household.
Thy wisdom I regarded high enough
To make thee tutor to mine only son—
Who now is gone.   Thus, and in various other
Ways, I've shown thy judgment great respect,
Albeit thou art a slave.   And now that I
Am ill, I place still greater import on
Thy wisdom.   Tell me, Decius, what thinkest
Thou of my misfortune?   Is't not too great?
Have not the Gods abased me much?

DECIUS

'Tis truly great.   Would thou could'st heap it
    all
Upon my head; most willingly I'd bear it.
So I love thee, master mine.

MARIUS

                              And yet,
A moment hence thou did'st remark: "Thou
    work'st
Thine own destruction."

DECIUS

                      'Twas an idle word.

257

MARIUS

'Twas not an idle word. Thou hast a mind
Which anyone might envy thee. Now come,
How dost thou mean I work mine own destruc-
tion?

DECIUS

I fear, oh, master, thou wilt be offended.

MARIUS

I'll be offended at thy prudish dalliance,
Which rears obstructions to mine understand
ing.
Thou art a good philosopher; come,
I'll forget thou art a slave. Come, come, speak
out.

DECIUS

Hast ever thought that in the world to-day
We dam the torrents of our grief until they wax
So turbulent, we turn with dazéd
Reasoning to blame the rancour of
The Gods, when we ourselves have been the
source?
For when the worst within us has o'ercome
The best, and when to poignancy we've yielded,
All the best seems but an atom in a
Sea of gall, wherein we float, and blindly
Groping, fall still lower in the bitter
Flood, which greedily devours us.
So thou dost only live in memory
Of sorrows thou hast known, and yield to moods
That fain would eat thy very soul away—

MARIUS

And should I smile when that from battle I
Returned one day to find mine only son
Was no more here?

DECIUS

        Not so; but now that he is
Gone, thou multiplyest much thy grief, by
    dwelling
On it over-long.

MARIUS

           Ah, "over-long!"
Into eternity would scarcely be long
Enough! I loved my child, my Claudius,
My son.

DECIUS

      And even I—

MARIUS

         His father, I—

DECIUS

And I, his slave.

MARIUS

        Indeed thou art a wise
Philosopher! Hast ever helped to bring
Into this world an offspring of thine own,
That thou might'st know the ties that bind a
    father
To his child? Hast ever felt the sweetness
Of paternal cares that wax as time
Goes on, as doth the grief that comes when such
Cares end? No, no, that hast thou not; and yet
Thou counsel'st thus? Out of my sight; be gone
Thou fool; out of my sight, be gone, be gone!

(*Decius retires to the background. The Messenger enters, followed by the Suevian prisoner between two Roman soldiers.*)

MESSENGER

Most noble sir: This is the leader of

A damnéd tribe that thrice hath ravished our
Cities, resting in the quiet of the
Night, with ne'er a thought of harm impending.
So the last atrocious deed was done
At Samaris, where scarce a peristyle
Remains, but that is smeared with blood which
    once
In veins of youth and noble manhood ran!
Not even helpless children did they spare,
And many a Roman maid, despondent grown
In pregnancy, now ends her life, ere yet
Her bastard Suevian offspring may be born!
And Samaris will not alone the mark
Of Suevian menace bear, for twice before
Hath Rome heard cries of mad despair,
Rising amid the smoke and flames
Of other devastated cities! But,
Each time the fiends had fled into the darkness
Of the night, before our soldiers could
Arrive. And now we have the leader of
Their tribe, with whom the Emperor hath sent
Me here, to say that Marius alone
Can justly treat so dastardly a crime.
Rome cries to thee from out the depths of shame,
That she should let such deed e'en once occur.
Avenge thou her, remove the tarnish from her
    name!

MARIUS

What hear I now? My breath, my breath, it
    fails!
'Though all the rage that mortal could possess
Now sears my soul, and kindles up a flame
Of keenest hate,
I count myself too much a weakling still

To punish thee. Thou hellish
Monster, thou—for every drop of Roman
Blood that thou didst spill, thy body shall
Receive a slash while hanging by its toes,
And for the Roman womanhood thou didst
Deflow'r, thy slashes shall be strewn with burn-
 ing
Sulphur! Now, my Suevian friend, how likest
Thou the wrath of Rome?

PRISONER
                    Thou slanderest Rome
To say thy shameful passion is her wrath.

MARIUS
My shameful passion then; how suits it thee?

PRISONER
Well, Roman, well; since I bear guilt of actions
Such as thine, I'm pleased to die.

MARIUS
                         Oh, thou
Germanic dog! 'Twas never known of Rome
To murder children in their sleep.

PRISONER
We even murder babes and women in
Their sleep, since murder deals a gentler blow
Than banishment to leprosy.

MARIUS
Ah, banishment to leprosy. So, now
I understand— My reputation travels fast.

PRISONER
Ne'er had our tribe an unfair battle waged,
And calmly were we e'er resigned to fates
Of honest war. But once because our loss
Was not so great as yours, and but a score

Of Suevian prisoners you had won, thy glut-
  tonous
Enmity thy reason stole and with
A fiendish mania thou didst condemn
Them to a living death, there in
The barren vales of that secluded isle,
With naught but cold gray hills to gaze upon,
And scores of wretches falling joint from joint.
'Twas then we swore that naught should stay
  our just
Revenge, not e'en the foulest trickery.
My daughter, too, was in that lot. Now she's
Unclean! Sweet child of rarest innocence!
Oh, how I wish that I might clasp her to
My heart just once again—just once again!
Now thou dost know why we bear guilt of
  damned
Deeds as black as thine.

MARIUS

                    Thou dar'st stand there
And damn what I have done! Since thou hast so
Declared thyself, I'll grant thy boon, that thou
May'st clasp thy daughter once more to thy
  breast.
Thou, too, shalt be unclean! Go drag him
  hence,
And when 'tis done, bring word in person here
  to me.
(*Exeunt the prisoner, messenger, and soldiers.*)
Now, Decius, put out the torch;
The moonbeams pierce the deep tenebrous
  clouds,
To woo the latent sorrow in my heart.
Now go; I'll count, alone, the tedious hours

That languish in the stillness of the air—
Creating vivid likenesses of pangs of
Passions ancient-born.

Curtain

SCENE TWO

> *Same as Scene One. Night.*
> *Discovered: Marius.*

MARIUS

                    When that the Gods
So prudently had wrought to manly youth
The only offspring of my flesh and blood—
I see him now, with head held high, darting
On nimble limbs as swift as winds that toss
His dark, abundant, curly hair;
With eyes a-sparkle, boyish smile, and gentle
Stroke of tender hand to smooth the time-worn
Furrows on my brow—my cup was filled!
Drunk with the joy of happiness supreme,
Unheedful of the source from whence it came,
I angered the immortal Gods, and reaped
The harvest of their quick and fearful doom!
And now my soul has fled to hazy spheres
Of everlasting memories, where happy
Dreams reiterate dear days that were
But are no more. Oh, Claudius, my son,
Return thy father's hideous gloom to cheer,
Or bid the Gods to open wide the black doors
Of foul mystery that thy dear presence
Doth conceal. I'd let the soothing zephyrs
Of the south waft thee my lamentations,
But the stream that yonder flows might rise

Enticing to my woeful words, and drown
Them in its buoyant waters. No, I'll face
The east; mayhap the first bright gleam of
Morning light will bring me hopeful word of
　　thee,
Or thou, thyself, wilt come again, dear son;
Yes, yes, thou'lt come, I know, I know thou'lt
　　come!

(*Decius and the Messenger have entered and overheard part of Marius' soliloquy.*)

DECIUS
　　You hear? And thus all through the night. And
　　Now this news. I fear, I fear, and yet
　　It must be done. Stand thou apart.
　　(*Decius cautiously approaches Marius.*)
　　　　　　　　　　　　　　　　Oh, master.
MARIUS (*after gazing about him in a dazed manner
addresses the messenger*)
　　What's in thy look that leers with mockery,
　　The while thy features ache with frowns and
　　　　fear?
MESSENGER
　　Oh, gruesome, soul-devouring sight that I
　　Beheld. Thy doom is sealed, and I the sealer,
　　Bound by thy command!
MARIUS
　　　　　　　　　　　　What is my doom?
　　Speak on, I am prepared for anything.
MESSENGER
　　We traveled fast and sped our sails, so that
　　We reached the wretched isle ere yet the sun
　　Had set, by whose slow-dying rays the peaks
　　Of those cold hills seemed steeped in gore.

The Suevian never spoke a word on all the way,
But once he said in tones that still are ringing
In mine ears: "He'll rue this day. For every act
Of violence we commit, we pay a ten-fold
Penalty before we quit." And then
He smiled, and entered fearlessly the heavy
Gate, which yawned and swallowed him.
I was about to turn and leave, when standing
There before me, at spear's length, I saw
A pair, now scarcely human as they looked,
She, from his fond embrace, sprang with a
    shriek
And fell into a heap before the prisoner,
Crying 'mid rasping sobs, "My father! Pity,
    Gods!"
The boy then came to me and when
He spoke, his tainted breath rose through the
    air
And stifled me. So frightfully distorted
Was his face, 'twas torture when he tried
To smile, which plainly I discerned, though low
He bowed his head. He dragged his limbs as if
To drop them would remove a weight of pain,
And bulging from their sockets with a piercing
Glare, his eyes shone through the lifeless strings
Of hair about his face. Sir, 'twas your son!
The girl whom he had followed there no earthly
Power could tear from him, nor him from her,
For so they loved—and so they went from life
    to death.
I knew him not, but he knew me. Oh, how I
    longed
To clasp him to my heart, and fold his swollen
    hands

In mine, but he's a thing unclean, unclean, un-
clean!
He asked with trembling lips concerning thee,
And quickly came the thought to me to lie.
I told him thou didst die in battle here
Of late; again he tried to smile and thanked
The Gods that thou should'st ne'er behold him
in
That piteous plight. And then he asked con-
cerning
Decius; and once again I lied,
And said thou gavest him his freedom at
Thy death; therefore I knew not where he was.
Then falling with his face upon the ground,
He clasped his hands in prayer, and thus I saw
Him lying still, while from the stern of our
Reluctant-moving barge I watched the scene of
sorrow fade.

MARIUS
Thy work is done, and well; return to Rome.
(*Exit the messenger.*)
Oh, God, a thing unclean, unclean, unclean!
And thou almighty Gods, art satisfied?
Oh, ne'er to come again, never again.
Ye Gods, ye mock me so. My heart doth
break,
And breaking still doth live. Can ye not still
Its beating, Gods? Why must it beat and
break?
No, no, I know thou'lt never come again, dear
son;
Ne'er more shall we behold thee! Decius,
When I am gone, what wilt thou do, and I
Thy freedom give to thee?

DECIUS

Ah, master mine, I'll stay with thee till thou
Art gone, and then I'll join my master Claudius,
To lave his wounds, and pray for comfort in
His last declining days of misery.

MARIUS

I'm faint—go, Decius, and fetch me wine.
(*Exit Decius.*)
Each twinkling star laughs at my sorry plight;
Each flower its perfume sends to throttle me;
Each fleeting cloud but mocks my waning life;
While each cool breath of breeze but fans the
    mad,
Devouring flame that in me burns. Ye triumph,
Mighty Gods.
(*He takes a sword from the wall.*)
Be not afraid, oh, sword, of this poor heart,
'Tis but a broken fluttering thing that fain
    would die.
Thou wilt disturb no feeling there, for all
Is gone, and thou art truly welcome—come!
(*He stabs himself and dies.*)

(*Enter Decius.*)

DECIUS

Here, master mine, take drink this wine,
And follow me, so that we three—
(*He sees that Marius is dead*)
Now, Claudius, my master, I will come.

FINIS

PEARL OF DAWN

A FANTASY IN TEN SCENES

by HOLLAND HUDSON

CHARACTERS

HAROUN AL RASCHID, *Caliph of Bagdad,*
    surnamed "the Good"
HIS VIZIER
HIS FAVORITE
HIS CHIEF EUNUCH
ALI ALI, *a Merchant, also called "the good"*
HIS ELDEST WIFE
HIS YOUNGEST WIFE
HAZAN, *his Brother-in-Law*
A ROBBER CAPTAIN
HIS LIEUTENANT
    Guards, robbers, wives, houri, ad lib.

ORDER OF SCENES

*The entire action takes place in one night.   Scenes 3 to 9
comprise the story within the play.*

PEARL OF DAWN

AUTHOR'S NOTE

"Pearl of Dawn" was written to provide a pictorial one-act play, neither tragic nor highfalutin, which might afford opportunity for rapid movement and adventure in a small compass of time and space. I have therefore placed the story in a period and a country about which the rising generation knows comparatively little, and have deliberately shifted the action constantly from street to shop or palace and back again.

Scenically, the street is a painted front curtain, and the shop a cyclorama drape. The palace scene is simply the shop, with different light, and its properties changed.

SCENE ONE: *A Street in Bagdad. Night.*

HAZAN (*comes down the street, making his way with difficulty, swaying with weakness. His clothes are shredded to ribbons. He has bandaged himself, here and there, with fragments of his garments*)
Allah, be merciful! Let me die! Let me die! Allah— (*He falls unconscious.*)

ALI (*runs out, carrying a lantern. He bends over the prostrate man and tries to rouse him.*)

HAZAN (*sprawls on his face, and his back, upon which no clothing remains, is revealed striped with marks of a whip.*)

18

271

ALI

Ah, poor man! Poor man!

HAZAN (*recovering consciousness, rolls over on his side, looks up*)

Ali!

ALI

What, you know me? Who are you?

HAZAN

You do not recognize me? I am Hazan. (*He faints again.*)

ALI

Hazan, good brother; wake again. It is I, Ali, Ali. I don't remember which wife it is whose brother you are, but I know you. Come, wake up, dear brother, you are much too heavy for me to carry. (*Nevertheless, he manages to pick up Hazan and stagger out with him, leaving his lantern behind.*)

HAROUN AL RASCHID (*enters from the opposite direction, with his Vizier, who carries a lantern*)

You say the man who carried him into that shop is Ali the good?

THE VIZIER (*salaaming*)

So people call him. As he is a merchant—you may believe it if you like.

HAROUN

Stop salaaming. I wish to remain incognito. So that is the man to whom they give my title? Not Haroun al Raschid the Good, but Ali the good! A merchant of women's wear for a rival!

VIZIER

The moon does not rival the sun, but reflects it.

HAROUN

But if he is called "the good," why does he now

give aid and comfort to a wretch who has been publicly whipped for violating his neighbor's harem?

VIZIER

Perhaps Ali's own harem is a little too much for him.

HAROUN

That is the most cynical thing you have said this evening. I shall have to present you with a brace of wives.

VIZIER

That is the most cynical threat you have made today. To keep you from remembering it, let me tell you that the man who was whipped is Ali's brother-in-law. Further, Ali undoubtedly does not know yet what he was whipped for. His wives keep all the scandal to themselves.

HAROUN

I should like to see this merchant sell his wares and yet earn his title of "the good."

VIZIER

You should have that opportunity soon. The guardian of your harem asked me where your favorite might buy some silks this evening at a reasonable price and I told him of Ali's shop. They may be there now.

HAROUN

And be defiled by the presence of Hazan the unclean! Let us go there quickly. (*They hurry off, Haroun taking Ali's lantern.*)

A patrol passes. The lights fade out.
The scene changes.

273

SCENE TWO: *The Shop of Ali*

Through the open doorway at the back one sees the sky of early night. In the foreground a curtained divan is lighted by a small lamp concealed in the canopy. The center of the shop is lighted by a brass hanging lamp. Under it Ali's wives are displaying silks to a veiled lady, who is guarded by Haroun's Chief Eunuch, a gigantic Nubian with a naked sword across one arm.

THE ELDEST WIFE
Lady, the silk is worth fifty pieces of silver, and it is yours for thirty.

HAROUN AL RASCHID'S FAVORITE
It does not interest me.

THE YOUNGEST WIFE
Lady, we could not cheat you. You are in the shop of Ali the good.

THE ELDEST WIFE
We are commanded to cheat no one and to speak to our customers no untrue word.

THE YOUNGEST WIFE
These are the commands of Ali the good.

THE FAVORITE
Is the merchant really so good?

THE ELDEST WIFE
I, the eldest wife, acknowledge it.

THE FAVORITE
Then he must be good, indeed. Are you sure this silk is of the best quality?

THE YOUNGEST WIFE
Lady, it is the jewel of China, whence it came.

ALI (*appears in the doorway carrying the uncon-scious Hazan*)
One of you, a cup of water, quickly!

THE ELDEST WIFE
But see, a customer, a great lady!

ALI
But I have found a brother—not yours? Well, a brother of one of you. Make haste! (*He brings Hazan down to the curtained divan.*)

THE YOUNGEST WIFE (*brings a cup of water.*)

THE ELDEST WIFE (*attends to her customer, screen-ing her from seeing more of the intruder.*)

THE FAVORITE
Is that the merchant, Ali?

THE ELDEST WIFE
Ali the good, lady. You must forgive him.
He is so tenderhearted that he forgets all busi-ness to help any creature in distress.

THE FAVORITE
What a wonderful husband he must be!

THE ELDEST WIFE
He is wonderful. Only sometimes we wish his heart would harden a little to the distress of others that he might take more thought for his own affairs.

ALI (*taking the cup from the Youngest Wife*)
Oh, he's your brother?

THE YOUNGEST WIFE
Dear husband, do not call him my brother again.
Let him tell you for what he was beaten. (*She rejoins the Eldest Wife.*)

ALI (*lifts Hazan and gives him a drink.*)

HAZAN (*not fully conscious*)

You may kill me if you like. It is the will of Allah.

ALI

Why should I kill you, brother?

HAZAN

Ah, it is you, Ali. Where have you brought me?

ALI

To my house.

HAZAN

No, no! You must not. (*Attempting to rise.*) My own sister, your youngest wife, would have me driven out.

ALI

What have you done, brother?

HAZAN

I was found—in the harem of my neighbor.

ALI

With his—wives?

HAZAN

His favorite.

ALI

Alas, brother, why did you do this?

HAZAN

Ali, you are too good; you do not know sin.

ALI

Do I not? Have I not eyes, brother?

HAZAN

I do not know, myself, why I sinned.

ALI

That is sin, indeed.

HAZAN

Yes, I have sinned and I have been caught, wounded with swords and beaten with whips.

Then, when the breath came back into my
body they stood before me with her—my beloved—and struck off her head before me so
that I was blinded with her blood. Oh Allah!
Allah! (*He weeps.*)

ALI

Shall I not arm you against them that did this?

HAZAN (*regaining some of his self-control*)

No, dear brother; it was done by decree of the
Caliph, Haroun al Raschid the Good.

ALI

Alas, then your case is hopeless.

HAZAN (*struggling up on one elbow, his eyes bright
with fever*)

No, it is not.

ALI

Indeed, I can see no hope for you.

HAZAN

Allah is merciful. I have learned it here in your
shop. That is why he would not answer my
prayers for death. That is why I shall leave
your house at once with my wounds healed.
(*He struggles to his feet.*)

ALI

A miracle?

HAZAN

The miraculous mercy of Allah! Listen, brother
—neither the sharp edges of the swords nor the
blows of whips have robbed me of my golden
hour. You say to yourself "but one hour?"
Why, it might have been but a minute. It is
written in the book of man's life that such things
shall not last long; we should then lose our interest in heaven. And look—

ALI

Where, brother?

HAZAN

Just before me.

ALI

I see nothing.

HAZAN

Ah, you cannot see her, but I do, and I shall never lose sight of her image while I live. I shall go to the desert, where my disgrace will not be known, and her ghost will lead the way and comfort me. Allah is merciful!

ALI

No! Do not go!

THE YOUNGEST WIFE (*has come down to them with a bag and a large cloak*)

Dear husband, I bring a cloak and food for this unfortunate man. You, dear husband, are Ali the merchant, and have a duty to your customers. Let the unfortunate man, who was my brother before his sin, go his way lest your customers think evil of Ali the good.

ALI

No, no!

HAZAN

The Youngest Wife is right, O Ali the good! Let me go my way in peace. (*He puts on the cloak, takes the bag and starts for the door.*)

HAROUN AND HIS VIZIER (*enter the shop, coming down toward Ali.*)

HAZAN (*turning in the doorway*)

The blessings of Allah on this household! (*Then to the moonlight outside.*) Lead on! (*He leaves the shop.*)

HAROUN
To whom did he speak the last words?

ALI
To a ghost. The unfortunate man has sinned and suffered.

HAROUN
Too bad, too bad!

ALI
Isn't it, now?

HAROUN
Don't you think the Caliph was too cruel?

ALI
Yes, of course. He has to be. People expect it of a man in his position. . . . I suppose that, personally, he is as merciful a man as any of us.

VIZIER
I am sure the Caliph would like to hear himself so well commended.

HAROUN
You are the merchant, Ali the good?

ALI (*simply*)
I am the merchant, Ali.

THE FAVORITE
I have been shopping in the bazaar all afternoon, and I am very tired. I must rest.

ALI
Conduct the lady to a place of rest.

THE ELDEST WIFE (*leads the Favorite to the curtained divan.*)

ALI (*to the Youngest Wife*)
Show her silks. Do not lose the sale. Is coffee ready?

THE YOUNGEST WIFE
   All ready to be poured. That Egyptian fabric
   —I cannot find it.
THE ELDEST WIFE (*joins her in the search*)
ALI (*handing a cup of coffee to Haroun*)
   May I offer you gentlemen a cup of coffee, since
   the Caliph has outlawed more stimulating hos-
   pitality?
THE VIZIER
   Do you mean to tell us that you have nothing
   in your cellar?
ALI (*giving him coffee*)
   I am unfortunate. My house was built without
   a cellar.
THE VIZIER
   Then you are, perforce, Ali the good.
ALI (*absently filling a third cup*)
   So I am called.
THE FAVORITE (*who has removed her cloak and veil*)
   Do I smell coffee?
THE WIVES (*busy with their search, do not hear her.*)
ALI (*comes down to her with the third cup.*)
THE FAVORITE (*snatches up her veil with a little
   start, then, lowering it with a smile, takes the
   coffee, which she sips*)
   How nice of you!
ALI (*devouring her with his eyes*)
   I am richly rewarded. O, how unfortunate are
   the blind!
HAROUN (*signals to the Chief Eunuch, who tiptoes
   stealthily toward Ali.*)
THE FAVORITE
   Tell me more.

ALI

Pearl of Dawn!

THE FAVORITE

But this is evening.

ALI

A night of miracles! Oh, that I—

THE FAVORITE

Be careful. We are watched. (*She raises her veil circumspectly.*) Has your shop ever been robbed?)

ALI

No, lady. My besetting vice is covetousness. I wish for what is my neighbor's. I dream of a jewel in a prince's turban.

THE FAVORITE

Such wishes sometimes come true. You should find ways.

THE WIVES (*come down with a piece of white silk.*)

THE FAVORITE

No, I want color. Show me all you have. (*She goes up with them to the other side of the shop.*)

THE NUBIAN (*stands regarding Ali, darkly.*)

ALI (*gazes, rapt, at the cushions where the Favorite rested. He becomes conscious of the Nubian, turns and smiles at him*)

Your master's lady is safe within my shop, good swordsman. (*He rejoins the Caliph and the Vizier.*)

HAROUN (*picking up the goods originally offered to the Favorite*)

This piece of silk. Is it good?

ALI

Gentlemen, no. That silk is of domestic make.

THE ELDEST WIFE (*signals frantically to Ali.*)

ALI (*disregarding her*)
It will turn yellow in a short time and the fabric will split.

VIZIER
Why, then, is it for sale in the shop of Ali the good?

ALI
Because it is cheap. The price is but ten pieces of silver. If you want silks for your turbans, buy *this*. If you do not find it good you may have, for the asking, another fabric or your money again.

THE FAVORITE
I will buy some new veils. And, mind you, do not try to cheat me again. This is the shop of Ali the good.

THE WIVES (*all talking at once*)
We would not think of cheating you.
Our husband knows the stock.
We made a mistake.
It takes an expert to tell the goods apart.
(*Grouped about the Favorite, they remove her outer cloak. One holds a mirror for her, the other a box of veils, which she tries on, frequently allowing her face to be seen by Ali.*)

HAROUN
Ali, you are a righteous man. Yet I have seen that you have compassion for the sinner. Can you not tell us why one man is righteous and another wicked?

ALI (*attempting to give his attention to the question, but letting his eyes stray frequently to the Favorite*)
No two men sin for the same reason. Some sin because they are stupid, which is a sin of itself.

Others sin because they live many years behind, or ahead, of the age in which they are born. Still others sin because all their lives they have cherished a dream, perhaps not a good dream, but the dream of their lives. When the chance comes for the dream to come true they do not stop to consider the consequences to the others, nor even to themselves. Sin has intrigued the philosophers of every age and nation. As for myself, I know that I might sin, and in this wise. Suppose two robbers met upon the street in Bagdad— (*As he talks the lights fade out.*)

The scene changes.

SCENE THREE: *A Street.*

A ROBBER CAPTAIN AND HIS LIEUTENANT (*enter from opposite directions—both carry lanterns.*)

CAPTAIN
Well, how many purses?

LIEUTENANT
None, yet, but I have news. Haroun al Raschid the Good is in the shop of the merchant Ali, also called "the good."

CAPTAIN
"The good"—to be cursed with a title like that! Was the Caliph spending freely there?

LIEUTENANT
He will, no fear. Ali is a shrewd merchant.

CAPTAIN
The more he spends, the more for us to take. But he doesn't spend fast enough. I wish I had force enough to swoop down on his treasury.

LIEUTENANT

It is well guarded.

CAPTAIN

Well guarded—yes, so is he. And well he need be, for banishing wine from Bagdad. My throat's dusty as a carpet in the bazaar. Who are these?

LIEUTENANT

The Caliph, his Vizier, and his Favorite. Hide quickly, the patrol will follow them. (*They hide at the end of the street.*)

THE NUBIAN (*enters and passes along the street, followed by the Favorite, carried in a tiny palanquin, with a lantern in its canopy.*)

THE CALIPH AND HIS VIZIER (*follow a few paces behind, also carrying lanterns.*)

THE VIZIER

You paid him too much for the silk.

HAROUN

I paid, not for the silk, but for the man. Such honesty is priceless. Had I more of it in Bagdad, I might dispense with guards and patrols.

THE VIZIER

Until you get it, though—ah, here they come.

THE PATROL (*enters, standing, ready to follow the Caliph.*)

HAROUN

Do you think he knew me for the Caliph?

THE VIZIER

Of course he did. I have told you a thousand times that your incognito deceives no one but yourself. (*They disappear, followed by the patrol.*)

THE ROBBER CAPTAIN (*comes out, with his Lieutenant, from their hiding-place*)
There goes the robber of wine. . . . Our way is
clear. Call the men. We'll fall upon the Ali
the moment his harem is alseep—be careful not
to wake the women—they're worse than any
dog—a bone will not silence them.

The lights fade out as they leave

SCENE FOUR: *The Shop—The lights are dim.*

ALI (*is discovered, standing beside the curtained
divan, lost in thought, alone.*)

THE WIVES (*from another room*)
Good-night, good-night!

ALI
Good-night! (*He draws the curtain across the
doorway to the street and comes down to the spot
where the Favorite tried on the veils. He finds on
the floor the veil which she wore, which he takes to
the chest in the center of the room, upon which he
sits with the veil at his lips, and is presently lost
in dreams.*)
(*A naked arm appears at the curtain to the street
and pulls it aside a little.*)

THE ROBBER CAPTAIN AND THE LIEUTENANT (*steal
into the room. They have left their cloaks outside
and their knives gleam wickedly in the dim light.
They waken Ali, presenting their knives to his ribs
to prevent outcry.*)

ALI
Mercy!

THE CAPTAIN

Tell us where your treasure is hid and no harm shall come to you.

ALI

In the box I sit on.

THE ROBBERS (*dump him unceremoniously off the chest and open it.*)

THE CAPTAIN (*lifting a bottle*)

By the beard of the Prophet, wine!

ALI

Even so.

THE CAPTAIN

Sly dog! Ali the good! Why, he has twenty varieties of bottled drunkenness!

LIEUTENANT

But how if it be poisoned?

THE CAPTAIN

In these days of forbidden wine, make the giver drink with you. Come, merchant. (*He fills a cup.*)

ALI

As I put by the wine, myself—may we all live to be extremely wicked! (*He drinks.*)

LIEUTENANT

The man is moonstruck!

CAPTAIN (*chuckling*)

Ali the good, extremely wicked? (*He drinks— wine dribbles down his chin.*)

ALI (*mopping it up with a napkin from the chest*)

Don't waste it, good Captain. There isn't much left.

CAPTAIN

Enough for the evening, good merchant. (*Pours himself another drink.*)

ALI

And after that?

CAPTAIN

After that, who cares? (*He drinks.*)

ALI

Could I but catch that thought! (*He drops the Favorite's veil.*)

LIEUTENANT (*snatches it up with a ribald exclamation.*)

ALI

Give it me!

CAPTAIN

I told you he was a sly dog! Ali the good, a harem robber, a beauty snatcher! Ah, old fox!

LIEUTENANT

Let it be, merchant, or I'll give you the knife instead. (*He thrusts at Ali.*)

ALI (*with a wrestler's trick, throws him on the floor. He retrieves the veil as the man sprawls.*)

CAPTAIN

Serves you right. Shouldn't interfere with another man's souvenirs. What's she like, merchant?

ALI

She is the Pearl of Dawn!

CAPTAIN

Marvelously accurate description! Identify her immediately. Where's she live?

ALI

That is my secret.

CAPTAIN

Must find this out. (*He places the point of his knife between Ali's ribs.*)

LIEUTENANT (*does the same on the other side.*)

ALI

It is the will of Allah. I will tell . . . All my
life I have been seeking for naughtiness.

CAPTAIN

Ali the good! (*He laughs boisterously.*)

ALI

That name was not of my own seeking. I own
the largest library of forbidden books in Bagdad.

CAPTAIN

Some day when I am sober——

ALI

If you are ever sober you may look at them. I
assure you they have been a great disappointment. None of them really come up to their
reputations.

CAPTAIN

But the censors——

ALI

The censors wouldn't know real naughtiness if
they met it. And I have wasted my substance
to see all the dancers and nautch girls of Turkey
and Egypt.

THE CAPTAIN (*rubbing his hands*)

Ah, an epicure!

ALI

Very, very stupid and not at all naughty. Dis-
appointments, every one. So I have thought
a great deal about naughtiness, and Allah has
given me the key to the riddle.

THE CAPTAIN

Well?

ALI

Naughtiness is like the kingdom of Heaven.
It lies within you. I have tended the naughti-

ness in my heart like a poppy garden until to-
day—

THE CAPTAIN

To-day you're a bolder fellow than I am, you
were going to say.

LIEUTENANT

Captain, he's tricked you. He's led you away
from the secret.

CAPTAIN (*his knife at Ali's ribs*)

Quickly—where does she live?

ALI

It is the will of Allah. She lives in the palace of
the Caliph.

CAPTAIN

Ah, the sly dog! No wonder he is vain!

ALI

The Pearl of Dawn!

CAPTAIN (*after emptying his cup*)

What would you give to hold the Pearl of
Dawn—to have her, perhaps.

ALI

Anything!

CAPTAIN

Now, perhaps, it might be managed if you—
No, no; it won't do. (*He finishes another cup.*)

ALI

Try me.

CAPTAIN

You are determined? Listen, then. About the
Caliph's house there is one place where the wall
may be reached from a neighboring roof. Once
inside, the harem is but one door away. The
treasury—but that is my affair. You have the

courage to climb that wall upon the shoulders
of my men and let a rope down after you?

ALI

Command me!

CAPTAIN

Come, then!

ALI

A moment only. A letter for my wives, lest they
grieve too loudly for my absence.

CAPTAIN (*looking over Ali's shoulder as he writes*)
"Am held captive by robbers. Give no alarm,
but send two thousand sequins at once to the
old gate of the city." Ah, sly dog! Lead on,
O Prince of Evil! (*The three men go out into the
street after putting out the light.*)

WOMEN'S VOICES (*rise in the next room from a murmur to an argument.*)

THE YOUNGEST WIFE (*coming from behind the curtains in her nightdress, with a lantern*)
But I'm sure I heard voices. (*She goes to the
divan, and, finding it empty, begins to search the
room.*) Husband is not here! The chest is
open! A letter! (*She reads it and screams.*)

THE OTHER WIVES (*run in; they all talk at once*)
Let me see it! How can I when you— But I
don't understand. It can't be true.
But think—robbers in here and gone without
noise. I knew there was something wrong. You
told me to be quiet. What shall we do? Ali says
to give no alarm. But they may murder him.
Two thousand sequins! Let's call the patrol!
Allah be merciful! Help! Robbers! Thieves!

(*Their chatter rises to a shriek, and the Youngest Wife goes tearing out into the street, followed by the others, all screaming.*)

The lights fade out.   The scene changes

SCENE FIVE: *A Street.*
A patrol passes.   The Captain, Ali, the Lieutenant, and sundry robbers enter warily, watching the patrol.

CAPTAIN (*stopping in a peevish, alcoholic reaction*)
I don't like it.   Something will go wrong, I know. Bagdad is alive with patrols.   Tomorrow night—

ALI (*with bravado—also slightly alcoholic*)
Tomorrow—why, tomorrow I may be
Myself with ten thousand yesterdays.

CAPTAIN
Stop quoting that damned Persian!   His verses are full of wine, and they make me thirsty. (*Struck by a happier thought.*)   Let's go back and have another drink!

ALI (*not budging, but pointing ahead*)
Have you forgotten the Caliph's treasury? Haroun al Raschid may feel generous in the morning and give half of it away to somebody. Think of taking, in one night, all the gold your men could carry!

CAPTAIN
Being wicked in large doses, aren't you?

ALI
I have been good for a long, long time.

LIEUTENANT (*starting sharply*)
What's that—

ALI (*laughing*)

Your shadow on the wall. What a bold company I have joined!

CAPTAIN (*roaring*)

Coward! Learn courage from this brave merchant, Ali the good! Let all brave men follow me. (*He struts off.*)

ALI

I follow

(*The party goes out—A patrol passes. From one side comes a murmur which swells in volume to the shrieks of Ali's wives, who now appear in their night robes.*)

THE WIVES (*all at once*)

Help, help, help! Thieves, thieves, Watch ho! Watch ho!
Thieves! Thieves! Watch ho! Watch ho! Help! Help!
Watch ho! Watch ho! Help! Help! Help! Thieves!

THE PATROL (*returns on the run.*)

THE WIVES (*loudly and all at once*)

Ali the merchant has been stolen by robbers while we slept, etc.
Robbers have kidnapped Ali the good for ransom, etc.
My husband is in the hands of robbers! He left this note, etc.

ONE OF THE PATROL (*bawling*)

One at a time—one at a time!

THE WIVES (*all at once, though less stridently*)

While we slept, robbers broke into our house.
They broke into my husband's chest and stole.

292

Not content with that they have taken him for
ransom, forcing him to leave this note here.
What shall we do?
You must help us to find our husband, etc.
How can you stand here and do nothing?
Don't you understand that robbers have entered
our house and stolen and taken away our hus-
band?
If we do not pay the ransom they will kill him;
and we can't pay it because all our money is
stolen, etc.
I shall die if you don't save him. Scour the
streets! Go at once! Spread the alarm! He is
our husband. If he dies our hearts perish also!
Draw your swords!
Read the letter!
Save him from the robbers!

THE PATROL (*puts its hands to its ears.*)

*The lights fade out. The gabble subsides to a
murmur, but does not stop, swelling again as the
lights come up on the next scene.*

SCENE SIX: *The Favorite's Chamber.*

*On the right, a draped bed. Cushions at intervals
on the floor. Several colored lamps hang from the
ceiling. As the lights come up the noise turns out
to be the chatter of three houri seated in the center
of the room.*

THREE HOURI (*all three at once*)
First: I don't see why on earth she paid fifty
sequins for that veil. I wouldn't trade at that
shop anyway. They're cheats. She doesn't use

any judgment at all in her shopping. That's why her clothes never look like anything.

Second: Did you smell the perfumery she bought? When the Caliph smells it, someone else will be the favorite until his nose gets well. I don't know how she gets away with it—a person with no more taste than that. Some women have all the luck.

Third: Then the Persian said to me, "Why are you content to be a maid for the Favorite? You should be favorite yourself. Run away with me and I will make you favorite over forty wives. The idea! I gave him one look and I told him—"

CHIEF EUNUCH (*appearing in the doorway*)
Silence. (*The chatter ceases abruptly.*) The husband comes!

THE HOURI (*prostrate themselves on the floor.*)

HAROUN AL RASCHID (*enters, followed by the Vizier*)
That will do, girls. Get up. Take them away, Captain.

THE HOURI (*go out, salamming, followed by the Chief Eunuch.*)

HAROUN (*sighing as he sits on a cushion*)
They're always underfoot.

VIZIER
Shall I have a hundred of them beheaded?

HAROUN
No, the executioner already complains of overwork.

VIZIER
I might give them away to the Bashaw.

HAROUN
No. No other potentate has my serene patience.

I must endure them. It is the will of Allah!
(*He looks toward the canopy.*)

VIZIER (*claps his hands.*)

HAROUN

She sleeps.

VIZIER (*chuckles audibly*)

HAROUN

You do not trust her.

VIZIER

I trust her to make an effective entrance always.

HAROUN

She sleeps. I will waken her. (*He strikes a bell.*)

VIZIER

Two more.

HAROUN (*strikes the bell again twice. On the third
stroke the curtains of the bed part, disclosing the
Favorite, becomingly costumed and well-lighted by
a lamp within the canopy.*)

THE FAVORITE (*affects to rub her eyes, then, seeing
Haroun, sinks gracefully to the floor and kisses
his slipper.*)

HAROUN (*to the Vizier*)

Well?

VIZIER

Perfect—I knew she would be.

HAROUN

Could you resist her?

VIZIER

In your place, I couldn't. In mine, I have to.

FAVORITE

That's the nicest thing he has said to me.

HAROUN

Doesn't he like you?

FAVORITE
 Ask him.

HAROUN
 Well?

VIZIER
 There is no lady in Turkey more delightful—

FAVORITE (*squeals and claps her hands.*)

VIZIER (*finishing*)
 —To look at.

HAROUN (*fondling the Favorite*)
 That's all you know about it.

THE CHIEF EUNUCH (*enters, prostrates himself before Haroun and hands him a parchment, which Haroun passes to the Vizier, who reads it and rises.*)

HAROUN
 Well?

VIZIER
 Robbers are at work in the city.

HAROUN (*abruptly drops the Favorite sprawling on the cushions, and jumps up*)
 I thought I had rid Bagdad of those vermin! Here is work for us. My chainmail and my sword! (*He rushes out, the other men following.*)

FAVORITE (*much injured, gets up and adjusts her hair*)
 Allah make me faithful to such a husband! (*She shakes her head, then dismisses the matter from her mind and disappears behind the bed curtains. A garment or two is flung out onto the cushion.*)

(*A rope drops from an unseen window in the top of the corridor. Ali comes down the rope, looks into the room and then around the turn. At his signal, the Robber Captain also descends the rope.*)

THE CAPTAIN

You're as good as your word. Well, your treasure is in here. (*Indicating the room.*) I'll let my men in by the door in the passage here. Allah be with you! We all go out by this door. (*He disappears around the corner.*)

ALI (*lifts the veil to his lips. As he lowers it, his eye falls on the garments lying on the cushions. He lifts these also to his lips and holds them there, intoxicated.*)

THE CHIEF EUNUCH (*tiptoes around the corridor, a bloody scimitar in his hands. Seeing Ali, he comes behind him and lifts his weapon.*)

THE FAVORITE (*looks out from the canopy*)

Behind you!

ALI (*turns and so does the Chief Eunuch. Ali pulls the Chief Eunuch's feet from under him.*)

THE FAVORITE (*still comparatively clothed, hands Ali scarves to bind the Chief Eunuch. When he is neatly trussed up, she says*)

I knew you'd come!

ALI

Pearl of Dawn! (*A great tumult is heard in the corridor.*)

THE FAVORITE

They are coming this way. Quickly, in the bed! (*They pick up the Chief Eunuch and hide him under the canopy. The Favorite pushes Ali in after him and sits hastily.*)

HAROUN (*enters, brandishing a sword and driving a robber before him, who is fighting desperately for his life. Haroun finishes him with a thrust, and, kicking him, wipes his sword on his sash.*)

The devils are in the palace. Have they disturbed you?

FAVORITE

I haven't heard a sound.

HAROUN

Guard! Guard!

A GUARD (*runs in, panting*)

HAROUN

Where are the rest?

GUARD

Fighting in the Treasury.

HAROUN

Remove this carrion! (*He storms out.*)

GUARD (*drags the corpse out by its feet.*)

FAVORITE (*looks around the corridor*)
Now!

ALI (*comes out from behind canopy*)
Pearl of Dawn!

THE ROBBER CAPTAIN (*darts in from the corridor and hides in the shadow at one side.*)

THE FAVORITE (*screaming, disappears under the canopy.*)

A GUARD (*dashes into the room.*)

THE CAPTAIN (*springing on him, stabs him in the back and hides again as.*)

TWO GUARDS (*run in. Seeing Ali, they attack him.*)

TWO HOURI (*run in, screaming, and seeing the mêlée run out again.*)

ALI (*has picked up the sword of the robber whom Haroun killed, and defends himself. He kills one guard. The other guard disarms him. He springs under the other guard's sword and they both go down with a crash.*)

THE CAPTAIN (*finishes the guard with his knife, and pulls him off Ali, whom he shakes*)
Come quickly! I left the door open.

ALI (*pulls himself up painfully on one elbow, much the worse for his fall.*)

THE CAPTAIN (*pulls the Favorite from behind the curtains and carries her off, struggling vigorously.*)

ALI (*staggers to his feet, looks under the canopy, and steps over the dead bodies*)
Must find her—must find— (*He disappears in the turn of the corridor.*)

HAROUN (*storms in, followed by the Vizier*)
I thought we had killed all of them, and look here! (*He darts to the bed and parts the curtains. The Chief Eunuch, bound and gagged, is sitting on the edge of the bed. Haroun releases him.*)

HAROUN
Where is she?

THE CHIEF EUNUCH (*points to the corridor.*)

THREE HOURI (*run in screaming and throw themselves at Haroun's feet.*)

HAROUN
Out, out of my way! (*He flings them off. He tears out, followed by the Vizier and the Chief Eunuch.*)

The lights fade out. The scene changes.

SCENE SEVEN: *A Street.*

Enter the Robber Captain, carrying the Favorite, whom he sets unceremoniously on her feet.

THE CAPTAIN
Stand awhile! Oof! What does Haroun feed his women to make them so heavy?

THE FAVORITE
Nobody asked you to carry me.

THE CAPTAIN
Oh, ho! You would have walked it, eh?

THE FAVORITE
With the right man.

THE CAPTAIN
I'm the right man. Ali thinks he is, but I brought you off and *I* keep you. What do you say to that?

THE FAVORITE
If Ali lets you keep me, then you are the right man.

THE CAPTAIN
What a mind you have! I like you better all the time.

THE FAVORITE
See, here comes Ali.

ALI (*enters hurriedly*)
The chase is close behind. We must hurry.

THE CAPTAIN
We must? Go on, no one will hinder vou!

ALI
Do you mean—then you don't—

THE CAPTAIN
You led me into a trap. My men are dead.

THE FAVORITE
He led you?

THE CAPTAIN
To find you. The treasury was full of armed men.

ALI
I could not know that. Do you forget that I, too, have fought—I, too, have stolen?

THE CAPTAIN
Stolen what?

ALI
The Pearl of Dawn.

THE CAPTAIN
Ha! It was my arms that carried her. I shall keep her myself. You—what does she want with you, a merchant—a dreamer? I am a man of action! She will come with me and of her own accord.

ALI (*to the Favorite*)
Speak!

THE FAVORITE
I go with him who takes me.

ALI (*stabs the Captain without warning and, straddling his body, lifts the Favorite in his arms*)
Pearl of Dawn!

THE FAVORITE
I knew you would! (*The pursuit sounds close at hand.*)

ALI (*hurries off with the Favorite.*)

HAROUN AL RASCHID (*enters, running with drawn sword, and with his retinue strung out behind him. He comes upon the captain's body*)
Lights! Lights here!

THE VIZIER (*holding a lantern to the Captain's face*)
It is the captain of the robbers. Now all of them are dead.

HAROUN
What have they done with her? Where is she?

THE VIZIER
She has possibly hidden from them. Did you search the palace?

HAROUN
  I tell you, she is stolen from me!

THE VIZIER
  This man's alive yet. He's trying to speak.

HAROUN (*leans close to listen.*)

THE CAPTAIN
  Find—Ali—(*summoning his strength for a final sneer*) the *good*! (*He dies.*)

HAROUN
  Ha!

  He goes tearing off, followed by his retinue, as the lights fade out.

SCENE EIGHT: *The Shop.*

ALI (*enters, badly out of breath, carrying the Favorite, whom he puts down as soon as they are inside.*)

THE FAVORITE (*not altogether pleased*)
  Is this where you were taking me?

ALI
  I know of no other place to go. I have thought of—this sort of thing—before, but I never got this far with it. (*His hand on his stomach.*) All this murder has upset me a little.

THE FAVORITE
  I thought you were a man! Now, what are we to do?

ALI (*sitting down on the chest, one hand on his stomach, ready to weep*)
  I'm sure I don't know.

THE FAVORITE
  Listen! (*The pursuit is heard in the street outside.*) The guards! They're coming here! Save me!

ALI (*rising uncertainly and pointing to the divan*)
Hide over there! (*He staggers up to the doorway, taking a sword from the chest.*)

HAROUN AL RASCHID (*dashes through the door, his sword whirling before him in vicious circles.*)

ALI (*defending himself as best he can, backs down into the middle of the room.*)

THE VIZIER (*following closely, strikes Ali's sword from his hand.*)

ALI (*recognizing his antagonist*)
Mercy on a poor merchant, O Haroun al Raschid the Good!

HAROUN
Where is she?

ALI
There, quite safe, and very angry.

THE FAVORITE (*is very angry, indeed, and beats the pillows with her fists.*)

HAROUN (*steps down to look at her.*)

THE NUBIAN (*elevates his sword over the prostrate merchant.*)

THE VIZIER
Stop! Let the Caliph give the word for his death!

ALI (*weeping*)
Sir, that was most unkind. I had already resigned myself to dying, and now I will have it to do all over again.

HAROUN
Take him to the street. Let him first be whipped with five hundred lashes. Then let one hundred lashes be laid upon the soles of his feet. After that, slit his tongue, cut off his hands and feet. After that, drag him through the

20

streets at the tail of a wild horse. When he dies, cut his body in twelve pieces and feed it to the lions.

THE VIZIER
Is that all?

HAROUN
No. Do all this in the streets of Bagdad at dawn, and do not begin until I give the word.

ALI
It is the will of Allah! (*He marches out, followed closely by the Vizier, the Nubian, and the guards.*)

HAROUN (*turning on the Favorite*)
You!

THE FAVORITE (*yawning*)
Why be angry with me? I've lost a whole night's sleep on account of the filthy robbers. Your house should be better guarded!

HAROUN (*partly mollified, but still suspicious*)
You and this dog of a merchant!

THE FAVORITE
He *is* a disappointment, isn't he? See, it is almost day. Let us go and see him whipped. (*As she speaks, she takes him by the hand and goes out talking to him.*)

The lights fade out. The scene changes.

SCENE NINE: *A Street.*

ALI (*lies on the ground, with his hands bound behind him. The Vizier stands watching him. The Nubian stands ready with a whip.*)

THE VIZIER
Are you sorry, merchant?

ALI

I shall be able to answer that truthfully only after I am dead.

THE VIZIER

That would be unusual.

ALI

Any truthful answer to that question would be unusual, sir. When men are sorry they pretend a defiance they do not feel and deny it. When they are not sorry they pretend repentance in the hope of getting off easier.

THE VIZIER

Can I do anything for you, merchant?

ALI

Yes. Persuade Haroun al Raschid, if you can, to leave out that part of my punishment in which the wild horse was mentioned. I shall be as dead by that time as I am ever going to be, and there is no need to annoy the poor horse with my domestic shortcomings.

HAROUN (*enters with the Favorite, who has reached the climax of a long and thrilling tale.*)

THE FAVORITE

Then the robber captain carried me off, fighting and struggling every step of the way. He must have carried me a thousand cubits. Then we heard steps behind us. The robber captain put me down and turned. Ali the merchant came running up with drawn sword. "Dog!" he shouted in a voice of thunder, "you have stolen the favorite of Haroun al Raschid the Good. Release her or perish." Then they fought and the merchant killed the robber captain. Then, as he fell, we heard others running up the street.

The merchant did not know whether they were friends or enemies, so he carried me to his shop, which was the nearest place of safety.

HAROUN (*looking at Ali doubtfully*)
But why did he fight me?

THE FAVORITE
You came in with a rush, and he did not know whether you were friend or foe.

HAROUN
Merchant, why didn't you tell me this?

ALI
How could I expect Haroun al Raschid the Good to believe anything so improbable?

HAROUN
I don't see yet, though. (*To the Vizier.*) Do you believe it?

THE VIZIER
I?

HAROUN
Why do I ask you? You never believe anything! Merchant, what shall I believe?

ALI
Believe what you would like to. That is the true secret of happiness.

HAROUN
Just one question—How came you with the robbers?

ALI'S WIVES (*come tearing in, all talking at once, at the top of their voices. One of them holds the letter.*)

THE VIZIER (*shouting*)
Silence!

HAROUN (*reading the letter*)
Held for ransom! Merchant, I have done you a great injustice. Come to my house this after-

noon, when I have had time for sleep, and you shall be richly rewarded. Unbind him. (*The Vizier liberates Ali.*)

THE ELDEST WIFE
Then he is not to be whipped?

HAROUN
By no means. Go to your home. It is not seemly for the wives of Ali the good to go out on the streets unveiled and unclad.

THE WIVES (*salaam and run out, very conscious of their attire.*)

THE FAVORITE (*steps into her palanquin and is carried off, followed by all of the retinue but the Vizier, who stands back, watching Ali.*)

HAROUN (*walking beside the palanquin*)
Try to get some sleep, merchant.

ALI (*salaams, then rises quickly to watch the Favorite.*)

THE VIZIER
I perceive that you are a man of some imagination.

ALI
That has always been my undoing. It is forever leading me into trouble.

THE VIZIER
And what led you out of it this time?

ALI
I don't know—it sounds like a riddle.

THE VIZIER
It is a riddle, merchant. I leave it you to think upon. The answer is: Your imagination led you into trouble—and your innocence led you out. (*He leaves.*)

ALI (*looking after him*)
Innocence?

A MUEZZIN (*shrieks his call to the faithful from a nearby tower.*)

ALI (*assumes the posture of a Mussulman at prayer*)
Allah il Allah! Allah il Allah! Make me bad! Make me bad!

The lights fade out. The scene changes.

SCENE TEN: *The Shop.*

Exactly as at the close of Scene Two, except that the Nubian has fallen asleep. Ali's voice is heard before the lights come up.

ALI (*concluding his tale*)
Allah il Allah! Make me bad! And thus I might pray until the last muezzin had called the faithful from his tower and further sin might follow unless—

THE NUBIAN (*snoring*)
Z—z—z—z!!

THE VIZIER
He has no interest in sin.

HAROUN
Poor fellow, it is past his bedtime. (*He rises and throws a purse to Ali.*) Bring that piece of silk tomorrow afternoon to my house. And think of other sins you might commit, were you not Ali the good.

ALI (*rising and looking at the Favorite*)
The thought shall not leave my mind.

THE VIZIER (*giving Ali a purse*)
And do not forget to bring something from your library.

ALI
Gentlemen, your pardon. I must ask the way to your house.

HAROUN (*delighted*)
  What, you do not recognize me? (*To the Vizier.*)
  I told you; I told you. (*To Ali with a flourish.*)
  I am the Caliph Haroun al Raschid.
ALI AND HIS WIVES (*salaaming*)
  Haroun al Raschid the Good!
HAROUN (*in the doorway*)
  The blessings of Allah on this household. (*The
  party goes out.*)
THE FAVORITE (*last to leave*)
  And bring, yourself, the veils I have selected.
  (*Gives Ali a purse.*)
ALI (*salaaming*)
  Pearl of Dawn!
THE FAVORITE (*rouses the Nubian with a kick, and
  leaves.*)
ALI (*rises, jingling the purses*)
  A fine night's business!   And more tomorrow!
  He! He! He thought we didn't know him!
THE ELDEST WIFE (*grimly*)
  Whom were you thinking of while you told that
  story?
THE YOUNGEST WIFE
  Just what I want to know!
ALI (*slipping his arms about them and displaying
  the purses*)
  Of new clothes for both of you, my loves. It is
  written that the want of money is the root of all
  evil.

CURTAIN

FINDERS-KEEPERS

A PLAY IN ONE ACT

by GEORGE KELLY

FINDERS-KEEPERS was presented at the Palace Theatre, New York City, on Monday, October 23, 1916, with the following cast:

EUGENE ALDRID	MR. GEORGE KELLY
MRS. ALDRID, *his wife*	MISS ANNE CLEVELAND
MRS. HAMPTON, *a neighbor*	MISS NORA O'CONNOR

The action of the play takes place in the living-room of Eugene Aldrid's home, which is located in an outlying suburb of the City of Philadelphia, Pennsylvania. The time is about five o'clock of a late-September afternoon. All curtains are of quiet cretonne, and there are sheaves of autumn-leaves about. The garden, through the window at the back, is bright with scarlet sage.

NOTE.—The form of the present manuscript is exactly that in which this play was presented continuously for a period of three years in the principal Keith and Orpheum Theatres of The United States of America and The Dominion of Canada.—AUTHOR.

FINDERS-KEEPERS

SCENE

SCENE

After a second's stillness, a door closes out at the right, and immediately Mrs. Aldrid enters through the archway, carrying several parcels, which she hastens to deposit on the center-table; then she straightens up and draws a deep breath. She is a trim blonde, in her late twenties, wearing a tailored coat-suit of fawn-colored serge, a toque of champagne silk, and a waist of very pale pink silk. Her slippers and stockings are of the lighter shades of brown, and she wears a quite long string of freakish black-and-yellow beads. Before she has had time to take the second breath, the bronze clock on the mantelpiece, at the left, strikes five. She glances at it.

MRS. ALDRID

Heavens! five o'clock! (*She hurriedly removes her coat and hat, lays them on the sofa in front of the mantelpiece, and, with a glance at herself in the mirror over the mantelpiece, vanishes through the door at the left. Then there is a slight pause; and Eugene Aldrid enters through the archway from the right, carrying a roll of blue-prints in one hand, and the evening paper in the other. He is a tall and thin, very intelligent-looking man of perhaps thirty-three, wearing a dark-blue, double-breasted business suit, dark shoes, and a dark tie. He sets the roll of blue-prints down on the center-table, and*

313

*then Mrs. Aldrid speaks to him from the room out
at the left)* Is that you, Gene?

ALDRID (*looking toward the left, and then starting
over towards his desk at the right*)
Yes.

MRS. ALDRID
You must have been right behind me.

ALDRID (*laying the newspaper on his desk.*)
Did you just get in?

MRS. ALDRID (*coming into the room from the left,
adjusting a bungalow apron*)
This minute,—I've been in town shopping; I
had no idea it was so late.

ALDRID (*picking up a telegram from his desk, and
opening it*)
It's after five.

MRS. ALDRID
I know it is; and there isn't a thing ready; you'll
have to wait a while for your dinner.

ALDRID (*with an exaggerated sigh of resignation*)
Ah—ho! (*Reads the telegram.*)

MRS. ALDRID
Did you come out on the four-fifty-three?

ALDRID (*without looking up*)
Yes; you weren't on it, were you?

MRS. ALDRID
No, I'd intended coming out on the train, but—
something happened that made me change my
mind.

ALDRID (*looking straight ahead, thinking; and tapping the telegram, which he has finished reading,
against his hand*)
Spaulding. (*Turning suddenly to Mrs. Aldrid.*)
What? Why—what happened?

MRS. ALDRID (*assuming an air of great confidence*)
Wait till I tell you! (*She steps to the back of the room and looks keenly out into the hallway, to assure herself that no one is within hearing—then comes down to the left of her husband, who watches her curiously.*) You know, I went into town this afternoon to get some Georgette Crepe for that new blouse of mine.

ALDRID
Yes.

MRS. ALDRID
Well,—as I went into the Market Street entrance of Blum's—you know, there's a glove-counter right inside the Market Street door. (*Aldrid nods.*) Well, I went over to ask the saleslady where I could get the Crepe; and, as I leaned over to ask her, I stepped on something: it felt like a bracelet or something—rather soft—and yet it was metallic.

ALDRID
Yes.

MRS. ALDRID
Well, I didn't pay any attention to it at first,—I thought it might be a joke or something,—you know, they're always doing that sort of thing in those Department Stores.

ALDRID
Yes, I know.

MRS. ALDRID
But, as I started away from the counter, I just glanced down at the floor; and, what do you suppose it was?

ALDRID
What?

MRS. ALDRID

A purse—one of those little gold, mesh purses.

ALDRID

Anything in it?

MRS. ALDRID

Well, now, wait till I tell you. I didn't open it right away; I was afraid someone might be looking; so I waited till I got up to the writing-room before I opened it: and, what do you suppose was in it?

ALDRID

What?

MRS. ALDRID

Four—hundred—dollars.

ALDRID (*after a slight pause*)

Four hundred dollars?

MRS. ALDRID

Hum—hum.

ALDRID (*incredulously*)

Where is it?

MRS. ALDRID

In my pocketbook.

ALDRID

Well, are you sure it's real money?

MRS. ALDRID

Of course it is; I'll show it to you in a minute. You know, I could scarcely believe my eyes at first; because, you know, I've never found anything in all my life; and then to suddenly pick up *eight* fifty-dollar bills. Positively, Gene, I don't know how I ever got home.

ALDRID

Were they all fifties?

MRS. ALDRID

Hum-hum; and brand-new ones at that; they look as though they'd just been taken out of a bank.

ALDRID (*turning suddenly and leaning on the chair in front of his desk, then looking at her*)

Can you imagine *losing* that!

MRS. ALDRID

Losing it? Can you imagine finding it? I thought I was seeing things. (*She starts towards the door at the left.*)

ALDRID

Did you say anything about it?

MRS. ALDRID (*stopping, and turning to him*)

How do you mean?

ALDRID

At the "Lost and Found"?

MRS. ALDRID

No, of course I didn't; what do you think I am.

ALDRID

You might have gotten in touch with the owner.

MRS. ALDRID (*smiling indulgently*)

Positively, Gene, you talk like a boy from the country.

ALDRID

Why so?

MRS. ALDRID (*with a touch of impatience, and coming to the left of the center-table*)

Because you do! Don't you know that if I were to turn that amount of money into a "Lost and Found" desk, I'd stand just about as much chance of ever seeing it again as I would of seeing the North Pole?

ALDRID
Well, you wouldn't expect ever to see it again
if it were returned to the owner?

MRS. ALDRID
And, how would I know that it *had* been returned to the owner?

ALDRID
Oh, everybody isn't dishonest! (*Glances through
the telegram again.*)

MRS. ALDRID
Well, you let people get their hands on four
hundred dollars—you'll find out how many of
them are honest! Turn that amount of money
over to one of those "Lost and Found" clerks—
he'd soon find an owner for it, believe me! (*She
starts for the door at the left.*)

ALDRID (*crushing the telegram in his hand*)
What are *you* going to do with it? (*She stops
at the door and looks back at him. He gracefully
tosses the telegram overhand into the waste-paper
basket below his desk.*)

MRS. ALDRID
I'm going to keep it!

ALDRID
Ho!

MRS. ALDRID (*surprised that he should ask such a
question*)
What do you suppose I'm going to do with it—
throw it away? It's as good in my pocket as it
is in anybody's else! (*He turns and looks at her
in a way that disconcerts her slightly, but, as he
withdraws his eyes in turning to his desk, she regains herself, and comes a step or two farther into*

the room.)   I can get awnings for this whole house for that—and a Victrola, too!

ALDRID (*coming over to the center-table for his blue-prints, after looking for them on his desk*)
You'd better not count your chickens before they're hatched.

MRS. ALDRID (*after looking at him for a second*)
What do you mean?

ALDRID (*picking up the roll of blue-prints from the table, and speaking rather abstractedly*)
Why, there'll very likely be an ad for it in one of the morning papers.

MRS. ALDRID
Well, what if there is?

ALDRID (*looking at the blue-prints*)
Nothing, only you'd simply have to return it, that's all.

MRS. ALDRID (*after thinking for a second, and with an expression of sullen calculation*)
I don't see why I should.   (*He raises his eyes from the blue-prints and looks at her quizzically.*)

ALDRID
You don't see why you should return lost property to the person who lost it?

MRS. ALDRID
That depends.

ALDRID (*in a level tone*)
Upon what?

MRS. ALDRID (*looking straight ahead*)
Whether or not I was sure he'd lost it.

ALDRID
Couldn't you make sure?

MRS. ALDRID (*after turning and looking at him*)
How?

ALDRID
Identification.

MRS. ALDRID
Not in this case.

ALDRID
Why not?

MRS. ALDRID
Because there isn't a solitary thing about it,
Gene, by which it could possibly be identified:
not a card or a paper of any kind!

ALDRID
How about the purse?

MRS. ALDRID
There are a million exactly like it; a plain, gold,
mesh bag. (*Indicating the desk at the right.*)
I've had one in that top drawer there for the
past year.

ALDRID
Couldn't the money be described?

MRS. ALDRID
That wouldn't be any identification.

ALDRID
Why not?

MRS. ALDRID
Why, because—money is simply money!—unless it's marked; and this isn't, because I've ex-
amined it very carefully.

ALDRID (*resting one end of the roll of blue-prints on
the table, and leaning his elbow on the other end*)
So you don't see any possible way by which
this money could be returned to its owner?

MRS. ALDRID
Not unless I took his word for it; (*turning and*

looking at him) and, really, I don't see why I should do that.

ALDRID (*evenly*)

What are you trying to do, make yourself believe it belongs to you?

MRS. ALDRID (*turning her head away*)

I found it.

ALDRID

And somebody else lost it.

MRS. ALDRID

I suppose so.

ALDRID

Possibly some poor man or woman.

MRS. ALDRID (*with a little toss of her head*)

Now, don't get sentimental, please!

ALDRID (*with a touch of impatience, and taking a couple of steps in front of the table towards her*)

That isn't sentiment at all!

MRS. ALDRID (*turning to him sharply, and speaking incisively*)

No very poor man or woman has any eight fifty-dollar bills to lose. (*She turns away, and secures a hairpin at the back of her head: he looks at her steadily.*) And no matter who lost it, it'll be a very good lesson to him to be a little more careful in the future.

ALDRID

I see. Well, why should he pay *you* four hundred dollars for that lesson?

MRS. ALDRID

Nobody's paying me any four hundred dollars.

ALDRID

You've often lost things yourself, haven't you?

MRS. ALDRID (*turning to him quickly*)
Yes, and I never got them back, either!

ALDRID
Whose fault was that?

MRS. ALDRID (*turning away again*)
I don't know whose fault it was.

ALDRID
Well, try and think.

MRS. ALDRID
Unless the people who found them weren't honest enough to return them. (*The door out at the right closes.*) Who's that? (*She starts for the archway at the right, tossing her apron onto the sofa as she goes.*)

ALDRID (*turning and crossing to his desk*)
Somebody at the door.

MRS. ALDRID (*in a lowered tone*)
Don't say anything about this. (*She reaches the archway.*) Oh, it's you, Mrs. Hampton! (*Aldrid half glances towards the archway, then picks up the evening paper and flips it open.*)

MRS. HAMPTON (*in the hallway*)
Yes, it's me.

MRS. ALDRID (*rather effusively*)
Come right in! (*She extends her arm and hand, and leads Mrs. Hampton into the room. Mrs. Hampton is a dark woman, with a pale but lovely face, and a certain Madonna quality about her generally. She is of the same build as Mrs. Aldrid, and, apparently, of the same age. She wears a coat-suit of good black, a white-silk waist, with a little string of purple beads at her throat, and a medium-sized hat of very dark, purple-colored*)

straw, trimmed with an ornament of itself. Her
slippers and stockings are black.)

MRS. HAMPTON
Good-evening.

MRS. ALDRID
Good-evening, dear, how are you?

ALDRID
Good-evening, Mrs. Hampton.

MRS. HAMPTON
Oh, good-evening, Mr. Aldrid, I didn't see you.
I hope you'll both excuse me for coming in with-
out ringing.

ALDRID (*tossing his paper onto the desk*)
Don't mention it.

MRS. ALDRID (*standing back of the center-table*)
Saved me the trouble of answering the door;
it's the girl's day out.

MRS. HAMPTON
Well, I *do* hope I haven't intruded.

MRS. ALDRID
You haven't at all, dear, really; I've just gotten
in from town.

MRS. HAMPTON
I've been in the city, too; I came out on the
four-fifty-three.

ALDRID (*placing a chair, which he has taken from
above his desk, about mid-way between the center-
table and the archway*)
Won't you take a chair, Mrs. Hampton?

MRS. HAMPTON
No, thank you, Mr. Aldrid, I can't stay a moment.

ALDRID

I'm sorry. (*He moves down to his desk again and picks up the paper.*)

MRS. ALDRID

Why not?

MRS. HAMPTON (*obviously troubled about something*)

Oh, I'm too upset.

MRS. ALDRID

Are you ill, dear?

MRS. HAMPTON

No,—but—I'd like to ask your advice about something.

MRS. ALDRID

Well, do sit down for a minute. (*Mrs. Hampton hesitates, then sits. Mrs. Aldrid takes a chair from the back, and, placing it above the center-table and slightly to the left of it, sits also. Aldrid stands at the lower corner of his desk, reading the paper. There is a slight pause.*) What is it?

MRS. HAMPTON (*speaking directly to Mrs. Aldrid*)

I've lost some money. (*Aldrid lifts his eyes over the top of his paper and looks straight out; Mrs. Aldrid looks straight into Mrs. Hampton's eyes for a second, then rises quietly, still holding her eyes, and moves to the center-table.*)

MRS. ALDRID

Much?

MRS. HAMPTON

Quite a bit, yes.

ALDRID (*without turning*)

Where did you lose it, Mrs. Hampton?

MRS. HAMPTON (*turning to him*)

I haven't an idea; (*Mrs. Aldrid has been looking intently at her, but, at this, she shifts her eyes to*

Aldrid, with a shade of relief.) but I think it was in town. (*Aldrid turns and glances at his wife, but she shifts her eyes back again to Mrs. Hampton.*)

ALDRID

How much was it?

MRS. HAMPTON

Why,—

MRS. ALDRID (*quickly*)

I suppose you don't know the exact amount, do you, dear?

MRS. HAMPTON (*turning to her*)

Four hundred dollars. (*Aldrid looks at his wife, but she's looking blankly at Mrs. Hampton.*) Isn't that dreadful! Of course, I know it would only be an item to some people,—but, to me! I feel terrible about it! (*She breaks down and cries. Aldrid turns and looks at her; then, tossing his paper onto the desk, and thrusting his hands into his trousers-pockets, he turns and strolls towards the back of the room, looking significantly at his wife.*)

MRS. ALDRID (*advancing and placing her hands on Mrs. Hampton's arms*)

Now, don't cry, Mrs. Hampton, it isn't that bad.

MRS. HAMPTON

Oh, I think it's *dreadful* to lose all that money!

MRS. ALDRID

I know it is, dear; I don't wonder you feel bad.

MRS. HAMPTON

Eight fifty-dollar bills! (*Mrs. Aldrid is frozen into stillness. Aldrid steps forward eagerly from the archway, where he has been standing.*)

ALDRID
  Eight fifties?
MRS. HAMPTON
  Yes.
ALDRID (*straightening up, and looking at his wife with an ingenuous smile*)
  Eight fifties.
MRS. HAMPTON
  And brand-new ones, too! It's awful! (*She begins crying again.*)
ALDRID (*to his wife, voicelessly, and indicating Mrs. Hampton with a nod*)
  Why don't you tell her? (*Mrs. Aldrid lifts her chin and looks at him icily; whereupon he indicates Mrs. Hampton again, with an austere point of his finger.*)
MRS. ALDRID (*choosing the better part of valor, and leaning over the back of Mrs. Hampton's chair*)
  Come now, Mrs. Hampton, you may not have lost it at all! (*Aldrid, who has been watching his wife narrowly, breaks slowly, and goes to his desk, where he espies a large scribbled note fastened to the desk-light, to attract his attention. Detaching this, he sits on the lower corner of his desk and reads it.*)
MRS. HAMPTON (*tearfully*)
  Oh, but I *have*, Mrs. Aldrid!
MRS. ALDRID
  I know, my dear, but, you know, sometimes we think we've lost a thing, and we find out later that we haven't lost it at all.
MRS. HAMPTON
  But, I've looked everywhere, and it's lost, I tell you!

MRS. ALDRID

But, you may find it again, honey.

MRS. HAMPTON

Oh, I don't think so!

MRS. ALDRID

Or someone else may find it.

MRS. HAMPTON

But, that wouldn't do me any good.

MRS. ALDRID

It would if the person who found it were honest.

MRS. HAMPTON

I'm afraid very few people are honest, if it cost them four hundred dollars. (*Aldrid finishes reading the note, and sits looking out, thinking.*)

MRS. ALDRID

Well, now, it may be one of those very few who has found it.

MRS. HAMPTON

I don't expect ever to get it again.

ALDRID

Nonsense, Mrs. Hampton!

MRS. HAMPTON

I don't.

ALDRID

Nonsense! Now, you wait and see. (*There is a pause: Mrs. Hampton touches her handkerchief to her eyes.*)

MRS. ALDRID (*looking away off*)

Of course, you'll have to advertise. (*There is a second before Aldrid grasps what she has said; then he turns his head sharply and looks at her; but she is still looking away off.*)

MRS. HAMPTON

Yes, that's what I wanted to see Mr. Aldrid

about; (*She turns to him.*) which would be the best paper for me to advertise in. (*He sits looking at his wife until she turns and meets his eyes: then he abstractedly extends his arm and hand in a gesture of interrogation, to which she responds by a sudden and taut pressing of her closed hand against her breast. He rises, to divert the attention of Mrs. Hampton, and, after leaning for a second upon the back of his desk-chair, starts slowly across the room in front of the center-table. As he passes Mrs. Hampton, she rises also.*) Now, don't let me worry you, Mr. Aldrid!

ALDRID (*abstractedly*)

No, no, it isn't that—I was just—wondering—

MRS. HAMPTON (*turning to Mrs. Aldrid*)

If I'd thought it would bother you folks, I shouldn't have told you at all.

MRS. ALDRID

That's perfectly all right, dear.

MRS. HAMPTON

But I was so troubled when I got home, I simply *couldn't* stay in the house! I just *had* to come out and tell someone! And, my dear, I don't know how I'm *ever* going to tell Frank when he comes home tonight; because he said to me this morning, when I told him I was going to town— he said, "Can I *trust* you to deposit this money for me?" And I said, "What do you think I am, a thief?" "Well," he said, "you're always *losing* things!" "Well," I said, "there's no danger of my losing four hundred dollars." "Well," he said, "I hope not, or we'll get a guardian for you!" (*Starting to cry again.*) And then I go straight into the city and lose it!

(*She cries a little, Mrs. Aldrid stands watching her; and Aldrid, who is leaning on his elbow on the mantelpiece, over at the left, watches Mrs. Aldrid.*) And, mind you, to make *sure* that nothing would happen to it, I didn't even put it with my other money!

MRS. ALDRID (*eagerly, but without moving*)
Where *did* you put it?

MRS. HAMPTON
In one of those little, gold, mesh purses. (*Aldrid accidentally tears the note-paper which he still has in his hand.*)

ALDRID
Mrs. Hampton!

MRS. HAMPTON
Yes?

ALDRID
Where did you first *miss* this money?

MRS. HAMPTON
When I was going up the steps into the bank.

ALDRID
Which bank?

MRS. HAMPTON
The Franklin National.

MRS. ALDRID
Where's that?

ALDRID
Broad and Chestnut. Where had you been before that?

MRS. HAMPTON
Why, when I came out of the station,—after I got off the train,—

ALDRID
Yes?

MRS. HAMPTON
  I went over to Wanamaker's—to get some gloves. (*Aldrid looks at her keenly.*)

MRS. ALDRID
  Wanamaker's?

MRS. HAMPTON (*turning to her*)
  Yes. (*Mrs. Aldrid gives a significant look at Aldrid, but he is looking at Mrs. Hampton.*) But they didn't have my size in what I wanted at Wanamaker's, so I crossed over to Blum's.

ALDRID (*quietly*)
  Blum's glove-counter?

MRS. HAMPTON
  Yes. (*Aldrid glances at his wife, but she is coughing into her handkerchief. He moves rather thoughtfully to the left of the center-table, and, picking up a book, stands it on its end on the table and leans upon it. Mrs. Hampton is standing on the opposite side of the table, and Mrs. Aldrid has moved quietly down to a point in front of Aldrid's desk.*)

ALDRID
  You hadn't missed this money up to that time?

MRS. HAMPTON
  No, and I'm quite sure I *had* it up to that time; because I hadn't opened my pocketbook from the time I left the house; and the money was *in* the big pocketbook.

ALDRID
  I see; and you went directly from there to the bank?

MRS. HAMPTON
  Yes, directly.

ALDRID

Then you think it was somewhere between Blum's glove-counter and the bank steps that you lost it?

MRS. HAMPTON

It must have been: I imagine I must have pulled it out without knowing it, when I was paying for the gloves at Blum's.

ALDRID

Very likely.

MRS. HAMPTON

Or else, possibly, someone opened my pocket-book and took out the little purse (*turning to Mrs. Aldrid*) when I wasn't looking. (*She begins to cry again, as she turns back to Mr. Aldrid.*) You know they do that, Mr. Aldrid.

ALDRID (*abstractedly*)

Yes, I know they do.

MRS. ALDRID (*standing at the right, quietly toying with her beads, and looking straight ahead, with a calculating expression*)

There wasn't a card or a paper of any kind in the purse, was there?

MRS. HAMPTON (*turning to her*)

No, there wasn't a thing in it but the money.

MRS. ALDRID

That's too bad: (*Aldrid watches her narrowly.*) no initials on it?

MRS. HAMPTON

No, I've always been going to have my initials put on it, but,—Oh, I don't know,—I never seemed to get round to it.

MRS. ALDRID

That makes it bad.

MRS. HAMPTON (*with the threat of a few more tears*)
Dear me, I wish I had, now.

MRS. ALDRID (*turning to her suddenly, with a kind of forced sincerity*)
Yes, because if someone find it, and answer your advertisement, he'll naturally expect you to be able to identify it—definitely; that is, before you could reasonably expect him to return it to you, I mean.

MRS. HAMPTON
Yes, I suppose he would; but, then, I could describe the purse and the money.

MRS. ALDRID (*with a tolerant smile*)
I know, my dear; but there may be a million purses exactly like it—

MRS. HAMPTON
That's true, too.

MRS. ALDRID
And, as far as the money is concerned, why,—money is simply money; unless it's marked; and this isn't, (*checking herself*) as you say.

MRS. HAMPTON
No, it isn't.

MRS. ALDRID
So that, really, a person would be more or less obliged to take your word for it, wouldn't he?

MRS. HAMPTON
I'm afraid he would.

MRS. ALDRID
And that's rather a lot for us to expect of people, isn't it, dear?

MRS. HAMPTON
Too much, I'm afraid.

MRS. ALDRID

Especially, when there's four hundred dollars in the bargain. (*She gives a little mirthless, self-conscious laugh, and settles the lace on Mrs. Hampton's lapelle. Aldrid, who has been watching her steadily, turns his head away slowly, and his eyes wander about the floor.*)

MRS. HAMPTON (*turning to the chair from which she arose*)

You're right, it is rather a poor prospect. (*Sits down.*)

MRS. ALDRID

Oh, well—

MRS. HAMPTON

Unless someone who is really honest find it.

MRS. ALDRID (*looking curiously at one of the beads in her necklace*)

Of course, the only thing you *can* do is to advertise.

MRS. HAMPTON (*rising*)

Yes, I must, right away. (*Moving to the right of the center-table.*) Which paper do you think it would be best for me to advertise in, Mr. Aldrid? (*He doesn't hear her.*) Mr. Aldrid?

ALDRID (*turning to her suddenly*)

I beg your pardon, Mrs. Hampton, what did—

MRS. ALDRID

She wants to know which paper you think it would be best for her to advertise in?

ALDRID (*directly to his wife*)

None of them— (*To Mrs. Hampton, with a change of tone*) until she hear from me.

MRS. ALDRID (*quickly, and laying her hands on Mrs. Hampton's shoulder and arm*)

He means, he'll look up the circulations later. (*Aldrid looks at her for a rather long pause, but she avoids his eyes; then, as Mrs. Hampton turns and looks at him, he speaks.*)

ALDRID

I'll telephone you after dinner, Mrs. Hampton. (*He starts towards the back of the room.*)

MRS. HAMPTON

Well, that's very charming of you, Mr. Aldrid.

ALDRID

Don't mention it. (*He passes out through the window into the garden; then stops abruptly, makes a taut, general movement of desperate irresolution, turns, and steps back in through the window again; where, gripping the draperies in his hands, he stands watching his wife with an expression of stony suspicion.*)

MRS. HAMPTON (*to Mrs. Aldrid*)

And I really feel that I owe you both a genuine apology for bothering you with my troubles. (*Starting for the archway at the right.*)

MRS. ALDRID (*turning, and following her*)

That's what neighbors are for, dear.

MRS. HAMPTON

Good-bye, Mr. Aldrid.

ALDRID (*coming a step or two out of the window-alcove*)

Good-bye, Mrs. Hampton.

MRS. HAMPTON

I'll be waiting to hear from you.

ALDRID

Right away, I'll call you.

MRS. HAMPTON (*turning at the archway*)
  And, be sure and ask for *me*, when you telephone,
  won't you?

ALDRID
  Yes, I shall.

MRS. HAMPTON
  Thank you very much.

ALDRID
  You're very welcome.

MRS. HAMPTON (*going out into the hallway at the
  right, followed by Mrs. Aldrid, who has been standing at the back of the room, just to the left of the
  archway.*
  I don't want Frank to know anything about this,
  if possible.

MRS. ALDRID
  No, there's no need of annoying him.

MRS. HAMPTON
  I suppose he'll have to be told soon enough.
  (*Aldrid, standing at the back of the room, watches
  his wife out into the hallway; then he turns
  sharply, and comes forward several steps, in
  a panic of indecision. Suddenly the impulse
  to recall Mrs. Hampton whirls him round into a
  literal spring in the direction of the hallway, but,
  at this point, the definite closing of the front door
  arrests him, and he stands taut and still for a second, gripping the back of the chair which Mrs.
  Aldrid occupied earlier in the action of the play.
  Then he shifts his position; and, gripping the
  chair with the other hand, leans upon it, and waits
  for his wife to come back from the door. Presently
  she darts into view between the archway portières,
  and stands regarding him with an expression of*

22

amused calculation. But he doesn't see her: so, after a glance over her shoulder into the hallway, she speaks.)

MRS. ALDRID
Did you see that?

ALDRID (*in a repressed, ominous tone*)
What?

MRS. ALDRID (*with a nod toward the hallway*)
She must have heard.

ALDRID
Have you told anybody?

MRS. ALDRID (*coming a little farther into the room*)
No!

ALDRID
I suppose the walls have ears?

MRS. ALDRID
Not necessarily.

ALDRID (*turning to her sharply and searching her with a look*)
Then, how would she know?

MRS. ALDRID
She must have heard me—there in the hallway!

ALDRID (*mercilessly*)
When?

MRS. ALDRID (*becoming slightly disconcerted under his gaze*)
A few minutes ago—when I was telling you I'd found a purse.

ALDRID (*after a fractional pause, and tilting his head a bit on one side, to look at her more quizzically*)
How would she overhear you—she wasn't in the hallway?

MRS. ALDRID

Wasn't she!

ALDRID (*whipping the chair upon which he is leaning out the way, and coming forward in a trembling rage*)

You know very well she wasn't! (*She crosses the back of the room towards the left, watching him. He stops in the middle of the room and forward, and continues speaking, but without looking at her.*) What are you trying to do, kid yourself, or me! (*He goes towards his desk at the right, and she comes forward at the left.*)

MRS. ALDRID (*picking up her apron from the sofa*)

I suppose you didn't take notice of the fact that she came in without ringing, did you?

ALDRID

Well, what of it, what of it, what of it!

MRS. ALDRID (*taking his tone*)

Nothing! Only just think it over while I'm getting your dinner! (*She starts towards the door at the left.*)

ALDRID (*leaning on the back of his desk-chair*)

You needn't get me any dinner. (*She stops and looks back at him.*)

MRS. ALDRID

Why not?

ALDRID

Because I don't want any.

MRS. ALDRID

Don't you want anything at all?

ALDRID (*turning sharply, and looking at her*)

Yes! (*Starting across towards the back of the center-table, and indicating the departed Mrs. Hampton with a wide gesture.*) I want to know

whether or not you intend to return that woman's property?

MRS. ALDRID
Her property?

ALDRID (*enraged, and lifting his voice*)
You heard me!

MRS. ALDRID (*lifting her hand to silence him*)
Sh—sh!

ALDRID (*disregarding her gesture*)
I want an answer, yes or no!

MRS. ALDRID (*flinging her apron back onto the sofa,
and stepping up very close to him*)
What's the matter with you, Gene, are you
blind?

ALDRID (*stonily*)
Not now; but I'm beginning to think I *have*
been—*terribly* blind.

MRS. ALDRID (*turning away from him, and taking a
couple of steps to the left*)
Well, I'm glad something has happened to open
your eyes. (*She feigns to be occupied with her
right cuff. He crosses to her rigidly, and, seizing
her by the arm, turns her sharply to him and looks
knowingly into her eyes.*)

ALDRID (*after a pause*)
If my eyes are not opened after this, it isn't
your fault. (*She attempts to move, but he pins
her to his side with another quick grip. She shows
a trace of fright.*) I want to know whether or not
you intend to return that money?

MRS. ALDRID (*with a mingling of fright and con-
ciliation*)
When I find the owner, yes!

ALDRID (*breaking from her in a wrath, and going towards the back of the room*)
Ah! more hedging!
Speaking together—

ALDRID (*turning at the back of the room, and coming forward again*)
God! how I hate that attitude!

MRS. ALDRID (*holding her right upperarm as though he had hurt her*)
I'd like to hand over four hundred dollars to every Tom, Dick, and Harry that says he lost it. You must think I'm a—

ALDRID (*whirling fiercely upon her, as he passes in front of the center-table*)
Please! (*She is instantly silenced.*) Don't drive me out of the house! (*He goes blindly up towards the hallway.*)

MRS. ALDRID (*regaining herself, and half crying*)
What do you think I am—some school-girl!

ALDRID (*stopping abruptly just inside the archway*)
No! (*Turning to her.*) I think you're a thief!

MRS. ALDRID (*freezing with resentment*)
Do you, really?

ALDRID
More contemptible than the out-and-outer, for he at least doesn't try to justify himself.

MRS. ALDRID
And I'm not trying to justify myself either.

ALDRID
You couldn't! There *is* no justification for your attitude.

MRS. ALDRID
There doesn't need to be any.

ALDRID
And there isn't—among honest people!

MRS. ALDRID (*sarcastically*)
So you don't consider me honest?

ALDRID (*moving a little nearer to her*)
You're like a million other people in this world,
honest, as long as you don't *lose* anything by it;
but as soon as you see where the principle of
honesty is going to *cost* you a dollar, you begin
to *hedge!*—just as you've been doing in this.

MRS. ALDRID
I've been doing nothing of the kind!

ALDRID (*bitterly*)
You've been *tinkering* with honesty.

MRS. ALDRID (*advancing a step or two towards him*)
I never took a cent in my life that didn't belong
to me!

ALDRID
There are rafts of people can say that. But
they wouldn't walk back a block to return ten
cents overchange that some clerk has given
them. (*She sniffs contemptuously, and turns
away*.) Pat themselves on the back, as I've
heard you do,—when the conductor on the
trolley doesn't ask them for their carfare!
(*Swings down towards his desk*.)

MRS. ALDRID
The trolley companies have enough!

ALDRID
There you are! (*Turning to her*.) That's the
psychology of a thief! (*He goes up to the
French window at the back of the room, and, after
glancing out to see that no one has heard them,
closes it*.)

MRS. ALDRID (*ready to cry with madness*)

Have I ever stolen anything from you? (*Evidently, he doesn't hear her, and starts back down towards the right of the center-table. She advances a bit towards him.*) Have I?

ALDRID (*stopping on a line with her, and looking at her witheringly*)

Now, don't start that, please. (*He continues on down to the right of the center-table, and stands, leaning upon it.*)

MRS. ALDRID (*stepping to the left of the center-table, and striking her fist upon it*)

Answer me! Have I ever stolen anything from you? (*There is a slight pause; then he sits down on the edge of the table—very weariedly—as though weighted with the conviction of having married an inferior woman.*)

ALDRID (*with a complete change of tone*)

Listen to me! (*He takes his left hand in his right, and looks at the back of it, with a kind of vacant curiosity; then he drops his clasped hands onto his leg and looks up and out and away off.*) A man's home, in the majority of cases, is founded upon his belief in the *honesty* of his wife; you've stolen that from me to-night.

MRS. ALDRID

What?

ALDRID

That *belief*—that I had in you, as an *honest* woman. (*With an impatient toss of her head, she crosses over in front of the table to the desk, and straightens the desk-pad; then stands with her back to him, with one hand resting on the back of the desk-chair, and the other on her hip.*) You know, there's a line in a book somewhere that says:

"What a little thing makes the world go wrong!
  A word too short, or a smile too long:
Then comes the mist, and the blinding rain,
  And life is never the same again."

Your—(*He feels for the word.*) attitude—in this affair to-night is that mist and blinding rain: it has shown me that my wife is not *strictly* honest—for the sake of being so; and honesty is such a passion with me that, as far as you are concerned, life will never be the same again; because I could never—absolutely *trust* you again. (*He rises slowly, and moves around in front of the table.*) Never. (*He continues to the window at the back, then stops and turns to her.*) I'm very sorry we found that out— (*He steps into the window-alcove and quietly pushes the window open; then, after glancing out, he leans against the side of the window-alcove and says, half to himself and half to her—*) I'm sorrier— than if I had lost a million dollars. (*There is a rather long stillness; then Mrs. Aldrid, who has been finding it difficult to encompass the situation, abandons the effort and crosses the room towards the door at the left.*)

MRS. ALDRID (*as she turns and starts across the room*)
Well, Gene, if you hadn't been so *strictly* honest all your life, we might have *had* a million dollars now.

ALDRID (*picking her up*)
Very true; but we'd have gotten it the way you are getting that four hundred.

MRS. ALDRID (*about to leave the room, and with a return to her former manner*)

And the way I'm going to hold on to it, incidentally. (*She starts to go out at the left.*)

ALDRID (*in a sudden rage, and seizing the telephone at his right*)

All right! Listen to this! Wait! (*She stops, and turns to him.*) I want you to hear this! (*He works the telephone hook violently.*) Give me Wayne one—three seven—D.—Wayne. Please? (*She recognizes the number, evidently, and takes a couple of frantic steps towards him; but he meets her startled expression with a look of quiet defiance, so she stops dead and turns away, waiting.*) Hello! Hello? (*He lowers the telephone again, and there is another pause: then, suddenly, he is answered.*) Hello!—Mrs. Hampton?—Is this Mrs. Hampton?—Mr. Aldrid. (*Mrs. Aldrid turns, and their eyes meet.*) I have some very good news for you.

MRS. ALDRID (*advancing in a panic*)

If you tell her I found that money, I'll deny it!

ALDRID (*into the telephone, and bitterly*)

Your money has been found!

MRS. ALDRID (*raising her arms and hands helplessly, and turning to the center-table*)

Oh, you silly fool!

ALDRID (*into the telephone*)

I found it.

MRS. ALDRID (*looking frantically among her parcels on the center-table*)

Well, if you did, you'll pay it!

ALDRID (*into the telephone, and half smiling*)

I wanted to give you a lesson.

MRS. ALDRID

    For I'm very sure I won't! (*Glancing under the center-table.*) Where's my pocketbook? (*Hurries over to the desk and looks.*)

ALDRID (*into the telephone*)

    I know, but I imagine you must be rather careless to drop that much money.

MRS. ALDRID (*hurrying back to the table, and becoming more excited every minute*)

    Where's my pocketbook?

ALDRID (*into the telephone*)

    All right, Mrs. Hampton, come ahead—it's here for you. (*Hangs up, and sets down the telephone.*)

MRS. ALDRID (*turning to him excitedly*)

    Listen! Have you seen anything of my pocketbook?

ALDRID

    No.

MRS. ALDRID (*looking among her parcels again, breathlessly*)

    I can't find it!

ALDRID

    Where'd you have it?

MRS. ALDRID

    Right here among these parcels!

ALDRID (*disinterestedly*)

    I haven't seen anything of it. (*He comes down to his desk.*)

MRS. ALDRID

    My God! I wonder if I've lost that! (*She looks again for a second, then stops dead and taps the table as though she has suddenly come to a conclusion.*) I wonder if *she* could have taken that—

ALDRID (*turning to her*)
Who?

MRS. ALDRID
Mrs. Hampton.

ALDRID
I'll ask her that—when she comes over.

MRS. ALDRID
Don't you dare!

ALDRID (*bitterly*)
Hum-hum. (*He shakes his head from side to side.*)

MRS. ALDRID
Well, it's gone!

ALDRID
Maybe you left it in the trolley-car.

MRS. ALDRID
Oh, wouldn't that be awful!—And that four hundred dollars is in it! (*Aldrid gives a short, dry sound of amusement, and, thrusting his hands into his trousers-pockets, starts across the room towards the left.*) I don't see anything to laugh at! (*He throws his head back and makes another little sound of intensely derisive laughter.*) And twenty-six dollars of my own! (*He laughs again.*) God! what's the matter with me?

ALDRID (*turning in front of the sofa*)
Maybe you dropped it out there in the hallway.

MRS. ALDRID
Call up the Rapid Transit "Lost and Found," and see if a lady's pocketbook has been turned in. I'll look out here. (*She vanishes into the hallway at the right. Aldrid stands still for a second, then picks up the telephone.*)

ALDRID (*into the telephone*)

Information, please. (*To Mrs. Aldrid*) Do you see anything of it?

MRS. ALDRID (*in the hallway*)

Not a sign!

ALDRID

Why don't you light that light? (*He stands looking into the hallway until a light is turned on: then into the telephone*) Hello? Information? What is the number of the Rapid Transit "Lost and Found?" Yes. Kensington one three— hundred? Will you ask the operator to ring it, please? If you please? (*He lowers the telephone, and Mrs. Aldrid appears at the entrance to the hallway, searching frantically. Aldrid laughs dryly.*)

MRS. ALDRID (*glancing up*)

Funny, isn't it! (*She disappears again into the hallway, and immediately there is the sound of a chair being knocked over, as though she had flung it aside in her anger. Aldrid looks sharply toward the hallway, then shakes his head slowly and conclusively.*)

ALDRID (*shifting his attitude, and sighing rather wearily*)

Ha, ho-ho— (*Into the telephone*) Hello? Information? (*Glances toward the hallway.*) Oh, this is "Lost and Found?" I'd like to know whether or not a lady's pocketbook has been turned in there this evening?

MRS. ALDRID (*rushing in from the hallway*)

Oh, it isn't out there! What do they say? (*He silences her with a gesture; then, after a slight pause, speaks suddenly into the telephone again.*)

ALDRID
  This minute?

MRS. ALDRID
  It *has* been turned in?

ALDRID (*to her*)
  Yes.

MRS. ALDRID (*turning and sinking onto the chair at her hand*)
  Oh, thank God!

ALDRID (*into the telephone*)
  No, my wife did.

MRS. ALDRID (*turning to him*)
  A regular, lady's, black-leather pocketbook!

ALDRID (*into the telephone*)
  Well, can you wait a minute? Please? (*To Mrs. Aldrid*) They want to know whether or not you can identify this?

MRS. ALDRID (*impatiently*)
  Oh, certainly I can! It's a regular, lady's black-leather pocketbook, with my initials E. A. on the outside!

ALDRID
  Yes.

MRS. ALDRID (*illustrating with her hands*)
  There's a small, gold-mesh purse inside, with four hundred dollars in it; and, in the side pocket, there are twenty-six dollars. Then, there's—

ALDRID (*to Mrs. Aldrid*)
  Wait a minute. (*Into the telephone*) Hello!

MRS. ALDRID
  A gold, mesh purse, with—

ALDRID (*to Mrs. Aldrid*)
  Wait a minute! (*Into the telephone.*) A lady's

black, leather pocketbook, with the initials,
E. A., on the outside. There's a gold—E. A.
No, no, no, no! E!—Yes.—Well, that's right.
Why— (*He looks at his wife.*)

MRS. ALDRID

A gold, mesh purse—

ALDRID (*into the telephone*)

A gold, mesh purse, with four hundred dollars
in it; and in the side pocket there are twenty-
six dollars—of her own. (*Mrs. Aldrid looks at
him suddenly.*)

MRS. ALDRID

Five fives and a one.

ALDRID (*into the telephone*)

In bills, yes. (*He looks at her, and she nods con-
firmation.*) Five fives and a one. One minute.
(*To his wife*) What else?—quick!

MRS. ALDRID (*becoming very nervous*)

Why, there's a silver vanity case—

ALDRID

Yes.

MRS. ALDRID

And a gold bracelet—with the clasp broken—
(*He makes a movement of interruption, but she
continues*) and a tax receipt, and a—
Aldrid and Mrs. Aldrid, speaking together—

ALDRID (*to Mrs. Aldrid*)

Wait a minute, now, till I get that! (*Into the
telephone*) Hello?

MRS. ALDRID

Sample of Georgette Crepe, and a face veil, and
a handkerchief, and two packages of hairpins,
and—

ALDRID (*to Mrs. Aldrid*)

I can't remember all those! (*She stops, and relaxes; then he speaks into the telephone*) Hello! There's a silver vanity case and a bracelet—

MRS. ALDRID

Broken!

ALDRID (*into the telephone*)

Broken!—A broken bracelet. (*With a touch of annoyance.*) The bracelet is broken. Yes. And there's a— (*He stops gradually and listens attentively—his eyes wandering to his wife's.*) I see.

MRS. ALDRID (*rising slowly and apprehensively*)

What is it?

ALDRID (*silencing her with a deft gesture, and continuing into the telephone*)

Why, yes, that *is* rather funny.

MRS. ALDRID (*impatiently*)

What does he say?

ALDRID (*into the telephone*)

How about tomorrow afternoon? No, no, I'll call for it myself. Well, if you will, please? Tha—nk you, very much. Thanks. (*He sets the telephone down.*)

MRS. ALDRID

Is everything all right?

ALDRID

Yes.

MRS. ALDRID (*sighing with relief, and leaning upon the center-table*)

Oh!—can you imagine if I'd lost that!

ALDRID (*coming down thoughtfully towards his desk*)

Everything but the money.

MRS. ALDRID (*turning and looking at him*)
  What'd you say?

ALDRID (*without meeting her eye*)
  He says that, evidently, the person who found
  your pocketbook took all the money out of it
  before turning it in.

MRS. ALDRID (*aghast*)
  What!

ALDRID (*indifferently, and turning to his desk*)
  That's what he says.

MRS. ALDRID (*morally and physically indignant*)
  Can you imagine anybody being that contemptible?

ALDRID (*turning and going up to the archway*)
  Please don't make me laugh—I'm not in the
  mood.

MRS. ALDRID
  You won't laugh when you have to pay that
  woman four hundred dollars out of your own
  pocket!

ALDRID (*turning to her sharply*)
  I'd have had to do that anyway!—there didn't
  seem to be very much chance of getting it away
  from you!

MRS. ALDRID
  Well, you're not going to give her four hundred
  dollars of your *own* money?

ALDRID
  That'll do! And, when she comes here, don't
  make it necessary for me to tell her who *found*
  her money. Now, be wise. (*He looks out the
  hallway, starts slightly, then steps quickly towards
  his desk.*) Where is that gold, mesh purse of
  yours?

MRS. ALDRID

There in that drawer—what are you going to do?

ALDRID (*speaking directly to her in a level tone*)

I'm going to give you a lesson in honesty. Where is it? (*Opens the middle drawer of his desk.*)

MRS. ALDRID

Right where you're looking: what do you want it for?

ALDRID (*whipping a little gold, mesh purse out of the drawer*)

Never mind! Is this it?

MRS. ALDRID

Yes; what are you going to do? (*He slams the drawer shut, and, simultaneously, there is a sharp ring at the front door. He lays his hand on Mrs. Aldrid's arm, and they stand still for a second*)

ALDRID

There she is. (*Then turning and urging Mrs. Aldrid across in front of the center-table towards the door at the left.*) Go up to my money-box and get me eight fifty-dollar bills—the newest you can find; and, hurry! (*He starts back towards the archway.*)

MRS. ALDRID (*recovering herself*)

I'll do nothing of the kind!

ALDRID (*whirling upon her, and indicating the left door with an imperative gesture*)

Quick! Now, you've lost enough tonight, I think!

MRS. ALDRID (*turns and goes to the left door, then stops again, defiantly*)

I will not!

23

ALDRID
  Very well, then; I shall be obliged to tell this
  woman the particulars.

MRS. ALDRID (*bitterly*)
  Oh, I'll get them! But I never knew, Gene,
  that you were such a fool! (*She starts to leave
  the room.*)

ALDRID
  Wait! (*She stops and looks at him.*) Wait a
  minute. (*He starts across towards her, passing
  back of the center-table.*) I'll get them myself.

MRS. ALDRID
  Why can't I get them?

ALDRID (*looking at her steadily as he passes above
  her and out the door*)
  Because I'd rather get them myself. (*She
  stands very still, realizing the implication, until
  the doorbell has rung three times; then with a
  rather slow, general gesture of sullenness and
  defeat, she moves up and across towards the archway to answer the door.*)

THE CURTAIN DESCENDS SLOWLY

SOLOMON'S SONG

A PASTORAL TRAGI-COMEDY IN ONE ACT

by HARRY KEMP

CHARACTERS

SHAMGAZAR	ABISHAG
MILCAH	ABIATHAR
SOLOMON	

SOLOMON'S SONG

Time: *The most flourishing period of Solomon's rule: about 1000 B. C.*

SCENE

The Throne-Room of Solomon's royal palace, built in that quarter of Ancient Jerusalem called Millo. The Throne-Room is a vast affair. The walls, from the floor to the ceiling, are covered with cedar wood and adorned with gold fretwork.

In the center stands Solomon's world-celebrated throne, of massive ivory, overlaid with gold. It is elevated on a platform, and a bronze lion stands on each side of it. An ascent of six steps leads up to it, and on each side of each step stands a bronze lion. They face toward the front, twelve in all, symbolizing the twelve tribes of Israel over which Solomon holds sway.

In the back, at the center, is an open balcony, giving on a garden of trees beneath. The tops of the trees come up to the edge of the balcony.

Enter Abishag. She is a young and slender, brown-bodied girl. She is dressed in simple shepherd costume, which consists of a skirt to the knees. Her legs and arms are bare. She has an agile girlish beauty that belongs to open fields and free hilltops. Stepping slowly and carefully about, she follows the contour of the room, with outspread

palms against the walls, like one seeking escape.
Her anklets and armlets make a tinkling sound.
Coming on the balcony, in the back, she looks out,
as if about to leap into the near tops of the trees.
But, in all her movements, she has been stealthily
followed, by the Chief Eunuch, Shamgazar, who
now, coming close to her, clutches her by the right
arm and slowly swings her back to the center of the
room. Abishag is brought to a kneeling position;
she pulls away from Shamgazar.

SHAMGAZAR
    Amend thy folly, girl! There is no maiden
    From the Euphrates to the river Nile
    But sorrows for the lack of what is thine,
    Yearns all her girlhood for the thing thou hast—
    The love of Solomon!

ABISHAG
              I sought it not!
    Let him have many maidens, yea, as many
    As almond blossoms putting forth in Spring,
    So that he come not nigh me with his arms,
    Nor touch me with the lips of his desire!

SHAMGAZAR (*impressively*)
    Abishag, he is ruler of the world!

ABISHAG
    Good—so he be not ruler of my heart! (*She*
    turns and looks out into garden.)

SHAMGAZAR
    Ten thousand bearded men guard Solomon;
    About his palace wait ten thousand men
    With shield and sword. Then, who can bring
        thee help?
    Be wise; accept the great king's love.

(*Dropping down disconsolately, Abishag seats herself on the first step of the throne. A pause. Then, the words inaudible, a song is heard without.*)

ABISHAG

I am
Abiathar's, and his alone, Shamgazar!
(*Softer.*)
That song—how could I hear it and say else?

SHAMGAZAR

'Tis Solomon's song of one and perfect love.

ABISHAG

It is the song we sang among the hills,
Tending our sheep. . . .

SHAMGAZAR

The world is singing it
From Tyre to Elath.

ABISHAG

'Twas our one hearts' song
At even, when the sheep were folded safe.

SHAMGAZAR

Put by all dreams of shepherds and green
hills. . . . .
A thousand towns and cities walled with stone
Have sent the whitest of their maidens hither,
And from the flower of these hast thou been
chosen,
The one bud to break into bloom for him. . . .
But wherefore trouble I my heart with thee?
Thou art a maiden, and thou dost but fear
What thou hast never known. (*Clapping his
hands.*) Come hither, Milcah!

357

(*Enter Milcah, who is to be handmaid to Abishag.
Milcah is tall. She is paler than Abishag, with
the pallor that comes from living an indoor life,
in the palace. She is dressed elaborately after the
Egyptian fashion, the style having been set by the
Egyptian Princess, daughter of King Psusennes,
for whom, a year previously, Solomon built a great
house, for her own private use, after her marriage
to him.*)

SHAMGAZAR (*to Milcah*)
Attend the Queen! (*Shamgazar goes out.*)

MILCAH (*rushing up to Abishag and embracing her*)
Abishag! Thou!

ABISHAG (*returning the embrace*)
As my soul liveth, Milcah of the Plains!
What dost thou here?

MILCAH
I am handmaid to the King. . . . (*Lower.*)
And hast thou thanked Jehovah yet?

ABISHAG
I pray,
With every thought, for my deliverance.

MILCAH (*astonished*)
For thy deliverance! Art thou not glad?

ABISHAG (*dumfounded*)
Glad, Milcah?

MILCAH (*reprovingly*)
Yea, that thou art chosen queen
To sit by Solomon on a throne of gold! . . .
Why, I, who was his but a day, rejoice!

ABISHAG (*smiling confidently*)
Didst know Abiathar?

358

MILCAH (*surprised*)
That tall, ill-favored shepherd lad?

ABISHAG (*severely*)
The same—but comely as the tents of Kedar

MILCAH
Thou lovedst him—but yet—

ABISHAG (*fervently*)
I'll have none other.

MILCAH (*looking about her, with a frightened air*)
If thou wouldst live
Then hold thy peace, lest thou be overheard.

ABISHAG
Nay, I'll speak out, ev'n if my words bring
death.

MILCAH
Doubt not but thou shalt die, thwarting the
King.
But be to him the thing that he desires
And he will make thy pathways delicate
And all thy goings-out and comings-in
As soft as wool. . . . Music will wait upon thee
Of divers instruments, and all the world
Will bow before thee. . . . Tyre will bring thee
purple;
All Egypt will be raiment unto thee;
Ivory and apes and gold will come by ships,
Crowding the sea with white like cloud on cloud,
While peacocks draw their fans down jacinth
courts
And make a sound like wind among blown
leaves. . . .

ABISHAG (*vehemently angry*)
Milcah, thou speakest with an harlot's tongue.
Go from me; I command thee, being Queen.

(Milcah goes out. Solomon's Song again comes from the garden under the balcony. But now a man's voice sings.)

I saw one star grow in the sky,
    I bent in worship to its light—
Then star on star, and star on star
    Drew here and there my sight;

The moon rose—to the moon I bowed;
    In its great light the stars were gone—
The moon, that, graying to a ghost,
    Went out before the sun. . . .

Women are many, thou, but one—
    The lights of heaven are but three,
The stars, the moon, and then—the sun! . . .
    O Love, make day for me!

(The singing ceases.)

ABISHAG *(recognizing Abiathar's voice, and leaning over)*
Abiathar!

ABIATHAR *(faintly, from below)*
Abishag!

(Abiathar is seen climbing in the very top of a tree near the edge of the veranda. Abishag reaches out her hand and helps him in. Abiathar holds her at arm's length, fondly gazing at her. Then they embrace.)

ABISHAG
                  How camest thou
Through all those eyes and spears that hedge
    with death
The gates and gardens of King Solomon?

ABIATHAR (*laughing boldly*)
Simple the deed was as the words that tell:
When the bright moon swam forth, I hid, and
    when
It hid, I ran, and slid from tree to tree,
From shade to shadow, climbing guarded walls,
Unseen, until, by chance, I heard your voice—
And then I sang!

ABISHAG
                        'Tis strange that thou alone
Couldst do so great a deed. . . . And didst thou
    fear not,
Singing?

ABIATHAR (*quickly*)
There is no hope for us but death!

ABISHAG
The prophets say that God is merciful.

ABIATHAR
The king, I think, is not.

ABISHAG
He has concubines,
And seven hundred wives.

ABIATHAR
                        Yet the new gift
Is ever prized the most—till others come.

(*Trumpets without; cries of* "The King," "King
Solomon.")

ABIATHAR (*showing dagger*)
Now death must take
Another, beside us!

ABISHAG
Thou slay the King!

361

ABIATHAR

 Aye, even Solomon, that mighty king. . . .
 And wherefore not? What pity hath he for
  thee,
 Or me, thy lover?

HERALD (*approaching from without*)

 Make way for Solomon!

ABISHAG (*hurriedly*)

 Convey thee hence behind yon throne and hide
  thee;
 Then, after I have sought the uttermost—

ABIATHAR (*embracing her*)

 —The dagger!
 (*Going.*)
 I will slay him with one thrust!

HERALD (*entering, crosses stage in stately and pomp-
ous fashion, as he chants:*)

 Make way for Solomon, that mighty king!
 Wiser than Ethan, the famed Ezrahite,
 Than Heman, Chalcol, and the sons of Mahol,
 Is Solomon, the Chosen of the Lord. . . .
 Hath he not made of songs a thousand and five?
 Hath he not spoken proverbs twice a thousand?
 (*Abishag seats herself on lower step to throne and
 waits. Herald chants as he disappears:*)
 Make way for Solomon! Make way for Solo-
  mon!

(*Trumpets are heard again. A momentary silence. Solomon appears. He is a tall, rather
stout man. He wears a turban, starry with jewels.
It is green. He has flashing black eyes and a
black beard. When he smiles his teeth flash white.
He walks as if with a sense of his own greatness*

362

and magnificence, with his arms folded. Yet his smile shows that, in spite of his unlimited power, he is, when he wills, whimsically human.)

SOLOMON (*standing over Abishag, and looking down at her*)
Abishag, lovest thou me?

ABISHAG (*looking up*)
I love thee not, nor will I bide thy wish.

SOLOMON
Others have vowed the same, nor kept that vow.

ABISHAG (*with slow determination*)
I have not vowed. I have no need of vows
To keep me from the thing I hate.

(Solomon ascends throne and sits down on it, resting his chin on his hand. From this position he studies Abishag, who remains seated on the lower step of the ascent.)

SOLOMON
Thou hast
Another lover?

ABISHAG
Nay, I know but one.

SOLOMON (*leaning down, seriously*)
One more, Abishag, than I've ever known!

ABISHAG (*looking up into his face with sudden vivacity. She is curious and would hear further*)
Nay, but the great King points a jest at me?

SOLOMON
Would it were so. Yet could I somewhere find
That love's perfection I have ever sought,
And never won, my seven hundred wives

Would I return to their far tribes again,
On seven hundred camels, royally.
(*Softly.*)
Abishag, hast thou ever heard my song,
"O Love, Make Day For Me?"

ABISHAG
All but the deaf have heard it, mighty king!

SOLOMON (*sadly dreaming*)
Yea, lovers sing it underneath the moon,
And in the latticed twilight it is sung,
Charming the evening air all hushed and still;
It is the world's one word of happy love,
The love which, hapless, I have never known.
(*Sighing.*)
A dream I shaped from a far dream's desire!

ABISHAG (*searching his thought*)
But thou hast gold from Ophir, and the wealth
Of twenty kingdoms ready at thy wish!

SOLOMON
But who has bought love since the world began?

ABISHAG
Yet, after God, thou hast the highest place.

SOLOMON
So 'tis the power I wear, not I, is loved.

ABISHAG
God gave thee wisdom passing all the world.

SOLOMON
Women love neither Wisdom nor the Wise.

ABISHAG (*with wonder and incredulity*)
Thou never hast been loved?

SOLOMON
By those I loved not,
The which is worse than hate.

ABISHAG (*with swift firmness*)
Thou hast said my thought.

SOLOMON (*rising and coming down to her*)
Handmaid, I will not reason with thee longer.
(*She rises, facing him.*)
Thou hast been sent to me as any gift,
And as a gift I'll use thee. If thou yield not
Thou shalt be made a handmaid to my hand-
    maids.
Yielding, thou shalt possess an equal throne.
. . .
And I have gold from Ophir and the wealth—

ABISHAG (*laughing*)
Nay, who hath bought love since the world be-
    gan?

SOLOMON
Yet, after God, mine is the highest place.

ABISHAG
Then would I love thy power and place, not
    thee.

SOLOMON
God gave me wisdom passing all mankind.

ABISHAG
Women love neither Wisdom nor the Wise.

SOLOMON
Thou mockest me?

ABISHAG
Thy wisdom I repeat!

SOLOMON (*entranced and flattered*)
Brown-bodied little woman from the hills,
Is there no way by which to win thy love?

ABISHAG
None but to be indeed the man I love.

SOLOMON
  What man is he?
ABISHAG
  A shepherd of my tribe. . . .
  I'll tell of him no further lest thou send
  Those who will come with swords and seek him
    out.
SOLOMON (*scornfully*)
  And make a slave my rival in men's eyes?
ABISHAG (*admiringly*)
  Ah, thou art wise, great king, in all but love.
SOLOMON
  What man knew woman since recorded time?
ABISHAG
  But thou, the wisest—
SOLOMON
                        Nay, I know them less
  Than my least slave, for, seven hundred times,
  I have shown lack of wisdom, marrying.
ABISHAG
  And still thou seekest love in me, great king?
SOLOMON (*earnestly*)
  For thou 'rt the only woman I have loved.
ABISHAG
  A lie repeated seven hundred times.
SOLOMON
  Nay, for now
  It springs, a living glory, born of truth:
  Not words lip-said, but brought deep from the
    heart
  As divers fetch up pearls from dangered seas. . . .
  (*A pause.*)
  Yea, and if thou wilt not come unto me
  Then I shall find ways out to bend thy will. . . .

Even now, even now thou livest at my word. . . .
Put by all thoughts of shepherds and green
    hills. . . .
A thousand towns and cities walled with stone
Have sent the whitest of their maidens hither,
And from the flower of these hast thou been
    chosen,
The one bud to break into bloom for me. . . .

ABISHAG

I am Abiathar's, and his alone . . .
I will speak out, ev'n if my words bring death.

SOLOMON (*angrily*)

Doubt not but thou shalt die, denying me:
(*Persuasively.*)
But be to me the thing that I desire,
And I will make thy pathways delicate,
And all thy goings-out and comings-in
As soft as wool. . . . Music shall wait on thee
Of divers instruments, and all the world
Will bow before thee. . . . Tyre will bring thee
    purple;
All Egypt will be raiment unto thee;
Ivory and apes and gold will come by ships
Crowding the sea with white like cloud on cloud.

(*Abiathar now suddenly and silently steps from
behind throne. Thrice he lifts dagger to stab the
King, and each time lowers it. As he is lowering
it the third time, Solomon turns, with slow imperial dignity, and laughs in his face.*)

SOLOMON

Abiathar, thou son of Zeruel,
Put up thy unsheathed dagger; 'tis a toy

Too perilous for youth to play with so.   .   .   .
Here!   Give it me!
(*He reaches for it.   Abiathar draws back.*)
What, child, thou thinkest to slay Solomon?

ABIATHAR
Aye, to slay Solomon, who steals my love.

SOLOMON
Thy love—?   And darest thou rival Israel's
king?

ABIATHAR
We have gone hand in hand since childhood,
sire.

SOLOMON (*admiringly*)
Thou art a bold youth.

ABIATHAR
Love hath made me so.

SOLOMON
So thou wouldst slay me?   But what held thy
hand?   .   .   .
Thrice thou assayedst.   .   .   .

ABIATHAR
Thou art God's Anointed.   .   .   .
(*Kneeling.*)
So to the merciful be merciful.   .   .   .
If not—even yet—

SOLOMON
And thinkest thou, bold young man,
That I was not aware?   Rash boy, I knew
The moment that thou wentest from thy tent,
Thy solitary tent among the hills,
Where thou didst guard thy flocks nigh Dabe-
rath,

On Tabor's morning heights . . . how thou
    didst track
The caravan which brought Abishag hither
By Harod's Well, Rabbith, and Lebonah. . . .
My secret watchers held thee in their eye
At Bethel, Beëroth, and Gibeon. . . .
And when thou didst assay the guarded walls
'Twas at my laughing wish the Watch with-
    drew . . .
Yea, in the light of intermittent moons,
And from the sinking of the day till dawn,
And through each golden passage of the sun,
Eyes watched thy goings-out and comings-in—
And, but I had reserved thee for my sport,
Thou hadst gone down to the forgotten Dark
Ten dawns ago.

ABIATHAR (*firmly*)
Do with me as thou wilt.

(*Kneeling, he offers up his dagger to King.*)

ABISHAG (*also kneeling*)
And do with me as thou wilt do with him.

SOLOMON (*triumphantly*)
Behold the wisdom of the King's device!
(*He waves his hand. The wall to the right slowly
opens, and five bearded and armed men are seen.
Another wave of the hand, and the wall closes
again.*)
Thou art taken fast like any silly bird
That drops upon a twig and finds a net. . . .
(*A pause. They still kneel, unspeaking.*)
Lovest thou not life, that thou dost rush on
    death? . . .
Bethink thee, thou art young, Abiathar!

ABIATHAR

Without love life is naught. . . . It was thy
song— (*Choking.*)
(*Solomon's face grows alit with sudden interest.
He leans forward.*)
Thy song—that taught me so!

SOLOMON (*pleased*)

How, boy? . . . My song?

ABIATHAR

Thy song that oft I sang on silver eves
And in the soft, rose-dappled dawns. . . .

ABISHAG (*taking up*)

Thy song
That thou didst make, of One and Perfect
Love . . .
(*In a soft, sweet voice.*)
How oft we sang that song among the hills
Tending our sheep. . . .
(*Solomon's face is bright with childlike pleasure.*)
It was our hearts' one song
At even, when the sheep were folded safe
And the long shadows marched down from the
hills.

SOLOMON (*smiling imperially*)

And so he won thee with (*fondly*) those words of
mine?

ABISHAG (*joyfully*)

'Twas so he won me. And, as with us, so is it
With all of Israel!

SOLOMON (*leaning forward eagerly*)

"With all of Israel!" What meanest thou?

ABIATHAR (*confidently answering for Abishag*)

Under the spell and music of thy song,

The world has turned to walking two by two
In perfect love, in simple happiness. . . „

SOLOMON (*half musing*)
That happiness which never will be mine,
That love, which, hapless, I shall never know—
Ah, Dream I shaped from a far dream's desire!
. . .

ABISHAG (*with a woman's quickness, pressing the
perceived advantage*)
Thou hast taught all the world this strange, new
thing—
That faithful love holds only room for two,
That every man, each woman, must create,
Anew, the garden of God's paradise
By walking hand in hand, like Adam and Eve,
Before mankind became a multitude. . . .

SOLOMON (*full of ecstasy at his fame*)
Abishag and Abiathar, arise!
(*They stand before him.*)
There's something makes my soul compassion-
ate. . . .
I know not what it is—but ye may go
Back to your hills!
(*They fall at his feet.*)
Aye, ye may go— (*Sadly; half to self.*)
'Tis I that am the one caught in a net. . . .
Nay, what am I, before this youth and love?
. . .

My only empire is an empty heart,
My lifted sceptre, but a gilded boast;
The glory that I have possesses me;
I am weighed down with splendor to my death,
Am sickened by the wasting of desire

For what my wisdom, seeking, cannot find—
And all is vanity of vanities!   .   .   .
(*A pause . . . then, with a proud, ringing voice.*)
Yet have I made a song that all men sing!

CURTAIN

MATINATA

A PLAY IN ONE ACT

by LAWRENCE LANGNER

MATINATA* was first produced by the Provincetown
Players at the Playwrights' Theatre, New York,
November 1, 1920, with the following cast:

COLUMBINE	NORMA MILLAY
PIERROT	JAMES LIGHT
HARLEQUIN	SYDNEY POWELL

*Owing to the general mispronunciation of the original title, "Matti-
nata," I have anglicized the spelling of the Italian word.—L. L.

MATINATA

SCENE

*A small room in a large city, in which Pierrot
and Columbine make their home. The room is
neither kitchen, bedroom, nor living-room; but
it serves as all three; it is, in fact, a room of a char-
acter which is denied to the rich.*

*There is a bed-couch, left front; door leading to
the bathroom, left rear; window, left center wall,
bed-couch against center wall; kitchen sink and
gas stove, right center wall; cupboard with dishes
and chest of drawers against right wall rear; and
door leading to staircase to street, right front.
In the center are a small table and a few chairs.*

AT RISE

*Pierrot is in bed; his head lies near the window.
Columbine is bustling around, setting the table on
which she has already placed some of the breakfast
dishes.*

COLUMBINE (*to Pierrot*)

Breakfast is nearly ready, Pierrot! Do wake
up. (*Pierrot takes no notice. Columbine goes
over to sit on the bed.*) Don't you want some
coffee? (*Pierrot grunts.*) I'm making a lovely
breakfast for you, Pierrot.

PIERROT (*sleepily*)

All right, dear! I'm getting up. (*She waits
expectantly; he rolls over and goes back to sleep.*)

COLUMBINE

I'm going to stay here and bother you until
you get up! See! I'm a mosquito! I'm buzzing
around you! Buzz, buzz, buzz!!! (*She kisses
him.*) I'm going to bite you! (*She attempts
to bite him.*)

PIERROT

Do go away, dear! Can't you see I'm making
up my mind to get up? It takes time. (*He
turns over so that his head is covered up, and all
one can see of him is his hunched-up back.*)

COLUMBINE

You'll never make up your mind! You know
.you've lots of things to do today. Please get
up, Pierrot! Please do! (*She begins to pull the
bedclothes off him.*)

PIERROT

Do leave me alone! I'm getting up. (*He winds
the covers around him.*)

COLUMBINE

But breakfast!

PIERROT

I don't want any breakfast. (*He settles down
in the bed in a determined manner.*)

COLUMBINE (*hurt*)

Very well!

(*She goes over to the gas stove and pours hot
water into the coffee-pot. She looks over at
Pierrot to see whether her new attitude will
make any difference. It does not. She pulls
up the blinds. She puts the coffee-pot on the table
with a thud and sits down, moving her chair*)

376

noisily. She pours herself a cup of coffee. Pierrot raises his head.)

PIERROT (*cheerfully*)
Hello!

(*Columbine drinks her coffee with great intensity.*)

PIERROT (*shouting*)
Didn't you hear what I said?

COLUMBINE (*coldly*)
What did you say?

PIERROT
I said, "Hello!"

COLUMBINE
I've heard you say that before. Do you know what time it is?

PIERROT
No!

COLUMBINE
It's nearly eleven o'clock.

PIERROT
Now, why did you tell me that? I've slept only —let me see—six hours. You're very irritating!

COLUMBINE
I meant to be.

PIERROT
Very well. I shall go back to sleep. (*He lies back on the bed.*)

COLUMBINE
I don't care. Your company isn't so charming, after all.

PIERROT
I have a lovely idea for a song. If I could write it, I might be able to sell it for a hundred dollars.

COLUMBINE

If only you could!

PIERROT

What couldn't we do with a hundred dollars! I know! We could go to a hotel and have breakfast, lunch, and dinner served in our room so we could stay in bed all day. I wish I could remember that song. Confound you, Columbine, why did you bother me! I was half dreaming of it—and now you've made me forget it. (*He sits up.*) It was a song to the dawn—"Matinata"!

COLUMBINE

What do *you* know about the dawn?

PIERROT

There is a great mystery about the dawn. It is seen only by people with very good habits, or by people with very bad habits.

COLUMBINE

It isn't difficult to see where you belong!

PIERROT

Isn't it? Well, I've never seen the dawn—that is, not for years!

COLUMBINE

You were out all night last Monday. Didn't you see it then?

PIERROT

No, I was playing poker. I think I shall get up.

COLUMBINE

I've finished my breakfast.

PIERROT (*gaily jumping out of bed*)

Isn't that fine! Just in time to get me mine!

COLUMBINE

I shall do nothing of the sort.

PIERROT (*pleading*)

But, Columbine, dear! I'm so hungry. I've had nothing to eat since two o'clock—and now it's eleven.

COLUMBINE

You should have gotten up when I called you!

PIERROT

My Columbine angry with me? Don't be angry, sweetheart. Your mouth is like a red rosebud when you smile—but when you're angry it gets thin, like a long, red worm.

COLUMBINE

Ugh! How can you say my mouth's like a worm!

PIERROT (*struck with the thought*)

A worm may hide in the reddest rose!

COLUMBINE

I'm angry with you!

PIERROT

I didn't say your mouth was like that. (*Gaily*) I meant I wanted you to smile—to be happy. It's morning, the sun is up!

COLUMBINE

It's been up for hours.

PIERROT (*jumping out of bed*)

And so am I! Here is your penitent Pierrot! If you'll only forgive me, I'll go to bed early, sleep all night, get up with the dawn, and bring you your breakfast in bed! Won't you like that? (*He takes off his pyjama jacket, disclosing his costume underneath.*)

COLUMBINE

It would be lovely—but it'll never happen! Goodness me, you've slept in your clothes!

PIERROT

Yes, I was too tired to take them off. Do they look bad?

COLUMBINE

The coat's creased terribly. I shall have to put the iron on. You can't go out looking like that! (*She goes over to the stove and puts on an iron.*)

PIERROT (*pulling on his stockings*)

Columbine, you are a dear! I don't deserve you. I know I don't. (*He looks around helplessly.*) Where are my shoes?

COLUMBINE

I don't know. I didn't take them off. Look where you least expect to find them.

(*Pierrot looks in his bed, under his pillow, and finally under the bed, where he finds them.*)

PIERROT

What are you going to give me for breakfast?

COLUMBINE

Would you like boiled eggs?

PIERROT (*with disgust*)

Eggs! Oh, Columbine, how could you suggest eggs? I want something dainty, something with a French name that will just waft its way gently into my insides.

COLUMBINE

I suppose you've been drinking!

PIERROT

Not more than was necessary!

COLUMBINE

I'll make you an omelette.

PIERROT

The French name! And it must be a frothy
one—clusters of air bubbles coated with egg!

COLUMBINE (*sighing*)

I shall have to dirty three extra dishes.

PIERROT

That makes me think of something. I know!
I haven't washed!

COLUMBINE (*breaking the eggs into a dish*)

Hurry, please! You'll begin to dress yourself
just when I have everything ready for you.

PIERROT

Don't hurry me, Columbine. There should be
something dignified about the way a man pre-
pares himself for the day. If he hurries and
skurries, it makes him fretful and nervous. A
great opportunity may come to me today, if I
preserve a calm in my soul. Would you have
me miss it, just so as not to keep breakfast
waiting for a few moments?

COLUMBINE

But you said you were hungry!

PIERROT

I *am* hungry. (*Rises.*) But I have a dignified
hunger. I shall enter the bathroom with a
stately air. Thus shall I begin the day and so
shall I end it. (*Exit Pierrot, bathroom door.*)

(*Columbine sighs, takes the egg-beater, mixes the
omelette and pours it into pan. She puts the
coffee-pot back on the stove. Enter Pierrot,
mopping his face with a towel. He dries it, then
stands up and exercises listlessly for a few
moments, using knife and fork as dumb-bells.*

MATINATA

He then tries rising up and down, hands on hips, body stiff; gets down but fails to rise; he staggers up. He repeats this twice, and finally falls into a chair at the table.)

PIERROT
Well! Where's the omelette?

COLUMBINE
It isn't ready yet.

PIERROT
I'm hungry.

COLUMBINE
Eat some bread.

PIERROT
Where is it?

COLUMBINE
Over here.

PIERROT
Well, why don't you bring it to me?

COLUMBINE
Can't you get it yourself?

PIERROT
Don't you see I'm sitting down to my break-fast? You've been hurrying me the whole morning, and now I'm here it isn't ready—.

COLUMBINE
It is ready. See, the omelette is done. (*She puts it on his plate.*)

PIERROT
Where's the salt?

COLUMBINE
Here you are!

PIERROT

And the bread. Do bring the bread!

(*She hands him bread*.)

COLUMBINE

You are bad tempered this morning.

PIERROT

I'm not. (*He eats the omelette ravenously*.)

COLUMBINE (*sitting at the table*)

Do you like the omelette?

PIERROT

It's all right. I nearly had that song. Listen:—
       "Rose-colored Dawn,
          My heart's forlorn—
Do you like that?

COLUMBINE

I don't. First of all, a dawn's not rose-colored;
and, secondly, the idea's absolutely unoriginal!

PIERROT

You do tell the truth terribly!

COLUMBINE

You need someone to tell you the truth.

PIERROT

Those weren't the words I was thinking of
in bed. If you don't like them, it's your own
fault for waking me up. What I said just now
was inspired by the omelette.

COLUMBINE

Don't be stupid, Pierrot. If I waked you up,
it was because I had to. I've worked all the
week and now it's your turn. There isn't a
thing in the place to eat.

PIERROT

Wouldn't it be wonderful if we could school

ourselves to live without food; one could do it
gradually.   After all, material functions are
merely matters of habit.

COLUMBINE

I wish you'd get the habit of working!

PIERROT (*hopelessly*)

Oh dear! (*He stretches.*)

COLUMBINE

You kicked me—right on the leg!

PIERROT (*indifferently*)

Did I?

COLUMBINE

Yes. You might say you're sorry.

PIERROT (*sharply*)

I suppose I am sorry.   Is it necessary to say so?

COLUMBINE (*indignantly*)

It certainly is!

PIERROT (*equally indignant*)

I might say equally, why did you have your leg
in my way? My desire to stretch was frustrated
—*and by your leg!*

COLUMBINE

Do you mean you're not sorry?

PIERROT

I mean that if your leg hadn't been there, I
wouldn't have kicked it.

COLUMBINE (*angrily*)

Where should I put my leg?

PIERROT (*more angrily still*)

Somewhere where it wouldn't be *in my way!*

COLUMBINE (*rising*)

Look here, Pierrot, I've just about had enough
of you. You don't care what you do, or what
you say!

PIERROT (*angrily*)

    I suppose I don't! Well, I'm going. (*He puts on his hat.*)

COLUMBINE (*alarmed*)

    Where are you going?

PIERROT (*bitterly*)

    To work. To sell my immortality for a mess of pottage.

COLUMBINE

    But I haven't ironed your coat—it is all creased. You look disreputable.

PIERROT

    I don't care how I look.

COLUMBINE

    And you haven't finished your breakfast.

PIERROT

    I'm not going to finish it.

    (*He goes out, slamming the door. Columbine sits at the table and weeps. After a pause, enter Harlequin. He stands at the door.*)

HARLEQUIN (*with aplomb*)

    Good morning!

COLUMBINE (*through her tears*)

    Hello, Harlequin!

HARLEQUIN

    Is that all you say to me, just "Hello"? Aren't you glad to see me?

COLUMBINE (*tearfully*)

    Yes, Harlequin!

    (*Harlequin approaches her.*)

HARLEQUIN

    What's the matter? You're crying.

COLUMBINE (*tearfully*)
Yes, Harlequin.

HARLEQUIN
Why are you crying? It's not over me, is it?

COLUMBINE
No, Harlequin.

HARLEQUIN (*disappointed*)
No? Oh! I thought it was!

COLUMBINE
Why, Harlequin?

HARLEQUIN
Well, I know I haven't been very nice to you lately. But it's all over now, Columbine. Tell me what you've been crying about.

COLUMBINE
I don't know.

(*Harlequin takes her hand.*)

HARLEQUIN (*sympathetically*)
Won't you tell Harlequin? Perhaps he can help you.

COLUMBINE
Oh, Harlequin, it's—it's Pierrot! (*She weeps again.*)

HARLEQUIN
It's too bad, dear. Pierrots are the same the world over. You may thank your stars that wherever there's a Pierrot you'll always find a Harlequin for consolation!

COLUMBINE
I'd like you to console me, Harlequin, but I don't think it would be right.

HARLEQUIN
Oh, yes it would. Harlequins are quite neces-

sary to the world. The Pierrots would be quite unbearable without them. And now tell me, what has Pierrot been doing?

COLUMBINE (*tearfully*)
It's what he hasn't been doing.

HARLEQUIN
Oh! Neglecting you!

COLUMBINE
Neglecting himself. Wasting his time. Going to parties, staying up late, working only when he has to. He's so—so inefficient with himself.

HARLEQUIN
Not with himself, Columbine, but with you. Columbine dear, if you were my wife, how I would devote myself to you! It would be the greatest pleasure for me to do little things for you, to make your life easier, instead of complicating it as Pierrot does. You make yourself a slave to him; you spoil him.

COLUMBINE
I know I do. He went away just now and left everything for me to do. The dishes aren't washed, the beds aren't made. He didn't get up 'til eleven o'clock!

HARLEQUIN
Eleven o'clock! (*With immense satisfaction.*) I've been up since five. What a way to treat you! Well, dear, I shall help you. Nobody can call *Me* inefficient!

COLUMBINE
How I wish Pierrot had some of your qualities!

HARLEQUIN (*with still more satisfaction*)
He never will have. (*Jumps up.*) Shall we begin?

COLUMBINE
Begin what?

HARLEQUIN
Tidying up. I hate to sit in a room that's disorderly.

COLUMBINE (*coaxing*)
Oh, let's talk for a while. I don't feel like tidying up yet.

HARLEQUIN
Don't you move! You stay right there. I'll do it. You've worked enough this morning.

COLUMBINE (*catches his arm*)
You are a dear to want to help me.

HARLEQUIN
There isn't anything I wouldn't do for you, Columbine. (*He bends his head down to her and kisses her.*)

COLUMBINE (*with a little cry of pleasure*)
Oh, Harlequin!

HARLEQUIN (*taking her hand*)
Columbine, dear, I love you. It's breaking my heart to see you so unhappy, to see your dear hands so hardened and stained by working and scrubbing for Pierrot, who doesn't appreciate you in the very least little bit.

COLUMBINE (*weeps*)
It's true. He doesn't.

HARLEQUIN
He stays out night after night, drinking and gambling, and when he's so tired that he can do nothing else, he comes back to you and offers

you the dregs of himself. Columbine, you are
too wonderful to be wasted on such a man.

COLUMBINE (*weepingly*)
I am! I know I am!

HARLEQUIN
Then leave him!

COLUMBINE (*amazed*)
Leave him?

HARLEQUIN
Yes, come with me.

COLUMBINE (*enthusiastically*)
Oh—an elopement!

HARLEQUIN
This wouldn't be an elopement exactly. We
should have to go through the form of a legal
separation.

COLUMBINE (*disappointed*)
But an elopement! I've always wanted an
elopement!

HARLEQUIN
I know, dear, but you must really leave this to
me. An elopement is very romantic and all that,
but a legal separation is really the most sensible
way of doing it.

COLUMBINE (*pouting*)
Very well, if you say so. I'm not sure I'm
very keen about a legal separation. It sounds
so—so—

HARLEQUIN (*interrupting*)
Practical. And that's just what it is.

COLUMBINE (*admiringly*)
You *are* practical, Harlequin. What do I have
to do?

HARLEQUIN

Sit right down and leave everything to me. I shall attend to every detail.

COLUMBINE

You *are* a dear, Harlequin. (*She sits down on a chair by the table.*) Kiss me, sweetheart.

(*Harlequin bends over and kisses her.*)

HARLEQUIN (*still bending over her*)

This isn't very comfortable.

COLUMBINE (*rising*)

You sit here and let me sit on your lap. (*Harlequin sits down, and she sits on his knee.*) Tell me, Harlequin, how was it you came to fall in love with me?

HARLEQUIN (*starting*)

Oh, dear, I've put my sleeve in the omelette I'm covered with egg. Do you mind if I clear off the table?

(*Columbine jumps off his knee and Harlequin rises.*)

COLUMBINE (*anxiously*)

Let me help you.

HARLEQUIN (*wiping his sleeve*)

No, I can manage, dear.

COLUMBINE

But Harlequin!

HARLEQUIN

But Columbine!

COLUMBINE

Oh, very well. (*She sits down.*)

HARLEQUIN

I'll clear them all off in a second.

(*He piles all the dishes on one arm, and in a few seconds has carried them all off, like an expert waiter.*)

COLUMBINE (*admiringly*)
How clever you are, Harlequin!

HARLEQUIN
While I'm up, I think I'll fix the beds.

COLUMBINE
But, Harlequin, what about the elopement?

HARLEQUIN (*rather sharply*)
The legal separation?

COLUMBINE
Yes, when shall we get started?

HARLEQUIN
When will Pierrot return?

COLUMBINE
I don't know.

HARLEQUIN
Didn't you ask him, dear?

COLUMBINE
No!

HARLEQUIN
That was rather thoughtless of you.

COLUMBINE
But, Harlequin, I didn't know we were going to elope when he left this morning.

HARLEQUIN
Of course you didn't, but on general principles, if you're living with a person constantly, Columbine, you ought to know just about what his habits are, and how long he may be expected to be away.

COLUMBINE
  But Pierrot has no habits.

HARLEQUIN
  That's true. I suppose you'd better get packed,
  so we can leave before he returns. Where is
  your suitcase, dear?

COLUMBINE (*pointing*)
  Under the bed.

HARLEQUIN (*pulls out the suitcase*)
  Lord, what a state it's in! Have you a duster?

COLUMBINE
  Let me do it.

HARLEQUIN
  Please, Columbine. Tell me where you keep the
  duster.

COLUMBINE
  Please let me do it.

HARLEQUIN
  Now, Columbine, didn't you say you'd leave
  everything to me?

COLUMBINE
  But I *want* to do it!

HARLEQUIN
  Very well, I know what we'll do. You pack the
  suitcase and I'll tidy the room.

  (*Columbine takes the suitcase and dusts it with
  her handkerchief.*)

  Using your handkerchief, dear?

COLUMBINE
  I have no duster.

HARLEQUIN
  No duster?

COLUMBINE
No!

HARLEQUIN (*expansively*)
When you are living with me, dear, we shall have large piles of dusters! We shall have small, striped ones, large tea cloths, dishcloths, towels, and washrags, and every kind of brush, broom, and cleaning appliance!

COLUMBINE
How wonderful!

HARLEQUIN (*begins making Pierrot's bed*)
Does Pierrot sleep in this bed?

COLUMBINE
Yes.

HARLEQUIN
I thought so. Nobody but Pierrot could stand such sheets.

COLUMBINE (*alarmed*)
They're clean, aren't they?

HARLEQUIN
Yes, but cotton and such cotton! When you live with me, Columbine, you shall sleep on linen. What's this? (*He takes out a photograph of Columbine in a silver frame from under pillow.*)

COLUMBINE (*taking the picture*)
Where did you find it?

HARLEQUIN
Under his pillow.

COLUMBINE
Silly Pierrot!

HARLEQUIN
Silly's too mild a name for a lazy sentimentalist like Pierrot. Sleeps with his wife's photograph!

COLUMBINE
  Hadn't we better hurry?

HARLEQUIN
  We can't go away and leave the place untidy—
  though I suppose Pierrot would never notice it.

COLUMBINE
  No—I don't think he would.

*(Columbine begins to bundle her underwear and
clothes into the suitcase. Harlequin continues
making up the bed.)*

HARLEQUIN *(making the bed)*
  Do you tuck the quilt under the mattress on
  both sides, or only on the left-hand side?

COLUMBINE *(carelessly)*
  Oh, any old way.

HARLEQUIN *(dogmatically)*
  The correct way is to tuck it under on the left-
  hand side only. *(Columbine attempts to close the
  suitcase. Harlequin sees her.)* Don't do that,
  Columbine. You're liable to strain yourself.
  Let me do it. *(Harlequin begins to struggle
  with the suitcase but fails to close it.)* You have
  too much in it. Do you mind if I open it?

COLUMBINE
  But, Harlequin, we must hurry. Pierrot may
  come back any moment.

HARLEQUIN
  We can't go away with all your things trailing
  out of the suitcase, dear! *(He opens it and turns
  to Columbine reproachfully.)* Columbine!

COLUMBINE
  Yes, it is untidy, isn't it? I was so excited I
  just pushed everything in.

HARLEQUIN

No wonder I couldn't close it. Columbine, dear, just leave this packing to me, will you? Look, here's a magazine. (*He gives it to her and guides her to chair.*) You sit down there and read it for a few minutes, and I'll have your suitcase packed like lightning.

COLUMBINE

But I feel so useless!

HARLEQUIN (*reproachfully*)

Columbine!

COLUMBINE

I do.

HARLEQUIN

But you want to go away with me, don't you, dear?

COLUMBINE (*dubiously*)

I suppose I do.

HARLEQUIN

You suppose? Don't you know, Columbine, darling?

COLUMBINE

Yes, of course I know.

HARLEQUIN

Very well. Leave everything to me and there won't be any hitch.

(*He begins packing up her clothes, which he has dumped out of the suitcase onto the floor. He is an expert packer; everything is folded up into the tiniest space. Columbine watches him apprehensively over the top of the magazine. Harlequin begins to fold up a very frilly nightgown.*)

395

COLUMBINE
Please don't look at that, Harlequin!

HARLEQUIN
Why not?

COLUMBINE
It embarrasses me.

HARLEQUIN
I've seen loads of them.

COLUMBINE
Harlequin!

HARLEQUIN
In shop windows. But isn't this rather a stupid one?

COLUMBINE
Pierrot doesn't think so.

HARLEQUIN
It is rather stupid, though. Look at all that frilly lace on the shoulders! It means that the gown lasts half as long. You are always liable to catch cold wearing it. Then again, the laundering is always more difficult and consequently more expensive, and it often scratches your skin when they put too much starch in it. (*His voice full of promise.*) I'll buy you some simple, practical ones, without any frills and fripperies.

COLUMBINE
But I like that one.

(*Harlequin has another frilly garment in his hand. She jumps up and takes it away from him.*)

HARLEQUIN (*amazed*)
Columbine, you don't mean to tell me you wear those!

COLUMBINE (*puzzled*)
Yes, I do; why not?

HARLEQUIN
Goodness me, they're mid-Victorian. You take me back to the days of my grandmother.

COLUMBINE
What's the matter with them?

HARLEQUIN
I shall have to buy you an entirely new trousseau!

COLUMBINE
I don't know that I want a new trousseau!

HARLEQUIN
Indeed you do. You need a new dress badly, too. When you live with me, I shall work hard and buy you loads of wonderful clothes. I shall select them myself. I want everybody to admire you and say what a faultlessly dressed woman you are! There! Everything's in, and there's room for a whole lot more. Are you sure you have everything?

COLUMBINE (*putting on coat and hat*)
Quite sure. Come along.

HARLEQUIN
Did you remember to put in your rubbers?

COLUMBINE (*puzzled*)
Rubbers—on an elopement?

HARLEQUIN
Yes, why not? It might rain.

COLUMBINE
Well, I won't put in rubbers!

HARLEQUIN
If it rains, you'd take cold without them.

COLUMBINE

I will *not* take rubbers.

HARLEQUIN

Columbine, I insist on rubbers.

COLUMBINE (*sarcastically*)

Very well, I *have* no rubbers. But I have an umbrella—perhaps you'd like me to take that!

HARLEQUIN

That would be an excellent idea!

COLUMBINE (*getting angry*)

And how about a small medicine chest with mustard plasters, hot water bottles, and all the necessary equipment for treating small wounds, sprains, bruises, burns, and chapped hands?

HARLEQUIN

Columbine, I believe you are angry with me.

COLUMBINE

Angry with you? No, Harlequin, I'm not angry with you. I'm angry with myself. Imagine eloping with a man who insists on packing rubbers and an umbrella. Oh, Lord!

HARLEQUIN

My dear, I'm simply trying to be practical!

COLUMBINE (*scornfully*)

Practical! Why haven't you brought a lawyer with you? Why haven't we signed the necessary legal documents? Why haven't you brought a doctor in case we have an accident, and a trained nurse, and a hospital, and an ambulance? Why haven't you been really practical?

HARLEQUIN

Columbine, you're making fun of me!

COLUMBINE

No, I'm not! If I elope, it must be with a

practical man, not an amateur.   I want him
to bring along railroad trains and seaside
hotels and ocean liners!

HARLEQUIN
You *are* making fun of me! Columbine, I shall
not go away with you.

COLUMBINE (*points to sink*)
How could you go away with me when the dishes
aren't washed? (*A noise is heard outside.*) Hist!
It's Pierrot!

HARLEQUIN
What shall I do?

COLUMBINE
Something practical!

HARLEQUIN
I'll hide in the bathroom.

(*Exit Harlequin, bathroom door.   Columbine
takes off her hat and coat and passes Harlequin's
hat and walkingstick into the bathroom.
Enter Pierrot.   He carries a small straggling bunch
of flowers.*)

PIERROT (*penitently*)
Columbine, dear, these are for you!

COLUMBINE
Pierrot, dear! (*They embrace.*)

PIERROT
Forgive me, darling!

COLUMBINE
There's nothing to forgive, dearest.

PIERROT
I was rude to you!

COLUMBINE

It was my fault, Pierrot. I had my leg in your way!

PIERROT

No, dearest, I was wrong in kicking my foot against you! I know I was. So I went out into the fields and picked these flowers for you. Then I sat on the grass and looked at them, and do you know, Columbine, dear, that the song came back to me, the one I was dreaming about when you woke me up this morning—"Matinata" I called it—so I wrote it down on a piece of paper and took it to the song publishers and would you believe it—they paid me ninety dollars and forty-seven cents for it!

COLUMBINE (*amazed*)

And forty-seven cents!

PIERROT

Three dollars and seven cents a line! Look, here's the money! (*He pulls out the roll of bills and shows them to her.*) Do you know what I'm going to do with it? I'm going to buy half a dozen of the laciest of lace nighties for you! The ones you have are nearly worn out.

COLUMBINE

But, darling, they are so impractical!

PIERROT

They're beautiful! And then I'm going to bring you half a dozen pairs of—

COLUMBINE (*glancing apprehensively at the bathroom door*)

Never mind, Pierrot!

PIERROT

And with the rest of the money we'll go on a

little trip together! You'll have to pack your suitcase!

COLUMBINE (*shows her suitcase*)
It *is* packed!

PIERROT
How did you come to do that?

COLUMBINE (*hesitating, then lying heroically*)
Woman's intuition! The moment you said those few lines at the breakfast table, I just knew the publisher would buy the song!

PIERROT
Have you any room for my things?

COLUMBINE (*opens suitcase*)
Lots!

PIERROT (*admiringly*)
How neatly you packed it! Here, drop these in.

(*He throws in some clothes and shuts the suitcase, stamps on it and goes to the door, right. Columbine puts on her hat and picks up the suitcase.*)

PIERROT
Columbine, you look charming in those old clothes. People will think we're eloping!

(*They kiss. Exit Pierrot. The bathroom door opens and Harlequin peeps through.*)

COLUMBINE (*calls dowstairs, looking at Harlequin*)
Pierrot, dear, shall I bring rubbers?

(*Exit Columbine. Enter Harlequin. He looks out of the window, sighs, goes over to the table, shrugs his shoulders, and begins to wash the dishes.*)

CURTAIN

THE CONFLICT

A DRAMA IN ONE ACT

by CLARICE VALLETTE McCAULEY

THE CONFLICT was first produced at the Vagabond
Theatre, Baltimore, Monday evening, December 6, 1920.

CHARACTERS

EMELIE, *Mrs. J. A. Dushane Penniman*

BESS, { *Rose Kohler*
{ *Harriet Gibbs*

BOB, *John Steuart*

MOTHER, *Mrs. S. Johnson Poe*

Produced by May Standish Rose.   Setting by
the Vagabond Workshop

THE CONFLICT

CHARACTERS (*in the order of their appearance*):

EMELIE, *the elder daughter of the house, who has already tested her wings in a first flight.*

BESS, *seventeen—just beginning to be aware of the worlds outside.*

BOBS, *thirteen—a vigorous young animal with no wings to speak of as yet.*

THE MOTHER, *guardian of the nest, and very jealous of the world—where her brood is concerned.*

SCENE: *The kitchen of an old-fashioned farmhouse.*

TIME: *Late afternoon of an April day.*

In the back wall, well to the right, is a door leading into the garden. Left of center a broad window curtained in crisp white muslin. In the right wall —down stage—a door leading to the living-rooms at the front of the house. Just opposite—in the left wall—a door which, when opened, reveals a narrow flight of stairs which turn and disappear —evidently the back stairway leading to the rear bedrooms.

In the upper left-hand corner a built-in kitchen range with copper preserving kettle above it. In the upper right a small sink with pump attachment—a little oak-framed mirror over it—a roller towel on the wall beside it. Further down, on the

*right, a cupboard filled with old-fashioned china
—a nest of yellow bowls—a pan of apples. A
drop-leaf table down right of center is covered with
a pretty blue and white cloth—a cane-seated
rocker on the right of it—on the left a straight
chair to match. Between outer door and window
is a little table with a workbasket on it—a clock
hangs on the wall above it. Near the window a
chair—on the sill potted geraniums in bloom. The
window is open and through it you get a glimpse
of a white lilac bush in flower. The square of sun-
shine on the floor is gradually cut off diagonally—
as though by a slanting roof—till near the end it
disappears entirely.*

*(Note.—The room should suggest by every detail
of its cheery, wholesome orderliness a certain sym-
pathetic plea for the mother. Otherwise, if the
home were unattractive, there would at once be
furnished a reason for the children's wish to leave
it; but there is no fundamental reason—other than
the primordial urge to try our wings, which gets
us all, sometime; and which no mother can success-
fully deny without forever crippling her child. In
contrast to the crisp, clear-cut details of the kitchen
is the vague, hazy sunshininess of the garden outside the door.)*

*As the curtain rises Emelie is discovered seated
at left of the center table writing a letter. On this
table stands a small black traveling-bag, and scat-
tered around it gloves, purse, a few letters.
Emelie is a tall girl of about twenty-three, not exactly beautiful, but with a certain nobility of pur-*

pose in her face that lends her distinction, and the lines of her slender figure in its solemn black are full of allurement. Her face quivers as she writes, and she stops a moment to wipe her eyes. There is the cheery, impudent call of a robin in the garden, and Bess enters from the living-room.

Bess is a girl of seventeen. She is not in mourning like her sister, but her white skirt and middy-blouse are set off by a black tie, and a black ribbon on her hair. She has emptied a vase of withered flowers on to a newspaper, and carries them care-fully before her.

EMELIE (*looking up and referring to the flowers*)
Gone—are they?

BESS
Yes—lilacs droop so soon. I cut these for you to take with you on the train.

EMELIE (*absent-mindedly, looking at her letter*)
I'm sorry, Puss—

BESS
I'm not; I'm, oh, so glad—you stayed! (*She has stopped back of the chair to give her sister a hug.*) You can't think how much even two days more means to us. You're surely going this time?

EMELIE
Yes.

BESS (*going up towards window*)
Then I'd better cut you some more. The white ones by the window—they're in bloom now—and they last longer, I think. Do you like them just as well?

EMELIE (*writing*)
Just as well, dear.

BESS (*raising the lid of the range and emptying news-paper*)
My! It's good I looked at this fire. It's almost gone. (*Reaches into wood-box and puts wood on fire as she speaks.*) And Mother *told* Bob to tend to it, but, of course, he's out—as usual—dear knows where. (*There's the sound of a rapidly passing train, and the sky above the window is darkened—as is the square of sunlight on the floor. Bess looks at the clock.*) There goes the express now. I suppose you'll take the 5.05?

EMELIE
Yes.

BESS
Well—You'll want supper before you go.

EMELIE
No, Bess, don't bother. I'm not hungry—I can get tea on the train.

BESS (*coming down*)
Sister, you haven't changed your mind?

EMELIE
No.

BESS
You're really going to New York?

EMELIE
Yes.

BESS
Does Mother know? (*Emelie nods.*) But she doesn't believe you'll do it?

EMELIE
I suppose not.

BESS

And when Mother sets her mind against anything we want to do—you know how it is—even Father always gave in to her—in the end. Don't you feel afraid—she'll persuade you not to go?

EMELIE

I hate to vex her, dear, but—well—neither of you quite understand. My whole future, my very life depends on this. (*Under her breath.*) More than my life, perhaps.

BESS (*who has caught the last phrase, looks at her searchingly*)

Sister— (*Coming down back of the table.*) you know that talk—we—had—last night? After we had gone to bed?

EMELIE

Yes—I kept you awake till all hours.

BESS

It was I kept you. Well—you know what you said—about how, sometimes, when you wanted something that wasn't good for you and didn't feel very strong—how it was awfully foolish to hang around in sight of it, and how it was much, much wiser to *run away* from temptation?

EMELIE

Yes.

BESS (*coming around and kneeling softly beside her*)

Are you—running away—from temptation?

EMELIE

Little sister, dear little sister, what are you saying?

BESS (*with the frank persistence of a child*)

Are you?

EMELIE (*frames the earnest face in her hands, and as she stoops to kiss her, whispers*)

Sh—yes.

BESS

Oh, I was sure of it! Then that's why you're not going back to Boston. I knew it—I knew it—It's those letters! (*Reaches towards them.*)

EMELIE (*checking her*)

Darling! You don't know what you're talking about. Those letters are from a very, very dear friend——

BESS (*convictingly*)

In Boston!

EMELIE

Well, yes——

BESS

And they always make you cry—such funny tears!

EMELIE

They spoke of Father—of our loss, dear. If they made me cry it was because they were so full of tenderness—of sympathy——

BESS

You think so much of him, sister?

EMELIE

So much, dear. He's the best, the truest friend I ever had.

BESS (*puzzled*)

Then why?

EMELIE

Don't, darling. I've no right—— I don't dare —— Oh, I can't explain——

BESS (*jealously*)

Well—just the same—I'm glad you're going to

New York instead. I wish I were. Is that really an honest-to-goodness contract—that long one? (*Indicating envelope.*)

EMELIE (*laughing and abandoning hope of writing for the time.*)
Not exactly. It's an offer, though—from one of the biggest magazines in New York—suggesting subjects for four of my kiddie pictures. If they like them—and they *shall* like them—they'll produce them in colors. And then—it's up to the public. If the public likes them—if it laughs —and applauds—and clamors for more—why, then I can ask, oh, just anything I want for my work—in reason, of course—and they'll give it to me. That's the way of the world.

BESS
Isn't is splendid? And that's when you'll send for me?

EMELIE
Yes, dear—if Mother will let you——

BESS (*despairingly*)
Oh, Mother——

EMELIE
Don't cross bridges, Honey. You know I must first be very sure that I can take care of you— before I talk to Mother.

BESS
You don't think I'll be too old, by then?

EMELIE
For music? You goosie, of course not! If you don't strain those sweet little vocal cords of yours, you'll be just right to begin. Pussy, run along now and cut the lilacs, won't you?—while

I finish my letter. And send Bobs if you see
him about.¶ I want him to mail this for me.

BESS (*going*)
   I shouldn't wonder if that's where he's gone—
   to the post-office. Shall I raise the shade?

EMELIE
   Yes, dear; and leave the door open—the air's so
   good to-day.

BESS (*taking a large scissors from a hook near the
   door—wistfully*)
   I wish I was going to New York. (*Goes out,
   leaving door open.*)

(*Through the open door the sun falls in a tessel-
lated square—as though through a trellis—across
the threshold. Emelie resumes her letter-writing.
Bess is seen through the window at the lilac bush.
There is no sound for a moment but the twittering
of birds and a little dry sob from the girl at the
table. Then a boy's clear whistle is heard, to which
Bess replies, and presently a boy's shadow falls
across the threshold, and an instant later he is apparently joined by Bess, who has gone to meet him.
By this time Emelie has sealed her letter and is ad-
dressing it.*)

EMELIE (*calling*)
   Bobbie!

BOB (*from outside*)
   All right, Sis! I'm coming. (*Entering.*) Bess
   said you wanted me.

(*Bobbie is a boy of twelve or thirteen—perfectly
clean but barefooted, and in the boyish dishabille
of a fellow that lives close to the ground. There is
no subtlety about Bobbie—he's just plain Boy.*)

EMELIE

Yes, I—goodness, Bobs! Bare feet, so early in Spring! Won't you catch cold?

BOB

Cold! Forget it! D'ye think I'm a girl? Say, Em! You're sure some letter writer. Gettin' 'em and sendin' 'em every mail—must keep you busy. Don't you want a secr'tary?

EMELIE

If I did, I wouldn't hire you—you fourth-grader, you!

BOB (*good-naturedly*)

Gee, what a wallop! Don't I make a pretty good fist at corresponding, though? Oh, well! Who wants to write, anyway? I got no use for a pen; but gimme a hammer an' saw an' some nails, an' I'll make you own up that I can't be beat turnin' out chick'n-coops. Ain't that right?

EMELIE (*laughing*)

It surely is; but, good gracious, Bobs, haven't you any ambition? Don't you ever think what you want to be when you're a man?

BOB

Sure I do! I'm goin' to stay right here and have the best little chick'n-farm in the county. Nothin' but Wy'ndottes an' Barr'd Rocks in mine! Well—mebbe some Leghorns f'r the eggs.

EMELIE (*smilingly*)

Oh, well! In that case, it's all right, I suppose. It's a good thing one of us wants to stick to the old place. If it were only Jim, now—— By the way, Bobs, where *is* Jim?   I haven't seen him all day.

BOB

Off with the gang, I guess.

EMELIE

Oh, dear!   That isn't right.   He ought to cut that out!—that's how he got into all that trouble.

BOB

You got it doped out wrong.   Cutting it out's what got him in Dutch!

EMELIE

Bob!   What do you mean?   I don't understand.

BOB (*loftily*)

No, and nobody takes the trouble to understand a fellow around here.

EMELIE

Robert!   I don't think that's quite fair—not to me!

BOB

Oh, well, it makes me sore.   Jim's all right— even if he does get pretty bossy sometimes. And Jim never got a square deal in this mixup —never, from nobody.   Seems to me anyone could understand that you can't go out with fellers one day an' cut 'em out the next—just like that! (*He makes a little perpendicular chopping-off gesture with one hand.*)   But you know how Mother is!   When she says cut it out—it means cut it out—*just like that!*   Not to-morror', or th' next day—or lettin' 'em down easy—but *now!*   Well, the night she said "No more of it!" the gang was meetin' at Dutch Heinie's for a game o' cards——

EMELIE

Oh, Bobbie!

BOB

Oh, well—they'd been meetin' all winter—
nothin' to it! But somebody must've got wind
of it—an' the whole crowd gets pinched!—an',
of course, just 'cause Jim had cut it out so sudden and shamefaced-like, they thought *he* was
the squealer—and mebbe they didn't have
trouble planted for *him* from that on. Say, he
didn't any more break into Martin's show-case
than I did.

EMELIE

Of course he didn't! My own brother! Don't I
know that, Bobs?

BOB

Well, if you'd heard Mother questioning him—
you'd a thought he was a liar as well as a thief.

EMELIE

Sh—Bobbie! That's the unfortunate part of it.
That's what he got for going with bad company.

BOB

Well—he sure had enough of 'em. When he got
out didn't he just beg Mother to let him get
away from here? He knows they're no good—
but in a little place like this what's a fellow goin'
to do? He wanted to go to Fall River; Uncle
Zack'd a got him a job there. But Mother said
he was too young to be *breaking home ties.*

EMELIE

Oh, Bobbie—you don't understand, dear.
Mother didn't want him away *then*, with Father
sick.

27

BOB (*sullenly*)

No, and she won't let him go *now*, with Father —— (*He stops, gulps, and turns away suddenly, brushing his eyes with his coat-sleeve.*)

EMELIE (*going to him*)

There, there, Bobbie—I know! It does seem as if everything was set against his getting a chance. But we will have to think hard—and stand together—and just be patient a little longer.

BOB

Well, I'll tell you something! It wouldn't surprise me none if he'd run away and enlist some day.

EMELIE

He can't! He's too young.

BOB

What's the matter with lying?

EMELIE

Bobby!

BOB

Oh, well, Jiminy Crickuts! If I wanted to get out of a place as bad as Jim does out 'a this one my brain 'u'd get so cracked I'd forget my name —let alone my birthday. Where's Mother? Out?

EMELIE

I think she's taking a nap, dear—she went up to lie down. You know she's all worn out with nursing——

BOB (*nodding and speaking quickly*)

Does she *take* it all right—you're going?

EMELIE

Bobs, dear! I don't like to hear you speak of Mother that way.

BOB

Aw, gee!

EMELIE

Well, I don't. It sounds so disrespectful. And you love her.

BOB

Course I do—you know it!

EMELIE

Sure I know it. Why, just think! You are *her baby!*

BOB (*slyly*)

Say, I don't get no chance to forget that neither.

EMELIE (*shaking him*)

Bobbie, you're incorrigible.

BOB (*purposely as ungrammatical as he knows how to be*)

I ain't never goin' to get no chance to grow up! I'm like that guy—what's his name? *Peter Pan!* That's me! Well, where's this letter you wanted me to mail? (*Going to table.*)

EMELIE

You haven't been to the post-office?

BOB

No. (*Half sheepishly.*) Mrs. Lane's. She promised to have something for me. (*Picks up letter.*) Bosting, eh? Well—Jumpin' *Jee*-hosaphat! What do you want to mail this here for? Why don't you take it along?

EMELIE

I'm not going that way.

BOB

> You ain't going by the 5.15 to Boston.

EMELIE

> No, dear youth—I take the 5.05 to New York.

BOB (*whistles*)

> Mother know?

(*Enter Bess with lilacs.*)

EMELIE

> Yes, *she—knows.*

BOB

> Well, I'm off. (*To Bess.*)   Shall we show her what I got? (*Exit.*)

BESS (*explaining Bob's last speech*)

> Pansies, Emelie.

EMELIE

> Oh, for Father. (*Taking the lilacs from Bess.*) Thank you, dear—they're beautiful—and like you. They'll go along to take care of me, Sweetheart.

(*Re-enter Bob with a broad, shallow basket filled with pansy plants.*)

BOB

> Pansies! Ain't they beauts? Mrs. Lane gave 'em to me. It looks so rough up there—no sod, nor nothin' growin'. Bess an' I were goin' to set 'em out this afternoon, but they can wait till morning. I won't have more'n time to get to the post-office and back before your train goes. Well—you don't have far to go—that's one comfort. Comes in sort o' handy this havin' a private railroad station at your back door, eh? Well—I'm off.

418

EMELIE

Wait, Bobbie. I don't want you to come back here.

BOB

What! Not to say good-bye?

EMELIE

I can't say good-bye to you children that way. I don't want either of you here when—they're going to be so hard—these last few moments with Mother. Bess will take the pansies and wait for you—you know the little siding where the train almost stops? I'll wave good-bye to you there; and after the train's gone, why, you two can go to the cemetery together, and all the way to New York I'll be seeing you setting out the pansies on Father's grave.

BOB

Don't, Em! Funny how a feller misses him— though he hardly ever *said* much—— Aw' Gee! (*Disgusted with himself for showing emotion.*) Take care of yourself, Em. Write soon! (*Rushes blindly off.*)

(*The two girls stand for a moment in each other's arms, then they break away with a guilty look at the clock.*)

BESS

Do you think she's sleeping?

EMELIE

No.

BESS

Then why——

EMELIE

Oh, it makes it so hard for me! It's her way,

you know—— Will you go up and tell her, dear, that I'm almost ready to go—and that there isn't much more time?

BESS (*crossing towards the door to the back stairway*)
Yes. What did you do with your suitcase, Sister?

EMELIE
I sent it over early this afternoon. And Bess—I don't want to go up to the room again—you might just bring my hat and coat, dear—I have everything else.

(*Bess runs up the back stairway, leaving the door swing open behind her. Emelie gathers up her writing materials, dropping the letters into the little satchel. One of these she stops to re-read; in the midst of it, with a little sob and a gesture of renunciation, she tears up the letter and drops the pieces into the fire. Coming back she stops and picks a pansy which she slips into the book on the table before she drops that into the satchel, too. Bess comes down the stairs carrying Emelie's hat and coat.*)

BESS
She'll be down in a minute. (*Then, in reply to the question in Emelie's face*) She was up— looking out of the window.

EMELIE
What did she say?

BESS
Only that she thought you'd given up going.

EMELIE (*sighs*)
Good-bye, dear.

BESS

You won't forget you're going to send for me?

EMELIE

I won't forget.

BESS (*taking up basket*)

Bobs and I'll be at the siding.

EMELIE

And I'll be sure to lean out of the window and throw you kisses as far as I can see you.

BESS (*tremulously*)

Good-bye. (*She goes out waving her hand and is seen passing the window.*)

EMELIE

Good-bye, little sister—and God keep you, darling—as you are. (*Emelie turns and sees Mother, who during the last speech has come down the stairway. She has taken down the kitchen apron that is hanging on nail inside of door, and is putting it on. There is a moment's embarrassed pause, then Emelie speaks.*) Mother—I hated to disturb you; but I was beginning to be afraid you might not waken till the last minute.

MOTHER (*placidly*)

I wasn't asleep. I thought you'd reconsidered going.

EMELIE

Mother—you make it *so hard* for me——

MOTHER

I mean to make it hard—very hard. (*She goes to the dresser and takes from it a large pan of apples, a knife, and a bowl. Then she draws the cane-seated rocker to the left of the table and proceeds to peel the apples in long, thin, unbroken curls—possibly only for the woman with a steady hand and no troublesome nerves.*) For that matter, I've never said that staying right here was going to be the *easy* thing for you to do; but you can't get out of the fact that it's your duty, Emelie. (*The rocker stops a moment, as though its occupant expected a reply; then, as there is none, it continues its placid rhythmic swing, as the Mother resumes her argument.*) You can't always have things the way you want them—and I don't think it would be good for you if you could. (*Emelie, who has come down behind the table, makes a sudden sharp movement as though to speak, then closes her lips firmly. She picks up one of her gloves, examines it mechanically for a moment—and then goes up stage to the work basket, and stands there finding needle and thread, etc., during next speeches. Meanwhile all the mother's attention appears to be centered on the careful coring and quartering of the apple in her hand. She leisurely selects another before continuing.*) Now that you've got used to your freedom and your own way, it's asking a sacrifice of you—I realize that; but you'll have to make lots of them before you're as old as I am.

EMELIE (*with a sudden lift of her head, and in a tone—crisp, clean-cut, that somehow shows the fight is on*)
It's your idea of life, isn't it, Mother?

MOTHER
Making sacrifices?

EMELIE
Yes.

MOTHER

Well, it's a pretty big part of it—as you'll find out.

EMELIE

I'm a poor scholar.

MOTHER

When you don't like the lesson?

EMELIE

Yes. For nearly twenty years I've tried to learn it, but—I can't do it.

MOTHER

How you exaggerate, Emelie.

(*There is nothing impetuous in the speech of these women—there is power—repose—at bottom both are very much alike.*)

EMELIE

Oh, no, I don't. Stop and think. I was three years old when Robert was born. I was expected to grow out of babyhood right then and there. And when he died—there was James to do for—and give in to. Do you remember what a naughty child I used to be? Poor little tempestuous mite—always being punished—hardly ever understanding what for——

MOTHER

Well, you *did* have a bad temper.

EMELIE

And, of course, *that had* to be sacrificed! (*At the little exclamation of surprise from her mother she continued hastily.*) Oh, I know that must sound absurd to you, because you don't—perhaps you can't see it as I do; but all the *little things* you didn't like about me—had to be lopped off, even if I was as surely maimed thereby as though you had cut off my arms and legs. Dear Mother! I know you meant everything for the best—always! You were determined I should be unselfish—well-disciplined —and self-controlled—cut out and fashioned by a pattern on your nail; weren't you? (*She has come down right of table during this speech, and on the last two words, to soften the unfilial tone of it, reaches out and just touches her mother's hand.*)

MOTHER (*not hurt at all by the criticism—and equally untouched by the caress*)

Do you think you're any the worse for it?

EMELIE

Who knows?

MOTHER

I don't think you understand, Emelie. Just what do you mean to complain of?

EMELIE

I don't mean to complain of anything, dear. You loved us all devotedly—no one could have been a better mother—if only— (*She hesitates, then finishes whimsically.*) If only you could have individualized us a bit, dear, instead of lumping us all together as just "*your children.*"

MOTHER (*her hands idle for a moment, she revolves what seemed to her an absurd arraignment; then, surrendering to the apparent need for justification*)

I suppose you will admit, Emelie, that you were a very jealous child?

EMELIE

Oh, undoubtedly! Frightfully so! Did you think you had cured me, Mother?

MOTHER

I tried——

EMELIE

On the contrary, you fed the flame—don't you see? You *exercised* the unlovely thing till it grew strong. I learnt jealousy as a fine art at the mature age of seven. It frightens me to think how I used to feel—how I could feel now if any—— (*She catches herself up and finishes rather lamely—as she goes back to the sewing-table*) anyone gave me cause.

MOTHER (*looking back after her a moment—then down at her work*)

Emelie! You've never told us—me—much about your friends.

EMELIE

No? (*She lingers a bit unnecessarily over the smoothing out of the gloves, but finally places them beside her hat and coat and comes slowly down to her mother's side.*) What is it you would like to know, Mother?

MOTHER

Something about the way you're living now—the people who have helped you in your work. That girl you roomed with first—for instance; what's become of her?

EMELIE

I don't know. I never see her any more.

MOTHER

Why not?

EMELIE

Mother! Let's not go into that. It's a long story—and it would have no bearing on the subject we are discussing.

MOTHER (*mildly*)

I thought that was settled.

EMELIE (*her eyes flashing ominously, but her voice quiet*)

Did you? You thought that all my life to come was to be narrowed within the limits of your "NO;" that I'd give up my plan to go to New York, to forego all the splendid opportunities this year is holding out to me, just because you believe my duty is here. And after all, is that your real reason, Mother? Isn't it rather that you're afraid—that you distrust your child—and your teaching? If not, why is it that you seem to resent each problem that I dare to solve for myself, each step I take unaided, each fresh proof that I'm no longer a child at your apron-strings?

MOTHER

Emelie!

EMELIE

Yes, Mother, I beg your pardon. I know I'm going to hate myself presently for talking to you like this—but can't you see that I've got to fight you? All my life with you has been a fight—a fight to keep true to myself—a constant conflict of wills—ideals and principles that clash and clash—it's terrible—terrible! Can't you see —— (*She stops to get hold of herself.*)

MOTHER

Can't I see what, Emelie?

EMELIE (*more gently*)

Can't you see that you can not hope to *always* have the ordering of your children's lives? We grow up; it is the way of children, Mother. We

have adult responsibilities—problems of our
own which we have a right to face ourselves;
and to each one of our battles we bring all that
we have inherited from our parents—and all
the teaching we've got at their hands—but
something of our own besides. And, Mother
— (*She kneels beside her.*) that something is the
God within us! Forever to do violence to that
something is to kill the individual. Can't you—
can't you try to understand before it's too late?
Jim—Bess—Bobs, even, will have his future
some day to decide for himself.

MOTHER

That's just why you're needed at home; you're
the eldest. You always were more like a boy
than a girl—Jim'll listen to you.

EMELIE

It took me a long time, Mother, to realize how
exacting your love was. Do you remember
how you opposed the idea of my studying in
Boston? Why, if I had not gotten that first
scholarship at the art school, I'd never have had
my chance at all—and *then* I had to go with the
bitter thought of your displeasure at my heart
like a stone all summer long.

MOTHER (*rather proudly*)

You had it in you! You'd have gotten there
just the same—no matter where you studied—
if a little later, perhaps.

EMELIE

Yes, but that's *such* a tragedy! The joy of battle and achievement belongs to youth! *I want
it now! Not when I'm forty.* And you know
that if I hadn't made good—right from the very

start—I should have had to come home. Not because my people couldn't afford it—that I would have understood—but just because Fate —in your own person—said "No!" Talk about signs from heaven! I fairly worshiped those first checks. Why, fifty dollars was a fortune that meant room-rent for a month—yes, and food, too. It took so little to live in a hall bedroom with the aid of a twenty-five-cent gas stove and the delicatessen around the corner.

MOTHER (*dryly*)

No wonder you've ruined your digestion.

EMELIE

Digestion depends upon the frame of mind, Mother. Mine was better in the hall bedroom than it has been here in my father's house, bottling up my sorrow and fighting your displeasure. (*The girl's lips quiver pitifully. The Mother rises, and, on her way back to the sink with the apples, she stops with a half clumsy caress and says gently*)

MOTHER

You're a good girl, Emelie, lots of ways. You mustn't think I'm always finding fault with you. It's strange how you've taken your father's death harder than any of the other children— though you were away from home so much— and never his favorite.

EMELIE

I guess there's no grief quite so bitter as the loss of someone we have loved imperfectly. Oh, it's all so irrevocable—and it's such a pity. Father —working, slaving all his life for us—unrecompensed, unappreciated.

MOTHER

Why, Emelie! I think we all did our duty by father.

EMELIE

Duty? Oh, yes. Duty—weighed—measured; so much politeness, so much service, so much tolerance of individual likings—with a sort of affection, too, of course. We all loved Father —Oh, as a father, all very much according to the letter of the law—but did any of us ever try to understand him—as an individual, like ourselves? And now it's too late! Oh, Mother, dear, I do wish *we* could understand each other a little better before I go.

MOTHER (*in the act of crossing to the range with the saucepan of apples*)

But I thought you'd come to see it my way— about going.

EMELIE (*with a little wail of hopeless desperation in her voice*)

Yes, yes, I know you did! And the pity of it is that you'll keep on thinking so till the whistle blows. We talk round and round in a circle— and my train will be here in fifteen minutes. Couldn't you just give in once—kiss me good-bye and wish me success? It takes lots of strength to travel the hard, lonely road in a strange city.

(*The Mother is through with her work. NOW they will have it out. She turns her back definitely upon the range, and for the first time speaks directly to the girl. All through the preceding scene she has made you feel that Emelie and her problem*

must take second place to this dish of apple sauce,
the duty of the moment.)

MOTHER

That's another thing I don't understand. You
might as well be frank with me, Emelie. I've
never liked secrecy—and you're mighty close
about your affairs. You were perfectly content
with Boston when you came here a month ago.
What's changed you—why, this sudden notion
for going to New York, instead?

EMELIE (*half-heartedly*)

We'll all need more money now that Father's
gone—and Jim's not making much yet. I think
I can earn more in New York.

MOTHER

And spend more, too. A year ago you were delighted with your place.

EMELIE

That was a year ago. Now, the drawing of in-
sipid faces and faultless figures in absurd gowns
seems intolerable—because I've grown and my
work has grown. Fashion-work was just a
means to keep me in food and lodging while I
studied.

MOTHER

Suppose you don't get anything to do—what
then?

EMELIE

I'm pretty sure to fall into something. If I fail,
there's always the fashion-work to fall back on.
But I have offers—good ones.

MOTHER

Who from?

EMELIE

Friends who have faith in me.

MOTHER

That's another thing I don't like. You never *talk* about your friends. 'Tain't natural—unless you're ashamed of them.

EMELIE

Mother!

MOTHER

I don't care—it doesn't look right. You've had letters and sent some every day—even the day of the funeral—but I notice how careful you were not to let them lie around none.

EMELIE (*looks nervously around the room—her eyes light on the clock*)

Mother, we're wasting time. You've known all along that I couldn't stay on here indefinitely.

MOTHER

I can't see why not. *Why is one place any better than another to make pictures in?* The boys are away all day. You needn't be afraid I'd expect much housework of you.

EMELIE (*looks at her mother in silence for a moment. There grows in her face a determination to force the issue, yet she reads the unspoken trouble at her mother's heart and her sense of justice counsels her to be very patient under the probe*)

Mother, suppose we quit fencing like this—get down to facts. Just why are you so determined to keep me here?

MOTHER

I *don't* trust you, Emelie, and that's the truth. You are changed somehow. You're older and more world-wise—and nervous—and there's something going on that you don't tell me. You never were one to talk much, but you don't give me your confidence at all, now.

EMELIE

And you think you can force it? Have I ever given you any real cause for not trusting me?

MOTHER (*reluctantly*)

Not as I know of.

EMELIE

Am I necessarily guilty of something unless I continually prove myself innocent?

MOTHER

I don't like it. You're not frank with me.

EMELIE

I'm all right, Mother. Oh, why should I worry *you* with my problems? I can't do it—though I love you, dear. (*She flings her arms impulsively around her mother's neck; but the whole unyielding figure is so prohibitive, so keenly censorious, that the next moment her hands fall limply to her side*) Well—what is it you want to know, Mother?

MOTHER (*grasping at the permission, without noticing what she pays for it*)

This man you've been getting letters from— who is he?

EMELIE

A gentleman I met through my work, Mother. He's been very good to me—in a business way—

MOTHER

Yes, but it don't look like *just business* to be writing letters back and forth every day——

EMELIE

Then it would be safe to conclude that there was more than *just business* between us.

MOTHER
  What's his name?
EMELIE (*flinching*)
  Is that necessary?
MOTHER
  Are you ashamed of him?
EMELIE
  No.
MOTHER (*after a dissatisfied pause*)
  What's he do?
EMELIE
  He's—he's on a magazine, Mother—what they call "Managing Editor."
MOTHER
  That how you came to meet him?
EMELIE
  Yes. I illustrated some articles for him.
MOTHER (*not looking at her*)
  Known him long—do you see much of him?
EMELIE
  About a year. Yes, I see quite a great deal of him. (*The girl's steady eyes have never wavered from her mother's face. There is a cold, bitter little smile about her lips. She could quicker understand a storm of passionate, anxious scolding than this inquisitorial skirmishing that keeps getting closer and closer to the vital question, but that dreads to ask it.*)
MOTHER
  I suppose he takes you out—sometimes?
EMELIE
  Frequently.
MOTHER
  You go—alone—with him?

EMELIE

Usually.

MOTHER

Of course—he's single?

EMELIE

No.

MOTHER

What!

EMELIE (*stiffening against the table—her nervous hands fingering the edge of the cloth, her coat, her gloves*)

He's married. I don't think I am hurting his wife. She does not care.

MOTHER (*indignantly*)

How do *you* know?

EMELIE

They have not lived together for years; she's abroad most of the time.

MOTHER (*speaking the word as though it were sacrilege*)

Divorced?

EMELIE

No—there's a child—a girl, just reaching womanhood. For her sake—well, they've never just happened to——

MOTHER

And you run around with him like this—*you*? I *want to know*—he says he loves you?

EMELIE (*laughing shortly*)

Yes.

MOTHER

And you?

EMELIE

I love him—yes. (*The last speeches have been spoken almost flippantly. Her attitude during the earlier part of the scene has been that of a child whistling in the dark. Now that her secret has been dragged boldly, nakedly into the daylight, her attitude becomes one of impregnable, hurt defiance. In her anxiety the mother is blind.*)

MOTHER

I can't grasp it! I've felt there was something like this in the wind all along—yet I couldn't believe it of you, Emelie. Mind you, I'm not saying you've done anything really bad——

EMELIE

Thank you. (*There is a flash of gratitude in her face, but it fades into bitterness as her mother quite unconsciously spoils it.*)

MOTHER

You've had too good training for that—but I didn't think you'd cheapen yourself so. How can you believe this man——

EMELIE

Because belief is the very life of love—something you've never learnt, Mother. You kill love by doubting it.

MOTHER

Can't very well believe in a married man who makes love——

EMELIE

Mother! Might I suggest that you do not know either the man or the circumstances?

MOTHER (*very emphatically*)

There aren't any circumstances that can make wrong right.

EMELIE

Oh! (*Pause.*) Very well. Then, since you've judged me, what do you propose to do?

MOTHER

I am trying to think. You want to go to New York. Why?

EMELIE

I told you——

MOTHER

You didn't! You told me a lot of nonsense. You never gave me the real reason.

EMELIE

Which is——

MOTHER

This man! He lives in New York—or he's going to live there. Ain't that why you want to go?

(*The girl looks at her mother incredulously—her whole attitude one of helpless aloofness. It is as though she looked across an ever-widening gulf at the dead.*)

EMELIE (*with a gesture of hopelessness*)

Well——

MOTHER

Do you think I can't put two and two together? Those big envelopes you got from New York yesterday and again today—and you walking about like one in a dream! He's on a magazine, you say—and look at *you*—so sure of getting work in a strange city. Well, why don't you speak? Isn't it so?

EMELIE

What's the use of speaking? You can't expect to extract truth with a probe—and get it out

436

undamaged. You have chosen to put your own construction on appearances—go on! I'm anxious to see what you're going to make of it. *Just what you will do to my life.*

(*The train is heard whistling in the distance.*)

MOTHER

You shall not go to New York tonight.

EMELIE

No? Well, that looks exceedingly probable. I should have to run now to catch the train. Yet I could make it! Quick, Mother! I know all that's worrying you. But of what good was your training if you can't trust me? I've made my choice—I want to abide by it. Just say that I may.

MOTHER

You see! Why are you so set on going by this very train if it isn't an appointment? If you are so determined on leaving home to-night it will have to be for Boston. You're playing on the brink of a precipice—and you don't know it!

EMELIE

Take care, Mother, that you don't push me over—

MOTHER

Oh, yes—I know you're stubborn—but after all, you're my child! Maybe when you've had a night to think——

(*The unwonted stimulus of opposition has aroused the Mother quite out of her quiet calm. All the majesty of outraged motherhood is in her bearing as she sweeps to the outer door and locks it. After the first little cry of "Mother,*

don't do that!" *the girl makes no protest. List-*
lessly she goes to the sink; as in a dream she
washes her hands and dries them on the roller-
towel, and at the little mirror studies her face cu-
riously while she fastens on her hat. While she is
doing this the smoke of the New York train dark-
ens the window. The girl parts the curtains and
stands watching. You hear the grinding of brakes,
the hissing of escaping air, the momentary por-
tentous silence, the clang of the bell, the exhaust—
and then the throbbing of the departing south-
bound train. The girl slips into her coat and picks
up her bag as the mother moves stolidly over to the
door and throws it open. Once more a shaft of sun-
light—a long, pale one this time—falls across the
threshold, and the birds break out into a joyous
twittering. The girl joins her mother in the door-
way, and for a moment they stand there in silence,
so incongruously out of it all—all that the spring
would tell them if they could but hear.)

EMELIE
Well, Mother—good-bye.

MOTHER
I suppose you'll have to go now. You wouldn't
care to stay till morning?

EMELIE
Hardly.

MOTHER (*flustered by the girl's steady eyes, takes*
refuge in a commonplace)
I'd a thought you'd have more pride, Emelie.
I had when I was your age. You'll write?

EMELIE
I don't know—it depends.

MOTHER

On what?

EMELIE

I can't see the outcome of this, Mother. But, whatever happens, I want you to feel that I'll not hold you responsible for *my* decisions.

MOTHER

Emelie!

EMELIE

Funny! You believe in predestination—don't you, Mother? I never did—before. I never could see Fate as a cat playing with a mouse— I never believed that God played with us in wanton sport, but what's the difference if he lets His creatures do it for Him?

MOTHER

You mustn't talk like that—I don't understand.

EMELIE

I hope you never will.

MOTHER (*drawing her quickly to her in alarm*)

Emelie!

EMELIE

Oh, don't! *Please* don't! (*In a sudden burst of anger she tears herself brusquely out of her mother's arms.*) You've faith in no one but yourself! Well, you can sleep tonight very sure of how beautifully you've managed everyone's life. (*Train whistles.*) Let me go! I don't want to miss my train. (*Emelie goes quickly out of the door and down the walk without a backward look.*)

MOTHER (*making a movement after her*)

Emelie! What a way for a girl to speak to her mother! (*Muttering to herself.*) Well, she needn't feel so bitter about it. I'm sure I did it all for her own good. But that's the way with children. (*Coming down.*) They never understand—till it's too late. She's forgot her flowers. Well, it's too late for them, too. I wonder what she meant by——

(*Bess is heard calling from right,* "Emelie!" Oh, Emelie! Where are you?" *She runs excitedly in at the door down right, and takes in her mother's appearance with an evident start of dismay. Train is heard stopping.*)

BESS

Why, Mother! Where's Emelie? Didn't she go? We waited for her at the siding. I'm sure she wasn't on the train, for it stopped an awful long time there. We ran all the way back. I came cross-lots and through the front because Bob got a——

BOB (*who has run around the house is seen passing window and runs in at kitchen door*)

Didn't she go?

(*Train is heard going rapidly in distance.*)

MOTHER (*after a pause*)

Yes—she went.

BESS

To New York?

MOTHER

No—to Boston

BESS

Oh! I wonder what made her change her mind.

BOB

Shucks! And I found this telegram for her at

the post-office, too! That chump of a green kid of Sweeny's put it in our mail box.

MOTHER

A telegram?

BOB

Yes; do you suppose it's anything important?

MOTHER

Give it to me. I'll see. (*She opens it—reads—looks stunned. Still clutching the envelope, in a dazed sort of way she drops the telegram, and crosses unsteadily towards the door, left.*) Emelie! My girl! Oh, why didn't you tell me? Why didn't you tell me? (*She goes heavily, brokenly up the stairs, muttering.*) I—I didn't understand her—she said—— Oh, my God—my God! What have I done?

BOB

Why, whatever's the matter with Mother? What's in the thing, anyway? (*Picks up telegram.*) That's funny—I don't see anything in this——

BESS (*faintly*)

What's—it say, Bobs?

BOB

Why, all it says is—"You can't mean to go out of my life like this. Think how I need you. I shall be waiting at South Station for you to-night, with what anxiety you can imagine. Don't fail me. Devotedly Craig." Who's Craig? Do you know? Well, anyway, it's from Boston. I don't see anything the matter with that. She'll meet him O. K. since she got that train. (*Goes to stairway.*) Oh, Mother! It's all right! That telegram was from Boston, you know. (*Waits a moment; then starts up the stairs.*) Say, Mother! What's the matter? Ain't you goin' to have any supper?

BESS (*staring down at the forgotten flowers, and speaking in a low, frightened voice*)
She—didn't take—my lilacs.

CURTAIN

TWO SLATTERNS AND A KING

A MORAL INTERLUDE

by EDNA ST. VINCENT MILLAY

PERSONS

The King
Chance, The Vice
Tidy, The False Slattern
Slut, The True Slattern

The Prologue *and the* Epilogue *are spoken by* Chance.

Two Slatterns and a King *was first produced at Vassar College.*

Two Slatterns and a King

PROLOGUE

I am that cunning infidel
By men called CHANCE,—you know me well.
It is through me you met your wives;
Through me your harvest blights or thrives;
And one and all, through me, to-day
Hither you came to see the play,
Which if your favor still you lend,
As now, so on until the end,
You shall be taught what way a King
Though a sublime and awful thing
And even wise, may come to be
A laughing-stock,—and all through me!

(Exit)

(ENTER KING)

KING

I am the King of all this land:
I hold a sceptre in my hand;
Upon my head I wear a crown;
Everybody stands when I sit down.   *(Sits)*

CHANCE *(Appearing to audience; he is invisible
throughout the play to the other players in it.)*
Excepting me,—please bear in mind
I sit whenever I feel inclined.   *(Sits)*

KING

Although my lands are wide and long,
My walls right thick, my armies strong,
I am not wholly satisfied.

445

CHANCE

That is because you have no bride.

KING

Who speaks?—Come forth and, if you dare,
Say once again what causes my care!
Why I am discontent with life!

CHANCE

It is because you have no wife.

KING

A woman in my royal house!
A woman! A wife! A bride! A spouse!
Bold stranger, this is not the cure,
For a woman I could never endure!

CHANCE

Per-CHANCE to-morrow you will find
You have altered your imperial mind.
    (*Exeunt* KING *and* CHANCE *severally*)

(ENTER TIDY)

TIDY

I am TIDY, I have been
All my life both neat and clean.
From my outside to my in
Clean am I unto my skin.
Every day into a bucket
My hands I dip, my head I duck it;
And if the water plenty be
I sometimes wet some more of me.
This is my kitchen, where you will find
All things pleasant and to your mind;
Against the wall in orderly pairs—
One, two,—one, two,—observe my chairs.

TWO SLATTERNS AND A KING

In the middle of the room my table stands:
I would not move it for many lands.
My basins and bowls are all in their places;
The bottoms of my pots are as clean as your
faces.
My kettle boils so cheerily,
It is like a friendly voice to me;
About my work I merrily sing,
And I brush my hearth with a white duck's wing.
Oh, full is every cupboard, sharp is every
knife!—
My bright, sunny kitchen is the pride of my life!

(*Exit* TIDY)

(ENTER SLUT)

SLUT

I am SLUT; I am a slattern,
You must not take me for your pattern.
I spend my days in slovenly ease;
I sleep when I like and I wake when I please.
My manners, they are indolent;
In clutter and filth I am quite content.
Here is my kitchen, where I stir up my messes,
And wear out my old shoes and soiled silk
dresses.
My table sags beneath the weight
Of stale food and unwashed plate;
The cat has tipped the pitcher o'er,—
The greasy stream drips onto the floor;
Under the table is a broken cup—
I am too tired to pick it up.

(*Exit* SLUT)

(ENTER KING)

KING

Now I will no longer tarry
For I think that I will marry.
Now the one thing in my life
Is to marry me a wife.
But I will not be content
With a wench that's indolent,
Or take a slattern for a spouse,—
I will go from house to house,
Unheralded—that there may be
No cleaning up because of me—
And that maid whose kitchen's neatest
Will I have to be my sweetest.

(*Exit* KING)

(CHANCE APPEARS)

CHANCE

That I am absent do not fear
For that you have not seen me here,
For know, I oft invisibly
Do move among the things you see;
And to confuse and thwart the King
Through Slut and Tidy, is a thing
Dear to my nature,—therefore heed,
And you shall see a show indeed!

(*Exit* CHANCE)

(*Enter* TIDY *in great disorder*)

TIDY

Oh, dear, oh, dear, what shall I do?
Oh, such a plight I never knew!
Though I arose as is my way
An hour before the break of day,

448

Here it is noon, and nothing done;
The milk has soured in the sun,
And the sweet, pretty duck I broiled
A neighbor's dog has dragged and spoiled;
I beat him with my hands and wept!
Straight through the window then he leapt,
And through the window after him,
With scratchéd face and bruiséd limb,
And on through mire and briar and bog
Hours and hours I chased that dog,
Stumbling, uttering awful cries—
While into my kitchen swarmed the flies!
I came back at half-past ten!
Oh, what a sight did greet me then!
My fair white sheets I hung so fine
Down in the black muck under the line!
And out of the oven from cakes 'n' pies 'n'
Beautiful tarts the thick smoke risin'!
I knelt down my tarts to remove,
And my quince jelly that stood on the stove
Up did boil, and, as you see,
Boiled itself all over me!—
All over the floor, all over the room,—
Whereat I ran to fetch the broom—
The broom! The broom—instead of the mop!
To fetch a broom to wipe up slop!
And with its handle smashed the clock's face,
Getting glass all over the place,
And knocked the dishes off the shelf,
And fell to my knees and cut myself,
And wept and cried and when I would rise
Could not see for the tears in my eyes;
So tripped on a chair and, to save a fall,
Caught at the table, then flat did sprawl,

Dragging the table down with me,
And everything on it, as well you may see!
I cannot live in such a state!
But where to begin is past my pate!

(*Enter* KING)

KING

I am the King of all these lands:
Down upon your knees and hands.
Wishing to marry me, I have said
That the tidiest maiden I would wed
In all my realm, wherefore I go
From kitchen to kitchen, that I may know
And judge for myself what maid is worth
To sit at my side in feasting and in mirth.
Untidy Spill-time, it is easy to see
That my fair bride you never will be.

TIDY

Oh, great King, hear me when I say
This has been a most unusual day!
It is by chance alone you see
In such a state my kitchen and me!
I can set us both to rights in a minute!

KING

In vain! I have set a trap and caught you in it!
Vain, wench, your lies and your pretense!
I see what I see and I hie me hence!

(*Exit* KING)

(*Exit* TIDY, *weeping*)

(ENTER SLUT)

SLUT

Lest you know me not in this disguise
I tell you I am SLUT, and I tell you no lies.

My face and my hands are clean and neat;
Fresh is my frock, trim are my feet.
But I assure you you are not wrong
To think that so tidy I shall not be for long.
And if the story you wish from me,
I will tell you how this came to be:
Dull was the day and tedious my book;
I saw no pleasure wherever I might look;
I had done everything that I knew how to do,
And I could think of nothing new.
But at last I thought of one
Thing that I had never done.
And I said, "I will take a broom,
And I will sweep this room!
I will wash this floor!"
I had never washed it before—
"All things in order will I arrange,
Although I hate order, for it will be a change."
So here I am, as you can see—
I and my kitchen as clean as can be.
But in a room as clean as this
My bones ache and I find no bliss.
So watch, and soon it will appear
Much less orderly and drear.

(Enter KING)

KING

Down upon your knees and hands!
I am the King of all these lands.
Wishing to marry me, I have said
That the tidiest maiden I would wed
In all my realms, wherefore I go
From kitchen to kitchen that I may know—
Yet stay! This kitchen is so tidy,
I think that you must be my bridey!

As far and wide as I have been
So neat a kitchen I have not seen;
Therefore I say you are my wife,
For the remainder of your life.

SLUT *(aside)*

To point him out his error at first I intended,
But least said is soonest mended.

(*Exit* KING *with* SLUT)

(*Enter* TIDY)

TIDY

Now once again with me
All is as it is wont to be.
Now once again you see me stand
The tidiest lady in the land.
If the King should see me now
He would tell a different tale, I trow.

(*Enter* KING)

KING

Oh, lovely lady, who are you,
That I am a talking to?

TIDY

She am I whom you did scorn
This very day at morn.

KING

It may not be as you have said,
For you would I gladly wed!

TIDY

I thank you for the favor, but
They tell me you have married SLUT!

KING

Oh, cock's bones!   And strike me dead!
Is it a Slut that I have wed?

(Enter SLUT *dressed as at first)*

SLUT

So here you dally whilst I sit at home!
Never any more abroad shall you roam,
But sit at home with me for the rest of your life,
For I am your lawful wedded wife!

KING

Oh, woe is me, what a life will be mine!

SLUT

It is too late now to repine:
Home with me you come for the rest of your
life,
For SLUT is your lawful wedded wife!

(Exit SLUT *with* KING*)*

TIDY

A slattern is a fearful sight,—ah, me!
What pleasure it gives so tidy to be!

(Exit TIDY*)*

EPILOGUE

Now that the play is at an end,
By CHANCE *you* have enjoyed it, friend;
By CHANCE to *you* his sweet was gall;
By CHANCE *you* slumbered through it all.
Howe'er it be, it was by CHANCE
The KING was led so merry a dance,
By CHANCE that TIDY met disgrace,
By CHANCE alone SLUT washed her face;

From morn to eve the whole day long
It was by CHANCE that things went wrong.
Wherefore, good friends, t' escape derision,
Be not o'er hasty in your decision,
For he who heedeth not this rule
BY CHANCE HE WILL BE CALLED A FOOL!

THURSDAY EVENING

A COMEDY IN ONE ACT

by CHRISTOPHER MORLEY

THURSDAY EVENING was first produced by the Stockbridge
Stocks, New York City, in November, 1921,
with the following cast:

GORDON JOHNS, *a Young Business Man,* HUBERT TEITMAN
LAURA, *Mrs. Gordon Johns,*   ELEANOR COATES TEITMAN
MRS. SHEFFIELD, *Laura's Mother,*   RACHEL LYMAN FIELD
MRS. JOHNS, *Gordon's Mother,*   LYSLE CLARK

THURSDAY EVENING

SCENE

A small suburban kitchen in the modest home of Mr. and Mrs. Gordon Johns. A meal has recently been cooked, as is shown by a general confusion of pots and pans and dish-cloths. At the rear, an icebox standing in the corner. Rear, center, two shelved cabinets, one containing groceries and household sundries, the other dishes and glassware. Rear, L, an oil range. Some baby linen and very small shirts (such as would be suitable for a child of about ten months) are hanging on a clothes-horse near the stove. Door R leads out to back porch; there are two windows in R wall, one each side of door. Door L to dining-room. At the corner in the rear, L, door opening on back stairs, which ascend to upper parts of the house. Down stage, L, against side wall, a sink and oil-cloth covered drain-board or shelf beside it. In the center of stage a small table covered with oil-cloth. A kitchen chair in corner, down R.

When the scene opens, GORDON and LAURA are carrying in soiled dishes through door, L. They come in and out several times, making methodical arrangements for cleaning up. They pile the dishes on the shelf by the sink. Gordon takes dishpan from a hook under the sink, and fills it with hot water from the kettle on the stove. LAURA, who is an attractive little person, aged about twenty-three, is in that slightly tense con-

dition of a young hostess who has had a long and trying day with house and baby, and has also cooked and served a dinner for four.

GORDON

All right, Creature, just wait till I light my pipe and we'll polish this up. (*Lights pipe and rolls up shirtsleeves.*)

LAURA (*taking an apron from chair in corner*)

Put this on first. That's the only decent pair of trousers you've got.

(*Enter Mrs. Sheffield, carrying dishes.*)

MRS. SHEFF

Now you children run along and take it easy. I'll do all this.

LAURA

No, no, mother. You go and talk to Mrs. Johns. (*Pointedly.*) Don't let her come in here.

MRS. SHEFF (*ultramaternally*)

Poor baby, she's tired. You've been on your feet all day, now let Mother wash up for you. That was a big dinner to cook.

LAURA

No tireder than you are, Mother darling. You cooked lunch.

GORDON

Both of you clear out; I can get this done in no time.

MRS. SHEFF (*patting Laura's cheek*)

Busy with the baby all afternoon, and then cooking such a delicious dinner— Dearie, won't you let Mother do this for you?

LAURA

There isn't room in this kitchen for everybody—
(*Enter Mrs. Johns, carrying dishes.*)

MRS. JOHNS

Gordon, you and Laura go and rest. Let the
two grandmothers—

GORDON

Now listen, little people, this is my job. I always wash up on Thursday evenings—

MRS. JOHNS

You go and read your newspaper. I can see
you're all fagged out after that long day in the
office—

MRS. SHEFF (*to Laura*)

Please go and lie down, Baby. You're *so* tired.

LAURA (*with waning patience*)

You two go and amuse yourselves; Gordon and
I'll attend to this. (*They gently eject the two
mothers-in-law.*)

GORDON

Come on, now, the good old system! (*He takes
the small table from center of stage, and puts it
carefully midway between sink and dish cabinet.
Takes chair from corner, down R, and sets it beside
table. Laura sits down on chair and wipes silver-
ware and dishes as he hands them to her after
washing.*)

LAURA

The silver first, while the water's clean.

GORDON

Right. We make a pretty good team at this,
don't we?

LAURA (*holds up a small silver jug*)

That darling old cream jug. Mother used that when she was a little girl.

GORDON

I love our little Thursday evening suppers. I think they're more fun than any other night.

LAURA

I'm glad, Gordie.

GORDON

We get better grub on Thursdays, when Ethel goes out, than we ever do when she's in.

LAURA

I tried to have everything specially nice to-night. Some visitors are very critical.

GORDON

It was lovely. I'm afraid it was hard for you, Creature, to have Mother come just now. (*A short pause.*) Especially when *your* Mother was here.

LAURA

Didn't she know Mother was here?

GORDON

No. I hadn't told her. You see your Mother is here so much more often. I didn't know your mother would still be here. I was afraid Mother might be a little hurt—

LAURA

Mother helps me a great deal. I think it's a queer thing if a wife can't have her mother stay with her once in a while—

GORDON (*aware of danger, changes the subject*)

Ye Gods, Ethel has cracked the Copenhagen

platter. (*Laura is silent.*) That's one of the set Mother gave us when we were married.

LAURA

It's a stock pattern. You can get another at any department store.

GORDON

I'll bet that coon didn't empty the icebox pan before she went. I never saw a cook yet who could remember to do that—

LAURA

If you had to go out and hunt for them you wouldn't be so particular. She's better than no one.

GORDON (*goes to icebox and removes a large, brimming pan from under it*)
What did I tell you! (*The water slops over from pan as he carries it gingerly to sink and empties it. He replaces the pan under icebox.*)

LAURA

You'd better heat some more water. You've poured that ice-water into the dishpan.

GORDON (*getting a little peevish; refills kettle and puts it on stove*)
It's perfectly absurd not having any pantry to keep the icebox in. In here, the heat of the stove melts the ice right away. (*Goes back to icebox and slams its doors shut.*) Of course, she never keeps the doors properly closed. (*He returns to sink and resumes dishwashing.*) It's a funny thing.

LAURA

What is?

GORDON

Why, that a presumably intelligent coon can't understand the doors of an icebox are meant to be kept tight shut, to save ice. What does she suppose those little clamps are for? (*Laura is silent. There is a pause, while Gordon scrapes portions of food off the soiled plates. He examines some of these plates rather carefully, and picks out several large pieces of meat, lettuce, butter, etc., which he puts on one plate at one side. Then he seems to resume his good humor and relights his pipe.*) Well, it's jolly to have both the grandmothers here together, isn't it?

LAURA

Gordon, dear, put the silver away in the sideboard before it gets wet again. (*He gathers up silver from the table in front of her and exit L. Laura steps outside door R, and returns, bringing garbage can, which she puts down by the sink. She begins to wash dishes, and sees the plate of odds and ends which Gordon has carefully put to one side. She scrapes its contents into the garbage pail. While she is washing, Gordon enter, L.*)

GORDON

Now, Creature, let me do that. You don't want to spoil those pretty hands. (*Takes them, with an attempt to be affectionate.*)

LAURA

I guess it isn't any worse for them than washing the baby's things.

GORDON

Come on, old man, let *me*. (*Gently removes her*

from sink, and pushes her to the chair by the table. She sits down and wipes dishes as he hands them to her.) It doesn't take long when there are two of us.

LAURA

Gordie, these dishes aren't properly clean. You can't get that grease off without hot water.

GORDON

I guess that kettle's hot by now. (*To stove, feels water in kettle.*) Give it a minute longer. (*Stands by stove and puffs at his pipe. In a moment of false security, he foolishly reopens a dangerous topic.*) You know, I'm a little worried about Mother.

LAURA (*putting away dishes*)
Why?

GORDON

I don't think she's as well as usual. She hardly ate any of her salad.

LAURA (*turns as though about to say something, but checks herself and pauses a moment. This time it is she who tries honorably to avert the gathering storm*)
Oh, Gordie, I forgot to tell you! Junior drank out of a cup to-day—the first time!

GORDON

He did! The little rascal!

LAURA

Look, here's the cup. (*Shows a small silver cup.*)

GORDON (*affectionately, putting his arm around her*)
Well, well. (*Looks at cup.*) What cup is that? I don't seem to remember it—

LAURA

Why—Mother brought it with her. She used it when she was a baby.

GORDON

Where's that nice old Christening mug of mine? I think Junior would like to use that once in a while, too.

LAURA

I put it away, dear. I was afraid Ethel might dent it.

GORDON (*takes kettle from stove, goes back to sink*)

I hope Mother isn't feeling poorly. I noticed at supper—

LAURA

When hot meat is served, refined people usually call it *dinner*—

GORDON (*looks at her cautiously, and suddenly seems to realize that they are on the edge of an abyss*)

Now, honey, you're tired. You go and rest, I'll finish up here.

LAURA

No, thank you. I like to see that everything gets cleaned up properly. Someone might come snooping out here, and then there'd be hints about my housekeeping. Of course, I'll admit I wasn't brought up to be a cook—

GORDON (*seeks inspiration by relighting his pipe, and takes up a handsome silver coffee pot*)

One thing I never can make out is, how to prevent coffee grounds from going down the sink. (*He talks desperately, trying to tide over the mutually realized danger point.*) Perhaps if I could

invent some kind of a little coffee-ground
strainer I'd make our fortune. That coffee was
delicious, Creature.

LAURA

Take care of that urn, it's one of the few handsome things we have.

GORDON

It *is* a beauty.

LAURA

Jack Davis gave it to me—

GORDON (*puts it down with distaste*)

I guess I'd better attend to the garbage.

LAURA (*nervously*)

It's all fixed.

GORDON

I always like Thursdays because that's the one
evening Ethel doesn't get a chance to throw
away about five dollars' worth of good food.

LAURA

I fixed the garbage. You can put the pail outside.

GORDON (*hunting among plates on the shelf beside
sink*)·

Where's that plate I put here? There was a lot
of perfectly good stuff I saved—

LAURA (*blows up at last*)

Well, if you think I'm going to keep a lot of half-
eaten salad your Mother picked over—

GORDON (*seizes garbage pail, lifts it up to the sink
and begins to explore its contents. His fuse also
is rapidly shortening.*)

My Lord, it's no wonder we never have any

465

money to spend if we chuck half of it away in waste. (*Picking out various selections.*) Waste! Look at that piece of cheese, and those potatoes. You could take those things, and some of this meat, and make a nice economical hash for lunch—

LAURA

It's a wonder you wouldn't get a job as a scavenger. I never *heard* of a husband like you, rummaging through the garbage pail.

GORDON (*blows up*)

Do you know what the one unforgivable sin is? The sin against the Holy Ghost? It's *Waste!* It makes me wild to think of working and working like a dog, and half of what I earn just thrown away by an ignorant coon. Look at this, just look at it! (*Displays a grisly object.*) There's enough meat on that bone to make soup. And ye gods, here's that jar of anchovy paste! (*Holds it up.*) I thought you got that for me as a little treat. I wondered where it had gone to. Why, I hadn't eaten more than just the top of it.

LAURA

Well, you left it, and left it, and it got mildewed.

GORDON

Scrape it off. A little mildew won't hurt anybody. There'll be mildew on my bank account if this kind of thing goes on. (*Still examining garbage pail.*) Look here, about half a dozen slices of bread. What's the matter with *them*, I'd like to know.

LAURA

I think it's the most disgusting thing I ever heard of. To go picking over the garbage pail like that. You attend to your affairs and I'll attend to mine.

GORDON

I guess throwing away good, hard-earned money is my affair, isn't it?

LAURA

You're always quick enough to find fault. I know Ethel's careless, but she's the best I can get out here in this godforsaken suburb. Maybe you'll be good enough to find me a better servant. A well-trained girl wouldn't work in this old dump, where there isn't even gas. You don't seem to know when you're lucky. You come back at night and find your home well cared for and me slaving over a hot dinner, and do you ever say a word of thanks? No, all you can think of is finding fault. I can't imagine how you were brought up. Your Mother—

GORDON

Just leave my mother out of it. I guess she didn't spoil me the way yours did you. Of course, I wasn't an only daughter—

LAURA

I wish you had been. Then I wouldn't have married you.

GORDON

I suppose you think that if you'd married Jack Davis or some other of those profiteers you'd never have had to see the inside of a kitchen—

LAURA

If Junior grows up with your disposition, all I can say is, I hope he'll never get married.

GORDON

If he gets married, I hope it'll be to some girl who understands something about economy—

LAURA

If he gets married, I hope he'll be man enough not to be always finding fault—

GORDON

Well, he *won't* get married! I'll put him wise to what marriage means, fussing like this all the time—

LAURA

Yes, he *will* get married. He *shall* get married!

GORDON

Oh, this is too absurd—

LAURA

He *shall* get married, just to be a humiliating example to his father. I'll bring him up the way a husband *ought* to be.

GORDON

In handcuffs, I suppose—

LAURA

And his wife won't have to sit and listen to perpetual criticism from his mother—

GORDON

If you're so down on mothers-in-law, it's queer you're anxious to be one yourself. The expectant mother-in-law!

LAURA

All right, be vulgar. I dare say you can't help it.

GORDON

Great Scott, what did you think marriage was like, anyway? Did you expect to go through life having everything done for you, without a little hard work to make it interesting?

LAURA

Is it necessary to shout?

GORDON

Now let me tell you something. Let's see if you can ratify it from your extensive observation of life. Is there anything in the world so cruel as bringing up a girl in absolute ignorance of housework, believing that all her days she's going to be waited on hand and foot, and that marriage is one long swoon of endearments—

LAURA

There's not much swooning while you're around.

GORDON

Why, I believe you actually think your life is wrecked if you aren't being petted and praised every minute. You pretend to think marriage is so sacred and yet you're buffaloed by a few greasy dishes. I like my kind of sacredness better than yours, and that's the sacredness of common sense. Marriage ought not to be performed before an altar, but before a kitchen sink.

LAURA (*furiously*)

I ought to have known that oil and water won't mix. I ought to have known that a vulgar, selfish, conceited man couldn't make a girl happy who was brought up in a refined family.

I was a Sheffield, and why I ever became a Johns is more than I can imagine. Johns—I suppose that's camouflage for Jones. You're too common, too ordinary, to know when you're lucky. You get a charming aristocratic wife and expect her to grub along like a washerwoman. You try to crush all the life and spirit out of her. You ought to have married an icebox—that's the only thing in this house you're really attentive to.

GORDON
Now listen—

LAURA (*will not be checked*)
Talk about being spoiled—why, your Mother babies you so, you think you're the only man on earth. (*Sarcastically.*) Her poor, overworked boy, who tries so hard and gets all fagged out in the office and struggles so nobly to support his family! I wonder how you'd like to run this house and bear a child and take care of it and shuffle along with an ignorant coon for a maid and then cook a big dinner and be sneered at and never a word of praise. All you can think of is picking over the garbage pail and finding fault—

GORDON (*like a fool*)
I didn't find fault. I found some good food being wasted.

LAURA
All right, if you love the garbage pail better than you do your wife, you can live with it. (*Flings her dishtowel on the floor and exit, L.*)

(Gordon stands irresolutely at the sink, and makes a few gloomy motions among the unfinished dishes. He glares at the garbage can. Then he carefully gathers those portions of food that he had chosen as being still usable, contemplates them grimly, then puts them on a plate and, after some hesitation, puts the plate in the icebox. He takes the garbage can and puts it outside door, R. He returns into the kitchen, but then a sudden fit of anger seizes him.)

GORDON

It's always the way! *(Tears off apron, throws it on the floor, and exit R, slamming door.)*

(After a brief pause, the door at the rear, opening onto the back stairs, is cautiously opened, and Mrs. Sheffield enters quietly. She takes one swift look around the disordered kitchen, picks up dish-towel and apron from the floor, and sets to work rapidly to clean up. Then the back stairs door is again opened in the same stealthy way, and Mrs. Johns enters. The two ladies seem to take each other's measure with instinctive shrewdness, and fall into a silent, businesslike team-play in putting things to rights. Mrs. Johns takes charge at the sink, and the remaining dishes spin under her capable hands. Mrs. Sheffield takes them from her, rapidly polishes them, and puts them away on the shelves. There is unconscious comedy in the trained precision and labor-saving method of their actions, which are synchronized so that every time Mrs. Johns holds out a washed dish, Mrs. Sheffield is moving back from the cabinet, ready to receive

it. They work like automatons, for perhaps two minutes not a word is said, and the two seem, by searching side-glances, to be probing each other's mood.)

MRS. JOHNS

If it wasn't so tragic I'd laugh. (*A pause, during which they work busily.*)

MRS. SHEFF

If it wasn't so comic I'd cry. (*Another pause.*) I guess it's my fault. Poor Laura, I'm afraid I *have* spoiled her.

MRS. JOHNS

My fault, I think. Two mothers-in-law at once is too much for any young couple. I didn't know you were here, or I wouldn't have come.

MRS. SHEFF

Laura is so dreadfully sensitive, poor child—

MRS. JOHNS

Gordon works so hard at the office. You know he's trying to get promoted to the sales department, and I suppose it tells on his nerves—

MRS. SHEFF

If Laura could afford to have a nurse to help her with the baby she wouldn't get so exhausted—

MRS. JOHNS

Gordon says he wants to take out some more insurance, that's why he worries so about economy. It isn't for himself, he's really very unselfish—

MRS. SHEFF (*a little tartly*)

Still, I do think that sometimes— (*They pause and look at each other quickly.*) My gracious, we'll be at it ourselves if we don't look out!

(*She goes to the clothes-horse and rearranges the garments on it. She holds up a lilliputian shirt, and they both smile.*)

MRS. JOHNS

That darling baby! I hope he won't have poor Gordon's quick temper. It runs in the Johns family, I'm afraid. I was an Armstrong before I married Gordon's father—I didn't know what temper was until I married—either my own or his.

MRS. SHEFF

I was a Thomson—Thomson without the P, you know, from Rhode Island. All families are hot tempered. All husbands' families, anyway.

MRS. JOHNS

Gordon's father used to say that Adam and Eve didn't know when they were well off. He said that was why they called it the Garden of Eden.

MRS. SHEFF

Why?

MRS. JOHNS

Because there was no mother-in-law there.

MRS. SHEFF

Poor children, they have such a lot to learn! I really feel ashamed, Mrs. Johns, because Laura is an undisciplined little thing, and I'm afraid I've always petted her too much. She had such a lot of attention before she met Gordon, and was made so much of, it gave her wrong ideas.

MRS. JOHNS

I wish Gordon was a little younger, I'd like to

turn him up and spank him. He's dreadfully stubborn and tactless—

MRS. SHEFF

But I'm afraid I *did* make a mistake. Laura was having such a good time as a girl, I was always afraid she'd have a hard awakening when she married. But Mr. Sheffield had a good deal of money at that time, and he used to say, 'She's only young once, let her enjoy herself.'

MRS. JOHNS

My husband was shortsighted, too. He had had to skimp so, that he brought up Gordon to have a terror of wasting a nickel.

MRS. SHEFF

Very sensible. I wish Mr. Sheffield had had a little more of that terror. I shall have to tell him what his policy has resulted in. But really, you know, when I heard them at it, I could hardly help admiring them. (*With a sigh.*) It brings back old times!

MRS. JOHNS

So it does! (*A pause.*) But we can't let them go on like this. A little vigorous quarreling is good for everybody. It's a kind of spiritual laxative. But they carry it too far.

MRS. SHEFF

They're awfully ingenious. They were even bickering about Junior's future mother-in-law. I suppose she's still in school, whoever she may be!

MRS. JOHNS

Being a mother-in-law is almost as painful as being a mother.

MRS. SHEFF

I think every marriage ought to be preceded by a treaty of peace between the two mothers. If they understand each other, everything will work out all right.

MRS. JOHNS

You're right. When each one takes sides with her own child, it's fatal.

MRS. SHEFF (*lowering her voice*)

Look here, I think I know how we can make them ashamed of themselves. Where are they now?

MRS. JOHNS (*goes cautiously to door L, and peeps through*)

Laura is lying on the couch in the living-room. I think she's crying—her face is buried in the cushions.

MRS. SHEFF

Splendid. That means she's listening with all her ears— (*Tiptoes to window, R.*) I can't see Gordon, but I think he's walking round the garden—

MRS. JOHNS (*quietly*)

If we were to talk a little louder he'd sit on the back steps to hear it—

MRS. SHEFF

Exactly. Now listen! (*They put their heads together and whisper; the audience does not hear what is said.*)

MRS. JOHNS

Fine! Oh, that's fine! (*Mrs. Sheffield whispers*

again, inaudible to the spectators.) But wait a moment. Don't you think it would be better if *I* praise Laura and *you* praise Gordon? They won't expect that, and it might shame them—

MRS. SHEFF

No, no! Don't you see— *(Whispers again, inaudibly.)*

MRS. JOHNS

You're right. Cunning as serpents and harmless as doves—*(They carefully set both doors, L and R, ajar.)*

MRS. SHEFF

I only hope we won't wake the baby— *(They return to the task of cleaning up, and talk very loud, in pretended quarrel.)*

MRS. JOHNS

Where do these dessert plates go?

MRS. SHEFF

On this shelf.

MRS. JOHNS

You're here so much more often than I, naturally you know Laura's arrangements better.

MRS. SHEFF

It's a lucky thing I *am* here. I don't know what poor Laura would do without me at such a dreadful time—

MRS. JOHNS

Poor Laura! I should say she's very fortunate, such a good husband—

MRS. SHEFF

I think it's rather sad for a girl who has had as much as she has, to come down to this—

MRS. JOHNS

It's perfectly wonderful how Gordon has got on in business—

MRS. SHEFF

He ought to, with such a lovely home, run like a clock—

MRS. JOHNS

Yes. An alarm clock.

MRS. SHEFF

Well, I'm not going to see my daughter's happiness ruined—

MRS. JOHNS

I always knew he'd make some girl a fine husband—

MRS. SHEFF

Perhaps. But he seems to have picked the wrong girl. Laura has too much spirit to be bullied—

MRS. JOHNS

Well, perhaps it was all a mistake. Poor Gordon, he works so hard. I believe his hair is going white over his ears already.

MRS. SHEFF

Stuff! That's lather from where he shaved this morning. He's too slovenly to wash it off.

MRS. JOHNS

It isn't right that a young man should have to slave the way he does—

MRS. SHEFF (*apparently in a passion*)

Do you think that business slavery can compare to household slavery? I think it's heart-

rending to see an attractive girl like Laura shut
up in a poky little house doing drudgery and tending a baby. Think of it, having to take care of
her own baby! Why, it's an outrage. If Gordon was half a man, he'd get her a trained baby
nurse so she wouldn't have to *look* at the poor
little thing—

MRS. JOHNS (*scathing*)
Yes, how sad that Gordon should have to en-
trust his son to amateur care when it needs scientific attention.

MRS. SHEFF
Poor darling Laura—she never ought to have
had a baby.

MRS. JOHNS
Gordon is too intellectual to be bothered with
these domestic details. He ought to be able
to concentrate on his work.

MRS. SHEFF (*coming close to Mrs. Johns, feigning
great rage, but grimacing to show it is merely acting*)
Well, if you don't think my daughter is good
enough for your son, I can always take her home
with *me*. I guess I can find room for her, and
we can put the child in an institution. (*Both
nearly laugh, but recover themselves.*)

MRS. JOHNS
Don't worry. *I'll* take the child. He's a Johns
anyway, not a Sheffield. And you just watch
Gordon, when he's relieved of all this family
worry and quarreling. He'll make his mark
in the world. He's too fine to be tied down by
a wife that doesn't understand him.

MRS. SHEFF

Oh, how happy Laura will be to hear this. My sweet, clever, attractive, economical, sensible little girl, free at last. Her married life has been a nightmare. That great, hulking, selfish man has tried to trample all the joy out of her. He shan't do it.

MRS. JOHNS

I never heard of a young husband as self-sacrificing as Gordon. I don't believe he *ever* goes out for an evening with other men, and he *never* spends anything on himself—

MRS. SHEFF

I think the way Laura runs her little home is just wonderful. See how she struggles to keep her kitchen in order—this miserable, inconvenient little kitchen, no gas, no pantry, no decent help. I think it's *terrible* she has had to put up with so much— (*They pause, and listen at the door, L. The kitchen is now spick and span. Mrs. Johns makes a gesture to indicate that Laura is taking it all in, offstage.*)

MRS. JOHNS

Well, then, it's all settled.

MRS. SHEFF

Yes. As Laura's mother, I can't let her go on like this. A husband, a home, and a baby—it's enough to ruin any woman.

MRS. JOHNS

It's only fair to both sides to end it all. I never heard of such brutal hardships. Gordon can't fight against these things any longer. Throwing

31

479

away a soupbone and three slices of bread! I
wonder he doesn't go mad.

MRS. SHEFF

We've saved them just in time. (*They look at
each other knowingly, with the air of those who
have done a sound bit of work. Then they stealthily
open the door at the rear, and exeunt up the back
stairs.*)

(*There is a brief pause; then the door L opens like
an explosion, and Laura bursts in. She stands
for a moment, wild-eyed, stamps her foot in a passion. Then she seizes one of the baby shirts from
the rack, and drops into the chair by the table, crying. She buries her head in her arms, concealing
the shirt. Enter Gordon, R. He stands uncertainly, evidently feeling like a fool.*)

GORDON

I'm sorry, I—I left my pipe in here. (*Finds it
by the sink.*)

LAURA (*her face still hidden*)

Oh, Gordie, *was* it all a mistake?

GORDON (*troubled, pats her shoulder tentatively*)

Now listen, Creature, don't. You'll make
yourself sick.

LAURA

I never thought I'd hear such things—from my
own mother.

GORDON

I never heard such rot. They must be mad,
both of them.

LAURA

Then you were listening, too—

GORDON

Yes. Why, they're deliberately trying to set us against each other.

LAURA

They wouldn't have *dared* speak like that if they had known we could hear. Gordon, I don't think it's *legal*—

GORDON

I'm afraid the law doesn't give one much protection against one's mothers.

LAURA (*miserably*)

I guess she's right. I *am* spoiled, and I *am* silly, and I *am* extravagant—

GORDON

Don't be silly, darling. That's crazy stuff. I'm *not* overworked, and even if I were I'd love it, for *you*—

LAURA

I don't *want* a nurse for Junior. I wouldn't have one in the house. (*Sits up, dishevelled, and displays the small shirt she has been clutching.*) Gordon, I'm *not* an amateur! I love that baby and I *am* scientific. I keep a chart of his weight every week.

GORDON

Yes, I know, ducky, Gordon understands. Soon we'll be able to buy that scales you want, and we won't have to weigh him on the meat balance.

LAURA

Nobody can take away my darling baby—

GORDON

It was my fault, dear. I *am* obstinate and disagreeable—

LAURA

I'll speak to Ethel about the garbage—

GORDON

Ethel's all right. We're lucky to have her.

LAURA

Gordon, you mustn't work too hard. You know you're all I have— (*A sob.*) since Mother's gone back on me.

GORDON (*patting her*)

I think it's frightful, the things they said. What are they trying to do, break up a happy home?

LAURA

We *are* happy, aren't we?

GORDON

Well, I should say so. Did you ever hear me complain? (*Takes her in his arms.*)

LAURA

No, Gordie. It was cruel of them to try to make trouble between us—but, perhaps, some of the things they said—

GORDON

Were true?—

LAURA

Well, not exactly true, dear, but—interesting! —your mother is right, you *do* have a hard time, and I'll try—

GORDON (*stops her*)

No, *your* mother is right. I've been a brute—

LAURA

I'm lucky to have such a husband— (*They are silent a moment.*)

GORDON

I suppose you'll think it an awful anticlimax—

LAURA

What, dear?

GORDON

Suppose we have something to eat?

LAURA (*happily*)

Good idea. Quarreling always makes me hungry. (*They go to the icebox.*) I didn't really get any supper to speak of, I was worrying about everything so—

GORDON (*opening icebox*)

You mean *dinner*, honey—among refined people!

LAURA

Don't be a tease. Come on, we'll have a snack— (*She discovers Gordon's plate of left-overs.*)

GORDON

Throw out that junk—I was idiotic to save it.

LAURA

No, Gordie, you were quite right. We must save everything we can. Four or five heads of lettuce would make a new shirt for Junior.

GORDON (*bewildered*)

' Lettuce?

LAURA

I mean, if we saved that much, it would make enough money to buy him a new little vest. He's getting so *enormous*— (*She puts plate of left-overs on the table, with some other cold food.*)

GORDON

There, now, this is better. (*They sit down at table.*)

LAURA (*thoughtfully*)

You know, Gordie, we mustn't let them know we heard them.

GORDON

No, I suppose not. But it's hard to forgive that sort of talk.

LAURA

Even if they did say atrocious things, I think they really love us—

GORDON

We'll be a bit cold and stand-offish until things blow over.

LAURA (*complacently*)

If I'm ever a mother-in-law, I shall try to be *very* understanding—

GORDON

Yes, Creature. Do you remember why I call you Creature?

LAURA

Do I not?

GORDON

There was an adjective omitted, you remember.

LAURA

Oh, Gordie, that's one of the troubles of married life. So many of the nice adjectives seem to get omitted.

GORDON

Motto for married men: Don't run short of adjectives!—You remember what the adjective was?

LAURA
Tell me.

GORDON
Adorable. It was an abbreviation for Adorable Creature— (*Holds her. They are both perfectly happy.*) I love our little Thursday evenings.

LAURA (*partly breaks from his embrace*)
Sssh! (*Listens.*) Was that the baby?

CURTAIN

THE DREAMY KID
(1918)

A PLAY

by EUGENE G. O'NEILL

CHARACTERS

Mammy Saunders
Abe, *her grandson, "The Dreamy Kid"*
Ceely Ann
Irene

Originally produced by the Provincetown Players in 1919

THE DREAMY KID

SCENE.—*Mammy Saunders' bedroom in a house just off of Carmine Street, New York City. The left of the room, forward, is taken up by a heavy, old-fashioned wooden bedstead with a feather mattress. A gaudy red-and-yellow quilt covers the other bedclothes. In back of the bed, a chest of drawers placed against the left wall. On top of the chest, a small lamp. A rocking-chair stands beside the head of the bed on the right. In the rear wall, toward the right, a low window, with ragged white curtains. In the right corner, a washstand with bowl and pitcher. Bottles of medicine, a spoon, a glass, etc., are also on the stand. Farther forward, a door opening on the hall and stairway.*

It is soon after nightfall of a day in early winter. The room is in shadowy half-darkness, the only light being a pale glow that seeps through the window from the arc lamp on the nearby corner, and by which the objects in the room can be dimly discerned. The vague outlines of Mammy Saunders' figure lying in the bed can be seen, and her black face stands out in sharp contrast from the pillows that support her head.

MAMMY SAUNDERS (*weakly*)

Ceely Ann! (*With faint querulousness*) Light de lamp, will you? Hits mighty dark in yere. (*After a slight pause*) Ain't you dar, Ceely Ann?

489

(Receiving no reply, she sighs deeply and her limbs move uneasily under the bedclothes. The door is opened and shut and the stooping form of another colored woman appears in the semi-darkness. She goes to the foot of the bed, sobbing softly, and stands there, evidently making an effort to control her emotion.)

MAMMY SAUNDERS
Dat you, Ceely Ann?

CEELY *(huskily)*
Hit ain't no yuther, Mammy.

MAMMY
Light de lamp, den. I can't see no whars.

CEELY
Des one second, till I finds a match. *(She wipes her eyes with her handkerchief, then goes to the chest of drawers and feels around on the top of it, pretending to grumble.)* Hit beat all how dem pesky little sticks done hide umse'fs. Shoo! Yere dey is. *(She fumbles with the lamp.)*

MAMMY *(suspiciously)*
You ain't been cryin', is you?

CEELY *(with feigned astonishment)*
Cryin'? I clar' ter goodness, you does git the mos' fool notions lyin' dar.

MAMMY *(in a tone of relief)*
I mos' thought I yeard you.

CEELY *(lighting the lamp)*
'Deed you aint.

(The two women are revealed by the light. Mammy Saunders is an old white-haired negress about ninety, with a weazened face furrowed by wrinkles and withered by old age and sickness. Ceely is a

stout woman of fifty or so, with gray hair and a round fat face. She wears a loose-fitting gingham dress and a shawl thrown over her head.

CEELY (*with attempted cheeriness*)

Bless yo' soul, I ain't got nothin' to cry 'bout. Yere. Lemme fix you so you'll rest mo' easy. (*She lifts the old woman gently and fixes the pillows.*) Dere. Now ain't you feelin' better?

MAMMY (*dully*)

My strenk don' all went. I can't lift a hand.

CEELY (*hurriedly*)

Dat'll all come back ter you, de doctor tole me des now when I goes down to de door with him. (*Glibly*) He say you is de mos' strongest 'oman fo' yo' years ever he sees in de worl'; and he tell me you gwine ter be up and walkin' agin fo' de week's out. (*As she finds the old woman's eyes fixed on her, she turns away confusedly and abruptly changes the subject.*) Hit ain't too wo'm in dis room, dat's a fac'.

MAMMY (*shaking her head—in a half-whisper*)

No, Ceely Ann. Hit ain't no use'n you tellin' me nothin' but de trufe. I feels mighty poo'ly. En I knows hit's on'y wid de blessin' er Gawd I kin las' de night out.

CEELY (*distractedly*)

Ain't no sich a thing! Hush yo' noise, Mammy!

MAMMY (*as if she hadn't heard—in a crooning sing-song*)

I'se gwine soon fum dis wicked yearth—and may de Lawd have mercy on dis po' ole sinner. (*After a pause—anxiously*) All I'se prayin' fer

is dat Gawd don' take me befo' I sees Dreamy
agin. Whar's Dreamy, Ceely Ann? Why ain't
he come yere? Ain't you done sent him word
I'se sick, like I tole you?

CEELY

I tole dem boys ter tell him speshul, and dey
swar dey would soon's dey find him. I s'pose
dey ain't kotch him yit. Don' yo' pester
yo'se'f worryin'. Dreamy 'ull come fo' ve'y
long.

MAMMY (*after a pause—weakly*)

Dere's a feelin' in my haid like I was a-floatin'
yander whar I can't see nothin', or 'member
nothin', or know de sight er any pusson I
knows; en I wants ter see Dreamy agin befo'—

CEELY (*quickly*)

Don' waste yo' strenk talkin'. Yo' git a wink
er sleep en I wake yo' when he comes. Yo'
heah me?

MAMMY (*faintly*)

I does feel mighty drowsy. (*She closes her eyes.*)

(*Ceely goes over to the window and, pulling the
curtains aside, stands looking down into the
street as if she were watching for someone coming.
A moment later there is a noise of footfalls from
the stairs in the hall, followed by a sharp rap on
the door.*)

CEELY (*turning quickly from the window*)

S-s-s-h-h! S-s-s-h-h!

(*She hurries to the door, glancing anxiously toward Mammy. The old woman appears to have
fallen asleep. Ceely cautiously opens the door a
bare inch or so and peeks out. When she sees*

who it is she immediately tries to slam it shut again, but a vigorous shove from the outside forces her back and Irene pushes her way defiantly into the room. She is a young, good-looking negress, highly rouged and powdered, dressed in gaudy, cheap finery.)

IRENE (*in a harsh voice, evidently worked up to a great state of nervous excitement*)
No you don't, Ceely Ann! I said I was comin' here, and it'll take mo'n you to stop me!

CEELY (*almost speechless with horrified indignation—breathing heavily*)
Yo' bad 'oman! Git back ter yo' bad-house, whar yo' b'longs!

IRENE (*raising her clenched hand—furiously*)
Stop dat talkin' to me, nigger, or I'll split yo' fool head! (*As Ceely shrinks away, Irene lowers her hand and glances quickly around the room.*) Whar's Dreamy?

CEELY (*scornfully*)
Yo' axe me dat! Whar's Dreamy? Axe yo'se'f. Yo's de one ought ter know whar he is.

IRENE
Den he ain't come here?

CEELY
I ain't tellin' de likes er you wedder he is or not.

IRENE (*pleadingly*)
Tell me, Ceely Ann, ain't he been here? He'd be sure to come here, 'count of Mammy dyin', dey said.

CEELY (*pointing to Mammy—apprehensively*)
S-s-shsh! (*Then lowering her voice to a whisper—suspiciously*) Dey said? Who said?

IRENE (*equally suspicious*)

None o' your business who said. (*Then pleading again*) Ceely Ann, I jest got ter see him dis minute, dis secon'! He's in bad, Dreamy is, and I knows somep'n I gotter tell him, somep'n I jest heard—

CEELY (*uncomprehendingly*)

In bad? What you jest heah?

IRENE

I ain't tellin' no one but him. (*Desperately.*) For Gawd's sake, tell me whar he is, Ceely!

CEELY

I don't know no mo'n you.

IRENE (*fiercely*)

You's lyin', Ceely! You's lyin' ter me jest 'cause I'se bad.

CEELY

De good Lawd bar witness I'se tellin' you de trufe!

IRENE (*hopelessly*)

Den I gotter go find him, high and low, some-wheres. (*Proudly*) You ain't got de right not ter trust me, Ceely, where de Dreamy's mixed in it. I'd go ter hell for Dreamy!

CEELY (*indignantly*)

Hush yo' wicked cussin'! (*Then, anxiously*) Is Dreamy in trouble?

IRENE (*with a scornful laugh*)

Trouble? Good Lawd, it's worser'n dat! (*Then in surprise*) Ain't you heerd what de Dreamy done last night, Ceely?

CEELY (*apprehensively*)

What de Dreamy do? Tell me, gal. Somep'n bad?

IRENE (*with the same scornful laugh*)

Bad? Worser'n bad, what he done!

CEELY (*lamenting querulously*)

Oh, good Lawd, I knowed it! I knowed with all his carryin's-on wid dat passel er tough young niggers—him so uppity 'cause he's de boss er de gang—sleepin' all de day 'stead er workin' an' Lawd knows what he does in de nights—fightin' wid white folks, an' totin' a pistol in his pocket—(*with a glance of angry resentment at Irene*) an' as fo' de udder company he's been keepin'—

IRENE (*fiercely*)

Shut your mouth, Ceely! Dat ain't your business.

CEELY

Oh, I knowed Dreamy'd be gittin' in trouble fo' long! De low-flung young trash! An' here's his ole Mammy don't know no dif'frunt but he's de mos' innercent young lamb in de worl'. (*In a strained whisper*) What he do? Is he been stealin' somep'n?

IRENE (*angrily*)

You go ter hell, Ceely Ann! You ain't no fren' of de Dreamy's, you talk dat way, and I ain't got no time ter waste argyin' wid your fool notions. (*She goes to the door.*) Dreamy'll go ter his death sho's yo' born, if I don't find him an' tell him quick!

CEELY (*terrified*)

Oh, Lawd!

IRENE (*anxiously*)

He'll sho'ly try ter come here and see his ole Mammy befo' she dies, don't you think, Ceely?

CEELY
Fo' Gawd, I hopes so! She's been a-prayin'
all de day—

IRENE (*opening the door*)
You hopes so, you fool nigger! I tells you it's
good-bye to de Dreamy, he come here! I
knows! I gotter find an' stop him. If he come
here, Ceely, you tell him git out quick and
hide, he don't wanter get pinched. You hear?
You tell him dat, Ceely, for Gawd's sake! I'se
got ter go—find him—high an' low—

(*She goes out leaving Ceely staring at her in
speechless indignation.*)

CEELY (*drawing a deep breath*)
Yo' street gal! I don' b'lieve one word you
says—stuffin' me wid yo' bad lies so's you kin
keep de Dreamy frum leavin' you! (*Mammy
Saunders awakes and groans faintly. Ceely
hurries over to her bedside.*) Is de pain hurtin'
agin, Mammy?

MAMMY (*vaguely*)
Dat you, Dreamy?

CEELY
No, Mammy, dis is Ceely. Dreamy's comin'
soon. Is you restin' easy?

MAMMY (*as if she hadn't heard*)
Dat you, Dreamy?

CEELY (*sitting down in the rocker by the bed and
taking one of the old woman's hands in hers*)
No. Dreamy's comin'.

MAMMY (*after a pause—suddenly*)
Does you 'member yo' dead Mammy, chile?

CEELY (*mystified*)
My dead Mammy?

MAMMY
Didn't I heah yo' talkin' jest now, Dreamy?

CEELY (*very worried*)
I clar ter goodness, she don' know me ary bit.
Dis is Ceely Ann talkin' ter yo', Mammy.

MAMMY
Who was yo' talkin' wid, Dreamy?

CEELY (*shaking her head—in a trembling voice*)
Hit can't be long befo' de en'. (*In a louder
tone*) Hit was me talkin' wid a pusson fum ovah
de way. She say tell you Dreamy comin' heah
ter see yo' right away. You heah dat, Mammy?

(*The old woman sighs, but does not answer.
There is a pause.*)

MAMMY (*suddenly*)
Does yo' 'member yo' dead Mammy, chile?
(*Then with a burst of religious exaltation*) De
Lawd have mercy!

CEELY (*like an echo*)
Bless de Lawd! (*Then in a frightened half-
whisper to herself*) Po' thing! Her min's done
leavin' her, jest like de doctor said.

(*She looks down at the old woman helplessly. The
door on the right is opened stealthily and the
Dreamy Kid slinks in on tiptoe.*)

CEELY (*hearing a board creak, turns quickly toward
the door and gives a frightened start*)
Dreamy!

DREAMY (*puts his fingers to his lips—command-
ingly*) S-s-s-h-h!

(He bends down to a crouching position and, holding the door about an inch open, peers out into the hallway in an attitude of tense waiting, one hand evidently clutching some weapon in the side pocket of his coat. After a moment he is satisfied of not being followed, and, after closing the door carefully and locking it, he stands up and walks to the center of the room, casting a look of awed curiosity at the figure in the bed. He is a well-built, good-looking young negro, light in color. His eyes are shifty and hard, their expression one of tough, scornful defiance. His mouth is cruel and perpetually drawn back at the corner into a snarl. He is dressed in well-fitting clothes of a flashy pattern. A light cap is pulled down on the side of his head.)

CEELY *(coming from the bed to meet him)*
Bless de Lawd, here you is at las'!

DREAMY *(with a warning gesture)*
Nix on de loud talk! Talk low, can't yuh? *(He glances back at the door furtively, then continues with a sneer)* Yuh're a fine nut, Ceely Ann! What for you sendin' out all ober de town for me like you was crazy? D'yuh want ter git me in de cooler? Don' you know dey're after me for what I done last night?

CEELY *(fearfully)*
I heerd somep'n — but — what you done, Dreamy?

DREAMY *(with an attempt at a careless bravado)*
I croaked a guy, dat's what! A white man.

CEELY *(in a frightened whisper)*
What you mean—croaked?

DREAMY (*boastfully*)

I shot him dead, dat's what! (*As Ceely shrinks away from him in horror—resentfully*) Aw say, don' gimme none o' dem looks o' yourn. 'T'warn't my doin' nohow. He was de one lookin' for trouble. I wasn't seekin' for no mess wid him dat I would help. But he tole folks he was gwine ter git me for a fac', and dat fo'ced my hand. I had ter git him ter pertect my own life. (*With cruel satisfaction*) And I got him right, you b'lieve me!

CEELY (*putting her hands over her face with a low moan of terror*)

May de good Lawd pardon yo' wickedness! Oh, Lawd! What yo' po' ole Mammy gwine say if she hear tell—an' she never knowin' how bad you's got.

DREAMY (*fiercely*)

Hell! You ain't tole her, is you?

CEELY

Think I want to kill her on the instant? An' I didn' know myse'f—what you done—till you tells me. (*Frightenedly*) Oh, Dreamy, what you gwine do now? How you gwine git away? (*Almost wailing*) Good Lawd, de perlice gon' kotch you suah!

DREAMY (*savagely*)

Shut yo' loud mouth, damn yo'! (*He stands tensely listening for some sound from the hall. After a moment he points to the bed.*) Is Mammy sleepin'?

CEELY (*tiptoes to the bed*)

Seems like she is. (*She comes back to him.*)

Dat's de way wid her—sleep fo' a few minutes, den she wake, den sleep again.

DREAMY (*scornfully*)

Aw, dere ain't nothin' wrong wid her 'ceptin' she's ole. What yuh wanter send de word tellin' me she's croakin', and git me comin' here at de risk o' my life, and den find her sleepin'. (*Clenching his fist threateningly.*) I gotter mind ter smash yo' face for playin' de damn fool and makin' me de goat. (*He turns toward the door.*) Ain't no use'n me stayin' here when dey'll likely come lookin' for me. I'm gwine out where I gotta chance ter make my git-away. De boy is all fixin' it up for me. (*His hand on the door knob*) When Mammy wakes, you tell her I couldn't wait, you hear?

CEELY (*hurrying to him and grabbing his arm— pleadingly*)

Don' yo' go now, Dreamy—not jest yit. Fo' de good Lawd's sake don' yo' go befo' you speaks wid her! If yo' knew how she's been a-callin' an' a-prayin' for yo' all de day—

DREAMY (*scornfully, but a bit uncertainly*)

Aw, she don' need none o' me. What good kin I do watchin' her do a kip? It'd be dif'frunt if she was croakin' on de level.

CEELY (*in an anguished whisper*)

She's gwine wake up in a secon' an' den she call: "Dreamy. Whar's Dreamy?" An' what I gwine tell her den? An' yo' Mammy is dyin', Dreamy, sho's fate! Her min' been wanderin' an' she don' even recernize me no mo', an' de doctor say when dat come it ain't but a sho't time befo' de en'. Yo' gotter stay wid yo'

Mammy long 'nuff ter speak wid her, Dreamy. Yo' jest gotter stay wid her in her las' secon's on dis yearth when she's callin' ter yo'. (*With conviction, as he hesitates*) Listen heah, yo' Dreamy! Yo' don' never git no bit er luck in dis worril ary agin, yo' leaves her now. De perlice gon' kotch yo' suah.

DREAMY (*with superstitious fear*)
S-s-s-h-h! Can dat bull, Ceely! (*Then boastfully*) I wasn't pinin' to beat it up here, git me? De boys was all persuadin' me not ter take de chance. It's takin' my life in my hands, dat's what. But when I heerd it was ole Mammy croakin' and axin' ter see me, I says ter myse'f: "Dreamy, you gotter make good wid ole Mammy, no matter what come— or you don' never git a bit of luck in yo' life no more." And I was game and come, wasn't I? Nary body in dis worril kin say de Dreamy ain't game ter de core, n'matter what. (*With sudden decision, walks to the foot of the bed and stands looking down at Mammy. A note of fear creeps into his voice*) Gawd, she's quiet 'nuff. Maybe she done passed away in her sleep like de ole ones does. You go see, Ceely; an' if she's on'y sleepin', you wake her up. I wanter speak wid her quick—an' den I'll make a break outa here. You make it fast, Ceely Ann, I tells yo'.

CEELY (*bends down beside the bed*)
Mammy! Mammy! Here's de Dreamy.

MAMMY (*opens her eyes—drowsily and vaguely, in a weak voice*)
Dreamy?

DREAMY (*shuffling his feet and moving around the bed*)

Here I is, Mammy.

MAMMY (*fastening her eyes on him with fascinated joy*)

Dreamy! Hits yo'! (*Then uncertainly*) I ain't dreamin' nor seein' ha'nts, is I?

DREAMY (*coming forward and taking her hand*)

'Deed I ain't no ghost. Here I is, sho' 'nuff.

MAMMY (*clutching his hand tight and pulling it down on her breast—in an ecstasy of happiness*)

Didn' I know you'd come! Didn' I say: "Dreamy ain't gwine let his ole Mammy die all 'lone by he'se'f an' him not dere wid her." I knows yo'd come. (*She starts to laugh joyously, but coughs and sinks back weakly.*)

DREAMY (*shudders in spite of himself as he realizes for the first time how far gone the old woman is—forcing a tone of joking reassurance*)

What's dat foolishness I hears you talkin', Mammy? Wha' d'yuh mean pullin' dat bull 'bout croakin' on me? Shoo! Tryin' ter kid me, ain't yo'? Shoo! You live ter plant de flowers on my grave, see if you don'.

MAMMY (*sadly and very weakly*)

I knows! I knows! Hit ain't long now. (*Bursting into a sudden weak hysteria*) Yo' stay heah, Dreamy! Yo' stay heah by me, yo' stay heah —till de good Lawd take me home. Yo' promise me dat! Yo' do dat fo' po' ole Mammy, won't yo'?

DREAMY (*uneasily*)

'Deed I will, Mammy, 'deed I will.

MAMMY (*closing her eyes with a sigh of relief—calmly*)

Bless de Lawd for dat. Den I ain't skeered no mo'. (*She settles herself comfortably in the bed as if preparing for sleep.*)

CEELY (*in a low voice*)

I gotter go home fo' a minute, Dreamy. I ain't been dere all de day, and Lawd knows what happen. I'll be back yere befo' ve'y long.

DREAMY (*his eyes fixed on Mammy*)

Aw right, beat it if yuh wanter. (*Turning to her—in a fierce whisper*) On'y don' be long. I can't stay here an' take dis risk, you hear?

CEELY (*frightenedly*)

I knows, chile. I come back, I swar!

(*She goes out quietly. Dreamy goes quickly to the window and cautiously searches the street below with his eyes.*)

MAMMY (*uneasily*)

Dreamy. (*He hurries back and takes her hand again.*) I got de mos' 'culiar feelin' in my head. Seems like de years done all roll away an' I'm back down home in de ole place whar you' was bo'n. (*After a short pause.*) Does yo' 'member yo' own mammy, chile?

DREAMY

No.

MAMMY

Yo' was too young, I s'pec'. Yo' was on'y a baby w'en she tuck 'n' die. My Sal was a mighty fine 'oman, if I does say hit my se'f.

DREAMY (*fidgeting nervously*)

Don' you talk, Mammy. Better you'd close yo' eyes an' rest.

MAMMY (*with a trembling smile—weakly*)

Shoo! W'at is I done come ter, wid my own gran'chile bossin' me 'bout. I wants ter talk. You knows you ain't give me much chance ter talk wid yo' dese las' years.

DREAMY (*sullenly*)

I ain't had de time, Mammy; but you knows I was always game ter give you anything I got. (*A note of appeal in his voice*) You knows dat, don' you, Mammy?

MAMMY

Sho'ly I does. Yo' been a good boy, Dreamy; an' if dere's one thing more'n 'nother makes me feel like I mighter done good in de sight er de Lawd, hits dat I raised yo' fum a baby.

DREAMY (*clearing his throat gruffly*)

Don' you talk so much, Mammy.

MAMMY (*querulously*)

I gotter talk, chile. Come times—w'en I git thinkin' yere in de bed—w'at's gwine ter come ter me a'mos' b'fore I knows hit—like de thief in de night—en den I gits skeered. But w'en I talks wid yo', I ain't skeered a bit.

DREAMY (*defiantly*)

You ain't got nothin' to be skeered of—not when de Dreamy's here.

MAMMY (*after a slight pause—faintly*)

Dere's a singin' in my ears all de time. (*Seized by a sudden religious ecstasy*) Maybe hits de singin' hymns o' de blessed angels I done heah fum above. (*Wildly*) Bless Gawd! Bless Gawd! Pity dis po' ole sinner!

MAMMY

DREAMY (*with an uneasy glance at the door*)
S-s-shsh, Mammy! Don' shout so loud.

MAMMY

De pictures keep a whizzin' fo' my eyes like de thread in a sewing machine. Seems 's if all my life fly back ter me all ter once. (*With a flickering smile—weakly*) Does you know how yo' come by dat nickname dey alls call yo'— de Dreamy? Is I ever tole yo' dat?

DREAMY (*evidently lying*)
No, Mammy.

MAMMY

Hit was one mawnin' b'fo' we come No'th. Me an' yo' mammy—yo' was des a baby in arms den—

DREAMY (*hears a noise from the hall*)
S-s-sh-h, Mammy! For Gawd's sake, don' speak for a minute. I hears somep'n. (*He stares at the door, his face hardening savagely, and listens intently.*)

MAMMY (*in a frightened tone*)
W'at's de matter, chile?

DREAMY

S-s-s-h-h! Somebody comin'. (*A noise of foot-steps comes from the hall stairway. Dreamy springs to his feet.*) Leggo my hand, Mammy— jest for a secon'. I come right back to you.

(*He pulls his hand from the old woman's grip. She falls back on the pillows, moaning. Dreamy pulls a large automatic revolver from his coat pocket and tiptoes quickly to the door. As he does so, there is a sharp rap. He stands listening at the crack for a moment, then noiselessly turns the key, unlocking the door. Then he crouches low down by the wall so that the door, when opened, will hide him from the sight of anyone entering. There is another and louder rap on the door.)*

MAMMY (*groaning*)
W'at's dat, Dreamy? Whar is yo'?

DREAMY
S-s-sh-h! (*Then muffling his voice, he calls*)
Come in. (*He raises the revolver in his hand.*)

(*The door is pushed open and Irene enters, her eyes peering wildly about the room. Her bosom is heaving as if she has been running, and she is trembling all over with terrified excitement.*)

IRENE (*not seeing him, calls out questioningly*)
Dreamy?

DREAMY (*lowering his revolver and rising to his feet roughly*)
Close dat door!

IRENE (*whirling about with a startled cry*)
Dreamy!

DREAMY (*shutting the door and locking it—aggressively*)
Shut yo' big mouth, gal, or I'll bang it shut for you! You wanter let de whole block know where I is?

IRENE (*hysterical with joy—trying to put her arms around him*)
Bless Gawd, I foun' you at last!

506

DREAMY (*pushing her away roughly*)

Leggo o' me! Why you come here follerin' me? Ain't yo' got 'nuff sense in yo' fool head ter know de bulls is liable ter shadow you when dey knows you's my gal? Is you pinin' ter git me kotched an' sent to de chair?

IRENE (*terrified*)

No, no!

DREAMY (*savagely*)

I gotter mind ter hand you one you won't forget! (*He draws back his fist.*)

IRENE (*shrinking away*)

Don' you hit me, Dreamy! Don' you beat me up now! Jest lemme 'xplain, dat's all.

MAMMY (*in a frightened whisper*)

Dreamy! Come yere to me. Whar is yo'? I'se skeered!

DREAMY (*in a fierce whisper to Irene*)

Can dat bull or I'll fix you. (*He hurries to the old woman and pats her hand.*) Here I is, Mammy.

MAMMY

Who dat yo's a-talkin' wid?

DREAMY

On'y a fren' o' Ceely Ann's, Mammy, axin' where she is. I gotter talk wid her some mo' yit. You sleep, Mammy? (*He goes to Irene.*)

MAMMY (*feebly*)

Don' yo' leave me, Dreamy.

DREAMY

I'se right here wid you. (*Fiercely to Irene*) You git the hell outa here, you Reeny, you heah— quick! Dis ain't no place for de likes o' you, wid ole Mammy dyin'.

IRENE (*with a horrified glance at the bed*)
Is she dyin'—honest?

DREAMY
S-s-s-h-h! She's croakin', I tells yo'—an' I
gotter stay wid her fo' a while—an' I ain't got
no time ter be pesterin' wid you. Beat it
now! Beat it outa here befo' I knocks yo'
cold, git me?

IRENE
Jest wait a secon', for de love o' Gawd. I got
somep'n ter tell you—

DREAMY
I don't wanter hear yo' fool talk. (*He gives her
a push toward the door.*) Git outa dis, you hear
me?

IRENE
I'll go. I'm gwine soon—soon's ever I've had
my say. Lissen, Dreamy! It's about de
coppers I come ter tell you.

DREAMY (*quickly*)
Why don' you say dat befo'? What you
know, gal?

IRENE
Just befo' I come here to find you de first time,
de madam sends me out to Murphy's ter git
her a bottle o' gin. I goes in de side door, but
I ain't rung de bell yet. I hear yo' name
spoken an' I stops ter lissen. Dey was three or
four men in de back room. Dey don't hear
me open de outside door, an' dey can't see me,
course. It was Big Sullivan from de Central
Office talkin'. He was talkin' 'bout de killin'
you done last night, and he tells dem odders
he's heerd 'bout de ole woman gittin' so sick,

and dat if dey don't fin' you none of de odder places dey's lookin', dey's goin' wait for you here. Dey s'pecs you come here say good-bye to Mammy befo' you make yo' git-away.

DREAMY

It's aw right, den. Dey ain't come yit. Twister Smith done tole me de coast was clear befo' I come here.

IRENE

Dat was den. It ain't now.

DREAMY (*excitedly*)

What you mean, gal?

IRENE

I was comin' in by de front way when I sees some pusson hidin' in de doorway 'cross de street. I gits a good peek at him and when I does—it's a copper, Dreamy, suah's yo' born, in his plain clo'se, and he's a watchin' de door o' dis house like a cat.

DREAMY (*goes to the window and, stealthily crouching by the dark side, peeks out. One glance is enough. He comes quickly back to Irene.*) You got de right dope, gal. It's dat Mickey. I knows him even in de dark. Dey're waitin'— so dey ain't wise I'm here yit, dat's suah.

IRENE

But dey'll git wise befo' long.

DREAMY

He don' pipe you comin' in here?

IRENE

I skulked roun' and sneaked in by de back way froo de yard. Dey ain't none o' dem dar yit. (*Raising her voice—excitedly*) But dere will be soon. Dey're boun' to git wise to dat back

door. You ain't got no time to lose, Dreamy.
Come on wid me now. Git back where yo'
safe. It's de cooler for you certain if you stays
here. Dey'll git you like a rat in de trap.
(*As Dreamy hesitates*) For de love of Gawd,
Dreamy, wake up to youse'f!

DREAMY (*uncertainly*)

I can't beat it—wid Mammy here alone. My
luck done turn bad all my life if I does.

IRENE (*fiercely*)

What good's you gittin' pinched and sent to
de chair gwine do her? Is you crazy mad?
Come away wid me, I tells you!

DREAMY (*half persuaded—hesitatingly*)

I gotter speak wid her. You wait a secon'.

IRENE (*wringing her hands*)

Dis ain't no time now for fussin' wid her.

DREAMY (*gruffly*)

Shut up! (*He makes a motion for her to remain
where she is and goes over to the bed—in a low
voice*) Mammy.

MAMMY (*hazily*)

Dat you, Dreamy? (*She tries to reach out her
hand and touch him.*)

DREAMY

I'm gwine leave you—jest for a moment,
Mammy. I'll send de word for Ceely Ann—

MAMMY (*wide awake in an instant—with intense
alarm*)

Don' yo' do dat. Don' yo' move one step out
er yere, or yo'll be sorry, Dreamy.

DREAMY (*apprehensively*)

I gotter go, I tells you. I'll come back.

MAMMY (*with wild grief*)
O good Lawd! W'en I's drawin' de las' bre'fs
in dis po' ole body. (*Frenziedly*) De Lawd have
mercy! Good Lawd, have mercy!

DREAMY (*fearfully*)
Stop dat racket, Mammy! You bring all o'
dem down on my head! (*He rushes over and
crouches by the window again to peer out—in
relieved tones*) He ain't heerd nothin'. He's
dar yit.

IRENE (*imploringly*)
Come on, Dreamy!

(*Mammy groans with pain.*)

DREAMY (*hurrying to the bed*)
What's de matter, Mammy?

IRENE (*stamping her foot*)
Dreamy! Fo' Gawd's sake!

MAMMY
Lawd have mercy! (*She groans.*) Gimme yo'
han', chile. Yo' ain't gwine leave me now,
Dreamy? Yo' ain't, is yo'? Yo' ole Mammy
won't bodder yo' long. Yo' know w'at yo'
promise me, Dreamy! Yo' promise yo' sacred
word yo' stay wid me till de en'. (*With an air
of somber prophecy—slowly*) If yo' leave me
now, yo' ain't gwine git no bit er luck s'long's
yo' live, I tells yo' dat!

DREAMY (*frightened—pleadingly*)
Don't you say dat, Mammy!

IRENE
Come on, Dreamy!

33

DREAMY (*slowly*)

   I can't. (*In awed tones*) Don' you hear de curse she puts on me if I does?

MAMMY (*her voice trembling with weak tears*)

   Don' go, chile!

DREAMY (*hastily*)

   I won't leave dis room, I swar ter you! (*Relieved by the finality in his tones, the old woman sighs and closes her eyes. Dreamy frees his hand from hers and goes to Irene. He speaks with a strange calm.*) De game's up, gal. You better beat it while de gwine's good.

IRENE (*aghast*)

   You gwine stay?

DREAMY

   I gotter, gal. I ain't gwine agin her dyin' curse. No, suh!

IRENE (*pitifully*)

   But dey'll git you, suah!

DREAMY (*slapping the gun in his pocket significantly*)

   Dey'll have some gittin'. I git some o' dem fust. (*With gloomy determination*) Dey don' git dis chicken alive! Lawd Jesus, no suh. Not de Dreamy!

IRENE (*helplessly*)

   Oh, Lawdy, Lawdy! (*She goes to the window—with a short cry*) He's talkin' wid someone. Dere's two o' dem.

   (*Dreamy hurries to her side.*)

DREAMY

   I knows him—de udder. It's Big Sullivan. (*Pulling her away roughly.*) Come out o' dat!

Dey'll see you. (*He pushes her toward the door.*)
Dey won't wait down here much longer. Dey'll
be comin' up here soon. (*Prayerfully, with a
glance at the bed*) I hopes she's croaked by den,
fo' Christ I does!

IRENE (*as if she couldn't believe it*)
Den you ain't gwine save youse'f while dere's
time? (*Pleadingly*) Oh, Dreamy, you can
make it yet!

DREAMY
De game's up, I tole you. (*With gloomy
fatalism*) I s'pect it hatter be. Yes, suh.
Dey'd git me in de long run, anyway—and wid
her curse de luck'd be agin me. (*With sudden
anger*) Git outa here, you Reeny! You ain't
aimin' ter git shot up, too, is you? Ain't no
sense in dat.

IRENE (*fiercely*)
I'se stayin', too, here wid you!

DREAMY
No you isn't! None o' dat bull! You ain't
got no mix in dis jamb.

IRENE
Yes, I is! Ain't you my man?

DREAMY
Don' make no dif. I don' wanter git you in
Dutch more'n you is. It's bad 'nuff fo' me.
(*He pushes her toward the door.*) Blow while
you kin, I tells you!

IRENE (*resisting him*)
No, Dreamy! What I care if dey kills me?
I'se gwine stick wid you.

DREAMY (*gives her another push*)
No, you isn't, gal. (*Unlocking the door—relentlessly*) Out wid you!

IRENE (*hysterically*)
You can't gimme no bum's rush. I'm gwine stay.

DREAMY (*gloomily*)
On'y one thing fo' me ter do, den. (*He hits her on the side of the face with all his might, knocking her back against the wall, where she sways as if about to fall. Then he opens the door and grabs her two arms from behind*) Out wid you, gal!

IRENE (*moaning*)
Dreamy! Dreamy! Lemme stay wid you! (*He pushes her into the hallway and holds her there at arm's length.*) Fo' Gawd's sake, Dreamy.

MAMMY (*whimperingly*)
Dreamy! I'se skeered!

IRENE (*from the hall*)
I'se gwine stay right here at de door. You might 's well lemme in.

DREAMY (*frowning*)
Don' do dat, Reeny. (*Then with a sudden idea*) You run roun' and tell de gang what's up. Maybe dey git me outa dis, you hear?

IRENE (*with eager hope*)
You think dey kin?

DREAMY
Never kin tell. You hurry—through de back yard, 'member—an' don' git pinched, now.

IRENE (*eagerly*)
I'm gwine! I'll bring dem back!

DREAMY (*stands listening to her retreating foot-*

steps—then shuts and locks the door—gloomily to himself)

Ain't no good. Dey dassent do nothin'—but I hatter git her outa dis somehow.

MAMMY (*groaning*)

Dreamy!

DREAMY

Here I is. Jest a secon'. (*He goes to the window.*)

MAMMY (*weakly*)

I feels—like—de en's comin'. Oh, Lawd, Lawd!

DREAMY (*absent-mindedly*)

Yes, Mammy. (*Aloud to himself*) Dey're sneakin' cross de street. Dere's anudder of 'em. Dat's tree.

(*He glances around the room quickly—then hurries over and takes hold of the chest of drawers. As he does so the old woman commences to croon shrilly to herself.*)

DREAMY

Stop dat noise, Mammy! Stop dat noise!

MAMMY (*wanderingly*)

Dat's how come yo' got dat—dat nickname— Dreamy.

DREAMY

Yes, Mammy.

(*He puts the lamp on the floor to the rear of the door, turning it down low. Then he carries the chest of drawers over and places it against the door as a barricade.*)

515

MAMMY (*rambling as he does this—very feebly*)
Does yo' know—I gives you dat name—w'en yo's des a baby—lyin' in my arms—

DREAMY
Yes, Mammy.

MAMMY
Down by de crik—under de ole willow—whar I uster take yo'—wid yo' big eyes a-chasin'—de sun flitterin' froo de grass—an' out on de water—

DREAMY (*takes the revolver from his pocket and puts it on top of the chest of drawers.*) Dey don't git de Dreamy alive—not for de chair! Lawd Jesus, no suh!

MAMMY
An' yo' was always—a-lookin'—an' a-thinkin' ter yo'se'f—an' yo' big eyes jest a-dreamin' an' a-dreamin'—an' dat's w'en I gives yo' dat nickname—Dreamy—Dreamy—

DREAMY
Yes, Mammy. (*He listens at the crack of the door—in a tense whisper*) I don' hear dem—but dey're comin' sneakin' up de stairs, I knows it.

MAMMY (*faintly*)
Whar is yo', Dreamy? I can't—ha'dly—breathe—no mo'. Oh, Lawd, have mercy!

DREAMY (*goes over to the bed*)
Here I is, Mammy.

MAMMY (*speaking with difficulty*)
Yo'—kneel down—chile—say a pray'r—Oh, Lawd!

DREAMY
Jest a secon' Mammy. (*He goes over and gets his revolver and comes back.*)

MAMMY

Gimme—yo' hand—chile. (*Dreamy gives her his left hand. The revolver is in his right. He stares nervously at the door.*) An' yo' kneel down—pray fo' me.

(*Dreamy gets on one knee beside the bed. There is a sound from the hallway as if someone had made a misstep on the stairs—then silence. Dreamy starts and half aims his gun in the direction of the door. Mammy groans weakly.*)

MAMMY

I'm dyin', chile. Hit's de en'. You pray for me—out loud—so's I can heah. Oh, Lawd! (*She gasps to catch her breath.*)

DREAMY (*abstractedly, not having heard a word she has said*)

Yes, Mammy. (*Aloud to himself, with an air of grim determination as if he were making a pledge*) Dey don't git de Dreamy! Not while he's 'live! Lawd Jesus, no suh!

MAMMY (*falteringly*)

Dat's right—yo' pray—Lawd Jesus—Lawd Jesus—

(*There is another slight sound of movement from the hallway.*)

THE CURTAIN FALLS

FORBIDDEN FRUIT

A COMEDY IN ONE ACT

Based on a Work of Octave Feuillet

by GEORGE JAY SMITH

PERSONS

CORISANDA, *a Countess*
BETTINA, *her Maid*
ANSELM, *her Notary*
ROSARIO, *a Stranger*
MAZETTO, *his Servant*

First produced at the Bandbox Theater, New York, 1915,
by The Washington Square Players.

FORBIDDEN FRUIT

*The scene shows an interior, a large living-room
in the château of the Countess Corisanda. Doors
right and left. A large window, left rear, in flat.
A large divan under the window, which is suitably
draped with curtains. A small writing desk right,
forward. A table left, near the side. A wall mirror
near it. Carpet, chairs, etc.*

*At rise, Corisanda is seated, LC, and Bettina is
engaged in putting the finishing touches on the
Countess' coiffure.*

CORISANDA

Oh, how bored I am! . . . What shall I read,
Bettina?—while you are doing my hair? Hand
me those verses that silly Marquis addressed to
me. . . . (*Bettina brings the paper from the
writing desk. After glancing at the verses, Corisanda throws them impatiently upon the table.*)
No; go call my notary. (*Bettina goes to door,
right, and summons Anselm. He enters, approaches and bows.*) Good day, Monsieur
Anselm. . . . Oh, pardon me, but what does
this mean? What's the color of your hair?

ANSELM

A blond brown, Madame.

CORISANDA

Ah, this is some joke. Yesterday it was black
as a crow.

ANSELM (*embarrassed*)

Madame the Countess is mistaken.

CORISANDA

I assure you, Mr. Notary, it was black as a crow.
Why should I try to deceive you?—Bettina,
haven't you almost finished?

BETTINA

Almost, Madame.

ANSELM

Madame the Countess had nothing else to say
to me?

CORISANDA

Oh, I ask your pardon. Please sit there. (*He
sits.*) Take this bundle of papers which came
yesterday by post. (*She hands him papers from
her table.*) They are about that law-suit of the
Count's for the lands. I spent half the night
going over these papers, and do you know what
I have discovered? That I have lost! Fifty
thousand francs, if you please.

ANSELM (*who has opened the papers*)

Pardon, Madame, but, on the contrary, you
have won.

CORISANDA (*bursting into laughter*)

Ah, so much the better! . . . Did I have anything
else to say to you? . . . Ah, no matter.

ANSELM (*aside*)

Can she have seen how I feel?

CORISANDA

Yes. . . . There is one matter I must speak of.

ANSELM

Yes, Madame?—(*Aside*) I tremble for fear my
love may be displeasing to her.

CORISANDA

I'm going to make my will.

ANSELM

Your will, Madame?

CORISANDA

I shall die of weariness tomorrow, or day after at latest. I shall be bored to death.

ANSELM

Weary? bored? Madame! In this magnificent château, beautiful, rich, a widow.

CORISANDA

Bettina, explain to Monsieur Anselm why I am bored.

BETTINA

Madame is bored, Monsieur, because she is beautiful, rich, and a widow. These are three very sufficient reasons. She is bored because she has no wish that may not be gratified, because there is no whim that her immense fortune does not permit her to carry out, no man whom her beauty does not make a lover, and no lover whom her liberty does not permit her to marry.

CORISANDA (*sighing*)

Ah, all that is only too true! (*Noise of horsemen is heard.*) What's that noise, Bettina? A troop of cavalry?

BETTINA (*running to the window*)

Madame, there are two strange gentlemen on horseback—one with feathers on his hat!

CORISANDA

Is he young, the one with feathers?

(*Anselm rises.*)

BETTINA

Young and fine-looking! But his valet has the look of a goose dressed in livery. They're entering the court.

CORISANDA (*who has gone to the window*)

He is handsome, that's true. How unfortunate! It would be fun to turn his head, but then he'd want to marry me, and what reason could I give for saying no? For, of course, I *am* a widow. . . . He'd take me for a coquette—he wouldn't know how bored I am.

BETTINA

That's a case when it would be most convenient to have a husband.

CORISANDA

Bettina, I can't refuse him hospitality if he asks it. (*She reflects a moment.*) Yes, that's it. Monsieur Anselm, *you* are my husband!

ANSELM (*starting*)

Good heavens! What, Madame!

CORISANDA

Yes, for an hour or two—for as long as this stranger is in my château. Listen now, and you, Bettina, give the word to all the servants. (*She comes forward with Anselm and Bettina.*) Monsieur Anselm, you are General Castelforte, my husband, whom false news reported dead in Bulgaria. . . . Now, then, this young stranger, whatever happens, can ask me nothing that I shall not be in a position to refuse him. Remember, Anselm, to speak as I speak.

ANSELM

Yes, Madame. Should I, in the course of conversation, call you "my angel"—before this young man?

CORISANDA

No. Put on this sword. (*She goes to the wall, right, and brings a sword and belt.*)

ANSELM (*aside*)

Is all this only a game to make me understand she knows of my love?—Why shouldn't I be the husband for her? I'm the only well-dressed man in the neighborhood.

CORISANDA

Here, get on your gloves, and give me your hand. (*Seizing his hand with a flourish she goes out, left, laughing, followed by Anselm, with the papers, grave, and Bettina.*)

(*Knocking on door, without, right. Re-enter Bettina, who admits the Chevalier de Rosario and Mazetto, his valet. They place their hats on the divan, rear. All three come forward.*)

ROSARIO

Whose is this château, my girl?

BETTINA

The Countess Corisanda's, sir.

ROSARIO

Is she young, this Countess?

BETTINA

Young as one of the Graces, and beautiful as all three.

ROSARIO

Take this purse for your mythology.

BETTINA

Thanks, Your Highness.

MAZETTO (*coming closer to Bettina*)
I must see a little closer here. Oh, good heavens, my child! What is that on your cheek there? (*He suddenly kisses her.*) Be easy, there's nothing there now.

ROSARIO
You have disgusting bad manners, Mazetto. My dear, will you announce the Chevalier de Rosario to your mistress?

BETTINA (*smiling*)
Yes, Your Excellency. She begs that you will await her here. (*She makes a saucy face at Mazetto, and goes out, left.*)

ROSARIO
Explain me one thing, Mazetto: you seem remarkably successful with women. . . .

MAZETTO (*laughing*)
Oh—fairly, fairly, that's a fact.

ROSARIO
And yet you have the face of a fool.

MAZETTO
Nothing is more certain; I have.

ROSARIO
Notwithstanding, you please women—you receive their favors?

MAZETTO
I should receive them if my master would only give me time enough. Yesterday, when you called me, if you had only given me ten minutes more my happiness would have been certain.

ROSARIO
You have a crazy idea of always wanting ten minutes more. Your "ten minutes more" is getting to be a little tiresome. But how is it

with a face like that you can win any woman's favor? I can't understand it.

MAZETTO

Oh, this face of mine gives me positive advantages. Women say, "Oh, he's only a poor fool, that Mazetto." And that gives me positively great advantages.

ROSARIO

That may be. Everything has its good side—except marriage.

MAZETTO

Oh, that thought torments you, sir! It has become a sort of refrain in your talk.

ROSARIO

But why are women such fools as to wish to bury their lovers in the guise of a husband? Disagreeable scientists will cut a beautiful flower in the sun to make of it an old dried-up thing in a herbarium. Women are the same way.

MAZETTO

Your excellency is not a marrying man, that's all.

ROSARIO

No, and when I make love to a pretty woman (which, of course, I can't help doing), it's most annoying to have her make an unpleasant scene when she discovers I'm not the marrying sort.

MAZETTO

Well, you have only to let them think from the first that you are already married.

ROSARIO

Married? No; that gives a fellow an awkward air. But there's one thing I might do. I'll say I'm a Knight of Malta. Everyone knows that the rule of this Order forbids marriage—that's a great idea!

MAZETTO

And I—I'll give myself out for a lay brother of of the same Order! We'll both be safe then.

ROSARIO

Be silent. She's coming.

(*Bettina opens the door, left, and admits Corisanda and Anselm.*)

BETTINA

My lady, gentlemen.

ROSARIO (*aside*)

Who's this melancholy fellow with her?—(*Aloud*) Madame, finding myself this morning on your road here with my valet—

CORISANDA

Sir, it is a piece of good fortune in this lonely region to—

ROSARIO (*bowing*)

To find a hostess so charming.

CORISANDA

The pleasure, I assure you, is mutual. But without more compliment, pray be seated. (*Aside to Anselm.*) Remember to back up all I say.

(*They all sit except Mazetto and Bettina.*)

ROSARIO (*aside*)

She's very beautiful.—(*To Mazetto, apart*). Don't forget to enlarge on what I say.

BETTINA (*to Corisanda, apart*)

His lackey is certainly a fool.

ROSARIO (*aside*)
I wonder who this silent duffer can be?—(*Aloud*)
Madame, permit me to introduce myself as the
Chevalier de Rosario, (*insistently*) Knight of
Malta.

MAZETTO (*bowing*)
Of the holy Order of Malta.

CORISANDA
Chevalier, let me present General Castelforte,
my husband, recently returned from his last
campaign in Bulgaria.

ANSELM (*bowing*)
In Bulgaria.

ROSARIO (*bowing*)
General.—(*Aside*) What an ass he is! But
since she's married, the Order of Malta was unnecessary, in fact embarrassing. Bah! she's
forgotten it already!

CORISANDA
Tell me, Chevalier, exactly what is your Order
of Malta? I confess my ignorance of it.

ROSARIO
Oh, Countess, it's an order of knighthood—like
all the orders.

MAZETTO
Except, Madame, that it forbids marriage.

ROSARIO (*aside*)
The idiot! When she's married!

CORISANDA
Ah!—(*Aside*.) If I'd known that, I shouldn't
have bothered with this stupid notary. But,
too late now.

ROSARIO (*looking furiously at Mazetto*)

My servant also, Madame, belongs to the same Order, and is bound by the same vows.

MAZETTO (*ogling Bettina*)

Yes, for my sins.

BETTINA (*aside*)

He's rather funny after all, this fellow.

CORISANDA

Did you choose this profession, Chevalier?

ROSARIO

Frankly, no, Madame. My father chose it for me, in my boyhood, because I was the youngest of my house.

MAZETTO

As I of mine.

ROSARIO (*apart to the Countess*)

Pardon, Countess. Would you mind sending this valet of mine to the servants' quarters?

CORISANDA

Bettina, take this young man and let him have some breakfast—unless his vows forbid food.

MAZETTO

Oh, no, Madame!

(*Bettina and Mazetto exeunt, right.*)

ROSARIO

A thousand thanks, Countess! When the boy sees me in peril of temptation, he becomes intolerable. Count, you appear troubled; pray, don't let me detain you. . . .

CORISANDA

You must pardon the Count, Chevalier de Rosario. The great suffering he endured in Bulgaria rendered him very taciturn.

ANSELM

Very taciturn.

CORISANDA

He was wounded and made prisoner in a skirmish, and, like everyone else, I, for a year, believed him dead.

ANSELM

Dead.

CORISANDA

Heaven was good enough to restore him to me one evening in the garb of a pilgrim.

ANSELM

Of a pilgrim.

ROSARIO (*aside*)

Good Lord! It's an echo dressed like a man! (*Aloud.*) General, it's very sad. Madame, will you permit me to express the great admiration I have for your park?—surely one of the most beautiful I have ever seen. It has the coquetry of a lovely woman, always inviting, yet always concealing and evading. I should like to explore this park, Madame.

CORISANDA (*smiling*)

But you would get lost, Chevalier, unless I serve you as guide; and if I guide you I should destroy the solitude.

ROSARIO

Countess! Do angels destroy paradise? Count, I am truly sorry for your indisposition.

CORISANDA (*rising*)

I take you at your word. Give me your arm. My dear Count, this walk would tire you. (*All have risen.*)

ANSELM

But, my loveliest one. . . .

CORISANDA

Silence, my dear. No unnecessary gallantry. The Chevalier will excuse you, I say.

ROSARIO

Certainly, General.

CORISANDA

Let us go out, Chevalier, by way of the library.

(*They go out, left. Anselm remains, pacing furiously up and down.*)

ANSELM (*alone*)

I'm their stalking horse, that's plain. I'm playing fool to them. This stranger with his pretentious talk must think me an ass. But, by heaven! I won't lose them from my sight. I'll make use of the advantage she's given me. It's not delicate, but love knows no law. Where the deuce have I seen that? No matter. After them.

(*He follows them, going out left. Enter, right, Bettina and Mazetto.*)

MAZETTO

Lovely Bettina! I admired you from the first glimpse I had of you!

BETTINA (*left center*)

Sorry I can't return the compliment.

MAZETTO

"Like mistress, like maid" proves true; only, if anything, I like your style a bit better than the Countess'.

BETTINA (*edging away from his arm*)
  Pity you don't share the Chevalier's good looks.
  What's the matter with your arm?

MAZETTO (*trying to embrace her*)
  It's nervous.

BETTINA
  And you a brother of a holy order, too!

MAZETTO
  Ah! But then you understand *my* vows were
  not so strict as the Chevalier's. Far from it.

BETTINA
  Evidently.

(*He seizes her and kisses her. She runs out, left,
followed by Mazetto. Enter, right, Corisanda
and Rosario.*)

ROSARIO
  We've eluded him, Countess.

CORISANDA
  Ah, the General is experienced in pursuit.

ROSARIO
  Madame, do you know you are maddeningly
  beautiful?

CORISANDA
  Pray, Chevalier, admire my park all you please,
  but let my face be.

ROSARIO
  Madame, in this world we admire what we must,
  whether we ought or not.

CORISANDA
  But surely it is not permitted a Knight of
  Malta . . . .

ROSARIO (*hastily*)
  Oh, beautiful Countess! I see you have a little

misunderstood that matter of the vows. (*She happens to look back to the window, at which the face of Anselm appears.*)

CORISANDA (*aside*)

Anselm! The impertinent meddler!

ROSARIO (*aside, also having perceived Anselm*)

The Count! Confound him! Fortunately his wife hasn't seen him.—(*Aloud*) Countess, if you will again enter the library, we may enjoy the view now more at leisure.

CORISANDA

Certainly, Chevalier. (*She looks back at the window, from which the face of Anselm disappears.*) This way! (*They go out again, left.*)

(*Enter Anselm, right, out of breath and irritated.*)

ANSELM

Where did they go? They have no shame! I'm eaten up with jealousy. (*Calling loudly.*) Corisanda! Oh, Corisanda!—I know well I'll lose the Countess' favor forever, but love doesn't reason. (*He calls into the door, left.*) Corisanda! Where are you? Corisanda! Oh, you are there, my dear one!

CORISANDA (*entering*)

You are an insolent fool, Anselm. Go away! What do you mean?

ANSELM (*in a loud voice*)

No, my adored angel!

CORISANDA (*low voice*)

What! You deserve a thrashing, you impudent fellow!

ANSELM (*very loud*)

No, joy of my life! No!

CORISANDA (*low voice*)
  I'll call the Chevalier and let him deal with you.
  (*Calling.*) Chevalier, here, if you please!

ANSELM (*low voice*)
  Countess! You will involve yourself in great
  embarrassment.

(*Enter Rosario, left.*)

CORISANDA (*aloud*)
  'Tis well, sir. You are right. A thousand par-
  dons, Chevalier. The General reminds me of
  an engagement. Pray excuse me. (*Exit, right.*)

ROSARIO (*striking Anselm on the shoulder*)
  What the Countess told me is the fact, General?

ANSELM
  What, sir?

ROSARIO
  Not only that the world believed you dead, but
  that you yourself shared in this tragic opinion?

ANSELM
  Maybe so.

ROSARIO
  You thought yourself dead, General? Very
  strange, indeed. But, shall I tell you? You
  don't seem to have recovered from that idea.

ANSELM
  Possibly not.

ROSARIO (*taking off his coat*)
  In that case, wouldn't it be just as well to bury
  you, by way of precaution? (*He takes his sword
  into his hand.*)

ANSELM (*coldly*)
  Underling! (*He goes out hastily, right.*)

ROSARIO (*stupefied*)

What! Are you crazy? I've insulted you and you run away! Sir, you are ridiculous! (*Louder*) General, you are a coward!—(*Alone.*) Well, I'll be—I never knew the like in all my life—and he a general! (*He puts on his coat. Noticing the desk, he sits and writes as follows:*) "Madame, I have deceived you: I have made no eternal vow save that of loving you. The union which binds you is monstrous. I will say nothing of the General. Either he is an idiot, or his mind is so far unbalanced that he refuses to fight me. I will rescue you from this bondage. I will go to Rome, to the Pope. I will do anything that is necessary, but I will recover liberty for you. Then do with me as you will. Your husband or your slave, Rosario." (*Calling*) Mazetto! (*Enter Mazetto, left.*) Take this to the Countess. (*Exit Mazetto, right.*) Oh, I am saved in this world and the next, if this woman will marry me. Thanks be to heaven for this second youth which I feel in my veins! O primitive faith, lost and sacred adoration, I feel you revive in my soul, and flood my heart!

MAZETTO (*returning*)

Sir, I met the Countess' servant, who was bringing this note from her mistress, and I gave her yours. That girl would make a musket fall in love!

ROSARIO

Go. (*Exit Mazetto, left.*)—(*Reading*) "I have deceived you, Chevalier. The Count, my husband, is dead. I am free, but you are not. I

536

will never see you again under any pretext. Adieu." Divine pity! She is free! and she loves me! (*The Countess appears at door, right, holding the open letter of Rosario. He perceives her.*) Oh, beloved vision! Tears, tears in your eyes! Oh, let me stop them forever!

CORISANDA

No, no let them flow, Chevalier! They are sweet. Come! (*The Chevalier kneels at her feet, LC.*) No, my friend, beside me; your hand in mine. Look into my eyes, since they please you. Talk to me of love, since I love you. Oh, my own, my own!

ROSARIO (*embracing her*)

Dear heart, how my mother will love you! The news that at last I love, love truly, blessedly, will make her happy. Oh, my darling—my life has not been all it should have been. Let me confess to you . . .

CORISANDA

No—no. It would only be to waste words. Let the past be. The present is enough!

ROSARIO

Oh, how I love you, love you! Till the end of the world!

CORISANDA

Some little ceremony is necessary for that, Chevalier. I have a mother, too, and her presence here now would be advisable. Come, sit there, write to your mother; I will write here, to mine.

(*Rosario sits at the desk, Corisanda at the table.*)

ROSARIO

It's far away from you, here.

CORISANDA

Well, in that case, make haste.

ROSARIO (*writing*)

"My dear Mother"—

CORISANDA (*writing*)

"Beloved Mamma"—

ROSARIO (*aside, thoughtful*)

Yes, yes, I love her, certainly—very probably.
I've spoken very feelingly to her.

CORISANDA (*aside*)

We shall be married. He wasn't a Knight of
Malta, after all. That probably excited me.

ROSARIO (*looking at her, aside*)

Assuredly, she's a beauty. Her mind has some
depth, too.

CORISANDA (*looking at him, aside*)

A good-looking man. His foot rather big: but a
well-looking man.

ROSARIO

"My dear Mother."—(*Aside.*) Who the devil
can that pretended general be? She has a rather
thin arm, like that of an actress I once knew.

CORISANDA

"Beloved Mamma." . . . You're not writing,
Chevalier?

ROSARIO

I ask your pardon. But when one wishes to be
brief, one seeks the right word, and that takes
time.—(*Aside.*) That shadow on her upper lip,
to an indifferent person, would look like a mous-
tache. Her arm is certainly thin. (*Pretends to
write.*)

CORISANDA (*aside*)

Somehow I don't feel very sure of him. He's had experiences. Do I really know anything about him? (*Pretends to write.*)

ROSARIO

She has seen life, this widow—for she *is* a widow . . .

CORISANDA

Chevalier, you're not writing?

ROSARIO

It seems to me we're playing the same game, Countess: your paper is blank, too.

CORISANDA

Do you know, Monsieur de Rosario, that your hesitation could be given an ill interpretation?

ROSARIO

How about yours, Madame?

CORISANDA (*abruptly, after a pause*)

Chevalier, you have an enormous foot.

ROSARIO (*rising*)

It is a reproach, Countess, which your arm will never merit!

CORISANDA

Your hat, sir, is on the divan.

ROSARIO (*bowing*)

If the dream has been half as agreeable to you, Madame, as to me, you will pardon me the awakening, as I pardon it to you. Mazetto! Blood and death! Mazetto!

(*Mazetto, redfaced, puts his head in at the door, left.*)

MAZETTO

My lord, in heaven's name! In the name of all that's most sacred! Ten minutes more!

ROSARIO (*putting on his hat*)

Fool! Will you come, or not?

MAZETTO (*entering*)

Oh! my cursed luck! You are harder than rock, sir!

ROSARIO

There's your hat! We're off! (*Exeunt, right.*)

CORISANDA (*seating herself languidly*)

Bettina! (*Enter Bettina, left.*) Hand me a novel, Bettina. . . . (*Corisanda regards herself in her hand mirror.*) . . . Oh, how bored I am!

CURTAIN

JEZEBEL

A PLAY

by DOROTHY STOCKBRIDGE

CHARACTERS

JEZEBEL   MELKAH   JEHU
MESSENGER   TWO SLAVES

First produced at Vassar College

JEZEBEL

A room in the royal palace in Jezreel overhanging the wall of the city. At back is a great window with steps leading up to it. D. R. is a statue of the Golden Bull on a pedestal. Jezebel is kneeling before it, her forehead bowed on its hoofs, side face to the audience. Melkah, a slave girl, not over young but very handsome, stands in the window looking down on the plain below. There are entrances through the curtains, R. and L. and a great chair, U. R. As the curtain rises, there is an instant's silence.

JEZEBEL

He whom I nursed as a child, forget not his name, O Heedless One.

He is riding forth into battle, Joram, Joram, my son.

With his hundred men of iron he is riding forth,
And Ahaziah, King of Judah, is with him,
I have served thee well, O thou golden Beast.
I have builded unto thee images and temples.
I have kept thy prophets, and in this way and in that,
Have I slain the priests of Him who would destroy thee.

(*More softly.*)

Forget not therefore his name, O Heedless One.
Joram, Joram, my son.
Remember him in the hour of battle.

His coat is red, red as the blood of his heart that
I gave him.

Thou canst see him afar off.

Be thou a shield to his heart, that no harm befall
him.

   (*Rises, turning to slave.*)

Girl, girl, rideth my son bravely? (*Taking a few
impatient steps, M. C.*)

Speak! Speak! What seest thou? Hath he
goodly following?

MELKAH

Aye, Queen. He is well attended. But the
army of his enemy numbereth many men.

JEZEBEL

His enemy. Would I knew his name. May he
be accursed forever. Tell me, girl, canst thou
not see who this man is that dare confront the
King, my son?

MELKAH (*slowly*)

Nay, O Jezebel. He standeth too far. (*A
quiver of excitement in her voice.*) But he beareth himself well—(*softly*) well.

JEZEBEL

Some upstart captain whom Joram trained to
war. What color weareth he?

MELKAH

A green coat. (*Turning and facing Jezebel with
covert triumph.*) And his hair is like flame in the
sun.

JEZEBEL (*venomously*)

Then it is Jehu. Jehu, the stranger, whom no
one knew. Cursed be his name and his house.
My son loved him and made him to be his captain, albeit he came none knew whence, and

now he turneth on him to rend him. (*Goes to chair and sits down.*)

MELKAH

Aye, he came none knew whence.

JEZEBEL

And Joram loved him.

MELKAH

Aye, O daughter of Kings. (*Maliciously.*) And thou, too, didst love him, ingrate that he is.

JEZEBEL (*quickly*)

I? I loved him?

MELKAH

Aye, Queen, and he hath returned thee this treachery. Cursed be he that could see love in thine eyes and return thee such treachery.

JEZEBEL

It is a lie, girl, I never loved him. (*The murmur of distant shouting is heard, softly at first.*)

MELKAH

True, true! Alas, that he should have dared to boast of thy love in the streets of Jezreel and among the captains.

JEZEBEL (*hoarse with rage*)

Ah, when I shall have him in these hands!

MELKAH

He will die, I doubt not, O Queen.

JEZEBEL

Die! (*Breaks off as murmur rises to a distant shout and then dies down again. The tempo, which began at a medium speed, has been slowly decreasing for the last ten lines or so. Now there is a sudden jump to quick tempo in the following lines.*)

545

MELKAH (*at window*)

 The messenger of King Joram hath ridden forth
to speak with Jehu.

JEZEBEL (*hoarsely*)

 What—what—tell me what befalleth, girl.

MELKAH

 A strange chance, truly. The messenger goeth
not back to the army of our King Joram, but
entereth the host of Jehu the traitor.

JEZEBEL (*rising*)

 Dogs that they are. And must my son perish
at the hands of traitors?—Perish—(*Again a
shout.*)

MELKAH (*breaks in*)

 Another messenger rideth forth.

JEZEBEL (*to the Bull in supplication*)

 Ah, send he may prosper and return. Tell me,
girl, dost thou see Joram? How fareth he?

MELKAH

 Well, O Queen—well. I see his red cloak shining right bravely among his captains.

JEZEBEL

 He is first of all, first of all. Is it not always so?
Men call me proud. Isn't it not so, girl?

MELKAH

 Aye, thou hast the pride of a Queen.

JEZEBEL

 Proud? Proud? Is he not always first? Doth
he not bear himself royally? Doth he bow to
any, even to me who gave him light? Is he not
the man of men whom all envy and admire?
Shall I not be proud? (*More softly.*) Because I
bore him under my heart—because I know how
small he was and helpless. Because he was the

only one, my only one—and I the only need of his life when he was so small. (*Murmur of battle dies away here.*)

MELKAH (*coming from window and speaking with unexpected sympathy*)
Ah, Jezebel, my heart bleedeth for thee!

JEZEBEL (*scornfully*)
Bleedeth for me. How, girl, what canst thou know of such things? (*Returns to chair and sits down.*)

MELKAH
What can I know? Hast thou forgotten that once thou gavest me—to him?

JEZEBEL (*indifferently*)
To Joram—Aye, I remember. He fancied thee, I think. Was it not honor enough for thee?

MELKAH
Aye, Queen, too great honor. My child died, dost thou remember? Since then I have not forgotten the prophecy of the man Elijah.

JEZEBEL (*startled; to herself, in a terrified whisper*)
The prophecy of Elijah! (*Then, turning to Melkah.*) Elijah is a prophet of the God of Israel, but no God of mine.

MELKAH
Who but a fool could believe in a God whom no one hath seen, whom no one can name? Who is everywhere, in the depths of the sea and the ends of the earth, but whom no one hath touched?

JEZEBEL
Out on thee, woman, what wouldst thou do to me?

MELKAH (*runs and throws herself at Jezebel's feet*)
I kiss thy feet if thou art enangered, O Queen.
I would ease thy heart, if thou thinkest of the
curse as I have thought of it. Hast thou not
dreamed of this curse in the night-time as I have
dreamed—

JEZEBEL
I have seen it sleeping and waking, sleeping and
waking—we will not speak of it. (*Rises.*)

MELKAH (*standing by chair.*)
Truly, O Queen, it is best to forget.

JEZEBEL
Forget! (*She paces restlessly about the room,
speaking with assumed indifference.*) Didst
thou see this Elijah?

MELKAH
Aye, Queen, I was a child then. In all these
years I have not forgotten.

JEZEBEL
A madman, I think he was, crying of wrongs
done. There was a *story* of some wrong, I think.

MELKAH
Aye, Queen—there *was* a story of wrong.

JEZEBEL
I have forgot. (*Returning slowly to chair.*)

MELKAH (*leaning over the chair*)
Shall I tell thee the whispers of the people, O
Queen?

JEZEBEL
Nay, Nay! What have I to do with their whis-
perings?

MELKAH (*with suppressed passion*)
They said thou gavest Naboth, the old man, to

death because he would not sell his vineyard to my lord Ahab, thine husband.

JEZEBEL

Naboth! (*Laughing in scorn.*) Now I do remember. He was in his dotage or else mad. My lord was too gracious to him.

MELKAH

Aye, he would have given him money for his father's acres.

JEZEBEL

He haggled with him like a merchant when he might have taken his desire like a king.

MELKAH (*obsequiously and stepping back a little*)

As thou wouldst have done.

JEZEBEL

As I would have done! Truly thou sayest well —Come hither, girl, come hither. (*Laughing wildly.*) And so I wrote to the elders and nobles and I said, "This Naboth is a blasphemer," and they hired men to bear witness against him and he was stoned to death in the market-place. It was so simple, so simple. (*Pauses, and then slowly, with clenched hands*) What sayest thou to that, thou God of Israel?

MELKAH

And then, O Queen?

JEZEBEL

And then Ahab went down and took the vineyard of Naboth as was his due.

MELKAH (*creeping up closer*)

Aye, he went down and took it. And when King Ahab was in the vineyard, Elijah came— (*Leaning near.*) Didst thou see him, O Jezebel?

JEZEBEL

Aye, I saw him.

MELKAH (*going back M C step by step as if in fear before a frightful vision*)

Ah, Queen, was not his presence a frightful thing? It haunteth me in the dark, and is with me all day long. Had I not seen him, perchance his prophecy would not be to me so black a thing.

JEZEBEL

Nay, what was there so frightful in him? I have seen beggars whose look offended me more.

MELKAH

But the look in his eyes. And he stood like a god or the messenger of a god. Canst thou forget, O Queen? (*Standing with arms raised, a figure vibrant with passion.*) "Hast thou killed and also taken possession? In the place where dogs licked the blood of Naboth shall dogs lick thy blood, even thine. Because thou hast sold thyself to work evil in the sight of the Lord I will bring evil upon thee and will take away thy posterity."

JEZEBEL (*rising*)

Nay—do not make an end. There is more to it than that. And when it is finished "the dogs shall eat Jezebel by the wall of Jezreel." When it is finished—(*Walking furiously towards Melkah.*) Why didst thou forget so much, girl?

MELKAH (*flinging herself at Jezebel's feet*)

O daughter of Kings, look not on me so. All, all could I endure but only that. How dared I frame it with my tongue? My child is dead. What have I to fear from the curse? (*The murmur*

of distant shouting begins very softly and contin-
ues during the next few pages.)

JEZEBEL (*thoughtfully*)

Aye, girl, *thy* child is dead. (*Wanders restlessly about, Melkah watching her covertly. For a mo-ment she stops before the image of the bull, then turns impatiently away. Murmur rises to shout-ing and the tempo which has again slowed down becomes very fast.*) Tell me, dost thou see my son?

MELKAH

The army of Jehu advanceth—Ah, grant the curse fall not today.

JEZEBEL

Be silent.

MELKAH

Nay, be not afraid. Doubtless there will be yet many years before my lord, thy son.

JEZEBEL

Silence, girl. Wouldst thou slay me? (*An-other shout. During the following lines the noise of distant shouting grows increasingly louder.*) What passeth without?

MELKAH

They are met. They clash in battle, the armies of my lord Joram and of Jehu the traitor.

JEZEBEL

Seest thou my son?

MELKAH

Aye, Queen, I see him.

JEZEBEL (*rushing to the window behind Melkah*)

Where, Where?

MELKAH

There among the plunging hosts and the white horses.

JEZEBEL

I see him not.

MELKAH

Dost thou not see the sun on his crown and his flashing blade? There, there in the forefront of battle. See, they press upon him, they surround him.

JEZEBEL

Nay, nay, there is a mist before my eyes. I see naught. (*Staggering from the window.*)

MELKAH (*watching her with furtive intensity*)

What, dost thou not even see the red cloak of Joram, of Joram the king?

JEZEBEL

Nay, nay, I have told thee, girl. I see naught, naught but a cloud of phantoms seething in a mist. (*Sinks exhaustedly in a chair, her back to Melkah. Noise culminates in a great shouting and sinks again to a murmur.*)

JEZEBEL (*frozen with fear, not turning in her chair*)

How fareth my son?

MELKAH

Well, O Queen, well. (*Melkah turns from window with narrowed eyes on Jezebel, but she speaks as though watching the battle below. The murmur of shouting rises very softly from the plain.*) He beareth himself royally, yet alas, how doth he defend himself? He is surrounded. Just Heavens! He is master of the sword. It is a wall of light around him. They attack him on all sides. They strike at him—he striketh their

552

weapons down and goeth unscathed. Yet how can he endure?

JEZEBEL (*speaking with difficulty*)
Do they not bring him succour? Where are his captains? (*Rising desperately.*) Ah, God, were I a man!

MELKAH
Thou dost well to call on a god. That is woman's work and help cometh so. Do thou pray to the Golden Bull—he belike will help thee. (*During the following speech the distant shouting is almost inaudible.*)

JEZEBEL
He? (*For a long moment she stands looking up at the golden image. Then suddenly she strikes it with her hand, half laughing, half shrieking hysterically.*) Thou? I strike thee with my hand. What then? My hand bleedeth a little. Bah! Dost thou destroy me? If I gave thee my heart to eat thou wouldst still grin and grin as the smith made thee. Thinkest thou I have forgotten how thou wert made of my jewels—the jewels King Ahab gave me when I was a bride? (*She leans close to the bull.*) That jewel that is thine eye—that sparkled on my bosom once. Faugh! Dost think that I do not know that they are jewels and not eyes? These I wore in my ears. Dost thou think I can believe that the goldsmith hath made a god of my vanities? (*Raises her arms and strikes down the incense jar from the stand, stamping upon it. Laughs wildly and threatens the beast with her hands.*) So much! (*Suddenly louder shouting. To Melkah, who has*

crept down from the steps watching her.) To thy place, girl. How fareth my son?

MELKAH (*running to window*)
Surprising well, O Queen. He hath rallied a few of his captains about him. Be not dismayed. He will yet win to the city gates.

JEZEBEL
Oh, if I could see! If I could see! Those cries are a thousand daggers stabbing my heart in darkness.

MELKAH (*leaning toward her from the window*)
Think not of them, O Queen.

JEZEBEL
Shall I not think of them? What shall cause me to forget? Prayers? Girl, girl, thou hast made a mock of me. (*Sits in chair. The murmur of shouting dies away altogether.*)

MELKAH (*craftily*)
Nay, I would not have spoken, O Queen, but that I feared thy wrath, had I said what it was in my mind to say.

JEZEBEL (*petulantly*)
Speak, speak.

MELKAH (*slowly and softly, watching Jezebel*)
In old days I used to think the God of Israel would answer prayer.

JEZEBEL
The God of Israel!

MELKAH
Nay, do not listen to those voices of the slain priests, close thine ears to them.

JEZEBEL
I hear them.

MELKAH

But they were servants of a God who was not thy God, O Queen. Indeed, indeed, thou didst right to order their deaths.

JEZEBEL

There were fifty of them.

MELKAH

Aye, fifty all told, but they spoke the truth unwisely; they prophesied unwisely. They spoke against thee, O Queen, and how may a state endure when tongues wag against its Queen?

JEZEBEL

True, they were unwise. (*In a half-whisper to herself.*) But doth *He* think of that, I wonder?

MELKAH

Perhaps he doth. I think he doth, O Queen. Do thou call thy name to him and he will not forget thee.

JEZEBEL (*she does not notice the half-hidden mockery. A pause, and then dully*)

Aye, so be it. Keep thou good watch, girl, and tell me what befalleth.

MELKAH

O Queen, I will.

(*Jezebel rises, starts toward the bull, covers her eyes as from some horror and crosses to the opposite side. Kneels, head bowed on her arms. Silence, except for the distant shouting which begins again very softly. Melkah creeps from window watching her.*)

JEZEBEL (*in a low voice, not moving*)

They cry very loud.

MELKAH

It is the noise of battle.

JEZEBEL (*dully*)

Nay, nay, it is the voices of the slain priests. I can not hear my praying for their cries. They cry to God against me.

MELKAH (*from behind, bending over her malignantly*)

Look up to Heaven, God will hear thee.

JEZEBEL (*raising her head slowly. Her senses are dulled. She is conscious only of the turmoil raging within. Her eyes fall on the bull*)

Nay, that way standeth the Golden Bull like a sign across the sky. I can not see God's face for the glitter of trivial things.

MELKAH

Call to Him. He will forget the slain priests and the golden idols. (*Very slowly.*) He is merciful.

JEZEBEL

Merciful. (*Rising, her pride stung to life.*) What have I to do with mercy? Shall I, who have given life and death, ask mercy? (*Restlessly.*) Bah! Mercy is the talk of weaklings and children.

MELKAH

Aye, it is true. (*Pauses, and then ventures with malice.*) The little daughter of Naboth prayed to thee for mercy, O Queen.

JEZEBEL (*turning sharply*)

How dost thou know that?

MELKAH

I have heard it said.

JEZEBEL (*pausing with her hand before her eyes*)

No matter, no matter. (*Half to herself.*) I had thought that none knew that.

MELKAH

Surely thou hast forgotten so small a thing.

JEZEBEL

Forgotten! (*Laughs oddly.*) Doth one then forget? She was very small, not so old as my son—so small. I struck her, I believe.

MELKAH

That, too, was justice—the daughter of one whom thou hadst condemned.

JEZEBEL (*laughing*)

Aye, that was justice. (*The murmur from the plain, which has been increasing in volume, rises to a great shouting.*)

JEZEBEL (*frantically*)

What is that? (*Again the sudden rise to very fast tempo.*)

MELKAH (*runs to the window*)

Alas, alas, King Joram is down—no, no, he holdeth his own. Ah, dear God, his men desert him—he is alone among his enemies. (*With wild exultation.*) Pray thou for him, O Queen, pray to God for him or he is indeed lost.

JEZEBEL (*raising her arms frantically*)

Pray to God! Fool! God hath spoken his justice against me. And when it is finished, "The dogs shall eat Jezebel by the walls of Jezreel." Doth *He* forget? Dost thou think he hath forgotten that I have slain His priests and blasphemed against His name? Have *I* forgotten? Shall I cry against his justice for mercy? (*She sinks exhausted into a chair, cowering and trembling convulsively. The tempo grows slower and slower through the next lines until entrance of messenger.*) I would do as He hath done, if I were

He and had power without limit. I would do it.
I would have no thought of mercy. Why, then,
should he? Shall I ask for mercy and be denied
—I, Jezebel, the Queen?

MELKAH
Nay, 'tis not for thyself thou shouldst ask
mercy, O Queen, but for the King, thy son.

JEZEBEL (*softly*)
"Because thou hast sold thyself to work in-
iquity I will bring evil upon thee, and (*hardly
above her breath*) I will take away thy posterity."

MELKAH
My child died, O Queen.

JEZEBEL (*furiously*)
Thy child! What of mine?

(*The curtain, R, is flung aside, the sound of
shouting increases, and a messenger enters, breathlessly, and flings himself down before Jezebel.
Fast tempo, which continues until the song.*)

MESSENGER
Alas! O Queen, the King's army is fled. (*A
short pause. Jezebel stands as though turned to
stone.*)

JEZEBEL
What sayest thou?

MESSENGER
My lord Joram's captains have fled before the
enemy.

JEZEBEL (*speaking with difficulty in a strange voice*)
And the King? What of him?

MESSENGER
The King! (*Jezebel sways uncertainly.*) Look

to thy mistress, girl, she is ill. (*Melkah does not stir.*)

JEZEBEL (*hoarsely*)
What of the King? Speak, fool!

MESSENGER
King Joram is taken prisoner in the hands of his enemies.

JEZEBEL
How knowest thou this?

MESSENGER
I stood by the King's orders in the gate of the city and saw it befall as I have said.

JEZEBEL (*raising her arms in futile passion*)
Traitors! Cowards!

MELKAH (*speaking slowly in emphatic contrast to the others*)
What of Jehu?

MESSENGER
He is riding into the city with his army, bringing King Joram with him.

JEZEBEL
Will he come here, thinkest thou?

MESSENGER
I fear so, O Jezebel.

JEZEBEL
Fear! Fear! (*Thinks a minute.*) We thank thee for thy good service. Now get thee gone. Bid them open the great doors of the palace and receive Jehu, the captain, in my name. And tell my musician, the lute player, I would have him play softly, here behind the curtains, love songs of the ancient gods and heroes. It is my command.

MESSENGER

   I obey. (*He withdraws to doorway, pauses.*) I crave thy pardon, O Queen.

JEZEBEL (*impatiently*)

   Speak, speak.

MESSENGER

   Would it not be well, O Queen—a small guard— behind the curtain?

JEZEBEL

   Are there still any who will serve me?

MESSENGER

   There are a few men in the palace, O Queen.

JEZEBEL

   Then a guard, an armed guard—behind the curtain, there, with all the speed thou knowest, Go!

MESSENGER

   I obey. (*Exit. After exit of messenger shouting gradually dies away.*)

JEZEBEL

   My robe and crown, Melkah. The jewels and the ointment for my face. (*Melkah goes to table.*) Quick, girl, quickly. Thou must paint me a new image in the mirror—young as I once was —and of a beauty to find favor in the eyes of Jehu.

MELKAH (*brings robe, puts it about Jezebel's shoulders and then steps away a few feet. Anxiously.*)

   Most gracious Queen, what hast thou in thy mind to do?

JEZEBEL (*with a hard, excited laugh*)

   Do? Am I then so old that I may not be loved? What, girl, didst thou not say that this Jehu boasted of my love? Is it not a wine a man

may be drunk withal? The crown, girl. I would
receive him meetly.

MELKAH (*speaking with real feeling*)

O Queen, thou knowest not what thou dost.

JEZEBEL

Do I not? Do I not? (*She laughs strangely.*)
Come near me, girl—near to me. Didst thou
hear what he said?

MELKAH

Aye, Queen.

JEZEBEL

They are bringing my son in—a captive—to the
city of his fathers—a captive.

MELKAH

Alas, it is true.

JEZEBEL

Shall I not win his safety for him?

MELKAH (*eagerly*)

Alas, how can that be?

JEZEBEL

My jewels, girl—bring them to me. The emer-
alds like green eyes. (*As Melkah brings the jewels, the sound of a harp softly touched sounds from
behind the curtain, R.*) Here, clasp them about
my neck—so. I will bring love back into his
heart. I will make it a flame to devour him—
and when he shall lie half fainting at my feet he
will give me again the life of my son. (*Raising
her clenched hands in exultant defiance.*) Aye, in
the teeth of thy prophets, O thou God of Israel,
I will have back the life of my son.

MELKAH (*softly from behind her*)

And what of that armed guard behind the curtain?

JEZEBEL (*with slow, exultant cruelty*)
When he hath released to me my son—then they
shall speak. (*Melkah, standing behind her,
draws a dagger from her bosom with swift, menac-
ing gesture, then slowly, hesitantly, slips it back
again.*) Look thou behind the curtains. Are
they in readiness? (*Melkah crosses R and holds
curtain back for Jezebel to see. Melkah comes
slowly back.*) It is well. Now the ointment, girl.

(*She sits in chair. As Melkah kneels to paint
Jezebel's face a voice is heard singing behind the
curtain. While the song is being sung, Melkah
anoints Jezebel's arms and feet, perfumes her hair
and clothes, paints her lips and eyes, etc. This
should be done with ceremony and unhurriedly.*)

Song

I have sought her all the night among the dark
    streets of the city.
Her for whose sake sleep hath forsaken me.
In the morning I spoke to the watchman at the
    gates.
I asked him, "Hast thou seen her for whose sake
    sleep hath forsaken me?"
The hair of my love is as the cedars of Lebanon,
    the black cedars of Lebanon:
Her eyes shine between her locks like stars
    among trees,
The blood of slain doves hath stained her
    narrow lip,
And her neck is white as the roses of Sharon in
    the dawn.

JEZEBEL
That will suffice. (*Melkah puts back the oint-
ments. As the song stops, the noise of triumphant
shouting commences and continues to the end.*)
Tell me what passeth without.

MELKAH (*in window, looking off, R*)
They are moving under the gate into the city.
O Queen.

JEZEBEL (*hoarsely*)
Dost thou—see—Joram?

MELKAH (*her voice quivering with passionate excitement*)
Aye, I see him. I see his red cloak clearly. (*A
louder shout. After the song is over, the tempo
should be kept very slow up to this point and then
very fast.*) What is that? (*Running down from
steps.*) Nay, nay, it cannot be true.

JEZEBEL
What is it? What seest thou?

MELKAH
O Queen, yon messenger lied to thee.

JEZEBEL (*trembling*)
Lied to me?

MELKAH
All is not lost. King Joram is riding back at the
head of his men. It is Jehu that walketh in
chains.

JEZEBEL (*rising*)
Jehu in chains! Ah, God, that I should live to
hear those words! Girl, thou art slaying me
with joy. Is it true? Look again. I could not
live if it were false.

MELKAH (*running back to window*)

True, Jezebel, as I live. Thou hast arrayed thyself for thy victorious son, not Jehu the traitor.

JEZEBEL

Why, it can not be true. What have I ever done that God should repent his words against me?

MELKAH

Belike thou hast loved thy son.

JEZEBEL

Loved him—Aye, I have loved him, and none other—all my life—none other. (*Very softly.*) He grew to life in my life, to childhood in my arms, to manhood under my care—Aye, belike I have loved him. God! God! I can ask Thy mercy for *him*. Dost Thou care for love, O Thou stern God? (*She is weeping softly, hysterically. Melkah in the window watches her with almost fiendish malignity.*)

MELKAH (*holding herself calm with difficulty*)

He rideth into the streets like a King, bearing himself proudly. Now he hath gone around the edge of the palace. I cannot see him now. He will be here soon.

JEZEBEL

Aye, he will come to me here—to me—I shall hold him in my arms whom I thought was dead. He was dead and is come alive again.

MELKAH

He is coming, O Queen, he is coming. (*Eagerly, running to Jezebel.*) Shall I not send the guard to meet him with honor?

JEZEBEL

Aye, send them that he may know there are still faithful men among us.

(*Melkah steps behind curtains, R, for a moment, and then back to window.*)

JEZEBEL (*pacing up and down, half crying, half laughing*)
My son, my son! O God of Israel, I thank Thee if indeed Thou hast brought him back to me. But, indeed, I think it was his own valor that made him victor.

MELKAH (*from the window*)
I have sent them forth.

JEZEBEL
It is well. Melkah, Melkah, he is returning to me!

MELKAH (*in a low voice, following Jezebel with cruel eyes*)
Aye, Queen. (*The shouting rises for an instant.*)

JEZEBEL
Hear them shout! The people love him so.

MELKAH (*with irony*)
Aye, so they do.

JEZEBEL
How canst thou be so calm, girl?

MELKAH (*with rising excitement*)
I was thinking that belike he, too, had forgotten me. (*Shouting dies away.*)

JEZEBEL (*stopping, D L*)
He, too?

MELKAH (*swift and catlike comes D C*)
As thou dost, daughter of Kings! (*With passionate calm.*) Thou hast forgotten that it was I who prayed to thee for mercy long since. Thou hast forgotten it was I whom thy hand struck—

565

years on years ago when I was a child. (*The tempo quickens again.*)

JEZEBEL (*her face filling with horror*)
Thou! What art thou?

MELKAH
Thou hast almost forgotten that Naboth had a daughter!

JEZEBEL (*almost shrieking*)
Thou the daughter of Naboth!

MELKAH
Aye, of Naboth whom thou hadst slain—by false witnesses.

JEZEBEL (*whispering*)
The daughter of Naboth.

MELKAH
He died—with blood on his white hair—stoned to death in the market-place. I saw it. I have never forgotten.

JEZEBEL (*dully*)
I, too, have never forgotten.

MELKAH (*her excitement at fever heat*)
And yet, yet I can be glad that thy son returneth to thee. (*Shouting outside.*) Hark! He cometh even now—he cometh. I rejoice that thy son is returned to thee. (*She laughs wildly. The shouts grow nearer and nearer. Jezebel faces the door from D L, with a presentiment of coming evil. Melkah, C, faces door backing down towards Jezebel and speaks in rising voice with unutterable triumph.*) He returneth to thee, O Queen—returneth to thee.

(*The curtain, R, is drawn back. Great shouting outside—"Make way for Jehu." Jehu comes in*

*from R, trailing the red cloak of Joram in his
hand and wearing Joram's crown. Two slaves
wait at the door. There is an instant's silence.
Jezebel stands rigid, swaying slightly. Then
Melkah creeps to the feet of Jehu, kissing his hand.
The tempo grows slow.)*

MELKAH
Thou art come, O Jehu, my beloved. *(His eyes
are on the Queen.)*

JEZEBEL
My son—*(It is all she can say.)*

JEHU
—Is dead. *(He raises the cloak, flinging it D C.)*

*(Jezebel walks slowly over; she stoops wearily after
a moment and with a low, crooning moan, gathers
the cloak in her arms as though it were the body of
her dead son. She straightens up, the red cloak
trailing from her side, and looks at Melkah.)*

JEZEBEL *(laughing oddly)*
Thou hast even sent the guard away.

JEHU
Will no one take this woman for me, or must I
take her with my own hands?

*(The two slaves start forward, one up stage and one
down. Jezebel steps quickly onto the step of
the window. They hesitate. Melkah watches,
crouched at Jehu's feet.)*

JEZEBEL
Are ye so impatient? God moveth only once
and then it is done. It will be all over in a moment.

JEHU
Seize her!

(*The slaves advance. Jezebel steps back into the window.*)

JEZEBEL
Nay, nay. (*At the ring of command in her voice the slaves hesitate again. Then to Jehu.*) Once thou couldst have had me for—a word, but thou wouldst not. Now thou shalt not. Take her who was the concubine of the King, my son— my son—take her. (*She throws back her head, laughing.*) Now I have finished my life. What sayest thou, girl? Have I asked for mercy? (*She raises her arms like a prophet.*) "When it is finished, the dogs shall eat Jezebel by the walls of Jezreel." (*Holding the cloak close to her left side.*) Well, it is finished,—(*she turns to the right, half facing the window*) now!

JEHU
Seize her!

(*The men advance on her to foot of steps. As they put out their hands to take her she raises her arm, stopping them again by her tremendous presence, and, facing the audience, the cloak held close in her arms she takes the last step back.*)

JEZEBEL
Have I asked mercy, O Thou God of Israel?

(*She flings herself out of the window. Melkah starts forward with a terrible indrawn scream of horror. The two slaves leap quickly forward, lean out, looking down, and fall back on each side of the window as Jehu rushes to the top of the steps. This happens almost instantaneously. Then the slaves stand stiffly and indifferently on each side of the window, and Jehu turns slowly away from it.)*

JEHU

So passeth Israel's beauty. She was betrayed of her gods, who gave her pride and moulded her in woman's form. Let her lie where she hath fallen, lest the prophecy go unfulfilled. (*Comes down from window and seats himself in the chair. Melkah crouches at his feet.*) Lord God, now am I King of Israel as thou hast ordained.

The light fades out and the curtain falls on the darkened stage.

SIR DAVID WEARS A CROWN

A PLAY IN ONE ACT

(*A sequel to "Six Who Pass While the Lentils Boil"*)

by STUART WALKER

First produced at the Murat Theatre, Indianapolis,
June 24, 1921, with the following cast:

PROLOGUE TO THE PERFORMANCE, TOM POWERS
THE PROLOGUE, - - - EDWIN NOEL
THE DEVICE-BEARER, - - JAMES MORGAN
YOU-IN-THE-AUDIENCE, - - YOU AND OTHERS

THE POPULATION, - - ALDRICH BOWKER
THE SOLDIERY, - - - JOHN WRAY
THE MIME, - - - - OSCAR DAVISSON
THE MILKMAID, - - - HELEN BURCH
THE BLINDMAN, - - - WALTER VONNEGUT
THE BALLAD-SINGER, - - STUART WALKER
THE KING'S TRUMPETER, - OAKLEY RICHEY
HIS MAJESTY, THE KING, - - GEORGE SOMNES
THE KING'S COUNCILLOR, - ROBERT MCGROARTY
THE KING'S GREAT-AUNT, - ELIZABETH PATTERSON
THE HEADSMAN, - - - McKAY MORRIS
HER MAJESTY, THE QUEEN, - JUDITH LOWRY
SIR DAVID LITTLE-BOY, - ROBERT MASTERS
HIS MOTHER, - - - - BLANCHE YURKA

The Scene is a gateway to the King's Castle.
The Time is when you will.

Scenery designed by Stuart Walker and Oakley Richey.
Costumes by Frank J. Zimmerer and Wilmot Heitland.
Properties by Frank J. Zimmerer.

An Outline of Six Who Pass While the Lentils Boil

While the Boy watches boiling lentils for his Mother, six people pass: The condemned Queen, whom he promises to hide until after the hour set for her decapitation; the Mime, who tempts him to leave his duty; the Milkmaid, who tells him of the reward offered for the Queen and makes him wish he had not made a promise; the Blindman, who shows him why it is best to keep a promise; the Ballad-Singer, who would rather wander all his life than break a promise; and the dreadful Headsman who, outwitted by the Boy, finds the Queen too late. Her Majesty gratefully knights Sir David Little-Boy and takes him in state to the King's castle. He is free to go, because by this time the lentils have boiled. He has done his duty and he has kept his promise.

LULLABY FROM SIR DAVID WEARS A CROWN

Music by Ethel Franklin Ellis

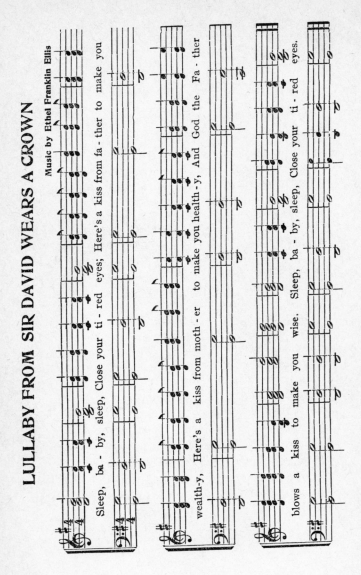

Sleep, ba - by, sleep, Close your ti - red eyes; Here's a kiss from fa - ther to make you wealth-y, Here's a kiss from moth - er to make you health-y, And God the Fa - ther blows a kiss to make you wise. Sleep, ba - by, sleep, Close your ti - red eyes.

SIR DAVID WEARS A CROWN

(The Prologue and the Device-Bearer enter.)

PROLOGUE

I am the Prologue. He is the Device-Bearer.
I am here to tell you about the play that hides
behind these curtains. He serves the simple
purpose of balancing me as a decoration.
*(The Prologue claps his hands and the Device-
Bearer sits at the side of the stage and henceforth
is nothing more than a small part of the picture.)*
It is possible that something difficult may creep
into this simple play. If there is anything you
do not understand I shall be glad to explain it
to you.

YOU *(in audience)*

While the play is going on?

PROLOGUE

Of course.

YOU

That will be disturbing.

PROLOGUE

Why? If one *must* talk in the theater everybody ought to be allowed to hear.
Now the interesting thing about this play is
that it isn't true at all. It is all make-believe.
Nobody in it *ever was*, and, unless you do your
part, no one in it ever will be.

YOU

What can we do?

PROLOGUE
 Believe.

YOU
 I can't believe what isn't real.

PROLOGUE
 Then make it real. . . . Here are the curtains. They divide you and them. . . . You are real, perhaps, and they are make-believe, surely. When these curtains open will you come here, shall they go there, or will you, both you and they, forget everything except the play?
 So, remove your hats, dear ladies, fix your hair once and for all. Clear your throats, you husky men, and cough now, for the play begins. Amongst you there are some so young, so eternally young, that they will soon be lost in the story. Do not disturb them if you have forgotten how to play. So, remove your hats, dear ladies, fix your hair for good and all. Clear your throats, you husky men, and cough now. See, the play begins.
 (*He claps his hands and the curtains open, disclosing the scene.*)
 This play is the story of what happens when one is guilty of a breach of etiquette.

YOU
 What is etiquette?

PROLOGUE
 Etiquette? Why, etiquette is living according to rules made by people who have never smiled.

. . . We are now outside the King's Palace.
. . . This is a gate. Through this the King
and the King's Great-Aunt will come. The
King will sit here, and the King's Great-Aunt
will sit here. . . . This is the Headsman's
block, and here the lovely Queen is to be beheaded before the clocks strike twelve at mid-
day, a half an hour from now.

YOU

Where is it?

PROLOGUE

Who can tell what country? I wish I knew.
. . . Are you ready? . . . Quiet, then.
. . . Here comes the Population; and here
the Soldiery.

(*The Prologue sits at the side of the curtains opposite the Device-Bearer.*)

(*The Population enters from one side of the
stage, the Soldiery from the other; the former
carries a bit of bread; the latter a lance and a
silken cord.*)

POPULATION

Good-morning, Soldiery.

SOLDIERY

Good-morning, Population.

POPULATION

I've come to see the beheading.

SOLDIERY

You're early.

POPULATION

I brought my lunch. I want to see it all.

SOLDIERY

That's good. Now help me stretch the ropes
to keep the Population back.

POPULATION

Why stretch the ropes to keep the Population
back?

SOLDIERY

It is the law.

POPULATION

I'm the Population, and I promise that I'll
stay back.

SOLDIERY

The Soldiery has *always* stretched the ropes to
hold the Population back. I shan't stop it
now, whether you number one or thousands.
Here, take this end and stretch the rope.
(*He sets his lance against the block, and he and
the Population stretch the rope, laying it very
carefully on the ground in a half-circle.*)

SOLDIERY (*taking up his lance and assuming a
professional pose, bellows*)

You can't come inside the ropes, on pain of
death. Do you hear?

POPULATION (*obsequiously, kneeling*)

Yes, sir.

SOLDIERY (*setting down his lance and assuming a
human tone*)

Thank you for your help.

POPULATION

That's all right.
(*He offers the Soldiery a crust of bread, which is
gratefully accepted.*)

(*Indeed, the Soldiery is a very excellent and human person, and his fierce attitude with the lance and his bellowing are merely official, like a uniform, and as easily removed. But the Soldiery has associated bellowing with taking up his lance so long that he is wholly automatic now, as he should be.*)

POPULATION
Who are they beheading?

SOLDIERY
What did you say?

POPULATION
I said, "Who are they beheading?"

SOLDIERY
Whom?

POPULATION
Yes, who?

SOLDIERY
You mustn't say "Who are they beheading?" You must say "Whom are they beheading?"

POPULATION
Nonsense. You don't say "Whom are you," do you?

SOLDIERY
Certainly not, but you ought to say "Whom are they beheading?"

POPULATION
Well, you can—

SOLDIERY (*taking up his lance, bellows*)
You say "Whom are they beheading!"

POPULATION

All right, if you are going to resort to force:
Whom are they beheading?

SOLDIERY (*putting his lance down*)

I don't know. That's the Headsman's business.

POPULATION

I heard it was the Queen.

SOLDIERY

May*be*. I wish it was the King's Great-Aunt.
(*The Mime and the Milkmaid enter.*)

POPULATION

Is the King's Great-Aunt very old?

SOLDIERY

She's very old and very meddlesome. She's
into everything, and she knows every law that's
ever passed, and she holds us to them.
(*The Mime steps forward.*)

MIME

Is this—

SOLDIERY (*seeing him and the Milkmaid for the first
time, leaps for his lance and, assuming his professional pose, bellows*)

You can't come inside the ropes, on pain of
death! Do you hear?
(*There is no answer.*)
(*Bellows again*)
You can't come inside the ropes, on pain of
death! Do you hear?
(*There is no answer. The Soldiery looks appeal-
ingly at the Population*)
Do you hear?

(*Again no answer, and again an appeal to the Population*)
Do you hear?

POPULATION (*to the Milkmaid*)
Say "Yes, sir."

MIME AND MILKMAID
Yes, sir.

SOLDIERY (*putting down his lance*)
Why didn't you answer me the first time?

MILKMAID
I didn't know you wanted me to.

SOLDIERY
Well, I did.

MILKMAID
But you shouted so loud I thought you weren't talking to anybody in particular.

SOLDIERY
It's the law.

MIME (*to the Population*)
Some laws are funny, don't you think?

POPULATION
I don't know. A law's a law, and I'm the Population, and a law is for the Population.

MIME
And now we know!

SOLDIERY
Who are you?

MIME
I'm a mime.

POPULATION
What's a mime?

MIME
   A mime's a mime.

SOLDIERY
   What's a mime?

MIME
   A mime's a mountebank.

MILKMAID
   And what's a mountebank?

MIME
   A mountebank's a strolling player.

SOLDIERY
   Are you going to perform for us?

MIME
   After the decapitation.

POPULATION
   What's your name?

MIME (*in action*)
   Ho, for Jack the Juggler! Would you miss him?

SOLDIERY
   We know all the rest of that.

MILKMAID
   You must let him finish.

SOLDIERY
   What's the use?

POPULATION
   Let's have it, Jack.

MIME
   How can I when you do not let me make my
   speech?

MILKMAID
   Go on, we'll let you finish.

MIME

Oh, no. I'll wait until the crowd is here.

POPULATION

I'm the crowd.

MILKMAID

Come on! Come on!

MIME

All right. . . . Ho, for Jack the Juggler!
Would you miss him—
(*A cry is heard, "Help the blind! Help the
blind!" and on top of it just the refrain "Old
King Cole was a merry old soul."*)
(*The Soldiery is on his guard immediately with
his lance as the Blindman and the Ballad-Singer
enter.*)

SOLDIERY (*bellowing*)

You can't come inside the ropes, on pain of
death! Do you hear?

MILKMAID

You'd better say, "Yes, sir," or he'll yell it
again.

SOLDIERY (*begins to bellow again*)

You can't—

BALLAD-SINGER AND BLINDMAN

Yes, sir.

SOLDIERY (*normally*)

I've got to finish it—(*and again starts*) come
inside—

MIME

We know the rest of it.

SOLDIERY

Don't interfere with the law. (*Continues bellow-*

ing) The ropes on pain of death! Do you
hear?

ALL (*eagerly*)
Yes, sir!

SOLDIERY (*putting down his lance*)
Thank you. . . . What are you doing here?

MILKMAID
I came to see the beheading.

BLINDMAN
And I, that I might tell about it.

SINGER
And I, that I might sing to the crowd.

MIME
And I, that I might dazzle you.

POPULATION
Everybody's here—except the Queen   Why
not begin?

MILKMAID
They can't find the Queen.

POPULATION
Where is she?

MILKMAID
They've offered a reward for her—

POPULATION
A reward?

MIME
How much?

MILKMAID
A pail of gold and a pair of finger-rings.

POPULATION
Why don't you find her, Soldiery?

SOLDIERY
No one told me to.

BLINDMAN
You say the reward is a pail of gold and a pair of finger-rings?

SINGER
That's what she said. I know—

SOLDIERY (*taking up his lance*)
What do you know?

BLINDMAN
Nothing.

SINGER
Nothing.

SOLDIERY
But you said "*I know*." Is it about the Queen? What do you know about the Queen?

SINGER
Shall I sing you a ballad?

POPULATION
Yes, sing a ballad.

SOLDIERY
What do you know about the Queen?

MILKMAID
Oh, let him sing a ballad.

SOLDIERY
I must do my duty. What do you know about the Queen?
(*The King's Trumpeter enters and stands at the center of the gate. He blows a noble blast on his trumpet.*)

TRUMPETER

His Majesty, the King!

(*All kneel except the Trumpeter as the King enters, followed by his Councillor.*)

(*The Trumpeter blows a lesser blast.*)

Her Highness, the King's Great-Aunt.

(*The King's Great-Aunt enters.*)

(*She and the King seat themselves ceremoniously.*)

(*The Councillor bows between the King and the King's Great-Aunt.*)

(*A mechanical chant is the official way of conducting cases here, and a man must learn by rote what he must say at trials, be he King or Councillor.*)

COUNCILLOR (*in a stiff, mechanical chant*)

Your Majesty, it is our duty to inform you that your wife, the Queen, is to be beheaded, in compliance with the law, while your Majesty's four clocks are striking twelve.

KING (*chanting*)

Who is the aggrieved person?

COUNCILLOR (*chanting*)

The aggrieved sits on your left.

MILKMAID (*whispering*)

Doesn't the King know his wife is to be beheaded?

POPULATION (*whispering*)

Of course he does.

MILKMAID

Then why do they tell him here?

POPULATION

It is the law.

SOLDIERY (*bellowing, after he is quite sure he has heard the entire conversation*)
Silence!

KING (*chanting*)
Then·let the aggrieved speak.

COUNCILLOR (*chanting*)
His Majesty the King bids you speak your grievance which is just cause for the Queen's beheading.

KING'S GREAT-AUNT (*chanting*)
Last night we were celebrating the second year of peace with the neighboring kingdom. We were dancing the minuet after the banquet—

MILKMAID (*whispering*)
Does the old lady dance?

POPULATION (*whispering*)
She tries to.

SOLDIERY (*bellowing*)
Silence!

KING'S GREAT-AUNT
When the Queen—(*forgetting to chant*) your wife—
(*The Councillor coughs and she chants again*)
stepped on the ring-toe of the King's Great-Aunt.

KING (*chanting*)
What is your demand?

KING'S GREAT-AUNT (*chanting*)
I demand that the aforesaid Queen be beheaded.

KING
By what authority?

KING'S GREAT-AUNT

According to the law.

KING

Is there such a law?

COUNCILLOR

There is.

KING

Read the law.

COUNCILLOR (*unrolling a parchment, reads*)

Whereas, if a Queen step on the ring-toe of the King's Great-Aunt, or any member of her family; Be it resolved, the aforesaid Queen must be beheaded while the King's four clocks are striking twelve at mid-day.

KING'S GREAT-AUNT

I demand the execution of the law.

KING

We, the King, decree that our wife the Queen be beheaded to-day while our four clocks are striking twelve at mid-day.

COUNCILLOR

The culprit will kneel.

MILKMAID (*whispering*)

Where is the culprit?

SOLDIERY (*bellowing*)

Silence!

(*Naturally*) She isn't here.

KING (*rising*)

It is not in our power to pardon you, oh, guilty Queen. Gracefulness is a royal possession, and when a Queen is no longer graceful she can no longer live.

KING'S GREAT-AUNT (*naturally*)
The Queen isn't here.

KING
The law will take its course.

KING'S GREAT-AUNT
Where is the Queen?

COUNCILLOR
I've offered a pail of gold and a pair of finger-rings for her apprehension.

KING'S GREAT-AUNT
Two pails of gold if she is found!

BLINDMAN
Is that a promise, your Highness?

SOLDIERY (*bellows*)
Silence!
(*Normally*) Royalty can't take back any statements.

KING'S GREAT-AUNT
I mean—

KING
We heard what you *said*. We shall judge what you *meant*.

COUNCILLOR
It is on the stroke of twelve, your Majesty, and there is no Queen, no culprit.

KING'S GREAT-AUNT
Are the laws of our country to be held up to ridicule? Find the Queen! Four pails of gold if she be found!
(*The kneeling commoners are excited.*)
Six pails of gold and *six* pairs of finger-rings!
(*The King's clocks begin to strike, but not in*

unison. First there is one large one, then two smaller ones, and finally a tiny one.)
(During the striking of the clocks there is great excitement. The spectators almost forget their manners before royalty. The Councillor buzzes around. The King's Great-Aunt cries out again and again, "Where is the Queen?" "Where is the culprit?" The Soldiery, lance in hand, bellows his familiar call, "You can't come inside the ropes." The Trumpeter blows his trumpet. The King stands up and counts the strokes of the clocks.)

KING *(at the twelfth stroke of the tiny clock)*
The Queen is free! I now decree a holiday to all the land. And everybody can go to hunt the Queen.

SINGER
And if I find the Queen I shall get six pails of gold and six pairs of finger-rings?

MILKMAID
That was the promise of the King's Great-Aunt.

SOLDIERY
Silence!

KING'S GREAT-AUNT
I said—

KING
You said just that. The King's Great-Aunt will give six pails of gold and six pairs of finger-rings to the one who finds the Queen.

KING'S GREAT-AUNT
I refuse—

KING

Royalty cannot refuse to fulfill a promise!
And to the offer of my aunt I shall add six
more pails of gold.

BLINDMAN

Can they behead the Queen now if they find
her?

KING

They can not.

BLINDMAN

Then I can find her, your Majesty.

KING

Where is she? Come here and tell me.
(*As the Blindman steps forward, the Soldiery
bellows "You can't come inside the ropes."*)

KING

Come here!

COUNCILLOR

He cannot approach your Majesty. . . . It
is the *law*.

SINGER

I can find the Queen, your Majesty!

KING'S GREAT-AUNT

Off with their worthless heads! They have
aided the escape of the culprit!

KING

No, I decree—

KING'S GREAT-AUNT

The law! The law!

COUNCILLOR

Her Highness is right, your Majesty. The law

states that anyone guilty of aiding a culprit to escape must be beheaded.

SINGER

We did not *aid*.

BLINDMAN

No, we did not.

KING'S GREAT-AUNT

The word of a commoner cannot stand.

COUNCILLOR

Soldiery, do your duty!

KING'S GREAT-AUNT

Now, we shall have a beheading after all!

SOLDIERY (*to Singer and Blindman*)

Come on, step up!

MILKMAID

Mercy, have mercy!

SOLDIERY

Step up.

(*The Ballad-Singer and the Blindman walk to the side of the block and there the Soldiery binds them together, all the while they protest their innocence.*)

(*At this moment the Headsman is heard, "Her Majesty the Queen and Sir David Little-Boy. Her Majesty the Queen and Sir David Little-Boy."*)

(*The Headsman, bearing his ax, enters in his own stately way, and with the utmost dignity starts to approach the King, but as he nears the rope, the Soldiery bellows his command, "You can't come inside the ropes." The Headsman stops short, but slays the Soldiery with a glance.*)

HEADSMAN
  The King's Headsman, the Winder of the King's
  Four Clocks—

SOLDIERY
  You can't come inside the ropes, on pain of
  death. Do you hear?

HEADSMAN
  Yes, I hear. (*Then he calls with refined dignity*)
  Her Majesty the Queen and Sir David Little-
  Boy!
  (*The Queen and the Boy enter. The boy suddenly
  becomes very conscious of being in the presence of
  the King.*)

KING'S GREAT-AUNT
  Oh, there you are!

KING
  My Queen!

COUNCILLOR
  It is not etiquette, your Majesty.

KING (*recalling the proper procedure, chants*)
  Who is this before us?

QUEEN (*chanting*)
  It is your wife, the Queen.

KING
  And who stands beside our Queen?

BOY
  I'm—

SOLDIERY
  Silence!

QUEEN
  This is Sir David Little-Boy.

COUNCILLOR
There is no Sir David Little-Boy in the royal
almanac, your Majesty.

KING
Who is this Sir David Little-Boy, Sir Headsman?

HEADSMAN
He helped the Queen to escape.

BLINDMAN
Is that the little boy who gave me the lentils
when I was hungry, and who would not break
a promise?

SINGER
It's the little boy to whom I sang two ballads.

BOY
Queen, why are my two friends bound together?

QUEEN
Sir David, first we must tell them who you are.

BOY (*stepping forward*)
I—

HEADSMAN
Address the King.

BOY
King—

HEADSMAN
That's not the way.

BOY
What do I do?

HEADSMAN
Watch me. (*He struts forward and kneels.*)
Your Majesty—see, that way.

BOY (*imitating the Headsman as only a little boy can imitate his elders*)
Your Majesty, I am the little boy who lives in the yellow cottage on the short-cut to the headsman's block.

KING'S GREAT-AUNT
How does it happen that you are called Sir David, upstart?

BOY
I'm not an upstart. The Queen called me Sir David Little-Boy.

KING'S GREAT-AUNT
What right has the Queen to create a knight? Well?

QUEEN
By the law passed by my great-great-grand-father.

KING'S GREAT-AUNT
There is no such law.

QUEEN
Oh, yes, there is, Aunt.

COUNCILLOR
I think your Majesty's memory fails.

QUEEN
It does not fail.

BOY
Queen, I won't be Sir David if it will cause you trouble.

QUEEN
A Queen has one trouble or another, but this will be my last.

KING'S GREAT-AUNT
Will you permit this insolence, your Majesty?

KING
Her Majesty the Queen claims a law. Can she produce the law?

QUEEN
I can, your Majesty.

KING
Where is it?

QUEEN
Here (*she takes a scroll from her dress*). I found it in the room of the King's Great-Aunt.

KING'S GREAT-AUNT
By what right does a Queen steal into my apartment? Seize her!
(*The Soldiery starts to take the Queen.*)

KING
Hands off the Queen!
(*The Queen takes a step to cross the ropes.*)

SOLDIERY (*bellows*)
You can't come inside the ropes, on pain of death. Do you hear?

QUEEN
But I'm the Queen.

SOLDIERY (*normally*)
Duty is duty, your Majesty, law is law. (*Bellowing*) You can't come inside the ropes, on pain of death. Do you hear?

QUEEN
Yes, I hear.

KING
> Sir Headsman, bring me the law.
> (*The Headsman is about to obey.*)

SOLDIERY (*bellows*)
> You can't come inside the ropes, on pain of death. Do you hear?

KING
> Then I shall go to the Queen.

COUNCILLOR
> Your Majesty, it is not fitting.

BLINDMAN
> I am about to die, oh, Queen; let me give the law.

QUEEN
> About to die?

BOY
> He is my friend! . . . If the ropes weren't there could I take the law to the King?

QUEEN
> Surely.

BOY
> Let's take the ropes away.

QUEEN
> Alas, it can't be done.

BOY
> Let's coil the ropes.

QUEEN
> How?

BOY
> So. (*He quickly coils the ropes.*)

SOLDIERY (*bellows*)
You can't come inside the ropes, on pain of death. Do you hear?

BOY
You can't get inside the ropes! There isn't any inside.

QUEEN (*going to the king*)
Here is the law, your Majesty.

KING (*about to embrace her*)
My Queen!

KING'S GREAT-AUNT
I protest.

COUNCILLOR
It is not seemly, your Majesty. . . . I'll take the law.

KING
Read the law.

COUNCILLOR
It may be better to discuss it first.

KING
Read the law!

COUNCILLOR (*reading*)
Whereas, all relatives have had an upper hand in my kingdom for three generations and have passed laws that make it difficult for our Queens; Be it resolved, that all such laws shall stand, because etiquette and discipline are good for all mankind, *but* should there ever be a Queen who can escape the punishments devised by relatives she shall be absolute, and thereafter her word will be the law, for any woman

who can outwit her husband's relatives is
worthy to rule a nation.

QUEEN

I have escaped. I claim the reward of the law.

KING

Your word is absolute. Henceforth you are
the law.

KING'S GREAT-AUNT (*feathering her nest*)

Dearest, mount the throne.

QUEEN

Nay, I shall mount the Headman's block.
(*She mounts the Headman's block, and she is
very beautiful.*)
I, the Queen—

COUNCILLOR

Your Majesty, it is proper to say "We, the
Queen"—

QUEEN

I, the Queen, do first hereby reiterate that this
brave knight is Sir David Little-Boy. Second,
that—

COUNCILLOR

You should chant it, your Majesty.

QUEEN (*still in normal tones*)

Second, that the office of King's Councillor be
vacant; third, that the King's Great-Aunt give
up her ring or her ring-toe—

KING'S GREAT-AUNT

Mercy! I am too old to lose my ring! I should
die without my ring-toe!

QUEEN

Very well, you shall keep your ring and your
toe; but when we dance the minuet you must

sit on your foot, for in future I shall step when
and where I please. . . . Sit on your foot!
(*The King's Great-Aunt sits on her foot and
wails.*)

KING'S GREAT-AUNT
What is the country coming to! (*But she is
very glad to save her toe.*)

YOU (*in the audience*)
Pshaw! this play is just like every other one.

PROLOGUE
It isn't over yet. You just wait.

QUEEN
Fourth, the Soldiery must lay down his arms.

SOLDIERY (*bellows*)
You can't come—

QUEEN
Lay down your arms!

SOLDIERY
Pardon me, your Majesty, it was habit. (*He
lays down his lance.*)

QUEEN
Loose the bonds from the Blindman and the
Ballad-Singer.
(*The Soldiery does so.*)
Sir David, your hand.
(*The Boy, in a glow of wonder, steps forward.*)
Here are your friends.

KING'S GREAT-AUNT
A noble cannot have friends among the commoners!

QUEEN
Quite true. Quite true. . . . Mime, step

forward. . . . Kneel. . . . Arise, Sir
Mime. Every Friday afternoon you shall have
an hour's sport with Sir David Little-Boy.

MIME

Please, your Majesty, I must wander far away
in search of farthings from the crowds of all
the world.

QUEEN

You make men happy with your play. We
give you farthings. You will not want.
(*As she speaks to each of the others, she makes
the gesture of knighting him.*)
(*They kneel together.*)

QUEEN

To you, sweet Lady Milkmaid, I give a spotted
cow; to you, Sir Blindman, a cushion and a
canopy at the castle gate; to you, Sir Ballad-
Singer, a vermilion cloak. Arise. And now,
Sir Little-Boy—(*She leans over him*) to you who
saved my life, to you who kept your promise,
for your mother I give a velvet gown, a silken
kerchief, and a cloth-of-gold bonnet, and for
yourself I give a milk-white palfrey, two pails
of gold, two finger-rings, a castle, and a sword.
Sir Councillor—
(*The Councillor comes forward and she whispers
in his ear.*)

COUNCILLOR

The little one, your Majesty?

QUEEN

The best one, Sir Councillor!
(*The Councillor goes into the Castle.*)

QUEEN

Court is dismissed! Your Highness, my husband's Great-Aunt, you may go to your room. You have caused us years of anguish; but I forgive you. Trumpeter, lead her Highness away in state.

(*The Trumpeter blows a little blast and exits, shouting "Make way for her Highness, the King's Great-Aunt!"*)

(*The King's Great-Aunt rises with difficulty and waddles away in defeat.*)

KING'S GREAT-AUNT (*mumbling*)

I never thought I'd live to see the day—but times have changed. (*Exits into the Castle.*)

QUEEN

The Population may go into the gardens. The Soldiery may take a holiday.

(*The Population and the Soldiery go out arm in arm.*)

Sir Headsman, you may take your ax to the museum.

BOY

Queen, can he come back and tell me stories?

QUEEN

Whenever you may wish. . . .

(*The Headsman starts to go*)

BOY

Sir Headsman—

HEADSMAN (*magnificent to the end*)

Sir *Headsman*—

BOY
Sir *Headsman*—

HEADSMAN
Alas, Sir Headsman, no more.   I am now only
the Winder of the King's Four Clocks.

BOY
Sir Winder of the King's Four Clocks, I—

HEADSMAN (*with the ghost of a smile*)
Sir Winder of the King's Four Clocks!   That
is the longest title in the kingdom.   There is
some consolation in that. . . . Well?

BOY (*looking at the Queen's neck*)
You said your ax was so sharp it would cut a
hair in two.

HEADSMAN
I did and it will.

BOY
How could it?

HEADSMAN
Easily.   This way.   (*He swings it downward
with all the grace of achieving his swan's song
with it.*)   See?

BOY
How do you spell hair?

HEADSMAN
H-A-R-E, of course.   How else?

BOY
Why, H-A-I-R.

HEADSMAN

I never quibble.

(*He bows to the Queen, the crowd, and You superbly; and he departs.*)

PROLOGUE

He is going to the Museum where other relics are; but civilization will always respect him and remember his ax and keep it sharp.

(*The Queen takes her place where the King's Great-Aunt had sat.*)

QUEEN

And now my friends and friends of Sir David, you may say good-bye. In an hour we shall meet in the banqueting hall for pies and cherry tarts and cakes and things.

(*The Mime steps forward.*)

MIME

Sir David Little-Boy, I am your slave.

(*He bows very deeply and lays his hand in the Boy's. When he has gone Sir David finds that he is clasping a golden ball.*)
(*The Milkmaid comes to Sir David.*)

MILKMAID

Isn't it wonderful!

(*And before he knows it she has thrown her arms around his neck and kissed him and passed on.*)
(*He doesn't know whether to smile or blush, but he does hang his head.*)
(*The Blindman shuffles up to him.*)

BLINDMAN
You only have to close your eyes to make
things true. (*And passes on.*)
(*The Ballad-Singer comes.*)

SINGER
Hello!

BOY
Sing me a ballad.

SINGER
Later—perhaps.

BOY
No, now.

QUEEN
Just for us.
(*The Boy sits between her and the King on the
step at their feet. The Ballad-Singer sits close
beside him.*)

SINGER
This is the Ballad of the Silver Star and the
Crescent Moon.
(*Sings to the wondering Boy.*)

Oh, a silver star and a crescent moon
Afloat in the sunset sky
Can make a smile on a scowling face,
Tho' the face be you or I.

For the silver star and the crescent moon
Are like memories afar—
We always dream at the guarded gate
And pass the gate ajar.

There's a moral to my little song,
For hearts bowed down and hearts in tune—
The silver star is a distant dream
And a waxing hope is the crescent moon.

Good-bye. And don't forget that the King's
Great-Aunt owes you six pails of gold. Good-
bye.
(*He dashes off.*)
(*The Boy sits in wonder a moment and then
looks first at the smiling Queen, then at the pleasant
King. He takes the knife from his pouch and
shows it to the King.*)

BOY
Have you seen my knife?
(*The King slips down beside him, which makes
the Boy gasp. It isn't everybody who sits beside
a King.*)

KING
We had a little boy like you, and he loved his
knife. . . . He was a Prince. . . . How
would you like to be a Prince?

BOY
I think—I'd like it.
(*He is almost breathless, talking to a King!*)
(*The Councillor enters and hands something to
the Queen.*)

KING
And would you like to be my son?

BOY
Yes, sir.

QUEEN
   And mine?
   (*As she sits beside him. Now they are not like
   King and Queen and a little Knight. They are
   just three people sitting together.*)
BOY (*to the lovely Queen*)
   Next to my mother I like *you*.

KING
   If you were our little boy, some day you would
   be a King.

BOY
   Oh—I couldn't be a King.

QUEEN
   Why not?

BOY
   I wouldn't know what to do.

KING
   There are many kings who do not know what
   to do.

QUEEN
   And think of all the happiness you could make.

BOY
   Could I do whatever I wanted to do?

KING
   If you were wise.

BOY
   Could I give a ring to the Blindman?

KING
   Oh, yes.

BOY
   And ask him in?

QUEEN
Surely.

BOY
Then—would I have to have a Great-Aunt?

KING
Not now.

BOY
Or a Councillor?

QUEEN
All that is abolished now.

BOY
Then—you're sure I wouldn't have a Great-Aunt?

QUEEN
Quite sure.

BOY
Then—I'd like to be a king!

QUEEN
All right. Shut your eyes.

BOY
Oh, I know—the Blindman told me to shut my eyes to make things come true.
(*He shuts his eyes very tight. The Queen unwraps the something which the Councillor brought. It is a beautiful crown. She places it on the boy's head.*)

QUEEN
Open your eyes!
(*He opens his eyes and his hands steal up to the crown. He can't believe his touch.*)

BOY
Oh!

QUEEN
  How do you feel?

BOY (*gasping*)
  All right.

KING
  You are a Prince now.
  (*He takes a cape from his shoulder and throws it about the Boy's shoulders.*)
  Arise, my Son and Prince.
  (*The Boy stands up, and he looks every inch a little king in his crown and robe.*)

BOY
  Am I a real prince?

QUEEN
  As real as the King or I.
  (*The Boy walks a princely step or two, when a voice is heard calling "David! David!" It is the sweetest voice in the world, and it is sad and troubled now. The Boy stops short.*)

BOY
  My mother!

VOICE
  David!

BOY
  I am here, Mother.
  (*The mother enters. She is the most beautiful woman in the world—like your mother and mine, but her eyes are wide with fear.*)

MOTHER
  David! Oh, I thought I had lost you! My boy! my boy!

609

BOY
Mother, I am a Prince.

MOTHER
Oh, my little dream-boy, you are always my Prince. Why did you run away?

BOY
I didn't run away. I came to save the Queen. And now I am a Prince.

MOTHER
The Queen? A Prince!
(*She sees the King and Queen.*)
Oh, your Majesties! (*And bows very low.*)

QUEEN
Arise, Lady Little-Boy. We have made your boy our son and heir.

MOTHER
Does that mean—I must—he must go from—me?

KING
When his country calls he must go.

BOY
You mean I must leave my mother?

KING
Some day you must leave her.

BOY (*to his mother*)
But don't you need me now?

MOTHER
David, if you are meant to be a king, I want you to be a king.

QUEEN

We'll leave you here together. You can tell him what you know.
(*She understands what all women understand.*)

KING

Farewell, my Prince.

QUEEN

My little boy!
(*They leave the mother and the boy together.*)

MOTHER

David, isn't it wonderful!

BOY

Mother, did they mean I had to leave you?

MOTHER

You will be a king.

BOY

I can't leave you.
(*He sits disconsolately on the step of the King's seat.*)

MOTHER (*sitting beside him*)

You are going to grow up to be a great, fine man, my David-Boy, and you will be a king. Some day you would have to leave me anyway —to go out into the world and seek your fortune.

BOY

But not so soon.

MOTHER

I'll be near, and I'll see you every day. You will be a king, my boy!

BOY
> You'll be all alone.

MOTHER
> Oh, no, my boy, never alone. For every hour
> of every day I'll think of you and dream of you.

BOY
> Who'll help you work?

MOTHER
> There'll be no work. It will all be play, for
> my boy is going to be a king.

BOY (*as he leans his head against her shoulder*)
> Oh, Mother, I'm so tired!

MOTHER (*placing her arm about him*)
> I know. Do you remember how I used to sing
> a little lullaby to you when you were tired?

BOY (*his eyes are heavy with sleep*)
> Uh-huh.
> (*The mother hums softly as she places her cheek
> against his head, but the crown interferes some-
> what.*)

BOY
> Sing it out. I like the words.

MOTHER (*singing*)
> Sleep, Davie, sleep—

BOY
> No, I like the old words—the ones when I was
> a little boy.

MOTHER
> Sleep, baby, sleep—
> Close your tired eyes;
> Here's a kiss from father,
> To make you wealthy;

Here's a kiss from mother,
To make you healthy;
And God the Father blows a kiss
To make you wise.
Sleep, baby, sleep.
Close your tired eyes.

(*The Boy snuggles against his mother and then
reaches up and takes off the crown. She carefully
places it beside her and continues her lullaby as
the curtains close.*)

YOU (*in the audience*)
Well, will he be a king or not?

PROLOGUE
His mother knows.

(*The Prologue and the Device-Bearer bow and
disappear.*)
(*The ladies may arrange their hair and the gentlemen may cough to their throats' content.*)

THE CURTAINS CLOSE

(3)